EXPERIENCES OF

E. Œ. SOMERVILLE & MARTIN ROSS

INTRODUCTION

Edith Œnone Somerville and Violet Florence Martin, the authors of this book, were second cousins, a convenient degree of relationship that can be acknowledged or ignored as may be desired. Their mothers were first cousins, which is a more serious affair that cannot be evaded. But in the case of these second cousins the question of evasion did not arise. A few details of their family history may not be considered out of place and shall be offered.

In the first place it may be said that they were both Irish, by birth and upbringing, and were proud of it. Their mutual great-grandfather was Lord Chief Justice of Ireland during the early years of the nineteenth century. He was Charles Kendal Bushe, a brilliant Irishman, a wit and an orator, and a man, in those days when bribery was rampant, so inflexibly honest, that the label 'Incorruptible' was attached to his name. His wife was Nancy Crampton, an artist and a musician, as brilliant in her own line as he in his. They had a large family of sons and daughters, to whom they transmitted no small share of brains, and an ever widening company of great-grandchildren feel themselves honoured in being able to claim descent from 'The Chief' and his Nancy.

And among these were the two descendants of whom I now propose to speak. Both of them were daughters of old families that had struck roots deep into Irish soil. The Martins had come to Ireland with Strongbow, and were one of the well-known Tribes of Galway. In the year 1500 they moved out of Galway Town to the lands of Ross, and built themselves a house there, and, incidentally, provided Violet with a handy *nom de plume*. She was born at Ross House, on 11th June 1862, and was the youngest of the eleven daughters of James Martin, D.L., of Ross, and of his wife, Anna Selina, daughter of Judge Fox and Katharine Bushe, a daughter of 'the Chief.'

Edith was born on 2nd May 1858, in Corfu, where her father was quartered with his regiment, the Buffs. She was the eldest of the seven children of Lieut.-Colonel Thomas Henry Somerville, D.L., and of his wife, Adelaide, daughter of Admiral Sir Josiah Coghill, Bart., R.N., and Anna Maria Bushe, who was a daughter of the Chief.

The first formative years of both young writers were spent in comfortable old-fashioned Irish country houses, whose atmosphere was surely enriched and mellowed by the pervading spirits of many generations of kindly ancestors. It would seem as though there had been deliberate intention on the part of Fate that these two cousins should write together, and that they should start their career as writers with a similar equipment of interests, tastes, and experiences. The children of the two old houses, Ross and Drishane, had happy lives, full of dogs and horses, and boating on sea and lake. The atmosphere of their homes was full of good talk, of books and music, of pictures and politics, and they learned from their fathers' tenants, in a mutual friendship as sincere as it was unselfconscious, the idiom of that delightful way of speech that among Irish country-people has sprung, like a wild flower, from the stiffer soil of the language of English 'Everyman' (and everywoman).

This was the life in which 'Martin Ross and E. Œ. Somerville' (to use their literary signatures) absorbed the spirit of the Ireland that they loved, which has saturated all that they have ever written. They met each other for the first time, in Castle Townshend, County Cork, in the year 1886, and almost immediately they were aware that Chance, or Fate, had done them a good turn, and that to the marriage of true minds there would be no impediment.

Nor was there. For the future, up to the year 1915, when, on 21st December, Martin Ross had to leave her colleague, they were seldom apart. Starting with the publication, by Bentley, of *An Irish Cousin*, which had a success that was, for two beginners, as surprising as it was delightful, they were commissioned by two or three illustrated papers to make tours in various countries, viz. France, Connemara, Denmark, and Wales. These very enjoyable tours were illustrated by E. Œ. S., who studied Art seriously in Paris and London, and has all her life combined the practices of Painting and Literature with what would seem an equal enthusiasm. (The Cousins' joint experiences in Denmark were recorded by Martin Ross, single-handed.)

Their first full-length three-volume novel, *The Real Charlotte*, was published in May 1894. It had a decidedly mixed reception. From those who may be described as 'High-brow' critics, it was received with much approval, even with respect. The writing was compared with Balzac's, and 'Charlotte' was said to recall the heroine of Balzac's *La Cousine Bette*. But by many readers it was detested, and by none more than by the cousins' nearest relations! Yet, after a decidedly stormy youth, it may now be said to have achieved classic rank, and in 1932, nearly fifty years after her original appearance, Charlotte received special honourable mention when Trinity College, Dublin, conferred the degree of Hon. Litt.D. on the surviving author, and the same distinction was bestowed, posthumously, on Martin Ross.

A short novel and some volumes of Irish stories and essays followed *The Real Charlotte*, and then, after a preliminary canter in the pages of the *Badminton Magazine*, the succession of stories of Irish life entitled *Some Experiences of an Irish R.M.* was published in a single volume, by Messrs. Longmans, Green & Co., in October 1899.

It is not too much to say that the authors awoke to find themselves famous. Gales of laughter wafted Major Yeates and his experiences round the world. One reviewer described it as a book no self-respecting person could read in a railway-carriage with any regard to decorum. A kind American critic said, picturesquely, that it 'had Shakespeare in a corner, screaming for mercy.' A reader wrote to assure the authors that she kept a copy of the book on both sides of her bed, so that she could, on waking, resume the study of what she felt to be its inspired pages without an instant of delay. Edition after edition poured forth, and presently the authors were assailed by letters from enthusiasts demanding to be told who were the originals of these priceless people and where they could be met with. And three readers, from three different Irish Hunts, each announced, in varying tones of triumph, that now they knew where the authors had found the originals of—; one character after another was claimed and identified as a member of the writers' county, while the authors themselves have more than once declared that of them all only Slipper and Maria had a right to assert that they were founded on fact.

Of all the many letters that the book has elicited those that may be described as Medical Testimonials have been almost the warmest and most persistent. No patent medicine has been credited with more various and remarkable cures. The Irish R.M. appears to have been especially successful in cases of quinsy. More than one grateful wife has written to the authors describing how her husband, suffering, suffocating, feeling literally at his last gasp, had panted a request for a farewell chapter to be read to him, and how, therewith, in that moment of extremity, an almost agonizing fit of laughter had overwhelmed him, the quinsy broke, and a generous testimonial was dispatched to the gratified authors.

For a considerable time the sex of the authors was a matter of heated interest, speculation, and controversy. One inquirer held that both writers were men: one of them an old man and the other a young one. Another, on what grounds it is difficult to determine, said that he knew one author was a very old lady, and the other was her nephew, a young soldier, but which was which he wasn't quite sure.

These cats are now out of the bag. Uncertainty is at an end, and this brief introduction may close with the candid admission of a fox-hunting gentleman. He said:

'The first time I read it, I read it at top speed. And the second time I read it *very* slowly, chewing every word. And then I read it a third time, going over the bits I liked best. And then—and I thank God not till then!—I heard it was written by two women!'

E. Œ. SOMERVILLE

January 1944.

P.S.—The arduous post of R.M., i.e. Resident Magistrate, exists no more in Ireland. Its duties consisted in attending the sittings of local magistrates and assisting in their deliberations. The post has been extinguished, like many other features of an earlier régime, and its incumbents no longer vie with the snipe and the dispensary doctor in endurance of conditions which test even those exponents of the art of being jolly in creditable circumstances.

BIBLIOGRAPHY

With the exception of those marked with an asterisk, the works in this list were published as by E. Œ. Somerville and Martin Ross. Many of them are illustrated by Dr. E. Œ. Somerville, including the 'Irish R.M.' books.

An Irish Cousin, 1889
Naboth's Vineyard, 1891
Through Connemara in a Governess Cart, 1892.
In the Vine Country, 1893
The Real Charlotte, 1894
Beggars on Horseback, 1895
The Silver Fox, 1897
Some Experiences of an Irish R.M., 1899
A Patrick's Day Hunt, 1902 (a sporting picture book)
*Slipper's A.B.C. of Foxhunting, 1903 (a sporting picture book)
All on the Irish Shore, 1903
Some Irish Yesterdays, 1906
Further Experiences of an Irish R.M., 1908
Dan Russel, the Fox, 1911
The Discontented Little Elephant, 1912 (a children's picture book)

In Mr. Knox's Country, 1915 (the third book of Irish R.M. Stories)
Irish Memories, 1917
Mount Music, 1919
Stray-Aways, 1920
*An Enthusiast, 1921
Wheel-Tracks, 1923 (reminiscences)
The Big House at Inver, 1925
French Leave, 1928
*The States through Irish Eyes, 1931
An Incorruptible Irishman (Charles Kendal Burke), 1932
The Smile and the Tear, 1933
The Sweet Cry of Hounds, 1936
Sarah's Youth, 1938
Notions in Garrison, 1942

For an autobiographical record of the families, lives, and careers of the authors, see *Irish Memories.*

PUBLISHER'S NOTE: *This volume is included in 'Everyman's Library' by kind permission of Messrs. Longmans, Green & Co. Ltd., the publishers of 'Some Experiences of an Irish R.M.' and 'Further Experiences of an Irish R.M.'*

CONTENTS

SOME EXPERIENCES OF AN IRISH R.M.

I

GREAT-UNCLE McCARTHY

A RESIDENT magistracy in Ireland is not an easy thing to come by nowadays; neither is it a very attractive job; yet on the evening when I first propounded the idea to the young lady who had recently consented to become Mrs. Sinclair Yeates, it seemed glittering with possibilities. There was, on that occasion, a sunset, and a string band playing *The Gondoliers*, and there was also an ingenuous belief in the omnipotence of a godfather of Philippa's—(Philippa was the young lady)—who had once been a member of the Government.

I was then climbing the steep ascent of the Captains towards my majority. I have no fault to find with Philippa's godfather: he did all and more than even Philippa had expected; nevertheless, I had attained to the dignity of mud major, and had spent a good deal on postage stamps, and on railway fares to interview people of influence, before I found myself in the hotel at Skebawn, opening long envelopes addressed to 'Major Yeates, R.M.'

My most immediate concern, as any one who has spent nine weeks at Mrs. Raverty's hotel will readily believe, was to leave it at the earliest opportunity; but in those nine weeks I had learned, amongst other painful things, a little, a very little, of the methods of the artisan in the west of Ireland. Finding a house had been easy enough. I had had my choice of several, each with some hundreds of acres of shooting, thoroughly poached, and a considerable portion of the roof intact. I had selected one; the one that had the largest extent of roof in proportion to the shooting, and had been assured by my landlord that in a fortnight or so it would be fit for occupation.

'There 's a few little odd things to be done,' he said easily; 'a lick of paint here and there, and a slap of plaster——'

I am short-sighted; I am also of Irish extraction; both facts that make for toleration—but even I thought he was understating the case. So did the contractor.

1

At the end of three weeks the latter reported progress, which mainly consisted of the facts that the plumber had accused the carpenter of stealing sixteen feet of his inch-pipe to run a bell-wire through, and that the carpenter had replied that he wished the divil might run the plumber through a wran's quill. The plumber having reflected upon the carpenter's parentage, the work of renovation had merged in battle, and at the next petty sessions I was reluctantly compelled to allot to each combatant seven days, without the option of a fine.

These and kindred difficulties extended in an unbroken chain through the summer months, until a certain wet and windy day in October, when, with my baggage, I drove over to establish myself at Shreelane. It was a tall, ugly house of three storeys high, its walls faced with weather-beaten slates, its windows staring, narrow, and vacant. Round the house ran an area, in which grew some laurustinus and holly bushes among ash heaps, and nettles, and broken bottles. I stood on the steps, waiting for the door to be opened, while the rain sluiced upon me from a broken eaveshoot that had, amongst many other things, escaped the notice of my landlord. I thought of Philippa, and of her plan, broached in to-day's letter, of having the hall done up as a sitting-room.

The door opened and revealed the hall. It struck me that I had perhaps overestimated its possibility. Among them I had certainly not included a flagged floor, sweating with damp, and a reek of cabbage from the adjacent kitchen stairs. A large elderly woman, with a red face, and a cap worn helmet-wise on her forehead, swept me a magnificent curtsy as I crossed the threshold.

'Your honour's welcome——' she began, and then every door in the house slammed in obedience to the gust that drove through it. With something that sounded like 'Mend ye for a back door!' Mrs. Cadogan abandoned her opening speech and made for the kitchen stairs. (Improbable as it may appear, my housekeeper was called Cadogan, a name made locally possible by being pronounced Caydogawn.)

Only those who have been through a similar experience can know what manner of afternoon I spent. I am a martyr to colds in the head, and I felt one coming on. I made a laager in front of the dining-room fire, with a tattered leather screen and the dinner table, and gradually, with cigarettes and strong tea, baffled the smell of must and cats, and fervently trusted that the rain might avert a threatened visit from my landlord. I was then but superficially acquainted with Mr. Florence McCarthy Knox and his habits.

At about four-thirty, when the room had warmed up, and my cold was yielding to treatment, Mrs. Cadogan entered and informed me that 'Mr. Flurry' was in the yard, and would be thankful if I 'd go out to him, for he couldn't come in. Many are the privileges of the female sex; had I been a woman I should unhesitatingly have said that I had a cold in my head. Being a man, I huddled on a mackintosh, and went out into the yard.

My landlord was there on horseback, and with him there was a man standing at the head of a stout grey animal. I recognized with despair that I was about to be compelled to buy a horse.

'Good afternoon, major,' said Mr. Knox in his slow, singsong brogue; 'it 's rather soon to be paying you a visit, but I thought you might be in a hurry to see the horse I was telling you of.'

I could have laughed. As if I were ever in a hurry to see a horse! I thanked him, and suggested that it was rather wet for horse-dealing.

'Oh, it 's nothing when you 're used to it,' replied Mr. Knox. His gloveless hands were red and wet, the rain ran down his nose, and his covert coat was soaked to a sodden brown. I thought that I did not want to become used to it. My relations with horses have been of a purely military character. I have endured the Sandhurst riding-school, I have galloped for an impetuous general, I have been steward at regimental races, but none of these feats have altered my opinion that the horse, as a means of locomotion, is obsolete. Nevertheless, the man who accepts a resident magistracy in the south-west of Ireland voluntarily retires into the prehistoric age; to institute a stable became inevitable.

'You ought to throw a leg over him,' said Mr. Knox, 'and you 're welcome to take him over a fence or two if you like. He 's a nice flippant jumper.'

Even to my unexacting eye the grey horse did not seem to promise flippancy, nor did I at all desire to find that quality in him. I explained that I wanted something to drive, and not to ride.

'Well, that's a fine raking horse in harness,' said Mr. Knox, looking at me with his serious grey eyes, 'and you'd drive him with a sop of hay in his mouth. Bring him up here, Michael.'

Michael abandoned his efforts to kick the grey horse's forelegs into a becoming position, and led him up to me.

I regarded him from under my umbrella with a quite unreasonable disfavour. He had the dreadful beauty of a horse in a toy-shop, as chubby, as wooden, and as conscientiously dappled, but it was unreasonable to urge this as an objection, and I was incapable of finding any more technical drawback. Yielding to circumstance, I 'threw my leg' over the brute, and after pacing gravely round the quadrangle that formed the yard, and jolting to my entrance gate and back, I decided that as he had neither fallen down nor kicked me off, it was worth paying twenty-five pounds for him, if only to get in out of the rain.

Mr. Knox accompanied me into the house and had a drink. He was a fair, spare young man, who looked like a stable boy among gentlemen, and a gentleman among stable boys. He belonged to a clan that cropped up in every grade of society in the county, from Sir Valentine Knox of Castle Knox down to the auctioneer Knox, who bore the attractive title of Larry the Liar. So far as I could judge, Florence McCarthy of that ilk occupied a shifting position about midway in the tribe. I had met him at dinner at Sir Valentine's, I had heard of him at an illicit auction, held by Larry the Liar, of brandy stolen from a wreck. They were 'Black Protestants,' all of them, in virtue of their descent from a godly soldier of Cromwell, and all were prepared at any moment of the day or night to sell a horse.

'You'll be apt to find this place a bit lonesome after the hotel,' remarked Mr. Flurry, sympathetically, as he placed his foot in its steaming boot on the hob, 'but it's a fine sound house anyway, and lots of rooms in it, though indeed, to tell you the truth, I never was through the whole of them since the time my great-uncle, Denis McCarthy, died here. The dear knows I had enough of it that time.' He paused, and lit a cigarette—one of my best, and quite thrown away upon him. 'Those top floors, now,' he resumed, 'I wouldn't make too free with them. There's some of them would jump under you like a spring bed. Many's the night I was in and out of those attics, following my poor uncle when he had a bad turn on him—the horrors, y' know—there were nights he never stopped walking through the house. Good Lord! will I ever forget the morning he said he saw the devil coming up the avenue! 'Look at the two horns on him,' says he, and he out with his gun and shot him, and, begad, it was his own donkey!'

Mr. Knox gave a couple of short laughs. He seldom laughed, having in unusual perfection the gravity of manner that is bred by horse-dealing, probably from the habitual repression of all emotion save disparagement.

The autumn evening, grey with rain, was darkening in the tall windows, and the wind was beginning to make bullying rushes among the shrubs in the area; a shower of soot rattled down the chimney and fell on the hearthrug.

'More rain coming,' said Mr. Knox, rising composedly; 'you 'll have to put a goose down these chimneys some day soon, it 's the only way in the world to clean them. Well, I 'm for the road. You 'll come out on the grey next week, I hope; the hounds 'll be meeting here. Give a roar at him coming in at his jumps.' He threw his cigarette into the fire and extended a hand to me. 'Good-bye, major, you 'll see plenty of me and my hounds before you 're done. There 's a power of foxes in the plantations here.'

This was scarcely reassuring for a man who hoped to shoot woodcock, and I hinted as much.

'Oh, is it the cock?' said Mr. Flurry; 'b'lieve me, there never was a woodcock yet that minded hounds, now, no more than they 'd mind rabbits! The best shoots ever I had here, the hounds were in it the day before.'

When Mr. Knox had gone, I began to picture myself going across country roaring, like a man on a fire-engine, while Philippa put the goose down the chimney; but when I sat down to write to her I did not feel equal to being humorous about it. I dilated ponderously on my cold, my hard work, and my loneliness, and eventually went to bed at ten o'clock full of cold shivers and hot whisky-and-water.

After a couple of hours of feverish dozing, I began to understand what had driven Great-Uncle McCarthy to perambulate the house by night. Mrs. Cadogan had assured me that the Pope of Rome hadn't a betther bed undher him than myself; wasn't I down on the new flog mattherass the old masther bought in Father Scanlan's auction? By the smell I recognized that 'flog' meant flock, otherwise I should have said my couch was stuffed with old boots. I have seldom spent a more wretched night. The rain drummed with soft fingers on my window-panes; the house was full of noises. I seemed to see Great-Uncle McCarthy ranging the passages with Flurry at his heels; several times I thought I heard him. Whisperings seemed borne on the wind through my keyhole, boards creaked in the room overhead, and once I could have sworn that a hand passed, groping, over the panels of my door. I am, I may admit, a believer in ghosts; I even take in a paper that deals with their culture, but I cannot pretend that on that night I looked forward to a manifestation of Great-Uncle McCarthy with any enthusiasm.

The morning broke stormily, and I woke to find Mrs. Cadogan's understudy, a grimy nephew of about eighteen, standing by my bedside, with a black bottle in his hand.

'There's no bath in the house, sir,' was his reply to my command; 'but me A'nt said, would ye like a taggeen?'

This alternative proved to be a glass of raw whisky. I declined it.

I look back to that first week of housekeeping at Shreelane as to a comedy excessively badly staged, and striped with lurid melodrama. Towards its close I was positively homesick for Mrs. Raverty's, and I had not a single clean pair of boots. I am not one of those who hold the convention that in Ireland the rain never ceases, day or night, but I must say that my first November at Shreelane was composed of weather of which my friend Flurry Knox remarked that you wouldn't meet a Christian out of doors, unless it was a snipe or a dispensary doctor. To this lamentable category might be added a resident magistrate. Daily, shrouded in mackintosh, I set forth for the Petty Sessions Courts of my wide district; daily, in the inevitable atmosphere of wet frieze and perjury, I listened to indictments of old women who plucked geese alive, of publicans whose hospitality to their friends broke forth uncontrollably on Sunday afternoons, of 'parties' who, in the language of the police sergeant, were subtly defined as 'not to say dhrunk, but in good fighting thrim.'

I got used to it all in time—I suppose one can get used to anything—I even became callous to the surprises of Mrs.

Cadogan's cooking. As the weather hardened and the wood-cock came in, and one by one I discovered and nailed up the rat holes, I began to find life endurable, and even to feel some remote sensation of home-coming when the grey horse turned in at the gate of Shreelane.

The one feature of my establishment to which I could not become inured was the pervading sub-presence of some thing or things which, for my own convenience, I summarized as Great-Uncle McCarthy. There were nights on which I was certain that I heard the inebriate shuffle of his foot overhead, the touch of his fumbling hand against the walls. There were dark times before the dawn when sounds went to and fro, the moving of weights, the creaking of doors, a far-away rapping in which was a workmanlike suggestion of the undertaker, a rumble of wheels on the avenue. Once I was impelled to the perhaps imprudent measure of cross-examining Mrs. Cadogan. Mrs. Cadogan, taking the preliminary precaution of crossing herself, asked me fatefully what day of the week it was.

' 'Friday!' she repeated after me. 'Friday! The Lord save us! 'Twas a Friday the old masther was buried!'

At this point a saucepan opportunely boiled over, and Mrs. Cadogan fled with it to the scullery, and was seen no more.

In the process of time I brought Great-Uncle McCarthy down to a fine point. On Friday nights he made coffins and drove hearses; during the rest of the week he rarely did more than patter and shuffle in the attics over my head.

One night, about the middle of December, I awoke, suddenly aware that some noise had fallen like a heavy stone into my dreams. As I felt for the matches it came again, the long, grudging groan and the uncompromising bang of the cross door at the head of the kitchen stairs. I told myself that it was a draught that had done it, but it was a perfectly still night. Even as I listened, a sound of wheels on the avenue shook the stillness. The thing was getting past a joke. In a few minutes I was stealthily groping my way down my own staircase, with a box of matches in my hand, enforced by scientific curiosity, but none the less armed with a stick. I stood in the dark at the top of the back stairs and listened; the snores of Mrs. Cadogan and her nephew Peter rose tranquilly from their respective lairs. I descended to the kitchen and lit a candle; there was nothing unusual there, except a great portion of the

Cadogan wearing apparel, which was arranged at the fire, and was being serenaded by two crickets. Whatever had opened the door, my household was blameless.

The kitchen was not attractive, yet I felt indisposed to leave it. None the less, it appeared to be my duty to inspect the yard. I put the candle on the table and went forth into the outer darkness. Not a·sound was to be heard. The night was very cold, and so dark, that I could scarcely distinguish the roofs of the stables against the sky; the house loomed tall and oppressive above me; I was conscious of how lonely it stood in the dumb and barren country. Spirits were certainly futile creatures, childish in their manifestations, stupidly content with the old machinery of raps and rumbles. I thought how fine a scene might be played on a stage like this; if I were a ghost, how bluely I would glimmer at the windows, how whimperingly chatter in the wind. Something whirled out of the darkness above me, and fell with a flop on the ground just at my feet. I jumped backwards, in point of fact I.made for the kitchen door, and, with my hand on the latch, stood still and waited. Nothing further happened; the thing that lay there did not stir. I struck a match. The moment of tension turned to bathos as the light flickered on nothing more fateful than a dead crow.

Dead it certainly was. I could have told that without looking at it; but why should it, at some considerable period after its death, fall from the clouds at my feet. But did it fall from the clouds? I struck another match, and stared up at the impenetrable face of the house. There was no hint of solution in the dark windows, but I determined to go up and search the rooms that gave upon the yard.

How cold it was! I can feel now the frozen musty air of those attics, with their rat-eaten floors and wallpapers furred with damp. I went softly from one to another, feeling like a burglar in my own house, and found nothing in elucidation of the mystery. The windows were hermetically shut and sealed with cobwebs. There was no furniture, except in the end room, where a wardrobe without doors stood in a corner, empty save for the solemn presence of a monstrous tall hat. I went back to bed, cursing those powers of darkness that had got me out of it, and heard no more.

My landlord had not failed of his promise to visit my coverts with his hounds; in fact, he fulfilled it rather more conscientiously than seemed to me quite wholesome for the cock-shooting. I maintained a silence which I felt to be magnanimous on the part of a man who cared nothing for hunting and a great deal for shooting, and wished the hounds more success in the slaughter of my foxes than seemed to be granted to them. I met them all, one red frosty evening, as I drove down the long hill to my demesne gates, Flurry at their head, in his shabby pink coat and dingy breeches, the hounds trailing dejectedly behind him and his half-dozen companions.

'What luck?' I called out, drawing rein as I met them.

'None,' said Mr. Flurry briefly. He did not stop, neither did he remove his pipe from the down-twisted corner of his mouth; his eye at me was cold and sour. The other members of the hunt passed me with equal hauteur; I thought they took their ill luck very badly.

On foot, among the last of the straggling hounds, cracking a carman's whip, and swearing comprehensively at them all, slouched my friend Slipper. Our friendship had begun in Court, the relative positions of the dock and the judgment-seat forming no obstacle to its progress, and had been cemented during several days' tramping after snipe. He was, as usual, a little drunk, and he hailed me as though I were a ship.

'Ahoy, Major Yeates!' he shouted, bringing himself up with a lurch against my cart; 'it's hunting you should be, in place of sending poor divils to gaol!'

'But I hear you had no hunting,' I said.

'Ye heard that, did ye?' Slipper rolled upon me an eye like that of a profligate pug. 'Well, begor, ye heard no more than the thruth.'

'But where are all the foxes?' said I.

'Begor, I don't know no more than your honour. And Shreelane—that there used to be as many foxes in it as there's crosses in a yard of check! Well, well, I'll say nothin' for it, only that it's quare! Here, Vaynus! Naygress!' Slipper uttered a yell, hoarse with whisky, in adjuration of two elderly ladies of the pack who had profited by our conversation to stray away into an adjacent cottage. 'Well, good-night, major. Mr. Flurry's as cross as briars, and he'll have me ate!'

He set off at a surprisingly steady run, cracking his whip,

and whooping like a madman.   I hope that when I also am fifty
I shall be able to run like Slipper. '

That frosty evening was followed by three others like unto it,
and a flight of woodcock came in.   I calculated that I could
do with five guns, and I dispatched invitations to shoot and
dine on the following day to four of the local sportsmen, among
whom was, of course, my landlord.   I remember that in my
letter to the latter I expressed a facetious hope that my bag of
cock would be more successful than his of foxes had been.

The answers to my invitations were not what I expected.
All, without so much as a conventional regret, declined my
invitation; Mr. Knox added that he hoped the bag of cock would
be to my liking, and that I need not be 'affraid' that the hounds
would trouble my coverts any more.   Here was war!   I gazed
in stupefaction at the crooked scrawl in which my landlord
had declared it.   It was wholly and entirely inexplicable, and
instead of going to sleep comfortably over the fire and my newspaper as a gentleman should, I spent the evening in irritated
ponderings over this bewildering and exasperating change of
front on the part of my friendly squireens.

My shoot the next day was scarcely a success.   I shot the
woods in company with my gamekeeper, Tim Connor, a
gentleman whose duties mainly consisted in limiting the poaching privileges to his personal friends, and whatever my offence
might have been, Mr. Knox could have wished me no bitterer
punishment than hearing the unavailing shouts of 'Mark cock!'
and seeing my birds winging their way from the coverts, far
out of shot.   Tim Connor and I got ten couple between us;
it might have been thirty if my neighbours had not boycotted
me, for what I could only suppose was the slackness of their
hounds.   .

I was dog-tired that night, having walked enough for three
men, and I slept the deep, insatiable sleep that I had earned.
It was somewhere about 3 a.m. that I was gradually awakened
by a continuous knocking, interspersed with muffled calls.
Great-Uncle McCarthy had never before given tongue, and I
freed one ear from blankets to listen.   Then I remembered
that Peter had told me the sweep had promised to arrive that
morning, and to arrive early.   Blind with sleep and fury I
went to the passage window, and thence desired the sweep to
go to the devil.   It availed me little.   For the remainder of the

night I could hear him pacing round the house, trying the windows, banging at the doors, and calling upon Peter Cadogan as the priests of Baal called upon their god. At six o'clock I had fallen into a troubled doze, when Mrs. Cadogan knocked at my door and imparted the information that the sweep had arrived. My answer need not be recorded, but in spite of it the door opened, and my housekeeper, in a weird *déshabille*, effectively lighted by the orange beams of her candle, entered my room.

'God forgive me, I never seen one I'd hate as much as that sweep!' she began; 'he's these three hours—arrah, what three hours!—no, but all night, raising tallywack and tandem round the house to get at the chimbleys.'

'Well, for heaven's sake let him get at the chimneys and let me go to sleep,' I answered, goaded to desperation, 'and you may tell him from me that if I hear his voice again I'll shoot him!'

Mrs. Cadogan silently left my bedside, and as she closed the door she said to herself, 'The Lord save us!'

Subsequent events may be briefly summarized. At 7.30 I was wakened anew by a thunderous sound in the chimney, and a brick crashed into the fireplace, followed at a short interval by two dead jackdaws and their nests. At eight I was informed by Peter that there was no hot water, and that he wished the divil would roast the same sweep. At 9.30, when I came down to breakfast, there was no fire anywhere, and my coffee, made in the coach-house, tasted of soot. I put on an overcoat and opened my letters. About fourth or fifth in the uninteresting heap came one in an egregiously disguised hand.

'Sir,' it began, 'this is to inform you your unsportsmanlike conduct has been discovered. You have been suspected this good while of shooting the Shreelane foxes, it is known now you do worse. Parties have seen your gamekeeper going regular to meet the Saturday early train at Salters Hill Station, with your grey horse under a cart, and your labels on the boxes, and we know as well as *your agent in Cork* what it is you have in those boxes. Be warned in time.—Your Wellwisher.'

I read this through twice before its drift became apparent, and I realized that I was accused of improving my shooting and my finances by the simple expedient of selling my foxes.

That is to say, I was in a worse position than if I had stolen
a horse, or murdered Mrs. Cadogan, or got drunk three times
a week in Skebawn.

For a few moments I fell into wild laughter, and then, aware
that it was rather a bad business to let a lie of this kind get a
start, I sat down to demolish the preposterous charge in a letter
to Flurry Knox. Somehow, as I selected my sentences, it was
borne in upon me that, if the letter spoke the truth, circum-
stantial evidence was rather against me. Mere lofty repudiation
would be unavailing, and by my infernal facetiousness about the
woodcock I had effectively filled in the case against myself.
At all events, the first thing to do was to establish a basis, and
have it out with Tim Connor. I rang the bell.

'Peter, is Tim Connor about the place?'

'He is not, sir. I heard him say he was going west the hill
to mend the bounds fence.' Peter's face was covered with
soot, his eyes were red, and he coughed ostentatiously. 'The
sweep's after breaking one of his brushes within in yer bedroom chimney, sir,' he went on, with all the satisfaction of his
class in announcing domestic calamity; 'he's above on the roof
now, and he'd be thankful to you to go up to him.'

I followed him upstairs in that state of simmering patience
that any employer of Irish labour must know and sympathize
with. I climbed the rickety ladder and squeezed through the
dirty trapdoor involved in the ascent to the roof, and was confronted by the hideous face of the sweep, black against the
frosty blue sky. He had encamped with all his paraphernalia
on the flat top of the roof, and was good enough to rise and put
his pipe in his pocket on my arrival.

'Good morning, Major. That's a grand view you have up
here,' said the sweep. He was evidently far too well-bred to
talk shop. 'I thravelled every roof in this counthry, and there
isn't one where you'd get as handsome a prospect!'

Theoretically he was right, but I had not come up to the roof
to discuss scenery, and demanded brutally why he had sent for
me. The explanation involved a recital of the special genius
required to sweep the Shreelane chimneys; of the fact that
the sweep had in infancy been sent up and down every one of
them by Great-Uncle McCarthy; of the three ass-loads of soot
that by his peculiar skill he had this morning taken from the
kitchen chimney; of its present purity, the draught being

such that it would 'dhraw up a young cat with it.' Finally—
realizing that I could endure no more—he explained that my
bedroom chimney had got what he called a 'wynd' in it, and he
proposed to climb down a little way in the stack to try 'would
he get to come at the brush.' The sweep was very small, the
chimney very large. I stipulated that he should have a rope
round his waist, and despite the illegality, I let him go. He
went down like a monkey, digging his toes and fingers into the
niches made for the purpose in the old chimney; Peter held the
rope. I lit a cigarette and waited.

Certainly the view from the roof was worth coming up to
look at. It was rough, heathery country on one side, with a
string of little blue lakes running like a turquoise necklet round
the base of a firry hill, and patches of pale green pasture were
set amidst the rocks and heather. A silvery flash behind the
undulations of the hills told where the Atlantic lay in immense
plains of sunlight. I turned to survey with an owner's eye
my own grey woods and straggling plantations of larch, and
espied a man coming out of the western wood. He had something on his back, and he was walking very fast; a rabbit poacher
no doubt. As he passed out of sight into the back avenue he
was beginning to run. At the same instant I saw on the hill
beyond my western boundaries half a dozen horsemen scrambling by zigzag ways down towards the wood. There was one
red coat among them; it came first at the gap in the fence that
Tim Connor had gone out to mend, and with the others was
lost to sight in the covert, from which, in another instant, came
clearly through the frosty air a shout of 'Gone to ground!'
Tremendous horn blowings followed, then, all in the same
moment, I saw the hounds break in full cry from the wood, and
come stringing over the grass and up the back avenue towards
the yard gate. Were they running a fresh fox into the stables?

I do not profess to be a hunting man, but I am an Irishman,
and so, it is perhaps superfluous to state, is Peter. We forgot
the sweep as if he had never existed, and precipitated ourselves
down the ladder, down the stairs, and out into the yard. One
side of the yard is formed by the coach-house and a long stable,
with a range of lofts above them, planned on the heroic scale
in such matters that obtained in Ireland formerly. These
join the house at the corner by the back door. A long flight of
stone steps leads to the lofts, and up these, as Peter and I

emerged from the back door, the hounds were struggling helter-skelter. Almost simultaneously there was a confused clatter of hoofs in the back avenue, and Flurry Knox came stooping at a gallop under the archway followed by three or four other riders. They flung themselves from their horses and made for the steps of the loft; more hounds pressed, yelling, on their heels, the din was indescribable, and justified Mrs. Cadogan's subsequent remark that 'when she heard the noise she thought 'twas the end of the world and the divil collecting his own!'

I jostled in the wake of the party, and found myself in the loft, wading in hay, and nearly deafened by the clamour that was bandied about the high roof and walls. At the farther end of the loft the hounds were raging in the hay, encouraged thereto by the whoops and screeches of Flurry and his friends. High up in the gable of the loft, where it joined the main wall of the house, there was a small door, and I noted with a transient surprise that there was a long ladder leading up to it. Even as it caught my eye a hound fought his way out of a drift of hay and began to jump at the ladder, throwing his tongue vociferously, and even clambering up a few rungs in his excitement.

'There's the way he's gone!' roared Flurry, striving through hounds and hay towards the ladder, 'Trumpeter has him! What's up there, back of the door, Major? I don't remember it at all.'

My crimes had evidently been forgotten in the supremacy of the moment. While I was futilely asserting that had the fox gone up the ladder he could not possibly have opened the door and shut it after him, even if the door led anywhere, which, to the best of my belief, it did not, the door in question opened, and to my amazement the sweep appeared at it. He gesticulated violently, and over the tumult was heard to asseverate that there was nothing above there, only a way into the flue, and any one would be destoyed with the soot——

'Ah, go to blazes with your soot!' interrupted Flurry, already half-way up the ladder.

I followed him, the other men pressing up behind me. That Trumpeter had made no mistake was instantly brought home to our noses by the reek of fox that met us at the door. Instead of a chimney, we found ourselves in a dilapidated bedroom, full of people. Tim Connor was there, the sweep was there, and a squalid elderly man and woman on whom I had never set eyes before: There was a large open fireplace, black with the soot the sweep had brought down with him, and on the table stood a bottle of my own special Scotch whisky. In one corner of the room was a pile of broken packing-cases, and beside these on the floor lay a bag in which something kicked.

Flurry, looking more uncomfortable and nonplussed than I could have believed possible, listened in silence to the ceaseless harangue of the elderly woman. The hounds were yelling like lost spirits in the loft below, but her voice pierced the uproar like a bagpipe. It was an unspeakably vulgar voice, yet it was not the voice of a countrywoman, and there were frowzy remnants of respectability about her general aspect.

'And is it you, Flurry Knox, that's calling me a disgrace! Disgrace, indeed, am I? Me that was your poor mother's own uncle's daughter, and as good a McCarthy as ever stood in Shreelane!'

What followed I could not comprehend, owing to the fact that the sweep kept up a perpetual undercurrent of explanation to me as to how he had got down the wrong chimney. I noticed that his breath stank of whisky—Scotch, not the native variety.

· · · · ·

Never, as long as Flurry Knox lives to blow a horn, will he hear the last of the day that he ran his mother's first cousin to ground in the attic. Never, while Mrs. Cadogan can hold a basting spoon, will she cease to recount how, on the same occasion, she plucked and roasted ten couple of woodcock in one torrid hour to provide luncheon for the hunt. In the glory of this achievement her confederacy with the stowaways in the attic is wholly slurred over, in much the same manner as the startling outburst of summons for trespass, brought by Tim Connor during the remainder of the shooting season, obscured the unfortunate episode of the bagged fox. It was, of course, zeal for my shooting that induced him to assist Mr. Knox's disreputable relations in the deportation of my foxes; and I have allowed it to remain at that.

In fact, the only things not allowed to remain were Mr. and Mrs. McCarthy Gannon. They, as my landlord informed me, in the midst of vast apologies, had been permitted to squat at Shreelane until my tenancy began, and having then ostentatiously and abusively left the house, they had, with the connivance of the Cadogans, secretly returned to roost in the corner attic, to sell foxes under the aegis of my name, and to make inroads on my belongings. They retained connection with the outer world by means of the ladder and the loft, and with the house in general, and my whisky in particular, by a door into the other attics—a door concealed by the wardrobe in which reposed Great-Uncle McCarthy's tall hat.

It is with the greatest regret that I relinquish the prospect of writing a monograph on Great-Uncle McCarthy for a Spiritualistic journal, but with the departure of his relations he ceased to manifest himself, and neither the nailing up of packing-cases, nor the rumble of the cart that took them to the station, disturbed my sleep for the future.

I understand that the task of clearing out the McCarthy Gannons' effects was of a nature that necessitated two glasses of whisky per man; and if the remnants of rabbit and jackdaw disinterred in the process were anything like the crow that was thrown out of the window at my feet, I do not grudge the restorative.

As Mrs. Cadogan remarked to the sweep, 'A Turk couldn't stand it.'

II

IN THE CURRANHILTY COUNTRY

It is hardly credible that I should have been induced to depart from my usual walk of life by a creature so uninspiring as the grey horse that I bought from Flurry Knox for twenty-five pounds.

Perhaps it was the monotony of being questioned by every other person with whom I had five minutes' conversation, as to when I was coming out with the hounds, and being further informed that in the days when Captain Browne, the late coastguard officer, had owned the grey, there was not a fence between this and Mallow big enough to please them. At all events, there came an epoch-making day when I mounted the Quaker and presented myself at a meet of Mr. Knox's hounds.

It is my belief that six out of every dozen people who go out hunting are disagreeably conscious of a nervous system, and two out of the six are in what is brutally called 'a blue funk.' I was not in a blue funk, but I was conscious not only of a nervous system, but of the anatomical fact that I possessed large, round legs, handsome in their way, even admirable in their proper sphere, but singularly ill adapted for adhering to the slippery surfaces of a saddle. By a fatal intervention of Providence, the sport, on this my first day in the hunting-field, was such as I could have enjoyed from a bath-chair. The hunting-field was, on this occasion, a relative term, implying long stretches of unfenced moorland and bog, anything, in fact, save a field; the hunt itself might also have been termed a relative one, being mainly composed of Mr. Knox's relations in all degrees of cousinhood. It was a day when frost and sunshine combined went to one's head like iced champagne; the distant sea looked like the Mediterranean, and for four sunny hours the Knox relatives and I followed nine couple of hounds at a tranquil footpace along the hills, our progress mildly enlivened by one or two scrambles in the shape of jumps. At three o'clock I jogged home, and felt within me the newborn desire to brag to Peter Cadogan of the Quaker's doings, as I dismounted rather stiffly in my own yard.

I little thought that the result would be that three weeks later I should find myself in a railway carriage at an early hour of a December morning, in company with Flurry Knox and four or five of his clan, journeying towards an unknown town, named Drumcurran, with an appropriate number of horses in boxes behind us and a van full of hounds in front. Mr. Knox's hounds were on their way, by invitation, to have a day in the country of their neighbours, the Curranhilty Harriers, and with amazing fatuity I had allowed myself to be cajoled into joining the party. A northerly shower was striking in long spikes on the glass of the window, the atmosphere of the carriage was blue with tobacco smoke, and my feet, in a pair of new butcher boots, had sunk into a species of Arctic sleep.

'Well, you got my letter about the dance at the hotel to-night?' said Flurry Knox, breaking off a whispered conversation with his amateur whip, Dr. Jerome Hickey, and sitting down beside me. 'And we're to go out with the Harriers to-day, and they've a sure fox for our hounds to-morrow. I tell you you'll have the best fun ever you had. It's a great country to ride. Fine honest banks, that you can come racing at anywhere you like.'

Dr. Hickey, a saturnine young man, with a long nose and a black torpedo beard, returned to his pocket the lancet with which he had been trimming his nails.

'They're like the Tipperary banks,' he said; 'you climb down nine feet and you fall the rest.'

It occurred to me that the Quaker and I would most probably fall all the way, but I said nothing.

'I hear Tomsy Flood has a good horse this season,' resumed Flurry.

'Then it's not the one you sold him,' said the doctor.

'I'll take my oath it's not,' said Flurry with a grin. 'I believe he has it in for me still over that one.'

Dr. Jerome's moustache went up under his nose and showed his white teeth.

'Small blame to him! when you sold him a mare that was wrong of both her hind legs. Do you know what he did, Major Yeates? The mare was lame going into the fair, and he took the two hind shoes off her and told poor Flood she kicked them off in the box, and that was why she was going tender, and he was so drunk he believed him.'

The conversation here deepened into trackless obscurities of horse-dealing. I took out my stylograph pen, and finished a letter to Philippa, with a feeling that it would probably be my last.

The next step in the day's enjoyment consisted in trotting in cavalcade through the streets of Drumcurran, with another northerly shower descending upon us, the mud splashing in my face, and my feet coming torturingly to life. Every man and boy in the town ran with us; the Harriers were somewhere in the tumult ahead, and the Quaker began to pull and hump his back ominously. I arrived at the meet considerably heated, and found myself one of some thirty or forty riders, who, with traps and bicycles and footpeople, were jammed in a narrow, muddy road. We were late, and a move was immediately made across a series of grass fields, all considerately furnished with gates. There was a glacial gleam of sunshine, and people began to turn down the collars of their coats. As they spread over the field I observed that Mr. Knox was no longer riding

with old Captain Handcock, the Master of the Harriers, but
had attached himself to a square-shouldered young lady with
effective coils of dark hair and a grey habit. She was riding
a fidgety black mare with great decision and a not disagreeable
swagger.

It was at about this moment that the hounds began to run,
fast and silently, and every one began to canter.

'This is nothing at all,' said Dr. Hickey, thundering alongside of me on a huge young chestnut; 'there might have been a
hare here last week, or a red herring this morning. I wouldn't
care if we only got what 'd warm us. For the matter of that,
I 'd as soon hunt a cat as a hare.'

I was already getting quite enough to warm me. The
Quaker's respectable grey head had twice disappeared between
his forelegs in a brace of most unsettling bucks, and all my
experiences at the riding-school at Sandhurst did not prepare
me for the sensation of jumping a briary wall with a heavy drop
into a lane so narrow that each horse had to turn at right angles
as he landed. I did not so turn, but saved myself from entire
disgrace by a timely clutch at the mane. We scrambled out
of the lane over a pile of stones and furze bushes, and at the
end of the next field were confronted by a tall, stone-faced bank.
Every one, always excepting myself, was riding with that
furious valour which is so conspicuous when neighbouring
hunts meet, and the leading half-dozen charged the obstacle at
steeplechase speed. I caught a glimpse of the young lady in
the grey habit, sitting square and strong as her mare topped
the bank, with Flurry and the redoubtable Mr. Tomsy Flood
riding on either hand; I followed in their wake, with a blind
confidence in the Quaker, and none at all in myself. He refused
it. I suppose it was in token of affection and gratitude that
I fell upon his neck: at all events, I had reason to respect his
judgment, as, before I had recovered myself, the hounds were
straggling back into the field by a gap lower down.

It finally appeared that the hounds could do no more with
the line they had been hunting, and we proceeded to jog inter-
minably, I knew not whither. During this unpleasant process
Flurry Knox bestowed on me many items of information,
chiefly as to the pangs of jealousy he was inflicting on Mr.
Flood by his attentions to the lady in the grey habit, Miss
'Bobbie' Bennett.

'She 'll have all old Handcock's money one of these days—
she 's his niece, y' know—and she 's a good girl to ride, but
she 's not as young as she was ten years ago. You 'd be looking
at a chicken a long time before you thought of her! She might
take Tomsy some day if she can't do any better.' He stopped
and looked at me with a gleam in his eye. 'Come on, and I 'll
introduce you to her!'

Before, however, this privilege could be mine, the whole
cavalcade was stopped by a series of distant yells, which apparently conveyed information to the hunt, though to me they only
suggested a Red Indian scalping his enemy. The yells travelled
rapidly nearer, and a young man with a scarlet face and a long
stick sprang upon the fence, and explained that he and Patsy
Lorry were after chasing a hare two miles down out of the hill
above, and ne'er a dog nor a one with them but themselves,
and she was lying, beat out, under a bush, and Patsy Lorry
was minding her until the hounds would come. I had a vision
of the humane Patsy Lorry fanning the hare with his hat, but
apparently nobody else found the fact unusual. The hounds
were hurried into the fields, the hare was again spurred into
action, and I was again confronted with the responsibilities of
the chase. After the first five minutes I had discovered several
facts about the Quaker. If the bank was above a certain height
he refused it irrevocably, if it accorded with his ideas he got his
forelegs over and ploughed through the rest of it on his stifle-
joints, or, if a gripe made this inexpedient, he remained poised
on top till the fabric crumbled under his weight. In the case
of walls he butted them down with his knees, or squandered
them with his hind legs. These operations took time, and the
leaders of the hunt streamed farther and farther away over the
crest of a hill, while the Quaker pursued at the equable gallop
of a horse in the Bayeux Tapestry.

I began to perceive that I had been adopted as a pioneer
by a small band of followers, who, as one of their number
candidly explained, 'liked to have someone ahead of them to
soften the banks,' and accordingly waited respectfully till the
Quaker had made the rough places smooth, and taken the raw
edge off the walls. They, in their turn, showed me alternative
routes when the obstacle proved above the Quaker's limit;
thus, in ignoble confederacy, I and the offscourings of the
Curranhilty hunt pursued our way across some four miles of

country. When at length we parted it was with extreme
regret on both sides. A river crossed our course, with boggy
banks pitted deep with the hoof marks of our forerunners;
I suggested it to the Quaker, and discovered that Nature had not
in vain endued him with the hind quarters of the hippopotamus.
I presume the others had jumped it; the Quaker, with abysmal
flounderings, walked through and heaved himself to safety on
the farther bank. It was the dividing of the ways. My friendly
company turned aside as one man, and I was left with the world
before me, and no guide save the hoof-marks in the grass.
These presently led me to a road, on the other side of which
was a bank, that was at once added to the Quaker's black list.
The rain had again begun to fall heavily, and was soaking in
about my elbows; I suddenly asked myself why, in heaven's
name, I should go any farther. No adequate reason occurred
to me, and I turned in what I believed to be the direction of
Drumcurran.

I rode on for possibly two or three miles without seeing a
human being, until, from the top of a hill I descried a solitary
lady rider. I started in pursuit. The rain kept blurring my
eye-glass, but it seemed to me that the rider was a schoolgirl
with hair hanging down her back, and that her horse was a
trifle lame. I pressed on to ask my way, and discovered that
I had been privileged to overtake no less a person than Miss
Bobbie Bennett.

My question as to the route led to information of a varied
character. Miss Bennett was going that way herself; her mare
had given her what she called 'a toss and a half,' whereby she
had strained her arm and the mare her shoulder, her habit
had been torn, and she had lost all her hairpins.

'I 'm an awful object,' she concluded; 'my hair 's the plague
of my life out hunting! I declare I wish to goodness I was bald!'

I struggled to the level of the occasion with an appropriate
protest. She had really very brilliant grey eyes, and her complexion was undeniable. Philippa has since explained to me
that it is a mere male fallacy that any woman can look well with
her hair down her back, but I have always maintained that Miss
Bobbie Bennett, with the rain glistening on her dark tresses,
looked uncommonly well.

'I shall never get it dry for the dance to-night,' she complained.

B 97⁸

'I wish I could help you,' said I.

'Perhaps you 've got a hairpin or two about you!' said she, with a glance that had certainly done great execution before now.

I disclaimed the possession of any such tokens, but volunteered to go and look for some at a neighbouring cottage.

The cottage door was shut, and my knockings were answered by a stupefied-looking elderly man. Conscious of my own absurdity, I asked him if he had any hairpins.

'I didn't see a hare this week!' he responded in a slow bellow.

'Hairpins!' I roared; 'has your wife any hairpins?'

'She has not.' Then, as an afterthought, 'She 's dead these ten years.'

At this point a young woman emerged from the cottage, and, with many coy grins, plucked from her own head some half-dozen hairpins, crooked, and grey with age, but still hairpins, and as such well worth my shilling. I returned with my spoil to Miss Bennett, only to be confronted with a fresh difficulty. The arm that she had strained was too stiff to raise to her head.

Miss Bobbie turned her handsome eyes upon me. 'It 's no use,' she said plaintively, 'I can't do it!'

I looked up and down the road; there was no one in sight. I offered to do it for her.

Miss Bennett's hair was long, thick, and soft; it was also slippery with rain. I twisted it conscientiously, as if it were a hay rope, until Miss Bennett, with an irrepressible shriek, told me it would break off. I coiled the rope with some success, and proceeded to nail it to her head with the hairpins. At all the most critical points one, if not both, of the horses moved; hairpins were driven home into Miss Bennett's skull, and were with difficulty plucked forth again; in fact, a more harrowing performance can hardly be imagined, but Miss Bennett bore it with the heroism of a pin-cushion.

I was putting the finishing touches to the coiffure when some sound made me look round, and I beheld at a distance of some fifty yards the entire hunt approaching us at a foot-pace. I lost my head, and, instead of continuing my task, I dropped the last hairpin as if it were red-hot, and kicked the Quaker away to the far side of the road, thus, if it were possible, giving the position away a shade more generously.

There were fifteen riders in the group that overtook us, and fourteen of them, including the Whip, were grinning from ear to ear; the fifteenth was Mr. Tomsy Flood, and he showed no sign of appreciation. He shoved his horse past me and up to Miss Bennett, his red moustache bristling, truculence in every outline of his heavy shoulders. His green coat was muddy, and his hat had a cave in it. Things had apparently gone ill with him.

Flurry's witticisms held out for about two miles and a half; I do not give them, because they were not amusing, but they all dealt ultimately with the animosity that I, in common with himself, should henceforth have to fear from Mr. Flood.

'Oh, he's a holy terror!' he said conclusively; 'he was riding the tails off the hounds to-day to best me. He was near killing me twice. We had some words about it, I can tell you. I very near took my whip to him. Such a bull-rider of a fellow I never saw! He wouldn't so much as stop to catch Bobbie Bennett's horse when I picked her up, he was riding so jealous. His own girl, mind you! And such a crumpler as she got too! I declare she knocked a groan out of the road when she struck it!'

'She doesn't seem so much hurt?' I said.

'Hurt!' said Flurry, flicking casually at a hound. 'You couldn't hurt that one unless you took a hatchet to her!'

The rain had reached a pitch that put further hunting out of the question, and we bumped home at that intolerable pace known as a 'hounds' jog.' I spent the remainder of the afternoon over a fire in my bedroom in the Royal Hotel, Drumcurran, official letters to write having mercifully provided me with an excuse for seclusion, while the bar and the billiard-room hummed below, and the Quaker's three-cornered gallop wreaked its inevitable revenge upon my person. As this process continued, and I became proportionately embittered, I asked myself, not for the first time, what Philippa would say when introduced to my present circle of acquaintances.

I have already mentioned that a dance was to take place at the hotel, given, as far as I could gather, by the leading lights of the Curranhilty Hunt. A less jocund guest than the wreck who at the pastoral hour of nine crept stiffly down to 'chase the glowing hours with flying feet' could hardly have been encountered. The dance was held in the coffee-room, and a conspicuous object outside the door was a saucer bath full of something that looked like flour.

'Rub your feet in that,' said Flurry; 'that's French chalk!
They hadn't time to do the floor, so they hit on this dodge.'

I complied with this encouraging direction, and followed him
into the room. Dancing had already begun, and the first sight
that met my eyes was Miss Bennett, in a yellow dress, waltzing
with Mr. Tomsy Flood. She looked very handsome, and, in
spite of her accident, she was getting round the sticky floor
and her still more sticky partner with the swing of a racing cutter.
Her eye caught mine immediately, and with confidence. Clearly
our acquaintance that, in the space of twenty minutes, had
blossomed tropically into hair-dressing, was not to be allowed
to wither. Nor was I myself allowed to wither. Men, known
and unknown, plied me with partners, till my shirt cuff was
black with names, and the number of dances stretched away into
the blue distance of to-morrow morning. The music was
supplied by the organist of the church, who played with
religious unction and at the pace of a processional hymn. I put
forth into the mêlée with a junior Bennett, inferior in calibre
to Miss Bobbie, but a strong goer, and, I fear, made but a sorry
début in the eyes of Drumcurran. At every other moment I
bumped into the unforeseen orbits of those who reversed, and
of those who walked their partners backwards down the room
with faces of ineffable supremacy. Being unskilled in these
intricacies of an elder civilization, the younger Miss Bennet
fared but ingloriously at my hands; the music pounded inter
minably on, until the heel of Mr. Flood put a period to our
sufferings.

'The nasty dirty filthy brute!' shrieked the younger Miss
Bennett in a single breath; 'he's torn the gown off my back!'

She whirled me to the cloak-room; we parted, mutually un
regretted, at its door, and by, I fear, common consent, evaded
our second dance together.

Many, many times during the evening I asked myself why
I did not go to bed. Perhaps it was the remembrance that my
bed was situated some ten feet above the piano in a direct line
but, whatever was the reason, the night wore on and found me
still working my way down my shirt cuff. I sat out as much as
possible, and found my partners to be, as a body, pretty, talka
tive, and ill-dressed, and during the evening I had many an
varied opportunities of observing the rapid progress of Mr
Knox's flirtation with Miss Bobbie Bennett. From No.

to No. 8 they were invisible; that they were behind a screen in the commercial-room might 'be inferred from Mr. Flood's thunder-cloud presence in the passage outside.

At No. 9 the young lady emerged for one of her dances with me; it was a barn dance, and particularly trying to my momently stiffening muscles; but Miss Bobbie, whether in dancing or sitting out, went in for 'the rigour of the game.' She was in as hard condition as one of her uncle's hounds, and for a full fifteen minutes I capered and swooped beside her, larding the lean earth as I went, and replying but spasmodically to her even flow of conversation.

'That 'll take the stiffness out of you!' she exclaimed, as the organist slowed down reverentially to a conclusion. 'I had a bet with Flurry Knox over that dance. He said you weren't up to my weight at the pace!'

I led her forth to the refreshment table, and was watching with awe her fearless consumption of claret cup that I would not have touched for a sovereign, when Flurry, with a partner on his arm, strolled past us.

'Well, you won the gloves, Miss Bobbie!' he said. 'Don't you wish you may get them!'

'Gloves without the *g*, Mr. Knox!' replied Miss Bennett, in a voice loud enough to reach the end of the passage, where Mr. Thomas Flood was burying his nose in a very brown whisky-and-soda.

'Your hair 's coming down!' retorted Flurry. 'Ask Major Yeates if he can spare you a few hairpins!'

Swifter than lightning Miss Bennett hurled a macaroon at her retreating foe, missed him, and subsided laughing on to a sofa. I mopped my brow and took my seat beside her, wondering how much longer I could live up to the social exigencies of Drumcurran.

Miss Bennett, however, proved excellent company. She told me artfully, and inch by inch, all that Mr. Flood had said to her on the subject of my hair-dressing; she admitted that she had, as a punishment, cut him out of three dances and given them to Flurry Knox. When I remarked that in fairness they should have been given to me, she darted a very attractive glance at me, and pertinently observed that I had not asked for them.

> As steals the dawn into a fevered room,
> And says 'Be of good cheer, the day is born!'

so did the rumour of supper pass among the chaperons, male and female. It was obviously due to a sense of the fitness of things that Mrs. Bennett was apportioned to me, and I found myself in the gratifying position of heading with her the procession to supper. My impressions of Mrs. Bennett are few but salient. She wore an apple-green satin dress and filled it tightly; wisely mistrusting the hotel supper, she had imported sandwiches and cake in a pocket-handkerchief, and, warmed by two glasses of sherry, she made me the recipient of the remarkable confidence that she had but two back teeth in her head, but, thank God, they met. When, with the other starving men, I fell upon the remains of the feast, I regretted that I had declined her offer of a sandwich.

Of the remainder of the evening I am unable to give a detailed account. Let it not for one instant be imagined that I had looked upon the wine of the Royal Hotel when it was red, or, indeed, any other colour; as a matter of fact, I had espied an inconspicuous corner in the entrance hall, and there I first smoked a cigarette, and subsequently sank into uneasy sleep. Through my dreams I was aware of the measured pounding of the piano, of the clatter of glasses at the bar, of wheels in the street, and then, more clearly, of Flurry's voice assuring Miss Bennett that if she'd only wait for another dance he'd get the R.M. out of bed to do her hair for her—then again oblivion.

At some later period I was dropping down a chasm on the Quaker's back, and landing with a shock; I was twisting his mane into a chignon, when he turned around his head and caught my arm in his teeth. I awoke with the dew of terror on my forehead, to find Miss Bennett leaning over me in a scarlet cloak with a hood over her head, and shaking me by my coat sleeve.

'Major Yeates,' she began at once in a hurried whisper, 'I want you to find Flurry Knox, and tell him there's a plan to feed his hounds at six o'clock this morning so as to spoil their hunting!'

'How do you know?' I asked, jumping up.

'My little brother told me. He came in with us to-night to see the dance, and he was hanging round in the stables, and he heard one of the men telling another there was a dead mule in an outhouse in Bride's Alley, all cut up ready to give to Mr. Knox's hounds.'

'But why shouldn't they get it?' I asked in sleepy stupidity.

'Is it fill them up with an old mule just before they're going out hunting?' flashed Miss Bennett. 'Hurry and tell Mr. Knox; don't let Tomsy Flood see you telling him—or any one else.'

'Oh, then, it's Mr. Flood's game?' I said grasping the situation at length.

'It is,' said Miss Bennett, suddenly turning scarlet; 'he's a disgrace! I'm ashamed of him! I'm done with him!'

I resisted a strong disposition to shake Miss Bennett by the hand.

'I can't wait,' she continued. 'I made my mother drive back a mile—she doesn't know a thing about it—I said I'd left my purse in the cloak-room. Good-night! Don't tell a soul but Flurry!'

She was off, and upon my incapable shoulders rested the responsibility of the enterprise.

It was past four o'clock, and the last bars of the last waltz were being played. At the bar a knot of men, with Flurry in their midst, were tossing 'Odd man out' for a bottle of champagne. Flurry was not in the least drunk, a circumstance worthy of remark in his present company, and I got him out into the hall and unfolded my tidings. The light of battle lit in his eye as he listened.

'I knew by Tomsy he was shaping for mischief,' he said coolly; 'he's taken as much liquor as'd stiffen a tinker, and he's only half drunk this minute. Hold on till I get Jerome Hickey and Charlie Knox—they're sober; I'll be back in a minute.'

I was not present at the council of war thus hurriedly convened; I was merely informed when they returned that we were all to 'hurry on.' My best evening pumps have never recovered the subsequent proceedings. They, with my swelled and aching feet inside them, were raced down one filthy lane after another, until, somewhere on the outskirts of Drumcurran, Flurry pushed open the gate of a yard and went in. It was nearly five o'clock on that raw December morning; low down in the sky a hazy moon shed a diffused light; all the surrounding houses were still and dark. At our footsteps an angry bark or two came from inside the stable.

'Whisht!' said Flurry, 'I'll say a word to them before I open the door.'

At his voice a chorus of hysterical welcome arose; without more delay he flung open the stable door, and instantly we were all knee-deep in a rush of hounds. There was not a moment lost. Flurry started at a quick run out of the yard with the whole pack pattering at his heels. Charlie Knox vanished; Dr. Hickey and I followed the hounds, splashing into puddles and hobbling over patches of broken stones, till we left the town behind and hedges arose on either hand.

'Here's the house!' said Flurry, stopping short at a low entrance gate; 'many's the time I've been here when his father had it; it'll be a queer thing if I can't find a window I can manage, and the old cook he has is as deaf as the dead.'

He and Doctor Hickey went in at the gate with the hounds; I hesitated ignobly in the mud.

'This isn't an R.M.'s job,' said Flurry in a whisper, closing the gate in my face; 'you'd best keep clear of house-breaking.'

I accepted his advice, but I may admit that before I turned for home a sash was gently raised, a light had sprung up in one of the lower windows, and I heard Flurry's voice saying, 'Over, over, over!' to his hounds.

There seemed to me to be no interval at all between these events and the moment when I woke in bright sunlight to find Dr. Hickey standing by my bedside in a red coat with a tall glass in his hand.

'It's nine o'clock,' he said. 'I'm just after waking Flurry Knox. There wasn't one stirring in the hotel till I went down and pulled the "boots" from under the kitchen table! It's well for us the meet's in the town; and, by the by, your grey horse has four legs on him the size of bolsters this morning; he won't be fit to go out, I'm afraid. Drink this anyway, you're in the want of it.'

Dr. Hickey's eyelids were rather pink, but his hand was as steady as a rock. The whisky-and-soda was singularly un-tempting.

'What happened last night?' I asked eagerly as I gulped it.

'Oh, it all went off very nicely, thank you,' said Hickey, twisting his black beard to a point. 'We benched as many of the hounds in Flood's bed as 'd fit, and we shut the lot into the room. We had them just comfortable when we heard his latch-key below at the door.' He broke off and began to snigger.

'Well?' I said, sitting bolt upright.

'Well, he got in at last, and he lit a candle then. That took him five minutes. He was pretty tight. We were looking at him over the banisters until he started to come up, and according as he came up, we went on up the top flight. He stood admiring his candle for a while on the landing, and we wondered he didn't hear the hounds snuffing under the door. He opened it then, and, on the minute, three of them bolted out between his legs.' Dr. Hickey again paused to indulge in Mephistophelian laughter. 'Well, you know,' he went on, 'when a man in poor Tomsy's condition sees six dogs jumping out of his bed he's apt to make a wrong diagnosis. He gave a roar, and pitched the candlestick at them, and ran for his life downstairs, and all the hounds after him. "Gone away!" screeches that devil Flurry, pelting downstairs on top of them in the dark. I believe I screeched too.'

'Good heavens!' I gasped, 'I was well out of that!'

'Well, you were,' admitted the doctor. 'However, Tomsy bested them in the dark, and he got to ground in the pantry. I heard the cups and saucers go as he slammed the door on the hounds' noses, and the minute he was in Flurry turned the key on him. "They're real dogs, Tomsy, my buck!" says Flurry, just to quiet him; and there we left him.'

'Was he hurt?' I asked, conscious of the triviality of the question.

'Well, he lost his brush,' replied Dr. Hickey. 'Old Merrylegs tore the coat-tails off him; we got them on the floor when we struck a light; Flurry has them to nail on his kennel door. Charlie Knox had a pleasant time too,' he went on, 'with the man that brought the barrow-load of meat to the stable. We picked out the tastiest bits and arranged them round Flood's breakfast table for him. They smelt very nice. Well, I'm delaying you with my talking——'

Flurry's hounds had the run of the season that day. I saw it admirably throughout—from Miss Bennett's pony cart. She drove extremely well, in spite of her strained arm.

* B 978

III

TRINKET'S COLT

IT was Petty Sessions day in Skebawn, a cold, grey day of
February. A case of trespass had dragged its burden of cross
summonses and cross swearing far into the afternoon, and when
I left the bench my head was singing from the bellowings of
the attorneys, and the smell of their clients was heavy upon my
palate.

The streets still testified to the fact that it was market day,
and I evaded with difficulty the sinuous course of carts full of
soddenly screwed people, and steered an equally devious one
for myself among the groups anchored round the doors of the
public-houses. Skebawn possesses, among its legion of public-
houses, one establishment which timorously, and almost imperceptibly, proffers tea to the thirsty. I turned in there, as
was my custom on court days, and found the little dingy den,
known as the Ladies' Coffee-room, in the occupancy of my
friend Mr. Florence McCarthy Knox, who was drinking strong
tea and eating buns with serious simplicity. It was a first and
quite unexpected glimpse of that domesticity that has now become a marked feature in his character.

'You 're the very man I wanted to see,' I said as I sat down
beside him at the oilcloth-covered table; 'a man I know in
England who is not much of a judge of character has asked me
to buy him a four-year-old down here, and as I should rather
be stuck by a friend than a dealer, I wish you 'd take over the job.'

'Flurry poured himself out another cup of tea, and dropped
three lumps of sugar into it in silence.

Finally he said, 'There isn't a four-year-old in this country
that I 'd be seen dead with at a pig fair.'

This was discouraging, from the premier authority on horseflesh in the district.

'But it isn't six weeks since you told me you had the finest
filly in your stables that was ever foaled in the County Cork,'
I protested; 'what 's wrong with her?'

'Oh, is it that filly?' said Mr. Knox with a lenient smile;
'she 's gone these three weeks from me. I swapped her and
six pounds for a three-year-old Ironmonger colt, and after that

I swapped the colt and nineteen pounds for that Bandon horse I rode last week at your place, and after that again I sold the Bandon horse for seventy-five pounds to old Welply, and I had to give him back a couple of sovereigns luck-money. You see I did pretty well with the filly after all.'

'Yes, yes—oh, rather,' I assented, as one dizzily accepts the propositions of a bimetellist; 'and you don't know of anything else——?'

The room in which we were seated was closely screened from the shop by a door with a muslin-curtained window in it; several of the panes were broken, and at this juncture two voices that had for some time carried on a discussion forced themselves upon our attention.

'Begging your pardon for contradicting you, ma'am,' said the voice of Mrs. McDonald, proprietress of the tea-shop, and a leading light in Skebawn Dissenting circles, shrilly tremulous with indignation, 'if the servants I recommend you won't stop with you, it's no fault of mine. If respectable young girls are set picking grass out of your gravel, in place of their proper work, certainly they will give warning!'

The voice that replied struck me as being a notable one, well-bred and imperious.

'When I take a barefooted slut out of a cabin, I don't expect her to dictate to me what her duties are!'

Flurry jerked up his chin in a noiseless laugh. 'It's my grandmother!' he whispered. 'I bet you Mrs. McDonald don't get much change out of her!'

'If I set her to clean the pigsty I expect her to obey me,' continued the voice in accents that would have made me clean forty pigsties had she desired me to do so.

'Very well, ma'am,' retorted Mrs. McDonald, 'if that's the way you treat your servants, you needn't come here again looking for them. I consider your conduct is neither that of a lady nor a Christian!'

'Don't you, indeed?' replied Flurry's grandmother. 'Well, your opinion doesn't greatly distress me, for, to tell you the truth, I don't think you're much of a judge.'

'Didn't I tell you she'd score?' murmured Flurry, who was by this time applying his eye to a hole in the muslin curtain. 'She's off,' he went on, returning to his tea. 'She's a great character! She's eighty-three if she's a day, and she's as sound on her legs as a three-year-old! Did you see that old shandrydan of hers in the street a while ago, and a fellow on the box with a red beard on him like Robinson Crusoe? That old mare that was on the near side—Trinket her name is—is mighty near clean bred. I can tell you her foals are worth a bit of money.'

I had heard of old Mrs. Knox of Aussolas; indeed, I had seldom dined out in the neighbourhood without hearing some new story of her and her remarkable *ménage*, but it had not yet been my privilege to meet her.

'Well, now,' went on Flurry in his slow voice, 'I 'll tell you a thing that 's just come into 'my head. My grandmother promised me a foal of Trinket's the day I was one-and-twenty, and that 's five years ago, and deuce a one I 've got from her yet. You never were at Aussolas? No, you were not. Well, I tell you the place there is like a circus with horses. She has a couple of score of them running wild in the woods, like deer.'

'Oh, come,' I said, 'I 'm a bit of a liar myself——'

'Well, she has a dozen of them anyhow, rattling good colts too, some of them, but they might as well be donkeys, for all the good they are to me or any one. It 's not once in three years she sells one, and there she has them walking after her for bits of sugar, like a lot of dirty lapdogs,' ended Flurry with disgust.

'Well, what 's your plan? Do you want me to make her a bid for one of the lapdogs?'

'I was thinking,' replied Flurry, with great deliberation, 'that my birthday 's this week, and maybe I could work a four-year-old colt of Trinket's she has out of her in honour of the occasion.'

'And sell your grandmother's birthday present to me?'

'Just that, I suppose,' answered Flurry with a slow wink.

A few days afterwards a letter from Mr. Knox informed me that he had ' squared the old lady, and it would be all right about the colt.' He further told me that Mrs. Knox had been good enough to offer me, with him, a day's snipe shooting on the celebrated Aussolas bogs, and he proposed to drive me there the following Monday, if convenient. Most people found it convenient to shoot the Aussolas snipe bog when they got the chance. Eight o'clock on the following Monday morning saw Flurry, myself, and a groom packed into a dogcart, with portmanteaus, gun-cases, and two rampant red setters.

It was a long drive, twelve miles at least, and a very cold one. We passed through long tracts of pasture country, fraught, for Flurry, with memories of runs, which were recorded for me, fence by fence, in every one of which the biggest dog-fox in the country had gone to ground, with not two feet—measured accurately on the handle of the whip—between him and the leading hound; through bogs that imperceptibly melted into lakes, and finally down and down into a valley, where the fir-trees of Aussolas clustered darkly round a glittering lake, and all but hid the grey roofs and pointed gables of Aussolas Castle.

'There's a nice stretch of a demesne for you,' remarked Flurry, pointing downwards with the whip, 'and one little old woman holding it all in the heel of her fist. Well able to hold it she is, too, and always was, and she'll live twenty years yet, if it's only to spite the whole lot of us, and when all's said and done goodness knows how she'll leave it!'

'It strikes me you were lucky to keep her up to her promise about the colt,' I said.

Flurry administered a composing kick to the ceaseless strivings of the red setters under the seat.

'I used to be rather a pet with her,' he said, after a pause; 'but mind you, I haven't got him yet, and if she gets any notion I want to sell him I'll never get him, so say nothing about the business to her.'

The tall gates of Aussolas shrieked on their hinges as they admitted us, and shut with a clang behind us, in the faces of an old mare and a couple of young horses, who, foiled in their break for the excitements of the outer world, turned and galloped defiantly on either side of us. Flurry's admirable cob hammered on, regardless of all things save his duty.

'He's the only one I have that I'd trust myself here with,' said his master, flicking him approvingly with the whip; 'there are plenty of people afraid to come here at all, and when my grandmother goes out driving she has a boy on the box with a basket full of stones to peg at them. Talk of the dickens, here she is herself!'

A short, upright old woman was approaching, preceded by a white woolly dog with sore eyes and a bark like a tin trumpet; we both got out of the trap and advanced to meet the lady of the manor.

I may summarize her attire by saying that she looked as if she had robbed a scarecrow; her face was small and incongruously refined, the skinny hand that she extended to me had the grubby tan that bespoke the professional gardener, and was decorated with a magnificent diamond ring. On her head was a massive purple velvet bonnet.

'I am very glad to meet you, Major Yeates,' she said with an old-fashioned precision of utterance; 'your grandfather was a dancing partner of mine in old days at the Castle, when he was a handsome young aide-de-camp there, and I was—— You may judge for yourself what I was.'

She ended with a startling little hoot of laughter, and I was aware that she quite realized the world's opinion of her, and was indifferent to it.

Our way to the bogs took us across Mrs. Knox's home farm, and through a large field in which several young horses were grazing.

'There now, that's my fellow,' said Flurry, pointing to a fine-looking colt, 'the chestnut with the white diamond on his forehead. He'll run into three figures before he's done, but we'll not tell that to the old lady!'

The famous Aussolas bogs were as full of snipe as usual, and a good deal fuller of water than any bogs I had ever shot before. I was on my day, and Flurry was not, and as he is ordinarily an infinitely better snipe shot than I, I felt at peace with the world and all men as we walked back, wet through, at five o'clock.

The sunset had waned, and a big white moon was making the eastern tower of Aussolas look like a thing in a fairy tale or a play when we arrived at the hall door. An individual, whom I recognized as the Robinson Crusoe coachman, admitted us to a hall, the like of which one does not often see. The walls were panelled with dark oak up to the gallery that ran round three sides of it, the balusters of the wide staircase were heavily carved, and blackened portraits of Flurry's ancestors on the spindle side stared sourly down on their descendant as he tramped upstairs with the bog mould on his hobnailed boots.

We had just changed into dry clothes when Robinson Crusoe shoved his red beard round the corner of the door, with the information that the mistress said we were to stay for dinner. My heart sank. It was then barely half-past five. I said

something about having no evening clothes and having to get
home early.

'Sure the dinner 'll be in another half hour,' said Robinson
Crusoe, joining hospitably in the conversation; 'and as for
evening clothes—God bless ye!'

The door closed behind him.

'Never mind,' said Flurry, 'I dare say you 'll be glad enough
to eat another dinner by the time you get home.' He laughed.
'Poor Slipper!' he added inconsequently, and only laughed
again when I asked for an explanation.

Old Mrs. Knox received us in the library, where she was
seated by a roaring turf fire, which lit the room a good deal more
effectively than the pair of candles that stood beside her in
tall silver candlesticks. Ceaseless and implacable growls from
under her chair indicated the presence of the woolly dog. She
talked with confounding culture of the books that rose all
round her to the ceiling; her evening dress was accomplished
by means of an additional white shawl, rather dirtier than its
congeners; as I took her in to dinner she quoted Virgil to me,
and in the same breath screeched an objurgation at a being whose
matted head rose suddenly into view from behind an ancient
Chinese screen, as I have seen the head of a Zulu woman peer
over a bush.

Dinner was as incongruous as everything else. Detestable
soup in a splendid old silver tureen that was nearly as dark in
hue as Robinson Crusoe's thumb; a perfect salmon, perfectly
cooked, on a chipped kitchen dish; such cut glass as is not easy
to find nowadays; sherry that, as Flurry subsequently remarked,
would burn the shell off an egg; and a bottle of port, draped in
immemorial cobwebs, wan with age, and probably priceless.
Throughout the vicissitudes of the meal Mrs. Knox's conversation flowed on undismayed, directed sometimes at me—
she had installed me in the position of friend of her youth—and
talked to me as if I were my own grandfather—sometimes at
Crusoe, with whom she had several heated arguments, and
sometimes she would make a statement of remarkable frankness
on the subject of her horse-farming affairs to Flurry, who, very
much on his best behaviour, agreed with all she said, and risked
no original remark. As I listened to them both, I remembered
with infinite amusement how he had told me once that 'a pet
name she had for him was "Tony Lumpkin," and no one but

herself knew what she meant by it.' It seemed strange that she made no allusion to Trinket's colt or to Flurry's birthday, but, mindful of my instructions, I held my peace.

As, at about half-past eight, we drove away in the moonlight, Flurry congratulated me solemnly on my success with his grandmother. He was good enough to tell me that she would marry me to-morrow if I asked her, and he wished I would, even if it was only to see what a nice grandson he'd be for me. A sympathetic giggle behind me told me that Michael, on the back seat, had heard and relished the jest.

We had left the gates of Aussolas about half a mile behind when, at the corner of a by-road, Flurry pulled up. A short squat figure arose from the black shadow of a furze bush and came out into the moonlight, swinging its arms like a cabman and cursing audibly.

'Oh murdher, oh murdher, Misther Flurry! What kept ye at all? 'Twould perish the crows to be waiting here the way I am these two hours——'

'Ah, shut your mouth, Slipper!' said Flurry, who, to my surprise, had turned back the rug and was taking off his driving coat, 'I couldn't help it. Come on, Yeates, we've got to get out here.'

'What for?' I asked, in not unnatural bewilderment.

'It's all right. I'll tell you as we go along,' replied my companion, who was already turning to follow Slipper up the by-road. 'Take the trap on, Michael, and wait at the River's Cross.' He waited for me to come up with him, and then put his hand on my arm. 'You see, Major, this is the way it is. My grandmother's given me that colt right enough, but if I waited for her to send him over to me I'd never see a hair of his tail. So I just thought that as we were over here we might as well take him back with us, and maybe you'll give us a help with him; he'll not be altogether too handy for a first go off.'

I was staggered. An infant in arms could scarcely have failed to discern the fishiness of the transaction, and I begged Mr. Knox not to put himself to this trouble on my account, as I had no doubt I could find a horse for my friend elsewhere. Mr. Knox assured me that it was no trouble at all, quite the contrary, and that, since his grandmother had given him the colt, he saw no reason why he should not take him when he wanted him; also, that if I didn't want him he'd be glad enough to keep him himself; and finally, that I wasn't the chap to go back on a friend, but I was welcome to drive back to Shreelane with Michael this minute if I liked.

Of course I yielded in the end. I told Flurry I should lose my job over the business, and he said I could then marry his grandmother, and the discussion was abruptly closed by the necessity of following Slipper over a locked five-barred gate.

Our pioneer took us over about half a mile of country, knocking down stone gaps where practicable and scrambling over tall banks in the deceptive moonlight. We found ourselves at length in a field with a shed in one corner of it; in a dim group of farm buildings a little way off a light was shining.

'Wait here,' said Flurry to me 'in a whisper; 'the less noise the better. It's an open shed, and we'll just slip in and coax him out.'

Slipper unwound from his waist a halter, and my colleagues glided like spectres into the shadow of the shed, leaving me to meditate on my duties as Resident Magistrate, and on the questions that would be asked in the House by our local member when Slipper had given away the adventure in his cups.

In less than a minute three shadows emerged from the shed, where two had gone in. They had got the colt.

'He came out as quiet as a calf when he winded the sugar,' said Flurry; 'it was well for me I filled my pockets from grandmamma's sugar basin.'

He and Slipper had a rope from each side of the colt's head; they took him quickly across a field towards a gate. The colt stepped daintily between them over the moonlit grass; he snorted occasionally, but appeared on the whole amenable.

The trouble began later, and was due, as trouble often is, to the beguilements of a short cut. Against the maturer judgment of Slipper, Flurry insisted on following a route that he assured us he knew as well as his own pocket, and the consequence was that in about five minutes I found myself standing on top of a bank hanging on to a rope, on the other end of which the colt dangled and danced, while Flurry, with the other rope, lay prone in the ditch, and Slipper administered to the bewildered colt's hind quarters such chastisement as could be ventured on.

I have no space to narrate in detail the atrocious difficulties and disasters of the short cut. How the colt set to work to buck, and went away across a field, dragging the faithful Slipper,

literally *ventre à terre*, after him, while I picked myself in
ignominy out of a briar patch, and Flurry cursed himself black
in the face.   How we were attacked by ferocious cur dogs, and
I lost my eye-glass; and how, as we neared the River's Cross,
Flurry espied the police patrol on the road, and we all hid behind
a rick of turf while I realized in fullness what an exceptional
ass I was, to have been beguiled into an enterprise that involved
hiding with Slipper from the Royal Irish Constabulary.

.Let it suffice to say that Trinket's infernal offspring was
finally handed over on the high road to Michael and Slipper,
and Flurry drove me home in a state of mental and physical
overthrow.

I saw nothing of my friend Mr. Knox for the next couple of
days, by the end of which time I had worked up a high polish
on my misgivings, and had determined to tell him that under no
circumstances would I have anything to say to his grandmother's
birthday present.   It was like my usual luck that, instead of
writing a note to this effect, I thought it would be good for my
liver to walk across the hills to Tory Cottage and tell Flurry
so in person.

It was a bright, blustery morning, after a muggy day.   The
feeling of spring was in the air, the daffodils were already in
bud, and crocuses showed purple in the grass on either side of
the avenue.   It was only a couple of miles to Tory Cottage by
the way across the hills; I walked fast, and it was barely twelve
o'clock when I saw its pink walls and clumps of evergreens
below me.   As I looked down at it the chiming of Flurry's
hounds in the kennels came to me on the wind; I stood still
to listen, and could almost have sworn that I was hearing again
the clash of Magdalen bells, hard at work on May morning.

The path that I was following led downwards through a
larch plantation to Flurry's back gate.   Hot wafts from some
hideous cauldron at the other side of a wall apprised me of the
vicinity of the kennels and their cuisine, and the fir-trees round
were hung with gruesome and unknown joints.   I thanked
heaven that I was not a master of hounds, and passed on as
quickly as might be to the hall door.

I rang two or three times without response; then the door
opened a couple of inches and was instantly slammed in my
face.   I heard the hurried paddling of bare feet on oil-cloth, and
a voice, 'Hurry, Bridgie, hurry!   There's quality at the door!'

Bridgie, holding a dirty cap on with one hand, presently arrived and informed me that she believed Mr. Knox was out about the place. She seemed perturbed, and she cast scared glances down the drive while speaking to me.

I knew enough of Flurry's habits to shape a tolerably direct course for his whereabouts. He was, as I had expected, in the training paddock, a field behind the stable yard, in which he had put up practice jumps for his horses. It was a good-sized field with clumps of furze in it, and Flurry was standing near one of these with his hands in his pockets, singularly unoccupied. I supposed that he was prospecting for a place to put up another jump. He did not see me coming, and turned with a start as I spoke to him. There was a queer expression of mingled guilt and what I can only describe as divilment in his grey eyes as he greeted me. In my dealings with Flurry Knox, I have since formed the habit of sitting tight, in a general way, when I see that expression.

'Well, who's coming next, I wonder!' he said, as he shook hands with me; 'it's not ten minutes since I had two of your d——d peelers here searching the whole place for my grandmother's colt!'

'What!' I exclaimed, feeling cold all down my back; 'do you mean the police have got hold of it?'

'They haven't got hold of the colt anyway,' said Flurry, looking sideways at me from under the peak of his cap, with the glint of the sun in his eye. 'I got word in time before they came.'

'What do you mean?' I demanded; 'where is he? For heaven's sake don't tell me you've sent the brute over to my place!'

'It's a good job for you I didn't,' replied Flurry, 'as the police are on their way to Shreelane this minute to consult you about it. *You!*' He gave utterance to one of his short diabolical fits of laughter. 'He's where they'll not find him, anyhow. Ho ho! It's the funniest hand I ever played!'

'Oh yes, it's devilish funny, I've no doubt,' I retorted, beginning to lose my temper, as is the manner of many people when they are frightened; 'but I give you fair warning that if Mrs. Knox asks me any questions about it, I shall tell her the whole story.'

'All right,' responded Flurry; 'and when you do, don't

forget to tell her how you flogged the colt out on to the road over her own bounds ditch.'

'Very well,' I said hotly, 'I may as well go home and send in my papers. They'll break me over this——'

'Ah, hold on, major,' said Flurry soothingly, 'it'll be all right. No one knows anything. It's only on spec the old lady sent the bobbies here. If you'll keep quiet it'll all blow over.'

'I don't care,' I said, struggling hopelessly in the toils; 'if I meet your grandmother, and she asks me about it, I shall tell her all I know.'

'Please God you'll not meet her! After all, it's not once in a blue moon that she——' began Flurry. Even as he said the words his face changed. 'Holy fly!' he ejaculated, 'isn't that her dog coming into the field? Look at her bonnet over the wall! Hide, hide for your life!' He caught me by the shoulder and shoved me down among the furze bushes before I realized what had happened.

'Get in there! I'll talk to her.'

I may as well confess that at the mere sight of Mrs. Knox's purple bonnet my heart had turned to water. In that moment I knew what it would be like to tell her how I, having eaten her salmon, and capped her quotations, and drunk her best port, had gone forth and helped to steal her horse. I abandoned my dignity, my sense of honour; I took the furze prickles to my breast and wallowed in them.

Mrs. Knox had advanced with vengeful speed; already she was in high altercation with Flurry at no great distance from where I lay; varying sounds of battle reached me, and I gathered that Flurry was not—to put it mildly—shrinking from that economy of truth that the situation required.

'Is it that curby, long-backed brute? You promised him to me long ago, but I wouldn't be bothered with him!'

The old lady uttered a laugh of shrill derision. 'Is it likely I'd promise you my best colt? And still more, is it likely that you'd refuse him if I did?'

'Very well, ma'am.' Flurry's voice was admirably indignant. 'Then I suppose I'm a liar and a thief.'

'I'd be more obliged to you for the information if I hadn't known it before,' responded his grandmother with lightning speed; 'if you swore to me on a stack of Bibles you knew nothing about my colt I wouldn't believe you! I shall go straight to

Major Yeates and ask his advice. I believe *him* to be a gentleman, in spite of the company he keeps!'

I writhed deeper into the furze bushes, and thereby discovered a sandy rabbit run, along which I crawled, with my cap well over my eyes, and the furze needles stabbing me through my stockings. The ground shelved a little, promising profounder concealment, but the bushes were very thick, and I laid hold of the bare stem of one to help my progress. It lifted out of the ground in my hand, revealing a freshly cut stump. Something snorted, not a yard away; I glared through the opening, and was confronted by the long, horrified face of Mrs. Knox's colt, mysteriously on a level with my own.

Even without the white diamond on his forehead I should have divined the truth; but how in the name of wonder had Flurry persuaded him to couch like a woodcock in the heart of a furze brake? For a full minute I lay as still as death for fear of frightening him, while the voices of Flurry and his grandmother raged on alarmingly close to me. The colt snorted, and blew long breaths through his wide nostrils, but he did not move. I crawled an inch or two nearer, and after a few seconds of cautious peering I grasped the position. They had buried him.

A small sandpit among the furze had been utilized as a grave; they had filled him in up to his withers with sand, and a few furze bushes, artistically disposed around the pit, had done the rest. As the depth of Flurry's guile was revealed, laughter came upon me like a flood; I gurgled and shook apoplectically, and the colt gazed at me with serious surprise, until a sudden outburst of barking close to my elbow administered a fresh shock to my tottering nerves.

Mrs. Knox's woolly dog had tracked me into the furze, and was now baying the colt and me with mingled terror and indignation. I addressed him in a whisper, with perfidious endearments, advancing a crafty hand towards him the while, made a snatch for the back of his neck, missed it badly, and got him by the ragged fleece of his hind quarters as he tried to flee. If I had flayed him alive he could hardly have uttered a more deafening series of yells, but, like a fool, instead of letting him go, I dragged him towards me, and tried to stifle the noise by holding his muzzle. The tussle lasted engrossingly for a few seconds, and then the climax of the nightmare arrived.

Mrs. Knox's voice, close behind me, said, 'Let go my dog this instant, sir! Who are you——'

Her voice faded away, and I knew that she also had seen the colt's head.

I positively felt sorry for her. At her age there was no knowing what effect the shock might have on her. I scrambled to my feet and confronted her.

'Major Yeates!' she said. There was a deathly pause. 'Will you kindly tell me,' said Mrs. Knox slowly, 'am I in Bedlam, or are you? And *what is that?*'

She pointed to the colt, and that unfortunate animal, recognizing the voice of his mistress, uttered a hoarse and lamentable whinny. Mrs. Knox felt around her for support, found only furze prickles, gazed speechlessly at me, and then, to her eternal honour, fell into wild cackles of laughter.

So, I may say, did Flurry and I. I embarked on my explanation and broke down; Flurry followed suit and broke down too. Overwhelming laughter held us all three, disintegrating our very souls. Mrs. Knox pulled herself together first.

'I acquit you, Major Yeates, I acquit you, though appearances are against you. It's clear enough to me you've fallen among thieves.' She stopped and glowered at Flurry. Her purple bonnet was over one eye. 'I'll thank you, sir,' she said, 'to dig out that horse before I leave this place. And when you've dug him out you may keep him. I'll be no receiver of stolen goods!'

She broke off and shook her fist at him. 'Upon my conscience, Tony, I'd give a guinea to have thought of it myself!'

IV

THE WATERS OF STRIFE

I KNEW Bat Callaghan's face long before I was able to put a name to it. There was seldom a court day in Skebawn that I was not aware of his level brows and superfluously intense expression somewhere among the knot of corner-boys who patronized the weekly sittings of the bench of magistrates. His social position appeared to fluctuate: I have seen him driving a car; he sometimes held my horse for me—that is to say, he sat on the counter of a public-house while the Quaker slumbered in the gutter; and, on one occasion, he retired, at my bidding, to Cork jail, there to meditate upon the inadvisability of defending a friend from the attentions of the police with the tailboard of a cart.

He next obtained prominence in my regard at a regatta held under the auspices of 'The Sons of Liberty,' a local football club that justified its title by the patriot green of its jerseys and its free interpretation of the rules of the game. The announcement of my name on the posters as a patron—a privilege acquired at the cost of a reluctant half-sovereign—made it incumbent on me to put in an appearance, even though the festival coincided with my Petty Sessions day at Skebawn; and at some five of the clock on a brilliant September afternoon I found myself driving down the stony road that dropped in zigzags to the borders of the lake on which the races were to come off.

I believe that the selection of Lough Lonen as the scene of the regatta was not unconnected with the fact that the secretary of the club owned a public-house at the cross roads at one end of it; none the less, the president of the Royal Academy could scarcely have chosen more picturesque surroundings. A mountain towered steeply up from the lake's edge, dark with the sad green of beech-trees in September; fir woods followed the curve of the shore, and leaned far over the answering darkness of the water; and above the trees rose the toppling steepnesses of the hill, painted with a purple glow of heather. The lake was about a mile long, and, tumbling from its farther end, a fierce and narrow river fled away west to the sea, some four or five miles off.

I had not seen a boat race since I was at Oxford, and the words still called up before my eyes a vision of smart parasols, of gorgeous barges, of snowy-clad youths, and of low slim outriggers, winged with the level flight of oars, slitting the water to the sway of the line of flat backs. Certainly undreamed-of possibilities in aquatics were revealed to me as I reined in the Quaker on the outskirts of the crowd, and saw below me the festival of the Sons of Liberty in full swing. Boats of all shapes and sizes, outrageously overladen, moved about the lake, with oars flourishing to the strains of concertinas. Black swarms of people seethed along the water's edge, congesting here and there round the dingy tents and stalls of green apples; and the club's celebrated brass band, enthroned in a wagonette, and stimulated by the presence of a barrel of porter on the box-seat, was belching forth *The Boys of Wexford*, under the guidance of a disreputable ex-militia drummer, in a series of crashing discords.

Almost as I arrived a pistol-shot set the echoes clattering round the lake, and three boats burst out abreast from the throng into the open water. Two of the crews were in shirt-sleeves, the third wore the green jerseys of the football club; the boats were of the heavy sea-going build, and pulled six oars apiece, oars of which the looms were scarcely narrower than the blades, and were, of the two, but a shade heavier. None the less, the rowers started dauntlessly at thirty-five strokes a minute, quickening up, incredible as it may seem, as they rounded the boat in the first lap of the two-mile course. The rowing was, in general style, more akin to the action of beating up eggs with a fork than to any other form of athletic exercise; but in its unorthodox way it kicked the heavy boats along at a surprising pace. The oars squeaked and grunted against the thole-pins, the coxswains kept up an unceasing flow of oratory, and, superfluous little boys in punts contrived to intervene at all the more critical turning-points of the race, only evading the flail of the oncoming oars by performing prodigies of 'waggling' with a single oar at the stern. I took out my watch and counted the strokes when they were passing the mark boat for the second time; they were pulling a fraction over forty; one of the shirt-sleeved crews was obviously in trouble, the other, with humped backs and jerking oars, was holding its own against the green jerseys amid the blended yells of friends and foes. When for the last time they rounded the green flag there were but two boats in the race, and the foul that had been imminent throughout was at length achieved with a rattle of oars and a storm of curses. They were clear again in a moment, the shirt-sleeved crew getting away with a distinct lead, and it was at about this juncture that I became aware that the coxswains had abandoned their long-handled tillers, and were standing over their respective 'strokes,' shoving frantically at their oars, and maintaining the while a ceaseless bawl of encouragement and defiance. It looked like a foregone conclusion for the leaders, and the war of cheers rose to frenzy. The word 'cheering,' indeed, is but

a euphemism, and in no way expresses the serrated yell, composed
of epithets, advice, and imprecations, that was flung like a live
thing at the oncoming boats. The green jerseys answered to
this stimulant with a wild spurt that drove the bow of their
boat within a measurable distance of their opponents' stroke oar.
In another second a thoroughly successful foul would have been
effected, but the cox of the leading boat proved himself equal
to the emergency by unshipping his tiller, and with it dealing
'bow' of the green jerseys such a blow over the head as effectu-
ally dismissed him from the sphere of practical politics.

A great roar of laughter greeted this feat of arms, and a voice
at my dogcart's wheel pierced the clamour:

'More power to ye, Larry, me owld darlin'!'

I looked down and saw Bat Callaghan, with shining eyes, and
a face white with excitement, poising himself on one foot on the
box of my wheel in order to get a better view of the race.
Almost before I had time to recognize him, a man in a green
jersey caught him round the legs and jerked him down. Callaghan fell into the throng, recovered himself in an instant, and
rushed, white and dangerous, at his assailant. The Son of
Liberty was no less ready for the fray, and what is known
in Ireland as 'the father and mother of a row' was imminent.
Already, however, one of those unequalled judges of the moral
temperature of a crowd, a sergeant of the R.I.C., had quietly
interposed his bulky person between the combatants, and the
coming trouble was averted.

Elsewhere battle was raging. The race was over, and the
committee boat was hemmed in by the rival crews, supplemented
by craft of all kinds. The 'objection' was being lodged, and
in its turn objected to, and I can only liken the process to the
screaming warfare of seagulls round a piece of carrion. The
tumult was still at its height when out of its very heart two four-
oared boats broke forth, and a pistol shot proclaimed that another race had begun, the public interest in which was specially
keen, owing to the fact that the rowers were stalwart country
girls, who made up in energy what they lacked in skill. It was
a short race, once round the mark boat only, and, like a successful farce, it 'went with a roar' from start to finish. Foul
after foul, each followed by a healing interval of calm, during
which the crews, who had all caught crabs, were recovering
themselves and their oars, marked its progress; and when the

two boats, locked in an inextricable embrace, at length passed the winning flag, and the crews, oblivious of judges and public, fell to untrammelled personal abuse and to doing up their hair, I decided that I had seen the best of the fun, and prepared to go home.

It was, as it happened, the last race of the day, and nothing remained in the way of excitement save the greased pole with the pig slung in a bag at the end of it. My final impression of the Lough Lonen Regatta was of Callaghan's lithe figure, sleek and dripping, against the yellow sky, as he poised on the swaying pole with the broken gold of the water beneath him.

Limited as was my experience of the south-west of Ireland, I was in no way surprised to hear on the following afternoon from Peter Cadogan that there had been 'sthrokes' the night before, when the boys were going home from the regatta, and that the police were searching for one Jimmy Foley.

'What do they want him for?' I asked.

'Sure it's according as a man that was bringing a car of bog-wood was tellin' me, sir,' answered Peter, pursuing his occupation of washing the dogcart with unabated industry; 'they say Jimmy's wife went roaring to the police, saying she could get no account of her husband.'

'I suppose he's beaten some fellow and is hiding,' I suggested.

'Well, that might be, sir,' asserted Peter respectfully. He plied his mop vigorously in intricate places about the springs, which would, I knew, have never been explored save for my presence.

'It's what John Hennessy was saying, that he was hard set to get his horse-past Cluin Cross, the way the blood was sthrewn about the road,' resumed Peter; 'sure they were fighting like wasps in it half the night.'

'Who were fighting?'

'I couldn't say, indeed, sir. Some o' thim low rakish lads from the town, I suppose,' replied Peter with virtuous respectability.

When Peter Cadogan was quietly and intelligently candid, to pursue an inquiry was seldom of much avail.

Next day in Skebawn I met little Murray, the district inspector, very alert and smart in his rifle-green uniform, going forth to collect evidence about the fight. He told me that the police were pretty certain that one of the Sons of Liberty, named Foley, had been murdered, but, as usual, the difficulty was to get any one to give information; all that was known was that he was gone, and that his wife had identified his cap, which had been found, drenched with blood, by the roadside. Murray gave it as his opinion that the whole business had arisen out of the row over the disputed race, and that there must have been a dozen people looking on when the murder was done; but so far no evidence was forthcoming, and after a day and a night of search the police had not been able to find the body.

'No,' said Flurry Knox, who had joined us, 'and if it was any of those mountainy men did away with him you might scrape Ireland with a small-tooth comb and you 'll not get him!'

That evening I smoked an after-dinner cigarette out of doors in the mild starlight, strolling about the rudimentary paths of what would, I hoped, some day be Philippa's garden. The bats came stooping at the red end of my cigarette, and from the covert behind the house I heard once or twice the delicate bark of a fox. Civilization seemed a thousand miles off, as far away as the falling star that had just drawn a line of pale fire half-way down the northern sky. I had been nearly a year at Shreelane House by myself now, and the time seemed very long to me. It was slow work putting by money, even under the austerities of Mrs. Cadogan's régime, and though I had warned Philippa I meant to marry her after Christmas, there were moments, and this was one of them, when it seemed an idle threat.

'Pether!' the strident voice of Mrs. Cadogan intruded upon my meditations. 'Go tell the Major his coffee is waitin' on him!' I went gloomily into the house, and, with a resignation born of adversity, swallowed the mixture of chicory and liquorice which my housekeeper possessed the secret of distilling from the best and most expensive coffee. My theory about it was that it added to the illusion that I had dined, and moreover that it kept me awake, and I generally had a good deal of writing to do after dinner.

Having swallowed it I went downstairs and out past the kitchen regions to my office, a hideous whitewashed room, in which I interviewed policemen, and took affidavits, and did most of my official writing. It had a door that opened into the yard, and a window that looked out in the other direction, among lanky laurels and scrubby hollies, where lay the cats' main thoroughfare from the scullery window to the rabbit holes in the wood. I had a good deal of work to do, and the time passed quickly. It was Friday night, and from the kitchen at the end of the passage came the gabbling murmur, in two alternate keys, that I had learned to recognise as the recital of a litany by my housekeeper and her nephew Peter. This performance was followed by some of those dreary and heart-rending yawns that are, I think, peculiar to Irish kitchens, then such of the cats as had returned from the chase were loudly shepherded into the back scullery, the kitchen door shut with a slam, and my retainers retired to repose.

It was nearly half an hour afterwards when I finished the notes I had been making on an adjourned case of 'stroke-hauling' salmon in the Lonen River. I learned back in my chair and lighted a cigarette preparatory to turning in; my thoughts had again wandered on a sentimental journey across the Irish Channel, when I heard a slight stir of some kind outside the open window. In the wilds of Ireland no one troubles themselves about burglars; 'More cats,' I thought, 'I must shut the window before I go to bed.'

Almost immediately there followed a faint tap on the window, and then a voice said in a hoarse and hurried whisper: 'Them that wants Jim Foley, let them look in the river!'

If I had kept my head I should have sat still and encouraged a further confidence, but unfortunately I acted on the impulse of the natural man, and was at the window in a jump, knocking down my chair, and making noise enough to scare a far less shy bird than an Irish informer. Of course, there was no one there. I listened, with every nerve as taut as a violin string. It was quite dark; there was just breeze enough to make a rustling in the evergreens, so that a man might brush through them without being heard; and while I debated on a plan of action there came from beyond the shrubbery the jar and twang of a loose strand of wire in the paling by the wood. My informant, whoever he might be, had vanished into the darkness from which he had come as irrecoverably as had the falling star that had written its brief message across the sky, and gone out again into infinity.

I got up very early next morning and drove to Skebawn to see Murray, and offer him my mysterious information for what it was worth. Personally, I did not think it worth much, and was disposed to regard it as a red herring drawn across the trail. Murray, however, was not in a mood to despise anything that had a suggestion to make, having been out till nine o'clock the night before without being able to find any clue to the hiding-place of James Foley.

'The river's a good mile from the place where the fight was,' he said, straddling his compasses over the Ordnance Survey map, 'and there's no sort of a road they could have taken him along, but a tip like this is always worth trying. I remember in the Land League time how a man came one Saturday night to my window and told me there were holes drilled in the chapel door to shoot a boycotted man through while he was at mass. The holes were there right enough, and you may be quite sure that chap found excellent reasons for having family prayers at home next day!'

I had sessions to attend on the extreme outskirts of my district, and could not wait, as Murray suggested, to see the thing out. I did not get home till the following day, and when I arrived I found a letter from Murray awaiting me.

'Your pal was right. We found Foley's body in the river, knocking about against the posts of the weir. The head was wrapped in his own green jersey, and had been smashed in by a stone. We suspect a fellow named Bat Callaghan, who has bolted, but there were a lot of them in it. Possibly it was Callaghan himself who gave you the tip; you never can tell how superstition is going to take them next. The inquest will be held to-morrow.'

The coroner's jury took a cautious view of the cause of the catastrophe, and brought in a verdict of 'death by misadventure,' and I presently found it to be my duty to call a magisterial inquiry to further investigate the matter. A few days before this was to take place, I was engaged in the delicate task of displaying to my landlord, Mr. Flurry Knox, the defects of the pantry sink, when Mrs. Cadogan advanced upon us with the information that the Widow Callaghan from Cluin would be thankful to speak to me, and had brought me a present of 'a fine young goose.'

'Is she come over here looking for Bat?' said Flurry, withdrawing his arm and the longest kitchen skewer from the pipe that he had been probing; 'she knows you're handy at hiding your friends, Mary; maybe it's he that's stopping the drain!'

Mrs. Cadogan turned her large red face upon her late employer.

'God knows I wish yerself was stuck in it, Master Flurry, the way ye 'd hear Pether cursin' the full o' the house when he 's striving to wash the things in that unnatural little trough.'

'Are you sure it 's Peter does all the cursing?' retorted Flurry. 'I hear Father Scanlan has it in for you this long time for not going to confession.'

'And how can I walk two miles to the chapel with God's burden on me feet?' demanded Mrs. Cadogan in purple indignation; 'the Blessed Virgin and Docthor Hickey knows well the hardship I gets from them. If it wasn't for a pair of the Major's boots he gave me, I 'd be hard set to thravel the house itself!'

The contest might have been continued indefinitely, had I not struck up the swords with a request that Mrs. Callaghan might be sent round to the hall door. There we found a tall, grey-haired countrywoman waiting for us at the foot of the steps, in the hooded blue cloak that is peculiar to the south of Ireland; from the fact that she clutched a pocket-handkerchief in her right hand I augured a stormy interview, but nothing could have been more self-restrained and even imposing than the reverence with which she greeted Flurry and me.

'Good-morning to your honours,' she began, with a dignified and extremely imminent snuffle. 'I ask your pardon for troubling you, Major Yeates, but I haven't a one in the counthry to give me an adwice, and I have no confidence only in your honour's experiments.'

'Experience, she means,' prompted Flurry. 'Didn't you get advice enough out of Mr. Murray yesterday?' he went on aloud. 'I heard he was at Cluin to see you.'

'And if he was itself, it 's little adwantage any one 'd get out of that little whipper-shnapper of a shnap-dhragon!' responded Mrs. Callaghan tartly; 'he was with me for a half-hour giving me every big rock of English till I had a reel in me head. I declare to ye, Mr. Flurry, after he had gone out o' the house, ye wouldn't throw three farthings for me!'

The pocket-handkerchief was here utilized, after which, with a heavy groan, Mrs. Callaghan again took up her parable.

'I towld him first and last I 'd lose me life if I had to go into the coort, and if I did itself sure th' attorneys could rip no more out o' me than what he did himself.'

'Did you tell him where was Bat?' inquired Flurry casually.
At this Mrs. Callaghan immediately dissolved into tears.
'Is it Bat?' she howled. 'If the twelve apostles came down
from heaven asking me where was Bat, I could give them no
satisfaction. The divil a know I know what's happened him.
He came home with me sober and good-natured from the
rogatta, and the next morning he axed a fresh egg for his breakfast, and God forgive me, I wouldn't break the score I was
taking to the hotel, and with that he slapped the cup o' tay into
the fire and went out the door, and I never got a word of him
since, good nor bad. God knows 'tis I got throuble with that
poor boy, and he the only one I have to look to 'in the world!'

I cut the matter short by asking her what she wanted me to
do for her, and sifted out from amongst much extraneous detail
the fact that she relied upon my renowned wisdom and clemency
to preserve her from being called as a witness at the coming
inquiry. The gift of the goose served its intended purpose of
embarrassing my position, but in spite of it I broke to the
Widow Callaghan my inability to help her. She did not, of
course, believe me, but she was too well-bred to say so. In
Ireland one becomes accustomed to this attitude.

As it turned out, however, Bat Callaghan's mother had nothing
to fear from the inquiry. She was by turns deaf, imbecile,
garrulously candid, and furiously abusive of Murray's principal
witness, a frightened lad of seventeen, who had sworn to having
seen Bat Callaghan and Jimmy Foley 'shaping at one another
to fight,' at an hour when, according to Mrs. Callaghan, Bat
was 'lying sthretched on the beddeen with a sick shtomach'
in consequence of the malignant character of the porter supplied by the last witness's father. It all ended, as such cases
so often do in Ireland, in complete moral certainty in the minds
of all concerned as to the guilt of the accused, and entire
impotence on the part of the law to prove it. A warrant was
issued for the arrest of Bartholomew Callaghan; and the clans
of Callaghan and Foley fought rather more bloodily than usual,
as occasion served; and at intervals during the next few months
Murray used to ask me if my friend the murderer had dropped
in lately, to which I was wont to reply with condolences on the
failure of the R.I.C. to find the Widow Callaghan's only son
for her; and that was about all that came of it.

Events with which the present story has no concern took

me to England towards the end of the following March. It so
happened that my old regiment, the —th Fusiliers, was quartered
at Whincastle, within a couple of hours by rail of Philippa's
home, where I was staying, and, since my wedding was now
within measurable distance, my former brothers - in - arms
invited me over to dine and sleep, and to receive a valedictory
silver claret jug that they were magnanimous enough to bestow
upon a backslider. I enjoyed the dinner as much as any man
can enjoy his dinner when he knows he has to make a speech
at the end of it; through much and varied conversation I strove,
like a nervous mother who cannot trust her offspring out of
her sight, to keep before my mind's eye the opening sentences
that I had composed in the train; I felt that if I could only
'get away' satisfactorily I might trust the Ayala ('89) to do the
rest, and of that fount of inspiration there was no lack. As it
turned out, I got away all right, though the sight of the double
line of expectant faces and red mess jackets nearly scattered
those precious opening sentences, and I am afraid that so far
as the various subsequent points went that I had intended to
make, I stayed away; however, neither Demosthenes, nor a
Nationalist member at a Cork election, could have been listened
to with more gratifying attention, and I sat down, hot and happy,
to be confronted with my own flushed visage, hideously reflected
in the glittering paunch of the claret jug.

Once safely over the presentation, the evening mellowed into
frivolity, and it was pretty late before I found myself settled
down to whist, at sixpenny points, in the ancient familiar way,
while most of the others fell to playing pool in the billiard-room
next door. I have played whist from my youth up; with the
preternatural seriousness of a subaltern, with the self-assurance
of a senior captain, with the privileged irascibility of a major;
and my eighteen months of abstinence at Shreelane had only
whetted my appetite for what I consider the best of games.
After the long lonely evenings there, with the rats for company,
and, for relaxation, a 'deck' of that specially demoniacal American variety of patience known as 'Fooly Ann,' it was wondrous
agreeable to sit again among my fellows, and 'lay the longs' on
a scientific rubber of whist, as though Mrs. Cadogan and the
Skebawn Bench of Magistrates had never existed.

We were in the first game of the second rubber, and I was
holding a very nice playing hand; I had early in the game moved

forth my trumps to battle, and I was now in the ineffable position of scoring with the small cards of my long suit. The cards
fell and fell in silence, and Ballantyne, my partner, raked in the
tricks like a machine. The concentrated quiet of the game was
suddenly arrested by a sharp, unmistakable sound from the
barrack yard outside, the snap of a Lee-Metford rifle.

'What was that?' exclaimed Moffat, the senior major.

Before he had finished speaking there was a second shot.

'By Jove, those were rifle-shots! Perhaps I'd better go and
see what's up,' said Ballantyne, who was captain of the week,
throwing down his cards and making a bolt for the door.

He had hardly got out of the room when the first long high
note of the 'assembly' sang out, sudden and clear. We all
sprang to our feet, and as the bugle-call went shrilly on, the
other men came pouring in from the billiard-room, and stampeded to their quarters to get their swords. At the same
moment the mess sergeant appeared at the outer door with a
face as white as his shirt-front.

'The sentry on the magazine guard has been shot, sir!' he
said excitedly to Moffat. 'They say he's dead!'

We were all out in the barrack square in an instant; it was clear
moonlight, and the square was already alive with hurrying
figures cramming on clothes and caps as they ran to fall in. I
was a free agent these times, and I followed the mess sergeant
across the square towards the distant corner where the magazine stands. As we doubled round the end of the men's
quarters, we nearly ran into a small party of men who were
advancing slowly and heavily in our direction.

''Ere he is, sir!' said the mess sergeant, stopping himself
abruptly.

They were carrying the sentry to the hospital. His busby
had fallen off; the moon shone mildly on his pale, convulsed
face, and foam and strange inhuman sounds came from his lips.
His head was rolling from side to side on the arm of the man
who was carrying him; as it turned towards me I was struck
by something disturbingly familiar in the face, and I wondered
if he had been in my old company.

'What's his name, sergeant?' I said to the mess sergeant.

'Private Harris, sir,' replied the sergeant; 'he's only lately
come up from the depot, and this was his first time on sentry
by himself.'

C 978

I went back to the mess, and in process of time the others straggled in, thirsting for whiskies-and-sodas, and full of such information as there was to give. Private Harris was not wounded; both the shots had been fired by him, as was testified by the state of his rifle and the fact that two of the cartridges were missing from the packet in his pouch.

'I hear he was a queer, sulky sort of chap always,' said Tomkinson, the subaltern of the day, 'but if he was having a try at suicide he made a bally bad fist of it.'

'He made as good a fist of it as you did of putting on your sword, Tommy,' remarked Ballantyne, indicating a dangling white strap of webbing, that hung down like a tail below Mr. Tomkinson's mess jacket. 'Nerves, obviously, in both cases!'

The exquisite satisfaction afforded by this discovery to Mr. Tomkinson's brother officers found its natural outlet in a bear fight that threatened to become more or less general, and in the course of which I slid away unostentatiously to bed in Ballantyne's quarters and took the precaution of barricading my door.

Next morning, when I got down to breakfast, I found Ballantyne and two or three others in the mess-room, and my first inquiry was for Private Harris.

'Oh, the poor chap's dead,' said Ballantyne; 'it's a very queer business altogether. I think he must have been wrong in the top storey. The doctor was with him when he came to out of the fit, or whatever it was, and O'Reilly—that's the doctor y' know, Irish, of course, and, by the way, poor Harris was an Irishman too—says that he could only gibber at first, but then he got out of him that when he had been on sentry-go for about half an hour, he happened to look up at the angle of the barrack wall near where it joins the magazine tower, and saw a face looking at him over it. He challenged and got no answer; but the face just stuck there staring at him; he challenged again, and then, as O'Reilly said, he "just oop with his royfle and blazed at it."' Ballantyne was not above the common English delusion that he could imitate an Irish brogue.

'Well, what happened then?'

'Well, according to the poor devil's own story, the face just kept on looking at him and he had another shot at it, and "My God Almighty," he said to O'Reilly, "it was there always!" While he was saying that to O'Reilly he began to chuck another fit, and apparently went on chucking them till he died a couple of hours ago.'

'One result of it is,' said another man, 'that they couldn't get a man to go on sentry there alone last night. I expect we shall have to double the sentries there every night as long as we 're here.'

'Silly asses!' remarked Tomkinson, but he said it without conviction.

After breakfast we went out to look at the wall by the magazine. It was about eleven feet high, with a coped top, and they told me there was a deep and wide dry ditch on the outside. A ladder was brought, and we examined the angle of the wall at which Harris said the face had appeared. He had made a beautiful shot, one of his bullets having flicked a piece off the ridge of the coping exactly at the corner.

'It 's not the kind of shot a man would make if he had been drinking,' said Moffat, regretfully abandoning his first simple hypothesis; 'he must have been mad.'

'I wish I could find out who his people are,' said Brownlow, the adjutant, who had joined us; 'they found in his box a letter to him from his mother, but we can't make out the name of the place. By Jove, Yeates, you 're an Irishman, perhaps you can help us.'

He handed me a latter in a dirty envelope. There was no address given, the contents were very short, and I may be forgiven if I transcribe them:

'My dear Son, I hope you are well as this leaves me at present, thanks be to God for it. I am very much unaisy about the cow. She swelled up this morning, she ran in and was frauding and I did not do but to run up for tom sweeney in the minute. We are thinking it is too much lairels or an eirub she took. I do not know what I will do with her. God help one that 's alone with himself I had not a days luck since ye went away. I am thinkin' them that wants ye is tired lookin' for ye. And so I remain,

YOUR FOND MOTHER.'

'Well, you don't get much of a lead from the cow, do you? And what the deuce is an eirub?' said Brownlow.

'It 's another way of spelling herb,' I said, turning over the envelope abstractedly. The postmark was almost obliterated, but it struck me it might be construed into the word Skebawn.

'Look here,' I said suddenly, 'let me see Harris. It's just possible I may know something about him.'

The sentry's body had been laid in the dead-house near the hospital, and Brownlow fetched the key. It was a grim little whitewashed building, without windows, save a small one of lancet shape, high up in one gable, through which a streak of April sunlight fell sharp and slender on the whitewashed wall. The long figure of the sentry lay sheeted on a stone slab, and Brownlow, with his cap in his hand, gently uncovered the face.

I leaned over and looked at it—at the heavy brows, the short nose, the small moustache lying black above the pale mouth, the deep-set eyes sealed in appalling peacefulness. There rose before me the wild dark face of the young man who had hung on my wheel and yelled encouragement to the winning coxswain at the Lough Lonen Regatta.

'I know him,' I said, 'his name is Callaghan.'

V

LISHEEN RACES, SECOND-HAND

It may or may not be agreeable to have attained the age of thirty-eight, but, judging from old photographs, the privilege of being nineteen has also its drawbacks. I turned over page after page of an ancient book in which were enshrined portraits of the friends of my youth, singly, in David and Jonathan couples, and in groups in which I, as it seemed to my mature and possibly jaundiced perception, always contrived to look the most immeasurable young bounder of the lot. Our faces were fat, and yet I cannot remember ever having been considered fat in my life; we indulged in low-necked shirts, in 'Jemima' ties with diagonal stripes; we wore coats that seemed three sizes too small, and trousers that were three sizes too big; we also wore small whiskers.

I stopped at last at one of the David and Jonathan memorial portraits. Yes, here was the object of my researches; this stout and earnestly romantic youth was Leigh Kelway, and that fatuous and chubby young person seated on the arm of his chair was myself. Leigh Kelway was a young man ardently believed in by a large circle of admirers, headed by himself and seconded by me, and for some time after I had left Magdalen for Sandhurst, I maintained a correspondence with him on large and abstract subjects. This phase of our friendship did not survive; I went soldiering to India, and Leigh Kelway took honours and moved suitably on into politics, as is the duty of an earnest young Radical with useful family connections and an independent income. Since then I had at intervals seen in the papers the name of the Honourable Basil Leigh Kelway mentioned as a speaker at elections, as a writer of thoughtful articles in the reviews, but we had never met, and nothing could have been less expected by me than the letter, written from Mrs. Raverty's Hotel, Skebawn, in which he told me he was making a tour in Ireland with Lord Waterbury, to whom he was private secretary. Lord Waterbury was at present having a few days' fishing near Killarney, and he himself, not being a fisherman, was collecting statistics for his chief on various points connected with the liquor question in Ireland. He had heard that I was in the neighbourhood, and was kind enough to add that it would give him much pleasure to meet me again.

With a stir of the old enthusiasm I wrote begging him to be my guest for as long as it suited him, and the following afternoon he arrived at Shreelane. The stout young friend of my youth had changed considerably. His important nose and slightly prominent teeth remained, but his wavy hair had withdrawn intellectually from his temples; his eyes had acquired a statesmanlike absence of expression, and his neck had grown long and birdlike. It was his first visit to Ireland, as he lost no time in telling me, and he and his chief had already collected much valuable information on the subject to which they had dedicated the Easter recess. He further informed me that he thought of popularizing the subject in a novel, and therefore intended to, as he put it, 'master the brogue' before his return.

During the next few days I did my best for Leigh Kelway. I turned him loose on Father Scanlan; I showed him Mohona, our champion village, that boasts fifteen public-houses out of twenty buildings of sorts and a railway station; I took him to hear the prosecution of a publican for selling drink on a Sunday,

which gave him an opportunity of studying perjury as a fine art,
and of hearing a lady, on whom police suspicion justly rested,
profoundly summed up by the sergeant as 'a woman who had
th' appairance of having knocked at a back door.'

The net result of these experiences has not yet been given
to the world by Leigh Kelway. For my own part, I had at
the end of three days arrived at the conclusion that his society,
when combined with a note-book and a thirst for statistics, was
not what I used to find it at Oxford. I therefore welcomed a
suggestion from Mr. Flurry Knox that we should accompany
him to some typical country races, got up by the farmers at a
place called Lisheen, some twelve miles away. It was the worst
road in the district, the races of the most grossly unorthodox
character; in fact, it was the very place for Leigh Kelway to
collect impressions of Irish life, and in any case it was a blessed
opportunity of disposing of him for the day.

In my guest's attire next morning I discerned an unbending
from the role of Cabinet minister towards that of sportsman;
the outlines of the note-book might be traced in his breast
pocket, but traversing it was the strap of a pair of field-glasses,
and his light grey suit was smart enough for Goodwood.

Flurry was to drive us to the races at one o'clock, and we
walked to Tory Cottage by the short cut over the hill, in the
sunny beauty of an April morning. Up to the present the
weather had kept me in a more or less apologetic condition;
any one who has entertained a guest in the country knows the
unjust weight of responsibility that rests on the shoulders of the
host in the matter of climate, and Leigh Kelway, after two
drenchings, had become sarcastically resigned to what I felt
he regarded as my mismanagement.

Flurry took us into the house for a drink and a biscuit, to
keep us going, as he said, till 'we lifted some luncheon out of
the Castle Knox people at the races,' and it was while we were
thus engaged that the first disaster of the day occurred. The
dining-room door was open, so also the window of the little
staircase just outside it, and through the window travelled
sounds that told of the close proximity of the stable-yard; the
clattering of hoofs on cobble stones, and voices uplifted in loud
conversation. Suddenly from this region there arose a screech
of the laughter peculiar to kitchen flirtation, followed by the
clank of a bucket, the plunging of a horse, and then an uproar

of wheels and galloping hoofs. An instant afterwards Flurry's
chestnut cob, in a dogcart, dashed at full gallop into view, with
the reins streaming behind him, and two men in hot pursuit.
Almost before I had time to realize what had happened,
Flurry jumped through the half-opened window of the dining-
room like a clown at a pantomime, and joined in the chase,
but the cob was resolved to make the most of his chance, and
went away down the drive and out of sight at a pace that dis-
tanced every one save the kennel terrier, who sped in shrieking
ecstasy beside him.

'Oh merciful hour!' exclaimed a female voice behind me.
Leigh Kelway and I were by this time watching the progress
of events from the gravel, in company with the remainder of
Flurry's household. 'The horse is desthroyed! Wasn't that
the quare start he took! And all in the world I done was to
shlap a bucket of wather at Michael out of the windy, and 'twas
himself got it in place of Michael!'

'Ye 'll never ate another bit, Bridgie Dunnigan,' replied the
cook, with the exulting pessimism of her kind. 'The master 'll
have your life!'

Both speakers shouted at the top of their voices, probably
because in spirit they still followed afar the flight of the cob.

Leigh Kelway looked serious as we walked on down the drive.
I almost dared to hope that a note on the degrading oppression
of Irish retainers was shaping itself. Before we reached the
bend of the drive the rescue party was returning with the fugitive
all, with the exception of the kennel terrier, looking extremely
gloomy. The cob had been confronted by a wooden gate,
which he had unhesitatingly taken in his stride, landing on his
head on the farther side with the gate and the cart on top of
him, and had risen with a lame foreleg, a cut on his nose, and
several other minor wounds.

'You 'd think the brute had been fighting the cats, with all
the scratches and scrapes he has on him!' said Flurry, casting
a vengeful eye at Michael, 'and one shaft 's broken and so is
the dashboard. I haven't another horse in the place; they 're
all out at grass, and so there 's an end of the races!'

We all three stood blankly on the hall-door steps and watched
the wreck of the trap being trundled up the avenue.

'I 'm very sorry you 're done out of your sport,' said
Flurry to Leigh Kelway, in tones of deplorable sincerity;

'perhaps, as there's nothing else to do, you'd like to see the hounds——?'

I felt for Flurry, but of the two I felt more for Leigh Kelway as he accepted this alleviation. He disliked dogs, and held the newest views on sanitation, and I knew what Flurry's kennels could smell like. I was lighting a precautionary cigarette, when we caught sight of an old man riding up the drive. Flurry stopped short.

'Hold on a minute,' he said; 'here's an old chap that often brings me horses for the kennels; I must see what he wants.'

The man dismounted and approached Mr. Knox, hat in hand, towing after him a gaunt and ancient black mare with a big knee.

'Well, Barrett,' began Flurry, surveying the mare with his hands in his pockets, 'I'm not giving the hounds meat this month, or only very little.'

'Ah, Master Flurry,' answered Barrett, 'it's you that's pleasant! Is it give the like o' this one for the dogs to ate! She's a vallyble strong young mare, no more than shixteen years of age, and ye'd sooner be lookin' at her goin' under a side-car than eatin' your dinner.'

'There isn't as much meat on her as 'd fatten a jackdaw,' said Flurry, clinking the silver in his pockets as he searched for a matchbox. 'What are you asking for her?'

The old man drew cautiously up to him.

'Master Flurry,' he said solemnly, 'I'll sell her to *your* honour for five pounds, and she'll be worth ten after you give her a month's grass.'

Flurry lit his cigarette; then he said imperturbably: 'I'll give you seven shillings for her.'

Old Barrett put on his hat in silence, and in silence buttoned his coat and took hold of the stirrup leather. Flurry remained immovable.

'Master Flurry,' said old Barrett suddenly, with tears in his voice, 'you must make it eight, sir!'

'Michael!' called out Flurry with apparent irrelevance, 'run up to your father's and ask him would he lend me a loan of his side-car.'

Half an hour later we were, improbable as it may seem, on our way to Lisheen races. We were seated upon an outside car of immemorial age, whose joints seemed to open and close again as it swung in and out of the ruts, whose tattered cushions stank of rats and mildew, whose wheels staggered and rocked like the legs of a drunken man. Between the shafts jogged the latest addition to the kennel larder, the eight-shilling mare. Flurry sat on one side, and kept her going at a rate of not less than four miles an hour; Leigh Kelway and I held on to the other.

'She 'll get us as far as Lynch's anyway,' said Flurry, abandoning his first contention that she could do the whole distance, as he pulled her on to her legs after her fifteenth stumble, 'and he 'll lend us some sort of a horse, if it was only a mule.'

'Do you notice that these cushions are very damp?' said Leigh Kelway to me, in a hollow undertone.

'Small blame to them if they are!' replied Flurry. 'I 've no doubt but they were out under the rain all day yesterday at Mrs. Hurly's funeral.'

Leigh Kelway made no reply, but he took his note-book out of his pocket and sat on it.

We arrived at Lynch's at a little past three, and were there confronted by the next disappointment of this disastrous day. The door of Lynch's farmhouse was locked, and nothing replied to our knocking except a puppy, who barked hysterically from within.

'All gone to the races,' said Flurry philosophically, picking his way round the manure heap. 'No matter, here 's the filly in the shed here. I know he 's had her under a car.'

An agitating ten minutes ensued, during which Leigh Kelway and I got the eight-shilling mare out of the shafts and the harness, and Flurry, with our inefficient help, crammed the young mare into them. As Flurry had stated that she had been driven before, I was bound to believe him, but the difficulty of getting the bit into her mouth was remarkable, and so also was the crab-like manner in which she sidled out of the yard, with Flurry and myself at her head, and Leigh Kelway hanging on to the back of the car to keep it from jamming in the gateway.

'Sit up on the car now,' said Flurry when we got out on to the road; 'I 'll lead her on a bit. She 's been ploughed anyway; one side of her mouth 's as tough as a gad!'

Leigh Kelway threw away the wisp of grass with which he had been cleaning his hands, and mopped his intellectual forehead; he was very silent. We both mounted the car, and
* C 978

Flurry, with the reins in his hand, walked beside the filly, who, with her tail clasped in, moved onward in a succession of short jerks.

'Oh, she's all right!' said Flurry, beginning to run, and dragging the filly into a trot; 'once she gets started——' Here the filly spied a pig in a neighbouring field, and despite the fact that she had probably eaten out of the same trough with it, she gave a violent side spring, and broke into a gallop.

'Now we're off!' shouted Flurry, making a jump at the car and clambering on; 'if the traces hold we'll do!'

The English language is powerless to suggest the view-halloo with which Mr. Knox ended his speech, or to do more than indicate the rigid anxiety of Leigh Kelway's face as he regained his balance after the preliminary jerk, and clutched the back rail. It must be said for Lynch's filly that she did not kick; she merely fled, like a dog with a kettle tied to its tail, from the pursuing rattle and jingle behind her, with the shafts buffeting her dusty sides as the car swung to and fro. Whenever she showed any signs of slackening, Flurry loosed another yell at her that renewed her panic, and thus we precariously covered another two or three miles of our journey.

Had it not been for a large stone lying on the road, and had the filly not chosen to swerve so as to bring the wheel on top of it, I dare say we might have got to the races; but by an unfortunate coincidence both these things occurred, and when we recovered from the consequent shock, the tyre of one of the wheels had come off; and was trundling with cumbrous gaiety into the ditch. Flurry stopped the filly and began to laugh; Leigh Kelway said something startlingly unparliamentary under his breath.

'Well, it might be worse,' Flurry said consolingly as he lifted the tyre on to the car; 'we're not half a mile from a forge.'

We walked that half-mile in funereal procession behind the car; the glory had departed from the weather, and an ugly wall of cloud was rising up out of the west to meet the sun; the hills had darkened and lost colour, and the white bog cotton shivered in a cold wind that smelt of rain.

By a miracle the smith was not at the races, owing, as he explained, to his having 'the toothaches,' the two facts combined producing in him a morosity only equalled by that of Leigh Kelway. The smith's sole comment on the situation was to unharness the filly, and drag her into the forge, where he tied her up. He then proceeded to whistle viciously on his fingers in the direction of a cottage, and to command, in tones of thunder, some unseen creature to bring over a couple of baskets of turf. The turf arrived in process of time, on a woman's back, and was arranged in a circle in a yard at the back of the forge. The tyre was bedded in it, and the turf was with difficulty kindled at different points.

'Ye'll not get to the races this day,' said the smith, yielding to a sardonic satisfaction; 'the turf's wet, and I haven't one to do a hand's turn for me.' He laid the wheel on the ground and lit his pipe.

Leigh Kelway looked pallidly about him over the spacious empty landscape of brown mountain slopes patched with golden furze and seamed with grey walls; I wondered if he were as hungry as I. We sat on stones opposite the smouldering ring of turf and smoked, and Flurry beguiled the smith into grim and calumnious confidences about every horse in the country. After about an hour, during which the turf went out three times, and the weather became more and more threatening, a girl with a red petticoat over her head appeared at the gate of the yard, and said to the smith:

'The horse is gone away from ye.'

'Where?' exclaimed Flurry, springing to his feet.

'I met him walking wesht the road there below, and when I thought to turn him he commenced to gallop.'

'Pulled her head out of the headstall,' said Flurry, after a rapid survey of the forge. 'She's near home by now.'

It was at this moment that the rain began; the situation could scarcely have been better stage-managed. After reviewing the position, Flurry and I decided that the only thing to do was to walk to a public-house a couple of miles farther on, feed there if possible, hire a car, and go home.

It was an uphill walk, with mild, generous raindrops striking thicker and thicker on our faces; no one talked, and the grey clouds crowded up from behind the hills like billows of steam. Leigh Kelway bore it all with egregious resignation. I cannot pretend that I was at heart sympathetic, but by virtue of being his host I felt responsible for the breakdown, for his light suit, for everything, and divined his sentiment of horror at the first sight of the public-house.

It was a long, low cottage, with a line of dripping elm-trees overshadowing it; empty cars and carts round its door, and a babel from within made it evident that the race-goers were pursuing a gradual homeward route. The shop was crammed with steaming countrymen, whose loud brawling voices, all talking together, roused my English friend to his first remark since we had left the forge.

'Surely, Yeates, we are not going into that place?' he said severely; 'those men are all drunk.'

'Ah, nothing to signify!' said Flurry, plunging in and driving his way through the throng like a plough. 'Here, Mary Kate!' he called to the girl behind the counter, 'tell your mother we want some tea and bread and butter in the room inside.'

The smell of bad tobacco and spilt porter was choking; we worked our way through it after him towards the end of the shop, intersecting at every hand discussions about the races.

'Tom was very nice. He spared his horse all along, and then he put into him——' 'Well, at Goggin's corner the third horse was before the second, but he was goin' wake in himself.' 'I tell ye the mare had the hind leg fasht in the fore.' 'Clancy was dipping in the saddle.' ''Twas a dam nice race whatever——'

We gained the inner room at last, a cheerless apartment, adorned with sacred pictures, a sewing-machine, and an array of supplementary tumblers and wineglasses; but, at all events, we had it so far to ourselves. At intervals during the next half-hour Mary Kate burst in with cups and plates, cast them on the table, and disappeared, but of food there was no sign. After a further period of starvation and of listening to the noise in the shop, Flurry made a sortie, and, after lengthy and unknown adventures, reappeared carrying a huge brown teapot, and driving before him Mary Kate with the remainder of the repast. The bread tasted of mice, the butter of turf-smoke, the tea of brown paper, but we had got past the critical stage. I had entered upon my third round of bread and butter when the door was flung open, and my valued acquaintance, Slipper, slightly advanced in liquor, presented himself to our gaze. His bandy legs sprawled consequentially, his nose was redder than a coal of fire, his prominent eyes rolled crookedly upon us, and his left hand swept behind him the attempt of Mary Kate to frustrate his entrance.

'Good evening to my vinerable friend, Mr. Flurry Knox!'
he began, in the voice of a town crier, 'and to the Honourable
Major Yeates, and the English gintleman!'

This impressive opening immediately attracted an audience
from the shop, and the doorway filled with grinning faces as
Slipper advanced farther into the room.

'Why weren't ye at the races, Mr. Flurry?' he went on, his
roving eye taking a grip of us all at the same time; 'sure the
Miss Bennetts and all the ladies was asking where were ye.'

'It 'd take some time to tell them that,' said Flurry, with his
mouth full; 'but what about the races, Slipper? Had you good
sport?'

'Sport is it? Divil so pleasant an afternoon ever you seen,'
replied Slipper. He leaned against a side-table, and all the
glasses on it jingled. Does your honour know Driscoll?'
he went on irrelevantly. 'Sure you do. He was in your
honour's stable. It 's what we were all sayin'; it was a great
pity your honour was not there, for the likin' you had to
Driscoll.'

'That 's thrue,' said a voice at the door.

'There wasn't one in the barony but was gethered in it,
through and fro,' continued Slipper, with a quelling glance at
the interrupter; 'and there was tints for sellin' porther, and
whisky as pliable as new milk, and boys goin' round the tints
outside, feeling for heads with the big ends of their black-
thorns, and all kinds of recreations, and the Sons of Liberty's
piffler and dhrum band from Skebawn; though faith! there
was more of thim runnin' to look at the races than what was
playin' in it; not to mintion different occasions that the bandmasther was atin' his lunch within in the whisky tint.'

'But what about Driscoll?' said Flurry.

'Sure it 's about him I 'm tellin' ye,' replied Slipper, with
the practised orator's watchful eye on his growing audience.
''Twas within in the same whisky tint meself was, with the
bandmasther and a few of the lads, an' we buyin' a ha'porth o'
crackers, when I seen me brave Driscoll landin' into the tint,
and a pair o' thim long boots on him; him that hadn't a shoe
nor a stocking to his foot when your honour had him picking
grass out o' the stones behind in your yard. "Well," says I
to meself, "we 'll knock some spoort out of Driscoll!"

'"Come here to me, acushla!" says I to him; "I suppose it 's some way wake in the legs y' are," says I, "an' the docther put them on ye the way the people wouldn't thrample ye!"

'"May the divil choke ye!" says he, pleasant enough, but I knew by the blush he had he was vexed.

'"Then I suppose 'tis a left-tenant colonel y' are," says I; "yer mother must be proud out o' ye!" says I, "an' maybe ye 'll lend her a loan o' thim waders when she's rinsin' yer bauneen in the river!" says I.

'"There 'll be work out o' this!' says he, lookin' at me both sour and bitther.

'"Well indeed, I was thinkin' you were blue-moulded for want of a batin'," says I. He was for fightin' us then, but afther we had him pacificated with about a quarther of a naggin o' sperrits, he told us he was goin' ridin' in a race.

'"An' what 'll ye ride?" says I.

'"Owld Bocock's mare," says he.

'"Knipes!" says I, sayin' a great curse; "is it that little staggeen from the mountains; sure she's somethin' about the one age with meself," says I. "Many's the time Jamesy Geoghegan and meself used to be dhrivin' her to Macroom with pigs an' all soorts," says I; "an' is it leppin' stone walls ye want her to go now?"

'"Faith, there's walls and every vari'ty of obstackle in it," says he.

'"It 'll be the best o' your play, so," says I, "to leg it away home out o' this."

'"An' who 'll ride her, so?" says he.

'"Let the divil ride her," says I.'

Leigh Kelway, who had been leaning back seemingly half asleep, obeyed the hypnotism of Slipper's gaze, and opened his eyes.

'That was now all the conversation that passed between himself and meself,' resumed Slipper, 'and there was no great delay afther that till they said there was a race startin' and the dickens a one at all was goin' to ride only two, Driscoll, and one Clancy. With that then I seen Mr. Kinahane, the Petty Sessions clerk, goin' round clearin' the coorse, an' I gethered a few o' the neighbours, an' we walked the fields hither and over till we seen the most of th' obstackles.

'"Stand aisy now by the plantation," says I; "if they get to come as far as this, believe me ye 'll see spoort," says I, "an' 'twill be a convanient spot to encourage the mare if she 's any-way wake in herself," says I, cuttin' somethin' about five foot of an ash sapling out o' the plantation.

'"That 's yer sort!" says owld Bocock, that was thravellin' the racecoorse, peggin' a bit o' paper down with a thorn in front of every lep, the way Driscoll 'd know the handiest place to face her at it.

'Well, I hadn't barely thrimmed the ash plant——'

'Have you any jam, Mary Kate?' interrupted Flurry, whose meal had been in no way interfered with by either the story or the highly-scented crowd who had come to listen to it.

'We have no jam, only thraycle, sir,' replied the invisible Mary Kate.

'I hadn't the switch barely thrimmed,' repeated Slipper firmly, 'when I heard the people screechin', an' I seen Driscoll an' Clancy comin' on, leppin' all before them, an' owld Bocock's mare bellusin' an' powdherin' along, an' bedad! whatever ob-stackle wouldn't throw *her* down, faith, she 'd throw *it* down, an' there 's the thraffic they had in it.

'"I declare to me sowl," says I, "if they continue on this way there 's a great chance some one o' thim 'll win," says I.

'"Ye lie!" says the bandmasther, bein' a thrifle fulsome after his luncheon.

'"I do not," says I, "in regard of seein' how soople them two boys is. Ye might observe," says I, "that if they have no convanient way to sit on the saddle, they 'll ride the neck o' the horse till such time as they gets an occasion to lave it," says I.

'"Arrah, shut yer mouth!" says the bandmasther; "they 're puckin' out this way now, an' may the divil admire me!" says he, "but Clancy has the other bet out, and the divil such leatherin' and beltin' of owld Bocock's mare ever you seen as what 's in it!" says he.

'Well, when I seen them comin' to me, and Driscoll about the length of the plantation behind Clancy, I let a couple of bawls.

'"Skelp her, ye big brute!" says I. "What good 's in ye that ye aren't able to skelp her?"'

The yell and the histrionic flourish of his stick with which Slipper delivered this incident brought down the house. Leigh Kelway was sufficiently moved to ask me in an undertone if 'skelp' was a local term.

'Well, Mr. Flurry, and gintlemen,' recommenced Slipper,

'I declare to ye when owld Bocock's mare heard thim roars she sthretched out her neck like a gandher, and when she passed me out she give a couple of grunts, and looked at me as ugly as a Christian.

'"Hah!" says I, givin' her a couple o' dhraws o' th' ash plant across the butt o' the tail, the way I wouldn't blind her; "I 'll make ye grunt!" says I, "I 'll nourish ye!"

'I knew well she was very frightful of th' ash plant since the winter Tommeen Sullivan had her under a side-car. But now, in place of havin' any obligations to me, ye' d be surprised if ye heard the blaspheemious expressions of that young boy that was ridin' her; and whether it was over-anxious he was, turnin' around the way I 'd hear him cursin', or whether it was some slither or slide came to owld Bocock's mare, I dunno, but she was bet up agin the last obstackle but two, and before ye could say "Shnipes," she was standin' on her two ears beyond in th' other field! I declare to ye, on the vartue of me oath, she stood that way till she reconnoithered what side would Driscoll fall, an' she turned about then and rolled on him as cosy as if he was meadow grass!'

Slipper stopped short; the people in the doorway groaned appreciatively; Mary Kate murmured: 'The Lord save us!'

'The blood was dhruv out through his nose and ears,' continued Slipper, with a voice that indicated the cream of the narration, 'and you 'd hear his bones crackin' on the ground! You 'd have pitied the poor boy.'

'Good heavens!' said Leigh Kelway, sitting up very straight in his chair.

'Was he hurt, Slipper?' asked Flurry casually.

'Hurt is it?' echoed Slipper in high scorn; 'killed on the spot!' He paused to relish the *dénouement* on Leigh Kelway. 'Oh, divil so pleasant an afthernoon ever you seen; and indeed, Mr. Flurry, it 's what we were all sayin', it was a great pity your honour was not there for the likin' you had for Driscoll.'

As he spoke the last word there was an outburst of singing and cheering from a car-load of people who had just pulled up at the door. Flurry listened, leaned back in his chair, and began to laugh.

'It scarcely strikes one as a comic incident,' said Leigh Kelway, very coldly to me; 'in fact, it seems to me that the police ought——'

'Show me Slipper!' bawled a voice in the shop; 'show me
that dirty little undherlooper till I have his blood! Hadn't I
the race won only for he souring the mare on me! What's
that you say? I tell ye he did! He left seven slaps on her with
the handle of a hay-rake——'

There was in the room in which we were sitting a second door,
leading to the back yard, a door consecrated to the unobtru-
sive visits of so-called 'Sunday travellers.' Through it Slipper
faded away like a dream, and, simultaneously, a tall young man,
with a face like a red-hot potato tied up in a bandage, squeezed
his way from the shop into the room.

'Well, Driscoll,' said Flurry, 'since it wasn't the teeth of the
rake he left on the mare, you needn't be talking!'

Leigh Kelway looked from one to the other with a wilder
expression in his eye than I had thought it capable of. I read
in it a resolve to abandon Ireland to her fate.

At eight o'clock we were still waiting for the car that we had
been assured should be ours directly it returned from the races.
At half-past eight we had adopted the only possible course that
remained, and had accepted the offers on the laden cars that
were returning to Skebawn, and I presently was gratified by
the spectacle of my friend Leigh Kelway wedged between a
roulette table and its proprietor on one side of a car, with
Driscoll and Slipper, mysteriously reconciled and excessively
drunk, seated, locked in each other's arms, on the other.
Flurry and I, somewhat similarly placed, followed on two other
cars. I was scarcely surprised when I was informed that the
melancholy white animal in the shafts of the leading car was
Owld Bocock's much-enduring steeplechaser.

The night was very dark and stormy, and it is almost superfluous to say that no one carried lamps; the rain poured upon
us, and through wind and wet Owld Bocock's mare set the pace
at a rate that showed she knew from bitter experience what
was expected from her by gentlemen who had spent the evening
in a public-house; behind her the other two tired horses followed closely, incited to emulation by shouting, singing, and a
liberal allowance of whip. We were a good ten miles from
Skebawn, and never had the road seemed so long. For mile
after mile the half-seen low walls slid past us, with occasional
plunges into caverns of darkness under trees. Sometimes from
a wayside cabin a dog would dash out to bark at us as we rattled

by; sometimes our cavalcade swung aside to pass, with yells and counter-yells, crawling carts filled with other belated race-goers.

I was nearly wet through, even though I received considerable shelter from a Skebawn publican, who slept heavily and irrepressibly on my shoulder. Driscoll, on the leading car, had struck up an approximation to *The Wearing of the Green*, when a wavering star appeared on the road ahead of us. It grew momently larger; it came towards us apace. Flurry, on the car behind me, shouted suddenly:

'That's the mail car, with one of the lamps out! Tell those fellows ahead to look out!'

But the warning fell on deaf ears.

> 'When laws can change the blades of grass
> From growing as they grow——'

howled five discordant voices, oblivious of the towering proximity of the star.

A Bianconi mail car is nearly three times the size of an ordinary outside car, and when on a dark night it advances, Cyclops-like, with but one eye, it is difficult for even a sober driver to calculate its bulk. Above the sounds of melody there arose the thunder of heavy wheels, the splashing trample of three big horses, then a crash and a turmoil of shouts. Our cars pulled up just in time, and I tore myself from the embrace of my publican to go to Leigh Kelway's assistance.

The wing of the Bianconi had caught the wing of the smaller car, flinging Owld Bocock's mare on her side, and throwing her freight headlong on top of her, the heap being surmounted by the roulette table. The driver of the mail car unshipped his solitary lamp and turned it on the disaster. I saw that Flurry had already got hold of Leigh Kelway by the heels, and was dragging him from under the others. He struggled up hatless, muddy, and gasping, with Driscoll hanging on by his neck, still singing *The Wearing of the Green*.

A voice from the mail car said incredulously: '*Leigh Kelway!*'

A spectacled face glared down upon him from under the dripping spikes of an umbrella.

It was the Right Honourable the Earl of Waterbury, Leigh Kelway's chief, returning from his fishing excursion.

Meanwhile Slipper, in the ditch, did not cease to announce that 'Divil so pleasant an afthernoon ever ye seen as what was in it!'

VI

PHILIPPA'S FOX-HUNT

No one can accuse Philippa and me of having married in haste. As a matter of fact, it was but little under five years from that autumn evening on the river when I had said what is called in Ireland 'the hard word,' to the day in August when I was led to the altar by my best man, and was subsequently led away from it by Mrs. Sinclair Yeates. About two years out of the five had been spent by me at Shreelane in ceaseless warfare with drains, eaveshoots, chimneys, pumps; all those fundamentals, in short, that the ingenuous and improving tenant expects to find established as a basis from which to rise to higher things. As far as rising to higher things went, frequent ascents to the roof to search for leaks summed up my achievements; in fact, I suffered so general a shrinkage of my ideals that the triumph of making the hall-door bell ring blinded me to the fact that the rat-holes in the hall floor were nailed up with pieces of tin biscuit boxes, and that the casual visitor could, instead of leaving a card, have easily written his name in the damp on the walls.

Philippa, however, proved adorably callous to these and similar shortcomings. She regarded Shreelane and its floundering, foundering *ménage* of incapables in the light of a gigantic picnic in a foreign land; she held long conversations daily with Mrs. Cadogan, in order, as she informed me, to acquire the language; without any ulterior domestic intention she engaged kitchenmaids because of the beauty of their eyes, and housemaids because they had such delightfully picturesque old mothers, and she declined to correct the phraseology of the parlourmaid, whose painful habit it was to whisper 'Do ye choose cherry or clarry?' when proffering the wine. Fast-days, perhaps, afforded my wife her first insight into the sterner realities of Irish housekeeping. Philippa had what are known as High Church proclivities, and took the matter seriously.

'I don't know how we are to manage for the servants' dinner to-morrow, Sinclair,' she said, coming to my office one Thursday morning; 'Julia says she "promised God this long time that she wouldn't eat an egg on a fast-day," and the kitchenmaid says she won't eat herrings "without they're fried with onions," and Mrs. Cadogan says she will "not go to them extremes for servants."'

'I should let Mrs. Cadogan settle the menu herself,' I suggested.

'I asked her to do that,' replied Philippa, 'and she only said she "thanked God *she* had no appetite!"'

The lady of the house here fell away into unseasonable laughter.

I made the demoralizing suggestion that, as we were going away for a couple of nights, we might safely leave them to fight it out, and the problem was abandoned.

Philippa had been much called on by the neighbourhood in all its shades and grades, and daily she and her trousseau frocks presented themselves at hall doors of varying dimensions in due acknowledgment of civilities. In Ireland, it may be noted, the process known in England as 'summering and wintering' a newcomer does not obtain; sociability and curiosity alike forbid delay. The visit to which we owed our escape from the intricacies of the fast-day was to the Knoxes of Castle Knox, relations in some remote and tribal way of my landlord, Mr. Flurry of that ilk. It involved a short journey by train, and my wife's longest basket-trunk; it also, which was more serious, involved my being lent a horse to go out cubbing the following morning.

At Castle Knox we sank into an almost forgotten environment of draught-proof windows and doors, of deep carpets, of silent servants instead of clattering belligerents. Philippa told me afterwards that it had only been by an effort that she had restrained herself from snatching up the train of her wedding-gown as she paced across the wide hall on little Sir Valentine's arm. After three weeks at Shreelane she found it difficult to remember that the floor was neither damp nor dusty.

I had the good fortune to be of the limited number of those who got on with Lady Knox, chiefly, I imagine, because I was as a worm before her, and thankfully permitted her to do all the talking.

'Your wife is extremely pretty,' she pronounced autocratically, surveying Philippa between the candle-shades; 'does she ride?'

Lady Knox was a short square lady, with a weather-beaten face, and an eye decisive from long habit of taking her own line across country and elsewhere. She would have made a very imposing little coachman, and would have caused her stable helpers to rue the day they had the presumption to be born; it struck me that Sir Valentine sometimes did so.

'I'm glad you like her looks,' I replied, 'as I fear you will find her thoroughly despicable otherwise; for one thing, she not only can't ride, but she believes that I can!'

'Oh, come, you're not as bad as all that!' my hostess was good enough to say; 'I'm going to put you up on Sorcerer to-morrow, and we'll see you at the top of the hunt—if there is one. That young Knox hasn't a notion how to draw these woods.'

'Well, the best run we had last year out of this place was with Flurry's hounds,' struck in 'Miss Sally, sole daughter of Sir Valentine's house and home, from her place half-way down the table. It was not difficult to see that she and her mother held different views on the subject of Mr. Flurry Knox.

'I call it a criminal thing in any one's great-great-grand-father to rear up a preposterous troop of sons and plant them all out in his own country,' Lady Knox said to me with apparent irrelevance. 'I detest collaterals. Blood may be thicker than water, but it is also a great deal nastier. In this country I find that fifteenth cousins consider themselves near relations if they live within twenty miles of one!'

Having before now taken in the position with regard to Flurry Knox, I took care to accept these remarks as generalities, and turned the conversation to other themes.

'I see Mrs. Yeates is doing wonders with Mr. Hamilton,' said Lady Knox presently, following the direction of my eyes, which had strayed away to where Philippa was beaming upon her left-hand neighbour, a mildewed-looking old clergyman, who was delivering a long dissertation, the purport of which we were happily unable to catch.

'She has always had a gift for the Church,' I said.

'Not curates?' said Lady Knox, in her deep voice.

I made haste to reply that it was the elders of the Church who were venerated by my wife.

'Well, she has her fancy in old Eustace Hamilton; he's elderly enough!' said Lady Knox. 'I wonder if she'd venerate him as much if she knew that he had fought with his sister-in-law, and they haven't spoken for thirty years! though for the matter of that,' she added, 'I think it shows his good sense!'

'Mrs. Knox is rather a friend of mine,' I ventured.

'Is she? H'm! Well, she's not one of mine!' replied my hostess, with her usual definiteness. 'I'll say one thing for her, I believe, she's always been a sportswoman. She's very rich, you know, and they say she only married old Badger Knox to save his hounds from being sold to pay his debts, and then she took the horn from him and hunted them herself. Has she been rude to your wife yet? No? Oh, well, she will. It's a mere question of time. She hates all English people. You know the story they tell of her? She was coming from London, and when she was getting her ticket the man asked if she had said a ticket for York. "No, thank God, Cork!" says Mrs. Knox.'

'Well, I rather agree with her!' said I; 'but why did she fight with Mr. Hamilton?'

'Oh, nobody knows. I don't believe they know themselves! Whatever it was, the old lady drives five miles to Fortwilliam every Sunday, rather than go to his church, just outside her own back gates,' Lady Knox said with a laugh like a terrier's bark. 'I wish I'd fought with him myself,' she said; 'he gives us forty minutes every Sunday.'

As I struggled into my boots the following morning, I felt that Sir Valentine's acid confidences on cub-hunting, bestowed on me at midnight, did credit to his judgment. 'A very moderate amusement, my dear Major,' he had said, in his dry little voice; 'you should stick to shooting. No one expects you to shoot before daybreak.'

It was six o'clock as I crept downstairs, and found Lady Knox and Miss Sally at breakfast, with two lamps on the table, and a foggy daylight oozing in from under the half-raised blinds. Philippa was already in the hall, pumping up her bicycle, in a state of excitement at the prospect of her first experience of hunting that would have been more comprehensible to me had she been going to ride a strange horse, as I was. As I bolted my food I saw the horses being led past the windows, and a faint twang of a horn told that Flurry Knox and his hounds were not far off.

Miss Sally jumped up.

'If I'm not on the Cockatoo before the hounds come up, I shall never get there!' she said, hobbling out of the room in the toils of her safety habit. Her small, alert face looked very

childish under her riding-hat; the lamp-light struck sparks óut
of her thick coil of golden-red hair: I wondered how I had
ever thought her like her prim little father.

She was already on her white cob when I got to the hall
door, and Flurry Knox was riding over the glistening wet grass
with his hounds, while his whip, Dr. Jerome Hickey, was having
a stirring time with the young entry and the rabbit-holes. They
moved on without stopping, up a back avenue, under tall and
dripping trees, to a thick laurel covert, at some little distance
from the house. Into this the hounds were thrown, and the
usual period of fidgety inaction set in for the riders, of whom
all told, there were about half a dozen. Lady Knox, square
and solid, on her big, confidential iron-grey, was near me, and
her eyes were on me and my mount; with her rubicund face and
white collar she was more than ever like a coachman.

'Sorcerer looks as if he suited you well,' she said, after a
few minutes of silence, during which the hounds rustled and
crackled steadily through the laurels; 'he's a little high on the
leg, and so are you, you know, so you show each other off.'

Sorcerer was standing like a rock, with his good-looking
head in the air and his eyes fastened on the covert. His
manners, so far, had been those of a perfect gentleman, and
were in marked contrast to those of Miss Sally's cob, who was
sidling, hopping, and snatching unappeasably at his bit.
Philippa had disappeared from view down the avenue ahead.
The fog was melting, and the sun threw long blades of light
through the trees; everything was quiet, and in the distance
the curtained windows of the house marked the warm repose
of Sir Valentine, and those of the party who shared his opinion
of cubbing.

'Hark! hark to cry there!'

It was Flurry's voice, away at the other side of the covert.
The rustling and brushing through the laurels became more
vehement, then passed out of hearing.

'He never will leave his hounds alone,' said Lady Knox
disapprovingly.

Miss Sally and the Cockatoo moved away in a series of
heraldic capers towards the end of the laurel plantation, and at
the same moment I saw Philippa on her bicycle shoot into view
on the drive ahead of us.

'I've seen a fox!' she screamed, white with what I believe

to have been personal terror, though she says it was excitement;
'it passed quite close to me!'

'What way did he go?' bellowed a voice which I recognized
as Dr. Hickey's, somewhere in the deep of the laurels.

'Down the drive!' returned Philippa, with a pea-hen quality
in her tones with which I was quite unacquainted.

An electrifying screech of 'Gone away!' was projected from
the laurels by Dr. Hickey.

'Gone away!' chanted Flurry's horn at the top of the
covert.

'This is what he calls cubbing!' said Lady Knox, 'a mere
farce!' but none the less she loosed her sedate monster into a
canter.

Sorcerer got his hind legs under him, and hardened his crest
against the bit, as we all hustled along the drive after the flying
figure of my wife. I knew very little about horses, but I
realized that even with the hounds tumbling hysterically out of
the covert, Sorcerer comported himself with the manners of
the best society. Up a side road I saw Flurry Knox opening
half of a gate and cramming through it; in a moment we also
had crammed through, and the turf of a pasture field was under
our feet. Dr. Hickey leaned forward and took hold of his
horse; I did likewise, with the trifling difference that my horse
took hold of me, and I steered for Flurry Knox with single-
hearted purpose, the hounds, already a field ahead, being
merely an exciting and noisy accompaniment of this endeavour.
A heavy stone wall was the first occurrence of note. Flurry
chose a place where the top was loose, and his clumsy-looking
brown mare changed feet on the rattling stones like a fairy.
Sorcerer came at it, tense and collected as a bow at full stretch,
and sailed steeply into the air; I saw the wall far beneath me,
with an unsuspected ditch on the far side, and I felt my hat
following me at the full stretch of its guard as we swept over it,
then, with a long slant, we descended to earth some sixteen
feet from where we had left it, and I was possessor of the gratifying fact that I had achieved a good-sized 'fly,' and had not
perceptibly moved in my saddle. Subsequent disillusioning
experience has taught me that but few horses jump like Sorcerer,
so gallantly, so sympathetically, and with such supreme mastery
of the subject; but none the less the enthusiasm that he imparted to me has never been extinguished, and that October

morning ride revealed to me the unsuspected intoxication of
fox-hunting.

Behind me I heard the scrabbling of the Cockatoo's little
hoofs among the loose stone, and Lady Knox, galloping on my
left, jerked a maternal chin over her shoulder to mark her
daughter's progress. For my part, had there been an entire
circus behind me, I was far too much occupied with ramming
on my hat and trying to hold Sorcerer, to have looked round,
and all my spare faculties were devoted to steering for Flurry,
who had taken a right-handed turn, and was at that moment
surmounting a bank of uncertain and briary aspect. I surmounted it also, with the swiftness and simplicity for which
the Quaker's methods of bank jumping had not prepared me,
and two or three fields, traversed at the same steeplechase pace,
brought us to a road and to an abrupt check. There, suddenly,
were the hounds, scrambling in baffled silence down into the
road from the opposite bank, to look for the line they had
overrun, and there, amazingly, was Philippa, engaged in excited
converse with several men with spades over their shoulders.

'Did ye see the fox, boys?' shouted Flurry, addressing the
group.

'We did! we did!' cried my wife and her friends in chorus;
'he ran up the road!'

'We'd be badly off without Mrs. Yeates!' said Flurry, as
he whirled his mare round and clattered up the road with a
hustle of hounds after him.

It occurred to me as forcibly as any mere earthly thing can
occur to those who are wrapped in the sublimities of a run,
that, for a young woman who had never before seen a fox out of
a cage at the Zoo, Philippa was taking to hunting very kindly.
Her cheeks were a most brilliant pink, her blue eyes shone.

'Oh, Sinclair!' she exclaimed, 'they say he's going for
Aussolas, and there's a road I can ride all the way!'

'Ye can, miss! Sure we'll show you!' chorused her cortège.

Her foot was on the pedal ready to mount. Decidedly my
wife was in no need of assistance from me.

Up the road a hound gave a yelp of discovery, and flung
himself over a stile into the fields; the rest of the pack went
squealing and jostling after him, and I followed Flurry over
one of those infinitely varied erections, pleasantly termed
'gaps' in Ireland. On this occasion the gap was made of three

razor-edged slabs of slate leaning against an iron bar, and Sorcerer conveyed to me his thorough knowledge of the matter by a lift of his hind quarters that made me feel as if I were being skilfully kicked downstairs. To what extent I looked it, I cannot say, nor providentially can Philippa, as she had already started. I only know that undeserved good luck restored to me my stirrup before Sorcerer got away with me in the next field.

What followed was, I am told, a very fast fifteen minutes; for me time was not; the empty fields rushed past uncounted, fences came and went in a flash, while the wind sang in my ears, and the dazzle of the early sun was in my eyes. I saw the hounds occasionally, sometimes pouring over a green bank, as the charging breaker lifts and flings itself, sometimes driving across a field, as the white tongues of foam slide racing over the sand; and always ahead of me was Flurry Knox, going as a man goes who knows his country, who knows his horse, and whose heart is wholly and absolutely in the right place.

Do what I would, Sorcerer's implacable stride carried me closer and closer to the brown mare, till, as I thundered down the slope of a long field, I was not twenty yards behind Flurry. Sorcerer had stiffened his neck to iron, and to slow him down was beyond me; but I fought his head away to the right, and found myself coming hard and steady at a stone-faced bank with broken ground in front of it. Flurry bore away to the left, shouting something that I did not understand. That Sorcerer shortened his stride at the right moment was entirely due to his own judgment; standing well away from the jump, he rose like a stag out of the tussocky ground, and as he swung my twelve stone six into the air the obstacle revealed itself to him and me as consisting not of one bank but of two, and between the two lay a deep grassy lane, half choked with furze. I have often been asked to state the width of the *bohireen,* and can only reply that in my opinion it was at least eighteen feet; Flurry Knox and Dr. Hickey, who did not jump it, say that it is not more than five. What Sorcerer did with it I cannot say; the sensation was of a towering flight with a kick back in it, a biggish drop, and a landing on cee-springs, still on the downhill grade. That was how one of the best horses in Ireland took one of Ireland's most ignorant riders over a very nasty place.

A sombre line of fir-wood lay ahead, rimmed with a grey wall, and in another couple of minutes we had pulled up on the

Aussolas road, and were watching the hounds struggling over
the wall into Aussolas demesne. —

'No hurry now,' said Flurry, turning in his saddle to watch
the Cockatoo jump into the road, 'he's to ground in the big
earth inside. Well, Major, it's well for you that's a big-jumped
horse. I thought you were a dead man a while ago when you
faced him at the *bohireen*!'

I was disclaiming intention in the matter when Lady Knox
and the others joined us.

'I thought you told me your wife was no sportswoman,'
she said to me, critically scanning Sorcerer's legs for cuts the
while, 'but when I saw her a minute ago she had abandoned her
bicycle and was running across country like——'

'Look at her now!' interrupted Miss Sally. 'Oh!—oh!'
In the interval between these exclamations my incredulous eyes
beheld my wife in mid air, hand in hand with a couple of
stalwart country boys, with whom she was leaping in unison
from the top of a bank on to the road.

Every one, even the saturnine Dr. Hickey, began to laugh;
I rode back to Philippa, who was exchanging compliments and
congratulations with her escort.

'Oh, Sinclair!' she cried, 'wasn't it splendid? I saw you
jumping, and everything! Where are they going now?'

'My dear girl,' I said, with marital disapproval, 'you're
killing yourself. Where's your bicycle?'

'Oh, it's punctured in a sort of lane, back there. It's all
right; and then they'—she breathlessly waved her hand at her
attendants—'they showed me the way.'

'Begor! you proved very good, miss!' said a grinning cavalier.

'Faith she did!' said another, polishing his shining brow with
his white flannel coat-sleeve, 'she lepped like a haarse!'

'And may I ask how you propose to go home?' said I.

'I don't know and I don't care! I'm not going home!'
She cast an entirely disobedient eye at me. 'And your eye-
glass is hanging down your back and your tie is bulging out
over your waistcoat!'

The little group of riders had begun to move away.

'We're going on into Aussolas,' called out Flurry; 'come
on, and make my grandmother give you some breakfast, Mrs.
Yeates; she always has it at eight o'clock.'

The front gates were close at hand, and we turned in under

the tall beech-trees, with the unswept leaves rustling round the horses' feet, and the lovely blue of the October morning sky filling the spaces between smooth grey branches and golden leaves. The woods rang with the voices of the hounds, enjoying an untrammelled rabbit hunt, while the Master and the Whip, both on foot, strolled along unconcernedly with their bridles over their arms, making themselves agreeable to my wife, an occasional touch of Flurry's horn, or a crack of Dr. Hickey's whip, just indicating to the pack that the authorities still took a friendly interest in their doings.

Down a grassy glade in the wood a party of old Mrs. Knox's young horses suddenly swept into view, headed by an old mare, who, with her tail over her back, stampeded ponderously past our cavalcade, shaking and swinging her handsome old head, while her youthful friends bucked and kicked and snapped at each other round her with the ferocious humour of their kind.

'Here, Jerome, take the horn,' said Flurry to Dr. Hickey; 'I 'm going to see Mrs. Yeates up to the house, the way these tomfools won't gallop on top of her.'

From this point it seems to me that Philippa's adventures are more worthy of record than mine, and as she has favoured me with a full account of them, I venture to think my version may be relied on.

Mrs. Knox was already at breakfast when Philippa was led, quaking, into her formidable presence. My wife's acquaintance with Mrs. Knox was, so far, limited to a state visit on either side, and she found but little comfort in Flurry's assurances that his grandmother wouldn't mind if he brought all the hounds in to breakfast, coupled with the statement that she would put her eyes on sticks for the Major.

Whatever the truth of this may have been, Mrs. Knox received her guest with an equanimity quite unshaken by the fact that her boots were in the fender instead of on her feet, and that a couple of shawls of varying dimensions and degrees of age did not conceal the inner presence of a magenta flannel dressing-jacket. She installed Philippa at the table and plied her with food, oblivious as to whether the needful implements with which to eat it were forthcoming or no. She told Flurry where a vixen had reared her family, and she watched him ride away, with some biting comment on his mare's hocks screamed after him from the window.

The dining-room at Aussolas Castle is one of the many rooms in Ireland in which Cromwell is said to have stabled his horse (and probably no one would have objected less than Mrs. Knox had she been consulted in the matter). Philippa questions if the room had ever been tidied up since, and she endorses Flurry's observation that 'there wasn't a day in the year you wouldn't get feeding for a hen and chickens on the floor.' Opposite to Philippa, on a Louis Quinze chair, sat Mrs. Knox's woolly dog, its suspicious little eyes peering at her out of their setting of pink lids and dirty white wool. A couple of young horses outside the windows tore at the matted creepers on the walls, or thrust faces that were half-shy, half-impudent, into the room. Portly pigeons waddled to and fro on the broad window-sill, sometimes flying in to perch on the picture-frames, while they kept up incessantly a hoarse and pompous cooing.

Animals and children are, as a rule, alike destructive to conversation; but Mrs. Knox, when she chose, *bien entendu*, could have made herself agreeable in a Noah's ark, and Philippa has a gift of sympathetic attention that personal experience has taught me to regard with distrust as well as respect, while it has often made me realize the worldly wisdom of Kingsley's injunction:

Be good, sweet maid, and let who will be clever.

Family prayers, declaimed by Mrs. Knox with alarming austerity, followed close on breakfast, Philippa and a vinegar-faced henchwoman forming the family. The prayers were long, and through the open window as they progressed came distantly a whoop or two; the declamatory tones staggered a little, and then continued at a distinctly higher rate of speed. 'Ma'am! Ma'am!' whispered a small voice at the window. Mrs. Knox made a repressive gesture and held on her way. A sudden outcry of hounds followed, and the owner of the whisper, a small boy with a face freckled like a turkey's egg, darted from the window and dragged a donkey and bath-chair into view. Philippa admits to having lost the thread of the discourse, but she thinks that the 'Amen' that immediately ensued can hardly have come in its usual place. Mrs. Knox shut the book abruptly, scrambled up from her knees, and said, 'They've found!'

In a surprisingly short space of time she had added to her

attire her boots, a fur cape, and a garden hat, and was in the bath-chair, the small boy stimulating the donkey with the success peculiar to his class, while Philippa hung on behind.

The woods of Aussolas are hilly and extensive, and on that particular morning it seemed that they held as many foxes as hounds. In vain was the horn blown and the whips cracked, small rejoicing parties of hounds, each with a fox of its own, scoured to and fro: every labourer in the vicinity had left his work, and was sedulously heading every fox with yells that would have befitted a tiger hunt, and sticks and stones when occasion served.

'Will I pull out as far as the big rosydandhrum, ma'am?' inquired the small boy; 'I seen three of the dogs go in it, and they yowling.'

'You will,' said Mrs. Knox, thumping the donkey on the back with her umbrella; 'here! Jeremiah Regan! Come down out of that with that pitchfork! Do you want to kill the fox, you fool?'

'I do not, your honour, ma'am,' responded Jeremiah Regan, a tall young countryman, emerging from a bramble brake.

'Did you see him?' said Mrs. Knox eagerly.

'I seen himself and his ten pups drinking below at the lake ere yestherday, your honour, ma'am, and he as big as a chestnut horse!' said Jeremiah.

'Faugh! Yesterday!' snorted Mrs. Knox; 'go on to the rhododendrons, Johnny!'

The party, reinforced by Jeremiah and the pitchfork, progressed at a high rate of speed along the shrubbery path, encountering *en route* Lady Knox, stooping on to her horse's neck under the sweeping branches of the laurels.

'Your horse is too high for my coverts, Lady Knox,' said the lady of the manor, with a malicious eye at Lady Knox's flushed face and dinged hat; 'I'm afraid you will be left behind like Absalom when the hounds go away!'

'As they never do anything here but hunt rabbits,' retorted her ladyship, 'I don't think that's likely.'

Mrs. Knox gave her donkey another whack, and passed on.

'Rabbits, my dear!' she said scornfully to Philippa. 'That's all she knows about it. I declare it disgusts me to see a woman of that age making such a Judy of herself! Rabbits indeed!'

Down in the thicket of rhododendron everything was very

quiet for a time. Philippa strained her eyes in vain to see any
of the riders; the horn-blowing and the whip-cracking passed
on almost out of hearing. Once or twice a hound worked
through the rhododendrons, glanced at the party, and hurried
on, immersed in business. All at once, Johnny, the donkey-
boy, whispered excitedly:

'Look at he! Look at he!' and pointed to a boulder of grey
rock that stood out among the dark evergreens. A big yellow
cub was crouching on it; he instantly slid into the shelter of
the bushes, and the irrepressible Jeremiah, uttering a rending
shriek, plunged into the thicket after him. Two or three hounds
came rushing at the sound, and after this Philippa says she finds
some difficulty in recalling the proper order of events; chiefly,
she confesses, because of the wholly ridiculous tears of excitement that blurred her eyes.

'We ran,' she said, 'we simply tore, and the donkey galloped,
and as for that old Mrs. Knox, she was giving cracked screams
to the hounds all the time, and they were screaming too; and
then somehow we were all out on the road!'

What seems to have occurred was that three couple of hounds,
Jeremiah Regan, and Mrs. Knox's equipage, amongst them
somehow hustled the cub out of Aussolas demesne and up on
to a hill on the farther side of the road. Jeremiah was sent
back by his mistress to fetch Flurry, and the rest of the party
pursued a thrilling course along the road, parallel with that of
the hounds, who were hunting slowly through the gorse on the
hill-side.

'Upon my honour and word, Mrs. Yeates, my dear, we have
the hunt to ourselves!' said Mrs. Knox to the panting Philippa,
as they pounded along the road. 'Johnny, d' ye see the fox?'

'I do, ma'am!' shrieked Johnny, who possessed the usual
field-glass vision bestowed upon his kind. 'Look at him over-
right us on the hill above! Hi! The spotty dog have him!
No, he's gone from him! *Gwan out o' that!*' This to the
donkey, with blows that sounded like the beating of carpets,
and produced rather more dust.

They had left Aussolas some half a mile behind, when, from
a strip of wood on their right, the fox suddenly slipped over the
bank on to the road just ahead of them, ran up it for a few yards,
and whisked in at a small entrance gate, with the three couple
of hounds yelling on a red-hot scent, not thirty yards behind.

The bath-chair party whirled in at their heels, Philippa and the donkey considerably blown, Johnny scarlet through his freckles, but as fresh as paint, the old lady blind and deaf to all things save the chase. The hounds went raging through the shrubs beside the drive, and away down a grassy slope towards a shallow glen, in the bottom of which ran a little stream, and after them over the grass bumped the bath-chair. At the stream they turned sharply and ran up the glen towards the avenue, which crossed it by means of a rough stone viaduct.

"'Pon me conscience, he's into the old culvert!' exclaimed Mrs. Knox; 'there was one of my hounds choked there once, long ago! Beat on the donkey, Johnny!'

At this juncture Philippa's narrative again becomes incoherent, not to say breathless. She is, however, positive that it was somewhere about here that the upset of the bath-chair occurred, but she cannot be clear as to whether she picked up the donkey or Mrs. Knox, or whether she herself was picked up by Johnny while Mrs. Knox picked up the donkey. From my knowledge of Mrs. Knox I should say she picked up herself and no one else. At all events, the next salient point is the palpitating moment when Mrs. Knox, Johnny, and Philippa successively applying an eye to the opening of the culvert by which the stream trickled under the viaduct, while five dripping hounds bayed and leaped around them, discovered by more senses than that of sight that the fox was in it, and furthermore that one of the hounds was in it too.

'There's a sthrong grating before him at the far end,' said Johnny, his head in at the mouth of the hole, his voice sounding as if he were talking into a jug, 'the two of them's fighting in it; they'll be choked surely!'

'Then don't stand gabbling there, you little fool, but get in and pull the hound out!' exclaimed Mrs. Knox, who was balancing herself on a stone in the stream.

'I'd be in dread, ma'am,' whined Johnny.

'Balderdash!' said the implacable Mrs. Knox. 'In with you!'

I understand that Philippa assisted Johnny into the culvert, and presume that it was in so doing that she acquired the two Robinson Crusoe bare footprints which decorated her jacket when I next met her.

'Have you got hold of him yet, Johnny?' cried Mrs. Knox up the culvert.

'I have, ma'am, by the tail,' responded Johnny's voice, sepulchral in the depths.

'Can you stir him, Johnny?'

'I cannot, ma'am, and the wather is rising in it.'

'Well, please God, they'll not open the mill dam!' remarked Mrs. Knox philosophically to Philippa, as she caught hold of Johnny's dirty ankles. 'Hold on to the tail, Johnny!'

She hauled, with, as might be expected, no appreciable result. 'Run, my dear, and look for somebody, and we'll have that fox yet!'

Philippa ran, whither she knew not, pursued by fearful visions of bursting mill-dams, and maddened foxes at bay. As she sped up the avenue she heard voices, robust male voices, in a shrubbery, and made for them. Advancing along an embowered walk towards her was what she took for one wild instant to be a funeral; a second glance showed her that it was a party of clergymen of all ages, walking by twos and threes in the dappled shade of the over-arching trees. Obviously she had intruded her sacrilegious presence into a Clerical Meeting. She acknowledges that at this awe-inspiring spectacle she faltered, but the thought of Johnny, the hound, and the fox, suffocating, possibly drowning together in the culvert, nerved her. She does not remember what she said or how she said it, but I fancy she must have conveyed to them the impression that old Mrs. Knox was being drowned, as she immediately found herself heading a charge of the Irish Church towards the scene of disaster.

Fate has not always used me well, but on this occasion it was mercifully decreed that I and the other members of the hunt should be privileged to arrive in time to see my wife and her rescue party precipitating themselves down the glen.

'Holy Biddy!' ejaculated Flurry, 'is she running a paper-chase with all the parsons? But look! For pity's sake will you look at my grandmother and my Uncle Eustace?'

Mrs. Knox and her sworn enemy the old clergyman, whom I had met at dinner the night before, were standing, apparently in the stream, tugging at two bare legs that projected from a hole in the viaduct, and arguing at the top of their voices. The bath-chair lay on its side with the donkey grazing beside it, on the bank a stout archdeacon was tendering advice, and the hounds danced and howled round the entire group.

D 978

'I tell you, Eliza, you had better let the archdeacon try,' thundered Mr. Hamilton.

'Then I tell you I will not!' vociferated Mrs. Knox, with a tug at the end of the sentence that elicited a subterranean lament from Johnny. 'Now who was right about the second grating? I told you so twenty years ago!'

Exactly as Philippa and her rescue party arrived, the efforts of Mrs. Knox and her brother-in-law triumphed. The struggling, sopping form of Johnny was slowly drawn from the hole, drenched, speechless, but clinging to the stern of a hound, who, in its turn, had its jaws fast in the hind quarters of a limp, yellow cub.

'Oh, it's dead!' wailed Philippa, 'I *did* think I should have been in time to save it!'

'Well, if that doesn't beat all!' said Dr. Hickey.

VII

A MISDEAL

THE wagonette slewed and slackened mysteriously on the top of the long hill above Drumcurran. So many remarkable things had happened since we had entrusted ourselves to the guidance of Mr. Bernard Shute that I rose in my place and possessed myself of the brake, and in so doing saw the horses with their heads hard in against their chests, and their quarters jammed crookedly against the splashboard, being apparently tied into knots by some inexplicable power.

'Someone's pulling the reins out of my hand!' exclaimed Mr. Shute.

The horses and pole were by this time making an acute angle with the wagonette, and the groom plunged from the box to their heads. Miss Sally Knox, who was sitting beside me, looked over the edge.

'Put on the brake! The reins are twisted round the axle!' she cried, and fell into a fit of laughter.

We all—that is to say, Philippa, Miss Shute, Miss Knox, and I—got out as speedily as might be; but, I think, without panic;

Mr. Shute alone stuck to the ship, with the horses struggling and rearing below him. The groom and I contrived to back them, and by so doing caused the reins to unwind themselves from the axle.

'It was my fault,' said Mr. Shute, hauling them in as fast as we could give them to him; 'I broke the reins yesterday, and these are the phaeton ones, and about six fathoms long at that, and I forgot and let the slack go overboard. It's all right, I won't do it again.'

With this reassurance we confided ourselves once more to the wagonette.

As we neared the town of Drumcurran the fact that we were on our way to a horse fair became alarmingly apparent. It is impossible to imagine how we pursued an uninjured course through the companies of horsemen, the crowded carts, the squealing colts, the irresponsible led horses, and, most immutable of all obstacles, the groups of countrywomen, with the hoods of their heavy blue cloaks over their heads. They looked like nuns of some obscure order; they were deaf and blind as ramparts of sandbags; nothing less callous to human life than a Parisian cabdriver could have burst a way through them. Many times during that drive I had cause to be thankful for the sterling qualities of Mr. Shute's brake; with its aid he dragged his over-fed bays into a crawl that finally, and not without injury to the varnish, took the wagonette to the Royal Hotel. Every available stall in the yard was by that time filled, and it was only by virtue of the fact that the kitchenmaid was nearly related to my cook that the indignant groom was permitted to stable the bays in a den known as the calf-house.

That I should have lent myself to such an expedition was wholly due to my wife. Since Philippa had taken up her residence in Ireland she had discovered a taste for horses that was not to be extinguished, even by an occasional afternoon on the Quaker, whose paces had become harder than rock in his many journeys to Petty Sessions; she had also discovered the Shutes, newcomers on the outer edge of our vast visiting district, and between them this party to Drumcurran Horse Fair had been devised. Philippa proposed to buy herself a hunter. Bernard Shute wished to do the same, possibly two hunters, money being no difficulty with this fortunate young man. Miss Sally Knox was of the company, and I also had been kindly invited, as to a missionary meeting, to come, and bring my cheque book. The only saving clause in the affair was the fact that Mr. Flurry Knox was to meet us at the scene of action.

The fair was held in a couple of large fields outside the town, and on the farther bank of the Curranhilty River. Across a wide and glittering ford, horses of all sizes and sorts were splashing, and a long row of stepping - stones was hopped, and staggered, and scrambled over by a ceaseless variety of foot-passengers. A man with a cart plied as a ferry-boat, doing a heavy trade among the apple-women and vendors of 'crubeens,' *alias* pigs' feet, a grisly delicacy peculiar to Irish open-air holiday-making, and the July sun blazed on a scene that even Miss Cecilia Shute found to be almost repayment enough for the alarms of the drive.

'As a rule, I am so bored by driving that I find it reviving to be frightened,' she said to me, as we climbed to safety on a heathery ridge above the fields dedicated to galloping the horses; 'but when my brother scraped all those people off one side of that car, and ran the pole into the cart of lemonade bottles, I began to wish for courage to tell him I was going to get out and walk home.'

'Well, if you only knew it,' said Bernard, who was spreading rugs over the low furze bushes in the touching belief that the prickles would not come through, 'the time you came nearest to walking home was when the lash of the whip got twisted round Nancy's tail. Miss Knox, you 're an authority on these things —don't you think it would be a good scheme to have a light anchor in the trap, and when the horses began to play the fool, you 'd heave the anchor over the fence and bring them up all standing?'

'They wouldn't stand very long,' remarked Miss Sally.

'Oh, that 's all right,' returned the inventor; 'I 'd have a dodge to cast them loose, with the pole and the splinter-bar.'

'You 'd never see them again,' responded Miss Knox demurely, 'if you thought that mattered.'

'It would be the brightest feature of the case,' said Miss Shute.

She was surveying Miss Sally through her pince-nez as she spoke, and was, I have reason to believe, deciding that by the end of the day her brother would be well on in the first stages of his fifteenth love affair.

It has possibly been suspected that Mr. Bernard Shute was
a sailor, had been a sailor, rather, until within the last year,
when he had tumbled into a fortune and a property, and out
of the Navy, in the shortest time on record. His enthusiasm
for horses had been nourished by the hirelings of Malta, and
other resorts of Her Majesty's ships, and his knowledge of them
was, so far, bounded by the fact that it was more usual to come
off over their heads than their tails. For the rest, he was a
clean-shaved and personable youth, with a laugh which I may,
without offensive intention, define as possessing a what-cheeri-
ness special to his profession, and a habit, engendered no doubt
by long sojourns at the Antipodes, of getting his clothes in
large hideous consignments from a naval outfitter.

It was eleven o'clock, and the fair was in full swing. Its
vortex was in the centre of the field below us, where a low bank
of sods and earth had been erected as a trial jump, with a yelling
crowd of men and boys at either end, acting instead of the usual
wings to prevent a swerve. Strings of reluctant horses were
scourged over the bank by dozens of willing hands, while
exhortation, cheers, and criticism were freely showered upon
each performance.

'Give the knees to the saddle, boy, and leave the heels slack.'
'That's a nice horse. He'd keep a jock on his back where
another'd throw him!' 'Well jumped, begor! She fled that
fairly!' as an ungainly three-year-old flounced over the bank
without putting a hoof on it. Then her owner, unloosing his
pride in simile after the manner of his race:

'Ah ha! when she give a lep, man, she's that free, she's like
a hare for it!'

A giggling group of country girls elbowed their way past us
out of the crowd of spectators, one of the number inciting her
fellows to hurry on to the other field 'until they'd see the lads
galloping the horses,' to which another responding that she'd
'be skinned alive for the horses,' the party sped on their way.
We—i.e. my wife, Miss Knox, Bernard Shute, and myself—
followed in their wake, a matter by no means as easy as it looked.
Miss Shute had exhibited her wonted intelligence by remaining
on the hill-top with the *Spectator*; she had not reached the
happy point of possessing a mind ten years older than her age,
and a face ten years younger, without also developing the gift
of scenting boredom from afar. We squeezed past the noses

and heels of fidgety horses, and circumnavigated their attendant groups of critics, while half-trained brutes in snaffles bolted
to nowhere and back again, and whinnying foals ran to and fro
in search of their mothers.

A moderate bank divided the upper from the lower fields,
and as every feasible spot in it was commanded by a refusing
horse, the choice of a place and moment for crossing it required
judgment. I got Philippa across it in safety; Miss Knox,
though as capable as any young woman in Ireland of getting
over a bank, either on horseback or on her own legs, had to
submit to the assistance of Mr. Shute, and the laws of dynamics
decreed that a force sufficient to raise a bower anchor should
hoist her seven stone odd to the top of the bank with such speed
that she landed half on her knees and half in the arms of her
pioneer. A group of portentously quiet men stood near, their
eyes on the ground, their hands in their pockets; they were all
dressed so much alike that I did not at first notice that Flurry
Knox was among them; when I did, I perceived that his eyes,
instead of being on the ground, were surveying Mr. Shute
with that measure of disapproval that he habitually bestowed
upon strange men.

'You're later than I thought you'd be,' he said. 'I have a
horse half-bought for Mrs. Yeates. It's that old mare of
Bobby Bennett's; she makes a little noise, but she's a good
mare, and you couldn't throw her down if you tried. Bobby
wants thirty pounds for her, but I think you might get her for
less. She's in the hotel stables, and you can see her when you
go to lunch.'

We moved on towards the rushy bank of the river, and
Philippa and Sally Knox seated themselves on a low rock,
looking, in their white frocks, as incongruous in that dingy
preoccupied assemblage as the dreamy meadow-sweet and
purple spires of loosestrife that thronged the river banks.
Bernard Shute had been lost in the shifting maze of men and
horses, who were, for the most part, galloping with the blind
fury of charging bulls; but presently, among a party who seemed
to be riding the finish of a race, we descried our friend, and a
second or two later he hauled a brown mare to a standstill in
front of us.

'The fellow's asking forty pounds for her,' he said to Miss
Sally; 'she's a nailer to gallop. I don't think it's too much.'

'Her grandsire was the Mountain Hare,' said the owner of the mare, hurrying up to continue her family history, 'and he was the grandest horse in the four baronies. He was forty-two years of age when he died, and they waked him the same as ye 'd wake a Christian. They had whisky and porther—and bread—and a piper in it.'

'Thim Mountain Hare colts is no great things,' interrupted Mr. Shute's groom contemptuously. 'I seen a colt once that was one of his stock, and if there was forty men and their wives, and they after him with sticks, he wouldn't lep a sod of turf.'

'Lep, is it!' ejaculated the owner in a voice shrill with outrage. 'You may lead that mare out through the counthry, and there isn't a fence in it that she wouldn't go up to it as indepindent as if she was going to her bed, and your honour's ladyship knows that dam well, Miss Knox.'

'You want too much money for her, McCarthy,' returned Miss Sally, with her little air of preternatural wisdom.

'God pardon you, Miss Knox! Sure a lady like you knows well that forty-five pounds is no money for that mare. Forty-five pounds!' He laughed. 'It 'd be as good for me to make her a present to the gentleman all out as take three farthings less for her! She 's too grand entirely for a poor farmer like me, and if it wasn't for the long weak family I have, I wouldn't part with her under twice the money.'

'Three fine lumps of daughters in America paying his rent for him,' commented Flurry in the background. 'That 's the long weak family!'

Bernard dismounted and slapped the mare's ribs approvingly. 'I haven't had such a gallop since I was at Rio,' he said. 'What do you think of her, Miss Knox?' Then, without waiting for an answer, 'I like her. I think I may as well give him the forty-five and have done with it!'

At these ingenuous words I saw a spasm of anguish cross the countenance of McCarthy, easily interpreted as the first pang of a lifelong regret that he had not asked twice the money. Flurry Knox put up an eyebrow and winked at me; Mr. Shute's groom turned away for very shame. Sally Knox laughed with the deplorable levity of nineteen.

Thus, with a brevity absolutely scandalous in the eyes of all beholders, the bargain was concluded.

Flurry strolled up to Philippa, observing an elaborate remoteness from Miss Sally and Mr. Shute.

'I believe I'm selling a horse here myself to-day,' he said; 'would you like to have a look at him, Mrs. Yeates?'

'Oh, are you selling, Knox?' struck in Bernard, to whose brain the glory of buying a horse had obviously mounted like new wine; 'I want another, and I know yours are the right sort.'

'Well as you seem fond of galloping,' said Flurry sardonically, 'this one might suit you.'

'You don't mean the Moonlighter?' said Miss Knox, looking fixedly at him.

'Supposing I did, have you anything to say against him?' replied Flurry.

Decidedly he was in a very bad temper. Miss Sally shrugged her shoulders, and gave a little shred of a laugh, but said no more.

In a comparatively secluded corner of the field we came upon Moonlighter, sidling and fussing, with flickering ears, his tail tightly tucked in and his strong back humped in a manner that boded little good. Even to my untutored eye, he appeared to be an uncommonly good-looking animal, a well-bred grey, with shoulders that raked back as far as the eye could wish, the true Irish jumping hind quarters, and a showy head and neck; it was obvious that nothing except Michael Hallahane's adroit chucks at his bridle kept him from displaying his jumping powers free of charge. Bernard stared at him in silence; not the pregnant and intimidating silence of the connoisseur, but the tongue-tied muteness of helpless ignorance. His eye for horses had most probably been formed on circus posters, and the advertisements of a well-known embrocation, and Moonlighter approximated in colour and conduct to these models.

'I can see he's a ripping fine horse,' he said at length; 'I think I should like to try him.'

Miss Knox changed countenance perceptibly, and gave a perturbed glance at Flurry. Flurry remained impenetrably unamiable.

'I don't pretend to be a judge of horses,' went on Mr. Shute. 'I dare say I needn't tell _you_ that!' with a very engaging smile at Miss Sally; 'but I like this one awfully.'

As even Philippa said afterwards, she would not have given herself away like that over buying a reel of cotton.

'Are you quite sure that he's really the sort of horse you want?' said Miss Knox, with rather more colour in her face than usual; 'he's only four years old, and he's hardly a finished hunter.'

The object of her philanthropy looked rather puzzled. 'What! can't he jump?' he said.

'Is it jump?' exclaimed Michael Hallahane, unable any longer to contain himself; 'is it the horse that jumped five foot of a clothes line in Heffernan's yard, and not a one on his back but himself, and didn't leave so much as the thrack of his hoof on the quilt that was hanging on it!'

'That's about good enough,' said Mr. Shute, with his large friendly laugh; 'what's your price, Knox? I must have the horse that jumped the quilt! I'd like to try him, if you don't mind. There are some jolly-looking banks over there.'

'My price is a hundred sovereigns,' said Flurry; 'you can try him, if you like.'

'Oh, don't!' cried Sally impulsively; but Bernard's foot was already in the stirrup. 'I call it disgraceful!' I heard her say in a low voice to her kinsman—'you know he can't ride.'

The kinsman permitted himself a malign smile. 'That's his look-out,' he said.

Perhaps the unexpected docility with which Moonlighter allowed himself to be manœuvred through the crowd was due to Bernard's thirteen stone; at all events, his progress through a gate into the next field was unexceptionable. Bernard, however, had no idea of encouraging this tranquillity. He had come out to gallop, and without further ceremony he drove his heels into Moonlighter's sides, and took the consequences in the shape of a very fine and able buck. How he remained within even visiting distance of the saddle it is impossible to explain; perhaps his early experience in the rigging stood him in good stead in the matter of hanging on by his hands; but, however preserved, he did remain, and went away down the field at what he himself subsequently described as 'the rate of knots.'

Flurry flung away his cigarette and ran to a point of better observation. We all ran, including Michael Hallahane and various onlookers, and were in time to see Mr. Shute charging the least advantageous spot in a hollow-faced furzy bank. Nothing but the grey horse's extreme activity got the pair safely over; he jumped it on a slant, changed feet in the heart of a furze-bush, and was lost to view. In what relative positions Bernard and his steed alighted was to us a matter of conjecture; when we caught sight of them again, Moonlighter was running away, with his rider still on his back, while the slope of the ground lent wings to his flight.

'That young gentleman will be apt to be killed,' said Michael Hallahane with composure, not to say enjoyment.

'He 'll be into the long bog with him pretty soon,' said Flurry, his keen eye tracking the fugitive.

'Oh!—I thought he was off that time!' exclaimed Miss Sally, with a gasp in which consternation and amusement were blended. 'There! He *is* into the bog!'

It did not take us long to arrive at the scene of disaster, to which, as to a dog-fight, other foot-runners were already hurrying, and on our arrival we found things looking remarkably unpleasant for Mr. Shute and Moonlighter. The latter was sunk to his withers in the sheet of black slime into which he had stampeded; the former, submerged to the waist three yards further away in the bog, was trying to drag himself towards firm ground by the aid of tussocks of wiry grass.

'Hit him!' shouted Flurry. 'Hit him! he 'll sink if he stops there!'

Mr Shute turned on his adviser a face streaming with black mud, out of which his brown eyes and white teeth gleamed with undaunted cheerfulness.

'All jolly fine,' he called back; 'if I let go this grass I 'll sink too!'

A shout of laughter from the male portion of the spectators sympathetically greeted this announcement, and a dozen equally futile methods of escape were suggested. Among those who had joined us was, fortunately, one of the many boys who pervaded the fair selling halters, and by means of several of these knotted together, a line of communication was established. Moonlighter, who had fallen into the state of inane stupor in which horses in his plight so often indulge, was roused to activity by showers of stones and imprecations but faintly chastened by the presence of ladies. Bernard, hanging on to his tail, belaboured him with a cane, and, finally, the reins proving good, the task of towing the victims ashore was achieved.

'He's mine, Knox, you know,' were Mr. Shute's first words as he scrambled to his feet; 'he's the best horse I ever got across—worth twice the money!'

'Faith, he's aisy plased!' remarked a bystander.

'Oh, do go and borrow some dry clothes,' interposed Philippa practically; 'surely there must be someone——'

'There's a shop in the town where he can strip a peg for 13s. 9d.,' said Flurry grimly; 'I wouldn't care myself about the clothes you'd borrow here!'

The morning sun shone jovially upon Moonlighter and his rider, caking momently the black bog stuff with which both were coated, and as the group disintegrated, and we turned to go back every man present was pleasurably aware that the buttons of Mr. Shute's riding breeches had burst at the knee, causing a large triangular hiatus above his gaiter.

'Well,' said Flurry conclusively to me as we retraced our steps, 'I always thought the fellow was a fool, but I never thought he was such a damned fool.'

It seemed an interminable time since breakfast when our party, somewhat shattered by the stirring events of the morning, found itself gathered in an upstairs room at the Royal Hotel, waiting for a meal that had been ordained some two hours before. The air was charged with the mingled odours of boiling cabbage and frying mutton; we affected to speak of them with disgust, but our souls yearned to them. Female ministrants, with rustling skirts and pounding feet, raced along the passages with trays that were never for us, and opening doors released roaring gusts of conversation, blended with the clatter of knives and forks, and still we starved. Even the ginger-coloured check suit, lately labelled 'The Sandringham. Wonderful value, 16s. 9d.' in the window of Drumcurran's leading mart, and now displayed upon Mr Shute's all too lengthy limbs, had lost its power to charm.

'Oh, don't tear that bell quite out by the roots, Bernard,' said his sister, from the heart of a lamentable yawn. 'I dare say it only amuses them when we ring, but it may remind them that we are still alive. Major Yeates, do you or do you not regret the pigs' feet?'

'More than I can express,' I said, turning from the window, where I had been looking down at the endless succession of horses' backs and men's hats, moving in two opposing currents in the street below. 'I dare say if we talk about them for a little we shall feel ill, and that will be better than nothing.'

At this juncture, however, a heavy-laden tray thumped against the door, and our repast was borne into the room by a hot young woman in creaking boots, who hoarsely explained that what kept her was waiting on the potatoes, and that the ould pan that was in it was playing Puck with the beefsteaks.

'Well,' said Miss Shute, as she began to try conclusions between a blunt knife and a bullet-proof mutton chop, 'I have never lived in the country before, but I have always been given to understand that the village inn was one of its chief attractions.' She delicately moved the potato dish so as to cover the traces of a bygone egg, and her glance lingered on the flies that dragged their way across a melting mound of salt butter. 'I like local colour, but I don't care about it on the tablecloth.'

'Well, I'm feeling quite anxious about Irish country hotels now,' said Bernard, 'they're getting so civilized and respectable. After all, when you go back to England no one cares a pin to hear that you've been done up to the knocker. That don't amuse them a bit. But all my friends are as pleased as anything when I tell them of the pothouse where I slept in my clothes rather than face the sheets, or how, when I complained to the landlady next day, she said, "Cock ye up! Wasn't it his Reverence the Dean of Kilcoe had them last!"'

We smiled wanly; what I chiefly felt was respect for any hungry man who could jest in presence of such a meal.

'All this time my hunter hasn't been bought,' said Philippa presently, leaning back in her chair, and abandoning the unequal contest with her beefsteak. 'Who is Bobby Bennett? Will his horse carry a lady?'

Sally Knox looked at me and began to laugh.

'You should ask Major Yeates about Bobby Bennett,' she said.

Confound Miss Sally! It had never seemed worth while to tell Philippa all that story about my doing up Miss Bobby Bennett's hair, and I sank my face in my tumbler of stagnant whisky-and-soda to conceal the colour that suddenly adorned it. Any intelligent man will understand that it was a situation calculated to amuse the ungodly, but without any real fun in it. I explained Miss Bennett as briefly as possible, and at all the

more critical points Miss Sally's hazel-green eyes roamed slowly
and mercilessly towards me.

'You haven't told Mrs. Yeates that she's one of the greatest
horse-copers in the country,' she said, when I had got through
somehow; 'she can sell you a very good horse sometimes, and
a very bad one too, if she gets the chance.'

'No one will ever explain to me,' said Miss Shute, scanning
us all with her dark, half-amused, and wholly sophisticated
eyes, 'why horse-coping is more respectable than cheating at
cards. I rather respect people who are able to cheat at cards;
if every one did, it would make whist so much more cheerful;
but there is no forgiveness for dealing yourself the right card,
and there is no condemnation for dealing your neighbour a
very wrong horse!'

'Your neighbour is supposed to be able to take care of
himself,' said Bernard.

'Well, why doesn't that apply to card-players?' returned his
sister; 'are they all in a state of helpless innocence?'

'I'm helplessly innocent,' announced Philippa, 'so I hope
Miss Bennett won't deal me a wrong horse.'

'Oh, her mare is one of the right ones,' said Miss Sally;
'she's a lovely jumper, and her manners are the very best.'

The door opened, and Flurry Knox put in his head. 'Bobby
Bennett's downstairs,' he said to me mysteriously.

I got up, not without consciousness of Miss Sally's eye, and
prepared to follow him. 'You'd better come too, Mrs. Yeates,
to keep an eye on him. Don't let him give her more than
thirty, and if he gives that she should return him two sovereigns.'
This last injunction was bestowed in a whisper as we descended
the stairs.

Miss Bennett was in the crowded yard of the hotel, looking
handsome and overdressed, and she greeted me with just that
touch of Auld Lang Syne in her manner that I could best
have dispensed with. I turned to the business in hand without
delay. The brown mare was led forth from the stable and
paraded for our benefit; she was one of those inconspicuous,
meritorious animals about whom there seems nothing particular
to say, and I felt her legs and looked hard at her hocks, and was
not much the wiser.

'It's no use my saying she doesn't make a noise,' said Miss
Bobby, 'because every one in the country will tell you she does.

You can have a vet if you like, and that's the only fault he can find with her. But if Mrs. Yeates hasn't hunted before now, I'll guarantee Cruiskeen as just the thing for her. She's really safe and confidential. My little brother Georgie has hunted her—*you* remember Georgie, Major Yeates?—the night of the ball, you know—and he's only eleven. Mr. Knox can tell you what sort she is.'

'Oh, she's a grand mare,' said Mr. Knox, thus appealed to; 'you'd hear her coming three fields off like a German band!'

'And well for you if you could keep within three fields of her!' retorted Miss Bennett. 'At all events, she's not like the hunter you sold uncle, that used to kick the stars as soon as I put my foot in the stirrup!'

'"Twas the size of the foot frightened him,' said Flurry.

'Do you know how uncle cured him?' said Miss Bennett, turning her back on her adversary; 'he had him tied head and tail across the yard gate, and every man that came in had to get over his back!'

'That's no bad one!' said Flurry.

Philippa looked from one to the other in bewilderment, while the badinage continued, swift and unsmiling, as became two hierarchs of horse-dealing; it went on at intervals for the next ten minutes, and at the end of that time I had bought the mare for thirty pounds. As Miss Bennett said nothing about giving me back two of them, I had not the nerve to suggest it.

After this Flurry and Miss Bennett went away, and were swallowed up in the fair; we returned to our friends upstairs, and began to arrange about getting home. This, among other difficulties, involved the tracking and capture of the Shutes' groom, and took so long that it necessitated tea. Bernard and I had settled to ride our new purchases home, and the groom was to drive the wagonette—an alteration ardently furthered by Miss Shute. The afternoon was well advanced when Bernard and I struggled through the turmoil of the hotel yard in search of our horses, and, the hotel hostler being nowhere to be found, the Shutes' man saddled our animals for us, and then withdrew, to grapple single-handed with the bays in the calf-house.

'Good business for me, that Knox is sending the grey horse home for me,' remarked Bernard, as his new mare followed him tractably out of the stall. 'He'd have been rather a handful in this hole of a place.'

He shoved his way out of the yard in front of me, seemingly
quite comfortable and at home upon the descendant of the
Mountain Hare, and I followed as closely as drunken carmen
and shafts of erratic carts would permit. Cruiskeen evinced
a decided tendency to turn to the right on leaving the yard,
but she took my leftward tug in good part, and we moved on
through the streets of Drumcurran with a dignity that was only
impaired by the irrepressible, determination of Mr. Shutes'
new trousers to run up his leg. It was a trifle disappointing
that Cruiskeen should carry her nose in the air like a camel, but
I set it down to my own bad hands, and to that cause I also
imputed her frequent desire to stop, a desire that appeared to
coincide with every fourth or fifth public-house on the line of
march. Indeed, at the last corner before we left the town, Miss
Bennett's mare and I had a serious difference of opinion, in
the course of which she mounted the pavement and remained
planted in front of a very disreputable public-house, whose
owner had been before me several times for various infringe-
ments of the Licensing Acts. Bernard and the corner-boys
were, of course, much pleased; I inwardly resolved to let Miss
Bennett know how her groom occupied his time in Drumcurran.

We got out into the calm of the country roads without further
incident, and I there discovered that Cruiskeen was possessed
of a dromedary swiftness in trotting, that the action was about
as comfortable as the dromedary's, and that it was extremely
difficult to moderate the pace.

'I say! This is something like going!' said Bernard, canter-
ing hard beside me with slack rein and every appearance of
happiness. 'Do you mean to keep it up all the way?'

'You 'd better ask this devil,' I replied, hauling on the futile
ring snaffle. 'Miss Bennett must have an arm like a prize-
fighter. If this is what she calls confidential, I don't want her
confidences.'

After another half-mile, during which I cursed Flurry Knox,
and registered a vow that Philippa should ride Cruiskeen in a
cavalry bit, we reached the cross-roads at which Bernard's way
parted from mine. Another difference of opinion between
my wife's hunter and me here took place, this time on the subject of parting from our companion, and I experienced that
peculiar inward sinking that accompanies the birth of the
conviction one has been stuck. There were still some eight

miles between me and home, but I had at least the consolation
of knowing that the brown mare would easily cover it in forty
minutes. But in this also disappointment awaited me. Dropping her head to about the level of her knees, the mare subsided
into a walk as slow as that of the slowest cow, and very similar
in general style. In this manner I progressed for a further mile,
breathing forth, like St. Paul, threatenings and slaughters
against Bobby Bennett and all her confederates; and then the
idea occurred to me that many really first-class hunters were
very poor hacks. I consoled myself with this for a further
period, and presently an opportunity for testing it presented
itself. The road made a long loop round the flank of a hill,
and it was possible to save half a mile or so by getting into the
fields. It was a short cut I had often taken on the Quaker, and
it involved nothing more serious than a couple of low stone
'gaps' and an infantine bank. I turned Cruiskeen at the first
of these. She was evidently surprised. Being in an excessively bad temper, I beat her in a way that surprised her even
more, and she jumped the stones precipitately and with an ease
that showed she knew quite well what she was about. I vented
some further emotion upon her by the convenient medium of
my cane, and galloped her across the field and over the bank,
which, as they say in these parts, she 'fled' without putting an
iron on it. It was not the right way to jump it, but it was
inspiriting, and when she had disposed of the next gap without
hesitation my waning confidence in Miss Bennett began to
revive. I cantered over the ridge of the hill, and down it towards the cottage near which I was accustomed to get out on to
the road again. As I neared my wonted opening in the fence,
I saw that it had been filled by a stout pole, well fixed into the
bank at each end, but not more than three feet high. Cruiskeen
pricked her ears at it with intelligence; I trotted her at it, and
gave her a whack.

Ages afterwards there was someone speaking on the blurred
edge of a dream that I was dreaming about nothing in particular.
I went on dreaming, and was impressed by the shape of a fat
jug, mottled white and blue, that intruded itself painfully, and
I again heard voices, very urgent and full of effort, but quite
outside any concern of mine.

I also made an effort of some kind; I was doing my very best
to be good and polite, but I was dreaming in a place that

whirred, and was engrossing, and daylight was cold and let in some unknown unpleasantness. For that time the dream got the better of the daylight, and then, apropos of nothing, I was standing up in a house with someone's arm round me; the mottled jug was there, so was the unpleasantness, and I was talking with most careful, old-world politeness.

'Sit down now, you're all right,' said Miss Bobby Bennett, who was mopping my face with a handkerchief dipped in the jug.

I perceived that I was asking what had happened.

'She fell over the stick with you,' said Miss Bennett; 'the dirty brute!'

With another effort I hooked myself on to the march of events, as a truck is dragged out of a siding and hooked to a train.

'Oh, the Lord save us!' said a grey-haired woman who held the jug, 'ye're desthroyed entirely, asthore! Oh, glory be to the merciful will of God, me heart lepped across me shesht when I seen him undher the horse!'

'Go out and see if the trap's coming,' said Miss Bennett; 'he should have found the doctor by this.' She stared very closely at my face, and seemed to find it easier to talk in short sentences.

'We must get those cuts looking better before Mrs. Yeates comes.'

After an interval, during which unexpected places in my head ached from the cold water, the desire to be polite and coherent again came upon me.

'I am sure it was not your mare's fault,' I said.

Miss Bennett laughed a very little. I was glad to see her laugh; it had struck me her face was strangely haggard and frightened.

'Well, of course, it wasn't poor Cruiskeen's fault,' she said. 'She's nearly home with Mr. Shute by now. That's why I came after you!'

'Mr. Shute!' I said; 'wasn't he at the fair that day?'

'He was,' answered Miss Bobby, looking at me with very compassionate eyes; 'you and he got on each other's horses by mistake at the hotel, and you got the worst of the exchange!'

'Oh!' I said, without even trying to understand.

'He's here within, your honour's ladyship, Mrs. Yeates, ma'am,' shouted the grey-haired woman at the door; 'don't

be unaisy, achudth; he 's doing grand.   Sure, I 'm telling Miss
Binnitt if she was his wife itself, she couldn't give him betther
care!'
The grey-haired woman laughed.

VIII

THE HOLY ISLAND

FOR three days of November a white fog stood motionless over
the country.   All day and all night smothered booms and bangs
away to the south-west told that the Fastnet gun was hard at
work, and the sirens of the American liners uplifted their
monstrous female voices as they felt their way along the coast of
Cork.   On the third afternoon the wind began to whine about
the windows of Shreelane, and the barometer fell like a stone.
At 11 p.m. the storm rushed upon us with the roar and the
suddenness of a train; the chimneys bellowed, the tall old house
quivered, and the yelling wind drove against it, as a man puts
his shoulder against a door to burst it in.

We none of us got much sleep, and if Mrs. Cadogan is to be
believed—which experience assures me she is not—she spent
the night in devotional exercises, and in ministering to the panic-
stricken kitchen-maid by the light of a Blessed candle.   All
that day the storm screamed on, dry-eyed; at nightfall the rain
began, and next morning, which happened to be Sunday,
every servant in the house was a messenger of Job, laden with
tales of leakages, floods, and fallen trees, and inflated with the
ill-concealed glory of their kind in evil tidings.   To Peter
Cadogan, who had been to early Mass, was reserved the crowning satisfaction of reporting that a big vessel had gone on the
rocks at Yokahn Point the evening before, and was breaking
up fast; it was rumoured that the crew had got ashore, but this
feature, being favourable and uninteresting, was kept as much
as possible in the background.   Mrs. Cadogan, who had been
to America in an ocean liner, became at once the latest authority
on shipwrecks, and was of opinion that 'whoever would be
dhrownded, it wouldn't be thim lads o' sailors.   Sure wasn't

there the greatest storm ever was in it the time meself was on the say, and what'd thim fellows do but to put us below entirely in the ship, and close down the doors on us, the way theirselves 'd leg it when we'd be dhrownding!'

This view of the position was so startlingly novel that Philippa withdrew suddenly from the task of ordering dinner, and fell up the kitchen stairs in unsuitable laughter. Philippa has not the most rudimentary capacity for keeping her countenance.

That afternoon I was wrapped in the slumber, balmiest and most profound, that follows on a wet Sunday luncheon, when Murray, our D.I. of police, drove up in uniform, and came into the house on the top of a gust that set every door banging and every picture dancing on the walls. He looked as if his eyes had been blown out of his head, and he wanted something to eat very badly.

'I 've been down at the wreck since ten o'clock this morning,' he said, 'waiting for her to break up, and once she does there 'll be trouble. She 's an American ship, and she 's full up with rum, and bacon, and butter, and all sorts. Bosanquet is there with all his coastguards, and there are five hundred country people on the strand at this moment, waiting for the fun to begin. I 've got ten of my fellows there, and I wish I had as many more. You 'd better come back with me, Yeates, we may want the Riot Act before all 's done!'

The heavy rain had ceased, but it seemed as if it had fed the wind instead of calming it, and when Murray and I drove out of Shreelane, the whole dirty sky was moving, full sailed, in from the south-west, and the telegraph wires were hanging in a loop from the post outside the gate. Nothing except a Skebawn car-horse would have faced the whooping charges of the wind that came at us across Corran Lake; stimulated mysteriously by whistles from the driver, Murray's yellow hireling pounded woodenly along against the blast, till the smell of the torn seaweed was borne upon it, and we saw the Atlantic waves come towering into the bay of Tralagough.

The ship was, or had been, a three-masted barque; two of her masts were gone, and her bows stood high out of water on the reef that forms one of the shark-like jaws of the bay. The long strand was crowded with black groups of people, from the bank of heavy shingle that had been hurled over on to the

road, down to the slope where the waves pitched themselves
and climbed and fought and tore the gravel back with them,
as though they had dug their fingers in. The people were
nearly all men, dressed solemnly and hideously in their Sunday
clothes; most of them had come straight from Mass without
any dinner, true to that Irish instinct that places its fun before
its food. That the wreck was regarded as a spree of the largest
kind was sufficiently obvious. Our car pulled up at a public-
house that stood askew between the road and the shingle; it was
humming with those whom Irish publicans are pleased to call
'Bona feeds,' and sundry of the same class were clustered
round the door. Under the wall on the lee side was seated a
bagpiper, droning out *The Irish Washerwoman* with nodding
head and tapping heel, and a young man was cutting a few
steps of a jig for the delectation of a group of girls.

So far Murray's constabulary had done nothing but exhibit
their imposing chest measurement and spotless uniforms to the
Atlantic, and Bosanquet's coastguards had only salvaged some
spars, the debris of a boat, and a dead sheep, but their time was
coming. As we stumbled down over the shingle, battered by
the wind and pelted by clots of foam, someone beside me shouted
'She's gone!' A hill of water had smothered the wreck, and
when it fell from her again nothing was left but the bows, with
the bowsprit hanging from them in a tangle of rigging. The
clouds, bronzed by an unseen sunset, hung low over her; in
that greedy pack of waves, with the remorseless rocks above
and below her, she seemed the most lonely and tormented of
creatures.

About half an hour afterwards the cargo began to come
ashore on the top of the rising tide. Barrels were plunging
and diving in the trough of the waves, like a school of porpoises; they were pitched up the beach in waist-deep rushes
of foam; they rolled down again, and were swung up and
shouldered by the next wave, playing a kind of Tom Tiddler's
ground with the coastguards. Some of the barrels were big
and dangerous, some were small and nimble like young pigs,
and the bluejackets were up to their middles as their prey
dodged and ducked, and the police lined out along the beach
to keep back the people. Ten men of the R.I.C. can do a
great deal, but they canot be in more than twenty or thirty places
at the same instant; therefore they could hardly cope with a

scattered and extremely active mob of four or five hundred, many of whom had taken advantage of their privileges as 'bona-fide travellers,' and all of whom were determined on getting at the rum.

As the dusk fell the thing got more and more out of hand; the people had found out that the big puncheons held the rum, and had succeeded in capturing one. In the twinkling of an eye it was broached, and fifty backs were shoving round it like a football scrummage. I have heard many rows in my time: I have seen two Irish regiments—one of them Militia—at each other's throats in Fermoy barracks; I have heard Philippa's water-spaniel and two fox-terriers hunting a strange cat round the dairy; but never have I known such untrammelled bedlam as that which yelled round the rum-casks on Tralagough strand. For it was soon not a question of one broached cask, or even of two. The barrels were coming in fast, so fast that it was impossible for the representatives of law and order to keep on any sort of terms with them. The people, shouting with laughter, stove in the casks, and drank rum at thirty-four degrees above proof, out of their hands, out of their hats, out of their boots. Women came fluttering over the hillsides through the twilight, carrying jugs, milk-pails, anything that would hold the liquor; I saw one of them, roaring with laughter, tilt a filthy zinc bucket to an old man's lips.

With the darkness came anarchy. The rising tide brought more and yet more booty: great spars came lunging in on the lap of the waves, mixed up with cabin furniture, seamen's chests, and the black and slippery barrels, and the country people continued to flock in, and the drinking became more and more unbridled. Murray sent for more men and a doctor, and we slaved on hopelessly in the dark; collaring half-drunken men, shoving pig-headed casks up hills of shingle, hustling in among groups of roaring drinkers—we rescued perhaps one barrel in half a dozen. I began to know that there were men there who were not drunk and were not idle; I was also aware, as the strenuous hours of darkness passed, of an occasional rumble of cart wheels on the road. It was evident that the casks which were broached were the least part of the looting, but even they were beyond our control. The most that Bosanquet, Murray, and I could do was to concentrate our forces on the casks that had been secured, and to organize charges upon the swilling

crowds in order to upset the casks that they had broached.
Already men and boys were lying about, limp as leeches,
motionless as the dead.

'They'll kill themselves before morning, at this rate!' shouted
Murray to me. 'They're drinking it by the quart! Here's
another barrel; come on!'

We rallied our small forces, and after a brief but furious
struggle succeeded in capsizing it. It poured away in a flood
over the stones, over the prostrate figures that sprawled on
them, and a howl of reproach followed.

'If ye pour away any more o' that, Major,' said an unctuous
voice in my ear, 'ye'll intoxicate the stones and they'll be
getting up and knocking us down!'

I had been aware of a fat shoulder next to mine in the throng
as we heaved the puncheon over, and I now recognised the
ponderous wit and Falstaffian figure of Mr. James Canty, a
noted member of the Skebawn Board of Guardians, and the
owner of a large farm near at hand.

'I never saw worse work on this strand,' he went on. 'I
considher these debaucheries a disgrace to the counthry.'

Mr. Canty was famous as an orator, and I presume that it
was from long practice among his fellow P.L.G.s that he was
able, without apparent exertion, to out-shout the storm.

At this juncture the long-awaited reinforcements arrived, and
along with them came Dr. Jerome Hickey, armed with a black
bag. Having mentioned that the bag contained a pump—not
one of the common or garden variety—and that no pump on
board a foundering ship had more arduous labour to perform,
I prefer to pass to other themes. The wreck, which had at first
appeared to be as inexhaustible and as variously stocked as
that in the *Swiss Family Robinson*, was beginning to fail in its
supply. The crowd were by this time for the most part incapable from drink, and the fresh contingent of police tackled
their work with some prospect of success by the light of a tar
barrel, contributed by the owner of the public-house. At about
the same time I began to be aware that I was aching with fatigue,
that my clothes hung heavy and soaked upon me, that my face
was stiff with the salt spray and the bitter wind, and that it was
two hours past dinner time. The possibility of fried salt herrings
and hot whisky and water at the public-house rose dazzlingly
before my mind, when Mr. Canty again crossed my path.

'In my opinion ye have the whole cargo under conthrol now, Major,' he said, 'and the police and the sailors should be able to account for it all now by the help of the light. Wasn't I the finished fool that I didn't think to send up to my house for a tar barrel before now! Well—we're all foolish sometimes! But indeed it's time for us to give over, and that's what I'm saying to the Captain and Mr. Murray. You're exhausted now the three of ye, and if I might make so bold, I'd suggest that ye'd come up to my little place and have what'd warm ye before ye'd go home. It's only a few perches up the road.'

The tide had turned, the rain had begun again, and the tar barrel illumined the fact that Dr. Hickey's dreadful duties alone were pressing. We held a council and finally followed Mr. Canty, picking our way through wreckage of all kinds, including the human variety. Near the public-house I stumbled over something that was soft and had a squeak in it; it was the piper, with his head and shoulders in an overturned rum-barrel, and the bagpipes still under his arm.

I knew the outward appearance of Mr. Canty's house very well. It was a typical southern farmhouse, with dirty white-washed walls, a slated roof, and small, hermetically-sealed windows staring at the morass of manure which constituted the yard. We followed Mr. Canty up the filthy lane that led to it, picked our way round vague and squelching spurs of the manure heap, and were finally led through the kitchen into a stifling best parlour. Mrs. Canty, a vast and slatternly matron, had evidently made preparations for us; there was a newly-lighted fire pouring flame up the chimney from layers of bogwood, there were whisky and brandy on the table, and a plateful of biscuits sugared in white and pink. Upon our hostess was a black silk dress which indifferently concealed the fact that she was short of boot-laces, and that the boots themselves had made many excursions to the yard and none to the blacking-bottle. Her manners, however, were admirable, and while I live I shall not forget her potato cakes. They came in hot and hot from a pot-oven, they were speckled with caraway seeds, they swam in salt butter, and we ate them shamelessly and greasily, and washed them down with hot whisky and water; I knew to a nicety how ill I should be next day, and heeded not.

'Well, gentlemen,' remarked Mr. Canty later on, in his best

Board of Guardians' manner, 'I 've seen many wrecks between this and the Mizen Head, but I never witnessed a scene of more disgraceful ex-cess than what was in it to-night.'

'Hear, hear!' murmured Bosanquet with unseemly levity.

'I should say,' went on Mr. Canty, 'there was at one time to-night upwards of one hundhred men dead dhrunk on the strand, or anyway so dhrunk that if they 'd attempt to spake they 'd foam at the mouth.'

'The craytures!' interjected Mrs. Canty sympathetically.

'But if they 're dhrunk to-day,' continued our host, 'it 's nothing at all to what they 'll be to-morrow and afther to-morrow, and it won't be on the strand they 'll be dhrinkin' it.'

'Why, where will it be?' said Bosanquet, with his discon-certing English way of asking a point-blank question.

Mr. Canty passed his hand over his red cheeks.

'There 'll be plenty asking that before all 's said and done, Captain,' he said, with a compassionate smile, 'and there 'll be plenty that could give the answer if they 'll like, but by dam I don't think ye 'll be apt to get much out of the Yokahn boys!'

'The Lord save us, 'twould be better to keep out from the likes o' thim!' put in Mrs. Canty, sliding a fresh avalanche of potato cakes on to the dish; 'didn't they pull the clothes off the gauger and pour potheen down his throath till he ran screeching through the streets o' Skebawn!'

James Canty chuckled.

'I remember there was a wreck here one time, and the undher-writers put me in charge of the cargo. Brandy it was—cases of the best Frinch brandy. The people had a song about it, what 's this the first verse was—

> One night to the rocks of Yokahn
> Came the barque *Isabella* so dandy,
> To pieces she went before dawn,
> Herself and her cargo of brandy,
> And all met a wathery grave
> Excepting the vessel's carpenther,
> Poor fellow, so far from his home.'

Mr. Canty chanted these touching lines in a tuneful if wheezy tenor. 'Well, gentlemen, we 're all friends here,' he continued, 'and it 's no harm to mention that this man below at the public-house came askin' me would I let him have some of it for a consideration. "Sullivan," says I to him, "if ye ran down gold in a cup in place of the brandy, I wouldn't give it to you. Of coorse," says I, "I'm not sayin' that if a bottle was to get a crack of a stick, and it to be broken, and a man to drink a glass out of it, that would be no more than an accident." "That's no good to me," says he, "but if I had twelve gallons of that brandy in Cork," says he, "by the Holy German!" says he, saying an awful curse, "I'd sell twenty-five out of it!" Well, indeed, it was true for him; it was grand stuff. As the saying is, it would make a horse out of a cow!'

'It appears to be a handy sort of place for keeping a pub,' said Bosanquet.

'Shut to the door, Margaret,' said Mr. Canty with elaborate caution. 'It'd be a queer place that wouldn't be handy for Sullivan!'

A further tale of great length wax in progress when Dr. Hickey's Mephistophelian nose was poked into the best parlour.

'Hullo, Hickey! Pumped out? eh?' said Murray.

'If I am, there's plenty more like me,' replied the doctor enigmatically, 'and some of them three times over! James, did these gentlemen leave you a drop of anything that you'd offer me?'

'Maybe ye'd like a glass of rum, Doctor?' said Mr. Canty with a wink at his other guests.

Dr. Hickey shuddered.

I had next morning precisely the kind of mouth that I had anticipated, and it being my duty to spend the better part of the day administering justice in Skebawn, I received from Mr. Flurry Knox and other of my brother magistrates precisely the class of condolences on my 'Monday head' that I found least amusing. It was unavailing to point out the resemblance between hot potato cakes and molten lead, or to dilate on their equal power of solidifying; the collective wisdom of the Bench decided that I was suffering from contraband rum, and rejoiced over me accordingly.

During the next three weeks Murray and Bosanquet put in a time only to be equalled by that of the heroes in detective romances. They began by acting on the hint offered by Mr. Canty, and were rewarded by finding eight barrels of bacon and three casks of rum in the heart of Mr. Sullivan's turf rick, placed there, so Mr. Sullivan explained with much detail, by enemies, with the object of getting his licence taken away.

They stabbed potato gardens with crowbars to find the buried
barrels, they explored the chimneys, they raided the cow-
houses; and in every possible and impossible place they found
some of the cargo of the late barque *John D. Williams*, and, as
the sympathetic Mr. Canty said, 'For as much as they found,
they left five times as much afther them!'

It was a wet, lingering autumn, but towards the end of
November the rain dried up, the weather stiffened, and a week
of light frosts and blue skies was offered as a tardy apology.
Philippa possesses, in common with many of her sex, an in-
appeasable passion for picnics, and her ingenuity for devising
occasions for them is only equalled by her gift for enduring
their rigours. I have seen her tackle a moist chicken pie with
a splinter of slate and my stylograph pen. I have known her
to take the tea-basket to an auction, and make tea in a four-
wheeled inside car, regardless of the fact that it was coming under
the hammer in ten minutes, and that the kettle took twenty
minutes to boil. It will therefore be readily understood that
the rare occasions when I was free to go out with a gun were
not allowed to pass uncelebrated by the tea-basket.

'You 'd much better shoot Corran Lake to-morrow,' my wife
said to me one brilliant afternoon. 'We could send the punt
over, and I would meet you on Holy Island with——'

The rest of the sentence was concerned with ways, means, and
the tea-basket, and need not be recorded.

I had taken the shooting of a long snipe bog that trailed from
Corran Lake almost to the sea at Tralagough, and it was my
custom to begin to shoot from the seaward end of it, and finally
to work round the lake after duck.

To-morrow proved a heavenly morning, touched with frost,
gilt with sun. I started early, and the mists were still smoking
up from the calm, all-reflecting lake, as the Quaker stepped out
along the level road, smashing the thin ice on the puddles with
his big feet. Behind the calves of my legs sat Maria, Philippa's
brown Irish water-spaniel, assiduously licking the barrels of
my gun, as was her custom when the ecstasy of going out
shooting was hers. Maria had been given to Philippa as a
wedding-present, and since then it had been my wife's ambition
that she should conform to the Beth Gelert standard of being
'a lamb at home, a lion in the chase.' Maria did pretty well as
a lion: she hunted all dogs unmistakably smaller than herself,

and whenever it was reasonably possible to do so she devoured
the spoils of the chase, notably jack snipe. It was as a lamb
that she failed; objectionable as I have no doubt a lamb would
be as a domestic pet, it at least would not snatch the cold beef
from the luncheon-table, nor yet, if banished for its crimes,
would it spend the night in scratching the paint off the hall
door. Maria bit beggars (who valued their disgusting limbs
at five shillings the square inch), she bullied the servants, she
concealed ducks' claws and fishes' backbones behind the sofa
cushions, and yet, when she laid her brown snout upon my knee,
and rolled her blackguard amber eyes upon me, and smote me
with her feathered paw, it was impossible to remember her
iniquities against her. On shooting mornings Maria ceased
to be a buccaneer, a glutton, and a hypocrite. From the
moment when I put my gun together her breakfast stood untouched until it suffered the final degradation of being eaten by
the cats, and now in the trap she was shivering with excitement,
and agonizing in her soul lest she should even yet be left behind.

Slipper met me at the cross-roads from which I had sent
back the trap; Slipper, redder in the nose than anything I had
ever seen off the stage, very husky as to the voice, and going
rather tender on both feet. He informed me that I should have
a grand day's shooting, the head-poacher of the locality having,
in a most gentlemanlike manner, refrained from exercising his
sporting rights the day before, on hearing that I was coming.
I understood that this was to be considered as a mark of high
personal esteem, and I set to work at the bog with suitable
gratitude.

In spite of Mr. O'Driscoll's magnanimity, I had not a very
good morning. The snipe were there, but in the perfect
stillness of the weather it was impossible to get near them, and
five times out of six they were up, flickering and dodging, before
I was within shot. Maria became possessed of seven devils
and broke away from heel the first time I let off my gun, ranging
far and wide in search of the bird I had missed, and putting up
every live thing for half a mile round, as she went splashing
and steeple-chasing through the bog. Slipper expressed his
opinion of her behaviour in language more appallingly picturesque and resourceful than any I have heard, even in the Skebawn court house; I admit that at the time I thought he spoke
very suitably. Before she was recaptured every remaining

snipe within earshot was lifted out of it by Slipper's steam-engine whistles and my own infuriated bellows; it was fortunate that the bog was spacious and that there was still a long tract of it ahead, where beyond these voices there was peace.

I worked my way on, jumping treacle-dark drains, floundering through the rustling yellow rushes, circumnavigating the bog-holes, and taking every possible and impossible chance of a shot; by the time I had reached Corran Lake I had got two and a half brace, retrieved by Maria with a perfection that showed what her powers were when the sinuous adroitness of Slipper's woodbine stick was fresh in her mind. But with Maria it was always the unexpected that happened. My last snipe, a jack, fell in the lake, and Maria, bursting through the reeds with kangaroo bounds, and cleaving the water like a torpedo-boat, was a model of all the virtues of her kind. She picked up the bird with a snake-like dart of her head, clambered with it on to a tussock, and there, well out of reach of the arm of the law, before our indignant eyes crunched it twice and bolted it.

'Well,' said Slipper complacently, some ten minutes after-wards, 'divil such a bating ever I gave a dog since the day Prince killed owld Mrs. Knox's paycock! Prince was a lump of a brown tarrier I had one time, and faith I kicked the toes out o' me owld boots on him before I had the owld lady composed!'

However composing Slipper's methods may have been to Mrs. Knox, they had quite the contrary effect upon a family party of duck that had been lying in the reeds. With horrified outcries they broke into flight, and now were far away on the ethereal mirror of the lake, among strings of their fellows that were floating and quacking in preoccupied indifference to my presence.

A promenade along the lake-shore demonstrated the fact that without a boat there was no more shooting for me; I looked across to the island where, some time ago, I had seen Philippa and her punt arrive. The boat was tied to an overhanging tree, but my wife was nowhere to be seen. I was opening my mouth to give a hail, when I saw her emerge precipitately from among the trees and jump into the boat; Philippa had not in vain spent many summers on the Thames, she was under way in a twinkling, sculled a score of strokes at the rate of a finish, then stopped at the peaceful island. I called to her, and in a minute or two the punt had crackled through the reeds, and shoved its blunt nose ashore at the spot where I was standing.

'Sinclair,' said Philippa in awestruck tones, 'there's something on the island!'

'I hope there's something to eat there,' said I.

'I tell you there *is* something there, alive,' said my wife with her eyes as large as saucers; 'it's making an awful sound like snoring.'

'That's the fairies, ma'am,' said Slipper with complete certainty; 'sure I known them that seen fairies in that island as thick as the grass, and every one o' them with little caps on them.'

Philippa's wide gaze wandered to Slipper's hideous pug face and back to me.

'It was not a human being, Sinclair!' she said combatively, though I had not uttered a word.

Maria had already, after the manner of dogs, leaped, dripping, into the boat: I prepared to follow her example.

'Major,' said Slipper, in a tragic whisper, 'there was a man was a night on that island one time, watching duck, and Thim People cot him, and dhragged him through Hell and through Death, and threw him in the tide——'

'Shove off the boat,' I said, too hungry for argument.

Slipper obeyed, throwing his knee over the gunwale as he did so, and tumbling into the bow; we could have done without him very comfortably, but his devotion was touching.

Holy Island was perhaps a hundred yards long, and about half as many broad; it was covered with trees and a dense growth of rhododendrons; somewhere in the jungle was a ruined fragment of a chapel, smothered in ivy and briars, and in a little glade in the heart of the island there was a holy well. We landed, and it was obviously a sore humiliation to Philippa that not a sound was to be heard in the spell-bound silence of the island, save the cough of a heron on a tree-top.

'It *was* there,' she said, with an unconvinced glance at the surrounding thickets.

'Sure, I'll give a thrawl through the island, ma'am,' volunteered Slipper with unexpected gallantry, 'an' if it's the divil himself is in it, I'll rattle him into the lake!'

He went swaggering on his search, shouting 'Hi, cock!' and whacking the rhododendrons with his stick, and after an interval returned and assured us that the island was uninhabited. Being provided with refreshments he again withdrew, and

Philippa and Maria and I fed variously and at great length, and washed the plates with water from the holy well. I was smoking a cigarette when we heard Slipper addressing the solitudes at the farther end of the island, and ending with one of his whisky-throated crows of laughter.

He presently came lurching towards us through the bushes, and a glance sufficed to show even Philippa—who was as incompetent a judge of such matters as many of her sex—that he was undeniably screwed.

'Major Yeates!' he began, 'and Mrs. Major Yeates, with respex to ye, I 'm bastely dhrunk! Me head is light since the 'fluenzy, and the docther told me I should carry a little bottle-een o' sperrits——'

'Look here,' I said to Philippa, 'I 'll take him across, and bring the boat back for you.'

'Sinclair,' responded my wife with concentrated emotion, 'I would rather die than stay on this island alone!'

Slipper was getting drunker every moment, but I managed to stow him on his back in the bows of the punt, in which position he at once began to uplift husky and wandering strains of melody. To this accompaniment we, as Tennyson says,

> moved from the brink, like some full-breasted swan,
> That, fluting a wild carol ere her death,
> Ruffles her pure cold plume, and takes the flood
> With swarthy web.

Slipper would certainly have been none the worse for taking the flood, and, as the burden of *Lannigan's Ball* strengthened and spread along the tranquil lake, and the duck once more fled in justifiable consternation, I felt much inclined to make him do so.

We made for the end of the lake that was nearest Shreelane, and, as we rounded the point of the island, another boat presented itself to our view. It contained my late entertainer, Mrs. Canty, seated bulkily in the stern, while a small boy bowed himself between the two heavy oars.

'It 's a lovely evening, Major Yeates,' she called out. 'I 'm just going to the island to get some water from the holy well for me daughter that has an impression on her chest. Indeed, I thought 'twas yourself was singing a song for Mrs. Yeates when I heard you coming, but sure Slipper is a great warrant himself for singing.'

'May the divil crack the two legs undher ye!' bawled Slipper in acknowledgment of the compliment.

Mrs. Canty laughed genially, and her boat lumbered away.

I shoved Slipper ashore at the nearest point; Philippa and I paddled to the end of the lake, and abandoning the duck as a bad business, walked home.

A few days afterwards it happened that it was incumbent upon me to attend the funeral of the Roman Catholic bishop of the diocese. It was what is called in France *un bel enterrement*, with inky flocks of tall-hatted priests, and countless yards of white scarves, and a repast of monumental solidity at the bishop's residence. The actual interment was to take place in Cork, and we moved in long and imposing procession to the railway station, where a special train awaited the cortège. My friend Mr. James Canty was among the mourners: an important and active personage, exchanging condolences with the priests, giving directions to porters, and blowing his nose with a trumpeting mournfulness that penetrated all the other noises of the platform. He was condescending enough to notice my presence, and found time to tell me that he had given Mr. Murray 'a sure word' with regard to some of '*the wreckage*'—this with deep significance, and a wink of an inflamed and tearful eye. I saw him depart in a first-class carriage and the odour of sanctity; seeing that he was accompanied by seven priests, and that both windows were shut, the latter must have been considerable.

Afterwards, in the town, I met Murray, looking more pleased with himself than I had seen him since he had taken up the unprofitable task of smuggler-hunting.

'Come along and have some lunch,' he said, 'I've got a real good thing on this time! That chap Canty came to me late last night, and told me that he knew for a fact that the island on Corran Lake was just stiff with barrels of bacon and rum, and that I'd better send every man I could spare to-day to get them into the town. I sent the men out at eight o'clock this morning; I think I've gone one better than Bosanquet this time!'

I began to realize that Philippa was going to score heavily on the subject of the fairies that she had heard snoring on the island, and I imparted to Murray the leading features of our picnic there.

'Oh, Slipper's been up to his chin in that rum from the first,' said Murray. 'I'd like to know who his sleeping partner was!'

It was beginning to get dark before the loaded carts of the salvage party came lumbering past Murray's windows and into the yard of the police-barrack. We followed them, and in so doing picked up Flurry Knox, who was sauntering in the same direction. It was a good haul, five big casks of rum, and at least a dozen smaller barrels of bacon and butter, and Murray and his Chief Constable smiled seraphically on one another as the spoil was unloaded and stowed in a shed.

'Wouldn't it be as well to see how the butter is keeping?' remarked Flurry, who had been looking on silently, with, as I had noticed, a still and amused eye. 'The rim of that small keg there looks as if it had been shifted lately.'

The sergeant looked hard at Flurry; he knew as well as most people that a hint from Mr. Knox was usually worth taking. He turned to Murray.

'Will I open it, sir?'

'Oh! open it if Mr. Knox wishes,' said Murray, who was not famous for appreciating other people's suggestions.

The keg was opened.

'Funny butter,' said Flurry.

The sergeant said nothing. The keg was full of black bog-mould. Another was opened, and another, all with the same result.

'Damnation!' said Murray, suddenly losing his temper. 'What's the use of going on with those? Try one of the rum casks.'

A few moments passed in total silence while a tap and a spigot were sent for and applied to the barrel. The sergeant drew off a mugful and put his nose to it with the deliberation of a connoisseur.

'Water, sir,' he pronounced, 'dirty water, with a small indication of sperrits.'

A junior constable tittered explosively, met the light blue glare of Murray's eye, and withered away.

'Perhaps it's holy water!' said I, with a wavering voice.

Murray's glance pinned me like an assegai, and I also faded into the background.

'Well,' said Flurry in dulcet tones, 'if you want to know where the stuff is that was in those barrels, I can tell you, for I was told it myself half an hour ago. It's gone to Cork with the bishop by special train!'

Mr. Canty was undoubtedly a man of resource. Mrs. Canty had mistakenly credited me with an intelligence equal to her own, and on receiving from Slipper a highly coloured account of how audibly Mr. Canty had slept off his potations, had regarded the secret of Holy Island as having been given away. That night and the two succeeding ones were spent in the transfer of the rum to bottles, and the bottles and the butter to fish boxes; these were, by means of a slight lubrication of the railway underlings, loaded into a truck as 'Fresh Fish, Urgent,' and attached to the bishop's funeral train, while the police, decoyed far from the scene of action, were breaking their backs over barrels of bog-water. 'I suppose,' continued Flurry pleasantly, 'you don't know the pub that Canty's brother has in Cork. Well, I do. I'm going to buy some rum there next week, cheap.'

'I shall proceed against Canty!' said Murray, with fateful calm.

'You won't proceed far,' said Flurry, 'you 'll not get as much evidence out of the whole country as 'd hang a cat.'

'Who was your informant?' demanded Murray.

Flurry laughed. 'Well, by the time the train was in Cork, yourself and the Major were the only two men in the town that weren't talking about it.'

IX

THE POLICY OF THE CLOSED DOOR

THE disasters and humiliations that befell me at Drumcurran Fair may yet be remembered. They certainly have not been forgotten in the regions about Skebawn, where the tale of how Bernard Shute and I stole each other's horses has passed into history. The grand-daughter of the Mountain Hare, bought by Mr. Shute with such light-hearted enthusiasm, was restored to that position between the shafts of a cart that she was so well fitted to grace; Moonlighter, his other purchase, spent the two months following on the fair in 'favouring' a leg with a strained sinew, and in receiving visits from the local vet, who, however uncertain in his diagnosis of Moonlighter's leg, had accurately estimated the length of Bernard's foot.

Miss Bennett's mare Cruiskeen, alone of the trio, was immediately and thoroughly successful. She went in harness like a hero, she carried Philippa like an elder sister, she was never sick or sorry; as Peter Cadogan summed her up, 'That one 'd live where another 'd die.' In her safe keeping Philippa made her debut with hounds at an uneventful morning's cubbing, with no particular result, except that Philippa returned home so stiff that she had to go to bed for a day, and arose more determined than ever to be a fox-hunter.

The opening meet of Mr. Knox's foxhounds was on 1st November, and on that morning Philippa on Cruiskeen, accompanied by me on the Quaker, set out for Ardmeen Cross, the time-honoured fixture for All Saints' Day. The weather was grey and quiet, and full of all the moist sweetness of an Irish autumn. There had been a great deal of rain during the past month; it had turned the bracken to a purple brown, and had filled the hollows wth shining splashes of water. The dead leaves were slippery under foot, and the branches above were thinly decked with yellow, where the pallid survivors of summer still clung to their posts. As Philippa and I sedately approached the meet the red coats of Flurry Knox and his whip, Dr. Jerome Hickey, were to be seen on the road at the top of the hill; Cruiskeen put her head in the air, and stared at them with eyes that understood all they portended.

'Sinclair,' said my wife hurriedly, as a straggling hound, flogged in by Dr. Hickey, uttered a grievous and melodious howl, 'remember, if they find, it 's no use to talk to me, for I shan't be able to speak.'

I was sufficiently acquainted with Philippa in moments of enthusiasm to exhibit silently the corner of a clean pockethandkerchief; I have seen her cry when a police constable won a bicycle race in Skebawn; she has wept at hearing Sir Valentine Knox's health drunk with musical honours at a tenants' dinner. It is an amiable custom, but, as she herself admits, it is unbecoming.

An imposing throng, in point of numbers, was gathered at the cross-roads, the riders being almost swamped in the crowd of traps, outside cars, bicyclists, and people on foot. The field was an eminently representative one. The Clan Knox was, as usual, there in force, its more aristocratic members dingily respectable in black coats and tall hats that went impartially to weddings, funerals, and hunts, and, like a horse that is past mark of mouth, were no longer to be identified with any special epoch; there was a humbler squireen element in tweeds and flat-brimmed pot-hats, and a good muster of farmers, men of the spare, black-muzzled, West of Ireland type, on horses that ranged from the cart mare, clipped trace high, to shaggy and leggy three-year-olds, none of them hunters, but all of them able to hunt. Philippa and I worked our way to the heart of things, where was Flurry, seated on his brown mare, in what appeared to be a somewhat moody silence. As we exchanged greetings I was aware that his eye was resting with extreme disfavour upon two approaching figures. I put up my eye-glass, and perceived that one of them was Miss Sally Knox, on a tall grey horse; the other was Mr. Bernard Shute, in all the flawless beauty of his first pink coat, mounted on Stockbroker, a well-known, hard-mouthed, big-jumping bay, recently purchased from Dr. Hickey.

During the languors of a damp autumn the neighbourhood had been much nourished and sustained by the privilege of observing and diagnosing the progress of Mr. Shute's flirtation with Miss Sally Knox. What made it all the more enjoyable for the lookers-on — or most of them — was, that although Bernard's courtship was of the nature of a proclamation from the housetops, Miss Knox's attitude left everything to the imagination. To Flurry Knox the romantic but despicable position of slighted rival was comfortably allotted; his sole sympathizers were Philippa and old Mrs. Knox of Aussolas, but no one knew if he needed sympathizers. Flurry was a man of mystery.

Mr. Shute and Miss Knox approached us rapidly, the latter's mount pulling hard.

'Flurry,' I said, 'isn't that grey the horse Shute bought from you last July at the fair?'

Flurry did not answer me. His face was as black as thunder. He turned his horse round, cursing two country boys who got in his way, with low and concentrated venom, and began to move forward, followed by the hounds. If his wish was to avoid speaking to Miss Sally it was not to be gratified.

'Good morning, Flurry,' she began, sitting close down to

Moonlighter's ramping jog as she rode up beside her cousin. '.What a hurry you 're in! We passed no end of people on the road who won't be here for another ten minutes.'

'No more will I,' was Mr. Knox's cryptic reply, as he spurred the brown mare into a trot.

Moonlighter made a vigorous but frustrated effort to buck, and indemnified himself by a successful kick at a hound.

'Bother you, Flurry! Can't you walk for a minute?' exclaimed Miss Sally, who looked about as large, in relation to her horse, as the conventional tomtit on a round of beef. 'You might have more sense than to crack your whip under this horse's nose! I don't believe you know what horse it is even!'

I was not near enough to catch Flurry's reply.

'Well, if you didn't want him to be lent to me you shouldn't have sold him to Mr. Shute!' retorted Miss Knox, in her clear, provoking little voice. •

·'I suppose he 's afraid to ride him himself,' said Flurry, turning his horse in at a gate. 'Get ahead there, Jerome, can't you? It 's better to put them in at this end than to have every one riding on top of them!'

Miss Sally's cheeks were still very pink when I came up and began to talk to her, and her grey-green eyes had a look in them like those of an angry kitten. ·

The riders moved slowly down a rough pasture-field, and took up their position along the brow of Ardmeen covert, into which the hounds had already hurled themselves with their customary contempt for the *convenances*. Flurry's hounds, true to their nationality, were in the habit of doing the right thing in the wrong way.

Untouched by autumn, the furze bushes of Ardmeen covert were darkly green, save for a golden fleck of blossom here and there, and the glistening grey cobwebs that stretched from spike to spike. The look of the ordinary gorse covert is familiar to most people as a tidy enclosure of an acre or so, filled with low plants of well-educated gorse; not so many will be found who have experience of it as a rocky, sedgy wilderness, half a mile square, garrisoned with brigades of furze bushes, some of them higher than a horse's head, lean, strong, and cunning, like the foxes that breed in them, impenetrable, with their bristling spikes, as a hedge of bayonets. By dint of infinite leisure and obstinate greed, the cattle had made paths for themselves through the bushes to the patches of grass that they hemmed in; their hoofprints were guides to the explorer, down muddy staircases of rock, and across black intervals of unplumbed bog. The whole covert slanted gradually down to a small river that raced round three sides of it, and beyond the stream, in agreeable contrast, lay a clean and wholesome country of grass fields and banks.

The hounds drew slowly along and down the hill towards the river, and the riders hung about outside the covert, and tried—I can answer for at least one of them—to decide which was the least odious of the ways through it, in the event of the fox breaking at the far side. Miss Sally took up a position not very far from me, and it was easy to see that she had her hands full with her borrowed mount, on whose temper the delay and suspense were visibly telling. His iron-grey neck was white from the chafing of the reins; had the ground under his feet been red-hot he could hardly have sidled and hopped more uncontrollably; nothing but the most impassioned conjugation of the verb to condemn could have supplied any human equivalent for the manner in which he tore holes in the sedgy grass with a furious forefoot. Those who were even superficial judges of character gave his heels a liberal allowance of sea-room, and Mr. Shute, who could not be numbered among such, and had, as usual, taken up a position as near Miss Sally as possible, was rewarded by a double knock on his horse's ribs that was a cause of heartless mirth to the lady of his affections.

Not a hound had as yet spoken, but they were forcing their way through the gorse forest and shoving each other jealously aside with growing excitement, and Flurry could be seen at intervals, moving forward in the direction they were indicating. It was at this juncture that the ubiquitous Slipper presented himself at my horse's shoulder.

"'Tis for the river he's making, Major,' he said, with an upward roll of his squinting eyes, that nearly made me sea-sick. 'He's a Castle Knox fox that came in this morning, and ye should get ahead down to the ford!'

A tip from Slipper was not to be neglected, and Philippa and I began a cautious progress through the gorse, followed by Miss Knox as quietly as Moonlighter's nerves would permit.

'Wishful has it!' she exclaimed, as a hound came out into view, uttered a sharp yelp, and drove forward.

'Hark! hark!' roared Flurry with at least three r's reverberating in each 'hark'; at the same instant came a holloa from the farther side of the river, and Dr. Hickey's renowned and bloodcurdling screech was uplifted at the bottom of the covert. Then babel broke forth, as the hounds, converging from every quarter, flung themselves shrieking on the line. Moonlighter went straight up on his hind legs, and dropped again with a bound that sent him crushing past Philippa and Cruiskeen; he did it a second time, and was almost on to the tail of the Quaker, whose bulky person was not to be hurried in any emergency.

'Get on if you can, Major Yeates!' called out Sally, steadying the grey as well as she could in the narrow pathway between the great gorse bushes.

Other horses were thundering behind us, men were shouting to each other in similar passages right and left of us, the cry of the hounds filled the air with a kind of delirium. A low wall with a stick laid along it barred the passage in front of me, and the Quaker firmly and immediately decided not to have it until someone else had dislodged the pole.

'Go ahead!' I shouted, squeezing to one side with heroic disregard of the furze bushes and my new tops.

The words were hardly out of my mouth when Moonlighter, mad with thwarted excitement, shot by me, hurtled over the obstacle with extravagant fury, landed twelve feet beyond it on clattering slippery rock, saved himself from falling with an eel-like forward buck on to sedgy ground, and bolted at full speed down the muddy cattle track. There are corners—rocky, most of them—in that cattle track, that Sally has told me she will remember to her dying day; boggy holes of any depth, ranging between two feet and half-way to Australia, that she says she does not fail to mention in the General Thanksgiving; but at the time they occupied mere fractions of the strenuous seconds in which it was hopeless for her to do anything but try to steer, trust to luck, sit hard down into the saddle and try to stay there. (For my part, I would as soon try to adhere to the horns of a charging bull as to the crutches of a side-saddle, but happily the necessity is not likely to arise.) I saw Flurry Knox a little ahead of her on the same track, jamming his mare into the furze bushes to get out of her way; he shouted something after her about the ford, and started to gallop for it himself by a breakneck short cut.

The hounds were already across the river, and it was obvious that, ford or no ford, Moonlighter's intentions might be simply expressed in the formula 'Be with them I will.' It was all downhill to the river, and among the furze bushes and rocks there was neither time nor place to turn him. He rushed at it with a shattering slip upon a streak of rock, with a heavy plunge in the deep ground by the brink; it was as bad a take-off for twenty feet of water as could well be found. The grey horse rose out of the boggy stuff with all the impetus that pace and temper could give, but it was not enough. For one instant the twisting, sliding current was under Sally, the next a veil of water sprang up all round her, and Moonlighter was rolling and lurching in the desperate effort to find foothold in the rocky bed of the stream.

I was following at the best pace I could kick out of the Quaker, and saw the water swirl into her lap as her horse rolled to the near-side. She caught the mane to save herself, but he struggled on to his legs again, and came floundering broadside on to the further bank. In three seconds she had got out of the saddle and flung herself at the bank, grasping the rushes, and trying, in spite of the sodden weight of her habit, to drag herself out of the water.

At the same instant I saw Flurry and the brown mare dashing through the ford, twenty yards higher up. He was off his horse and beside her with that uncanny quickness that Flurry reserved for moments of emergency, and, catching her by the arms, swung her on to the bank as easily as if she had been the kennel terrier.

'Catch the horse!' she called out, scrambling to her feet.

'Damn the horse!' returned Flurry, in the rage that is so often the reaction from a bad scare.

I turned along the bank and made for the ford; by this time it was full of hustling, splashing riders, through whom Bernard Shute, furiously picking up a bad start, drove a devastating way. He tried to turn his horse down the bank towards Miss Knox, but the hounds were running hard, and, to my intense amusement, Stockbroker refused to abandon the chase, and swept his rider away in the wake of his stable companion, Dr. Hickey's young chestnut. By this time two country boys had, as is usual in such cases, risen from the earth, and fished Moonlighter out of the stream. Miss Sally wound up an acrimonious

argument with her cousin by observing that she didn't care
what he said, and placing her water-logged boot in his obviously
unwilling hand, in a second was again in the saddle, gathering
up the wet reins with the trembling, clumsy fingers of a person
who is thoroughly chilled and in a violent hurry. She set
Moonlighter going, and was away in a moment, galloping him at
the first fence at a pace that suited his steeple-chasing ideas.

'Mr. Knox!' panted Philippa, who had by this time joined
us, 'make her go home!'

'She can go where she likes as far as I 'm concerned,' responded Mr. Knox, pitching himself on to his mare's back and
digging in the spurs.

Moonlighter had already glided over the bank in front of us,
with a perfunctory flick at it with his heels; Flurry's mare and
Cruiskeen jumped it side by side with equal precision. It was
a bank of some five feet high; the Quaker charged it enthusiastically, refused it abruptly, and, according to his infuriating
custom at such moments, proceeded to tear hurried mouthfuls
of grass.

'Will I give him a couple o' belts, your honour?' shouted one
of the running accompaniment of country boys.

'You will!' said I, with some further remarks to the Quaker
that I need not commit to paper.

Swish! Whack! The sound was music in my ears, as the
good, remorseless ash sapling bent round the Quaker's dappled
hind quarters. At the third stripe he launched both his heels
in the operator's face; at the fourth he reared undecidedly; at
the fifth he bundled over the bank in a manner purged of
hesitation.

'Ha!' yelled my assistants, 'that 'll put the fear o' God in
him!' as the Quaker fled headlong after the hunt. 'He 'll
be the betther o' that while he lives!'

Without going quite as far as this, I must admit that for the
next half-hour he was astonishingly the better of it.

The Castle Knox fox was making a very pretty line of it over
the seven miles that separated him from his home. He headed
through a grassy country of Ireland's mild and brilliant green,
fenced with sound and buxom banks, enlivened by stone walls,
uncompromised by the presence of gates, and yet comfortably
laced with lanes for the furtherance of those who had laid to
heart Wolsey's valuable advice: 'Fling away ambition: by

that sin fell the angels.' The flotsam and jetsam of the hunt pervaded the landscape: standing on one long bank, three dismounted farmers flogged away at the refusing steeds below them like anglers trying to rise a sulky fish; half a dozen hats, bobbing in a string, showed where the road rider followed the delusive windings of a *bohireen*. It was obvious that in the matter of ambition they would not have caused Cardinal Wolsey a moment's uneasiness; whether angels or otherwise, they were not going to run any risk of falling.

Flurry's red coat was like a beacon, two fields ahead of me, with Philippa following in his tracks; it was the first run worthy of the name that Philippa had ridden, and I blessed Miss Bobby Bennett as I saw Cruiskeen's undefeated fencing. An encouraging twang of the doctor's horn notified that the hounds were giving us a chance; even the Quaker pricked his blunt ears and swerved in his stride to the sound. A stone wall, a rough patch of heather, a boggy field, dinted deep and black with hoof marks, and the stern chase was at an end. The hounds had checked on the outskirts of a small wood, and the field, thinned down to a panting dozen or so, viewed us with the disfavour shown by the first flight towards those who unexpectedly add to their select number. In the depths of the wood Dr. Hickey might be heard uttering those singular little yelps of encouragement that to the irreverent suggest a milkman in his dotage. Bernard Shute, who neither knew nor cared what the hounds were doing, was expatiating at great length to an uninterested squireen upon the virtues and perfections of his new mount.

'I did all I knew to come and help you at the river.' he said, riding up to the splashed and still dripping Sally, 'but Stockbroker wouldn't hear of it. I pulled his ugly head round till his nose was on my boot, but he galloped away just the same!'

'He was quite right,' said Miss Sally; 'I didn't want you in the least.'

As Miss Sally's red gold coil of hair was turned towards me during this speech, I could only infer the glance with which it was delivered, from the fact that Mr. Shute responded to it with one of those firm gazes of adoration in which the neighbourhood took such an interest, and crumbled away into incoherency.

A shout from the top of a hill interrupted the amenities of the check; Flurry was out of the wood in half a dozen seconds, blowing shattering blasts upon his horn, and the hounds rushed to him, knowing the 'gone away' note that was never blown in vain. The brown mare came out through the trees and the undergrowth like a woodcock down the wind, and jumped across a stream on to a more than questionable bank; the hounds splashed and struggled after her, and, as they landed, the first ecstatic whimpers broke forth. In a moment it was full cry, discordant, beautiful, and soul-stirring, as the pack spread and sped, and settled to the line. I saw the absurd dazzle of tears in Philippa's eyes, and found time for the insulting proffer of the clean pocket-handkerchief, as we all galloped hard to get away on good terms with the hounds.

It was one of those elect moments in fox-hunting when the fittest alone have survived; even the Quaker's sluggish blood was stirred by good company, and possibly by the remembrance of the singing ash-plant, and he lumbered up tall stone-faced banks and down heavy drops, and across wide ditches, in astounding adherence to the line cut out by Flurry. Cruiskeen went like a book—a story for girls, very pleasant and safe, but rather slow. Moonlighter was pulling Miss Sally on to the sterns of the hounds, flying his banks, rocketing like a pheasant over three-foot walls—committing, in fact, all the crimes induced by youth and over-feeding; he would have done very comfortably with another six or seven stone on his back.

Why Bernard Shute did not come off at every fence and generally die a thousand deaths I cannot explain. Occasionally I rather wished he would, as, from my secure position in the rear, I saw him charging his fences at whatever pace and place seemed good to the thoroughly demoralized Stockbroker, and in so doing cannon heavily against Dr. Hickey on landing over a rotten ditch, jump a wall with his spur rowelling Charlie Knox's boot, and cut in at top speed in front of Flurry, who was scientifically cramming his mare up a very awkward scramble. In so far as I could think of anything beyond Philippa and myself and the next fence, I thought there would be trouble for Mr. Shute in consequence of this last feat. It was a half-hour long to be remembered, in spite of the Quaker's ponderous and unalterable gallop, in spite of the thump with which he came down off his banks, in spite of the confiding manner in which he hung upon my hand.

We were nearing Castle Knox, and the riders began to edge

away from the hounds towards a gate that broke the long barrier of the demesne wall. Steaming horses and purple-faced riders clattered and crushed in at the gate; there was a moment of pulling up and listening, in which quivering tails and pumping sides told their own story. Cruiskeen's breathing suggested a cross between a grampus and a gramophone; Philippa's hair had come down, and she had a stitch in her side. Moonlighter, fresher than ever, stamped and dragged at his bit; I thought little Miss Sally looked very white. The bewildering clamour of the hounds was all through the wide laurel plantations. At a word from Flurry, Dr. Hickey shoved his horse ahead and turned down a ride, followed by most of the field.

'Philippa,' I said severely, 'you've had enough, and you know it.'

'Do go up to the house, and make them give you something to eat,' struck in Miss Sally, twisting Moonlighter round to keep his mind occupied.

'And as for you, Miss Sally,' I went on, in the manner of Mr. Fairchild, 'the sooner you get off that horse and out of those wet things the better.'

Flurry, who was just in front of us, said nothing but gave a short and most disagreeable laugh. Philippa accepted my suggestion with the meekness of exhaustion, but in the circumstances it did not surprise me that Miss Sally did not follow her example.

Then ensued an hour of woodland hunting at its worst and most bewildering. I galloped after Flurry and Miss Sally up and down long glittering lanes of laurel, at every other moment burying my face in the Quaker's coarse white mane to avoid the slash of the branches, and receiving down the back of my neck showers of drops stored up from the rain of the day before; playing an endless game of hide-and-seek with the hounds, and never getting any nearer to them, as they turned and doubled through the thickets of evergreens. Even to my limited understanding of the situation it became clear at length that two foxes were on foot; most of the hounds were hard at work a quarter of a mile away, but Flurry, with a grim face and a faithful three couple, stuck to the failing line of the hunted fox.

There came a moment when Miss Sally and I—who through many vicissitudes had clung to each other—found ourselves at a spot where two rides crossed. Flurry was waiting there, and a little way up one of the rides a couple of hounds were hustling to and fro, with thwarted whimpers half breaking from them; he held up his hand to stop us, and at that identical moment Bernard Shute, like a bolt from the blue, burst upon our vision. It need scarcely be mentioned that he was going at full gallop —I have rarely seen him ride at any other pace—and as he bore down upon Flurry and the hounds, ducking and dodging to avoid the branches, he shouted something about a fox having gone away at the other side of the covert.

'Hold hard!' roared Flurry; 'don't you see the hounds, you fool?'

Mr. Shute, to do him justice, held hard with all the strength in his body, but it was of no avail. The bay horse had got his head down and his tail up, there was a piercing yell from a hound as it was ridden over, and Flurry's brown mare will not soon forget the moment when Stockbroker's shoulder took her on the point of the hip and sent her staggering into the laurel branches. As she swung round, Flurry's whip went up, and with a swift backhander the cane and the looped thong caught Bernard across his broad shoulders.

'O Mr. Shute!' shrieked Miss Sally, as I stared dumb-founded; 'did that branch hurt you?'

'All right! Nothing to signify!' he called out as he bucketed past, tugging at his horse's head. 'Thought someone had hit me at first! Come on, we'll catch 'em up this way!'

He swung perilously into the main ride and was gone, totally unaware of the position that Miss Sally's quickness had saved.

Flurry rode straight up to his cousin, with a pale, dangerous face.

'I suppose you think I'm to stand being ridden over and having my hounds killed to please you,' he said; 'but you're mistaken. You were very smart, and you may think you've saved him his licking, but you needn't think he won't get it. He'll have it in spite of you, before he goes to his bed this night!'

A man who loses his temper badly because he is badly in love is inevitably ridiculous, far though he may be from think-ing himself so. He is also a highly unpleasant person to argue with, and Miss Sally and I held our peace respectfully. He turned his horse and rode away.

Almost instantly the three couple of hounds opened in the underwood near us with a deafening crash, and not twenty yards ahead the hunted fox, dark with wet and mud, slunk across the ride. The hounds were almost on his brush; Moonlighter reared and chafed; the din was redoubled, passed away to a little distance, and suddenly seemed stationary in the middle of the laurels.

'Could he have got into the old ice-house?' exclaimed Miss Sally, with reviving excitement. She pushed ahead, and turned down the narrowest of all the rides that had that day been my portion. At the end of the green tunnel there was a comparatively open space; Flurry's mare was standing in it, riderless, and Flurry himself was hammering with a stone at the padlock of a door that seemed to lead into the heart of a laurel clump. The hounds were baying furiously somewhere back of the entrance, among the laurel stems.

'He 's got in by the old ice drain,' said Flurry, addressing himself sulkily to me, and ignoring Miss Sally. He had not the least idea of how absurd was his scowling face, draped by the luxuriant hart's-tongues that overhung the doorway.

The padlock yielded, and the opening door revealed a low, dark passage, into which Flurry disappeared, lugging a couple of hounds with him by the scruff of the neck; the remaining two couple bayed implacably at the mouth of the drain. The croak of a rusty bolt told of a second door at the inner end of the passage.

'Look out for the steps, Flurry, they 're all broken,' called out Miss Sally in tones of honey.

There was no answer. Miss Sally looked at me; her face was serious, but her mischievous eyes made a confederate of me.

'He 's in an *awful* rage!' she said. 'I 'm afraid there will certainly be a row.'

A row there certainly was, but it was in the cavern of the icehouse, where the fox had evidently been discovered. Miss Sally suddenly flung Moonlighter's reins to me and slipped off his back.

'Hold him!' she said, and dived into the doorway under the overhanging branches.

'Things happened after that with astonishing simultaneousness. There was a shrill exclamation from Miss Sally, the inner door was slammed and bolted, and at one and the same moment the fox darted from the entry, and was away into the wood before one could wink.

'What's happened?' I called out, playing the refractory Moonlighter like a salmon.

Miss Sally appeared at the doorway, looking half scared and half delighted.

'I 've bolted him in, and I won't let him out till he promises to be good! I was only just in time to slam the door after the fox bolted out!'

'Great Scott!' I said helplessly.

Miss Sally vanished again into the passage, and the imprisoned hounds continued to express their emotions in the echoing vault of the ice-house. Their master remained mute as the dead, and I trembled.

'Flurry!' I heard Miss Sally say. 'Flurry, I—I 've locked you in!'

This self-evident piece of information met with no response.

'Shall I tell you why?'

A keener note seemed to indicate that a hound had been kicked.

'I don't care whether you answer me or not, I 'm going to tell you!'

There was a pause; apparently telling him was not as simple as had been expected.

'I don't let you out till you promise me something. Ah, Flurry, don't be so cross! What do you say?—Oh, that 's a ridiculous thing to say. You know quite well it 's not on his account!'

There was another considerable pause.

'Flurry!' said Miss Sally again, in tones that would have wiled a badger from his earth. 'Dear Flurry——'

At this point I hurriedly flung Moonlighter's bridle over a branch and withdrew.

My own subsequent adventures are quite immaterial, until the moment when I encountered Miss Sally on the steps of the hall door at Castle Knox.

'I 'm just going in to take off these wet things,' she said airily.

This was no way to treat a confederate.

'Well?' I said, barring her progress.

'Oh—he—he promised. It 's all right,' she replied, rather breathlessly.

There was no one about; I waited resolutely for further information. It did not come.

'Did he try to make his own terms?' said I, looking hard at her.

'Yes, he did.' She tried to pass me.

'And what did you do?'

'I refused them!' she said, with the sudden stagger of a sob in her voice, as she escaped into the house.

Now what on earth was Sally Knox crying about?

X

THE HOUSE OF FAHY

NOTHING could shake the conviction of Maria that she was by nature and by practice a house dog. Every one of Shreelane's many doors had, at one time or another, slammed upon her expulsion, and each one of them had seen her stealthy, irrepressible return to the sphere that she felt herself so eminently qualified to grace. For her the bone, thriftily interred by Tim Connor's terrier, was a mere diversion; even the fruitage of the ash-pit had little charm for an accomplished *habitué* of the kitchen. She knew to a nicety which of the doors could be burst open by assault, at which it was necessary to whine sycophantically; and the clinical thermometer alone could furnish a parallel for her perception of mood in those in authority. In the case of Mrs. Cadogan she knew that there were seasons when instant and complete self-effacement was the only course to pursue; therefore when, on a certain morning in July, on my way through the downstairs regions to my office, I saw her approach the kitchen door with her usual circumspection, and, on hearing her name enunciated indignantly by my cook, withdraw swiftly to a city of refuge at the back of the hay-rick, I drew my own conclusions.

Had she remained, as I did, she would have heard the disclosure of a crime that lay more heavily on her digestion than her conscience.

'I can't put a thing out o' me hand but he's watching me to whip it away!' declaimed Mrs. Cadogan, with all the disregard of her kind for the accident of sex in the brute creation. ''Twas only last night I was back in the scullery when I heard Bridget let a screech, and there was me brave dog up on the table eating the roast beef that was after coming out from the dinner!'

'Brute!' interjected Philippa, with what I well knew to be a simulated wrath.

'And I had planned that bit of beef for the luncheon,' continued Mrs. Cadogan in impassioned lamentation, 'the way we wouldn't have to inthrude on the cold turkey! Sure he has it that dhragged, that all we can do with it now is run it through the mincing machine for the Major's sandwiches.'

At this appetizing suggestion I thought fit to intervene in the deliberations.

'One thing,' I said to Philippa afterwards, as I wrapped up a bottle of Yanatas in a Cardigan jacket and rammed it into an already apoplectic Gladstone bag, 'that I do draw the line at, is taking that dog with us. The whole business is black enough as it is.'

'Dear,' said my wife, looking at me with almost clairvoyant abstraction, 'I could manage a second evening dress if you didn't mind putting my tea-jacket in your portmanteau.'

Little, thank Heaven! as I know about yachting, I knew enough to make pertinent remarks on the incongruity of an ancient sixty-ton hireling and a fleet of smart evening dresses; but none the less I left a pair of indispensable boots behind, and the tea-jacket went into my portmanteau.

It is doing no more than the barest justice to the officers of the Royal Navy to say that, so far as I know them, they cherish no mistaken enthusiasm for a home on the rolling deep when a home anywhere else presents itself. Bernard Shute had unfortunately proved an exception to this rule. During the winter, the invitation to go for a cruise in the yacht that was in process of building for him hung over me like a cloud; a timely strike in the builder's yard brought a respite, and, in fact, placed the completion of the yacht at so safe a distance that I was betrayed into specious regrets, echoed with an atrocious sincerity by Philippa. Into a life pastorally compounded of Petty Sessions and lawn tennis parties, retribution fell when it was least expected. Bernard Shute hired a yacht in Queenstown, and one short week afterwards the worst had happened, and we were packing our things for a cruise in her, the only alleviation being the knowledge that, whether by sea or land, I was bound to return to my work in four days.

We left Shreelane at twelve o'clock, a specially depressing hour for a start, when breakfast has died in you, and lunch is still remote. My last act before mounting the dogcart was to put her collar and chain on Maria and immure her in the potato-house, whence, as we drove down the avenue, her wails rent the heart of Philippa and rejoiced mine. It was a very hot day, with a cloudless sky; the dust lay thick on the white road, and on us also, as, during two baking hours, we drove up and down the long hills and remembered things that had been left behind, and grew hungry enough to eat sandwiches that tasted suspiciously of roast beef.

The yacht was moored in Clountiss Harbour; we drove through the village street, a narrow and unlovely thoroughfare, studded with public-houses, swarming with children and poultry, down through an ever-growing smell of fish, to the quay.

Thence we first viewed our fate, a dingy-looking schooner, and the hope I had secretly been nourishing that there was not wind enough for her to start, was dispelled by the sight of her topsail going up. More than ever at that radiant moment —as the reflection of the white sail quivered on the tranquil blue, and the still water flattered all it reproduced, like a fashionable photographer—did I agree with George Herbert's advice, 'Praise the sea, but stay on shore.'

'We must hail her, I suppose,' I said drearily. I assailed the *Eileen Oge*, such being her inappropriate name, with desolate cries, but achieved no immediate result beyond the assembling of some village children round us and our luggage.

'Mr. Shute and the two ladies was after screeching here for the boat awhile ago,' volunteered a horrid little girl, whom I had already twice frustrated in the attempt to seat an infant relative on our bundle of rugs. 'Timsy Hallahane says 'twould be as good for them to stay ashore, for there isn't as much wind outside as 'd out a candle.'

With this encouraging statement the little girl devoted herself to the alternate consumption of gooseberries and cockles.

All things come to those who wait, and to us arrived at length the gig of the *Eileen Oge*, and such, by this time, were the temperature and the smells of the quay that I actually welcomed the moment that found us leaving it for the yacht.

'Now, Sinclair, aren't you glad we came?' remarked Philippa, as the clear green water deepened under us, and a light briny air came coolly round us with the motion of the boat.

As she spoke, there was an outburst of screams from the children on the quay, followed by a heavy splash.

'Oh stop!' cried Philippa in an agony; 'one of them has fallen in! I can see its poor little brown head!'

'Tis a dog, ma'am,' said briefly the man who was rowing stroke.

'One might have wished it had been that little girl,' said I, as I steered to the best of my ability for the yacht.

We had traversed another twenty yards or so, when Philippa, in a voice, in which horror and triumph were strangely blended, exclaimed, 'She's following us!'

'Who? The little girl?' I asked callously.

'No,' returned Philippa; 'worse!'

I looked round, not without a prevision of what I was to see, and beheld the faithful Maria swimming steadily after us, with her brown muzzle thrust out in front of her, ripping through the reflections like a plough.

'Go home!' I roared, standing up and gesticulating in fury that I well knew to be impotent. 'Go home, you brute!'

Maria redoubled her efforts, and Philippa murmured uncontrollably:

'Well, she *is* a dear!'

Had I had a sword in my hand I should undoubtedly have slain Philippa; but before I could express my sentiments in any way, a violent shock flung me endways on top of the man who was pulling stroke. Thanks to Maria, we had reached our destination all unawares; the two men, respectfully awaiting my instructions, had rowed on with disciplined steadiness, and, as a result, we had rammed the *Eileen Oge* amidships, with a vigour that brought Mr. Shute tumbling up the companion to see what had happened.

'Oh, it's you, is it?' he said, with his mouth full. 'Come in; don't knock! Delighted to see you, Mrs. Yeates; don't apologize. There's nothing like a hired ship after all—it's quite jolly to see the splinters fly—shows you're getting your money's worth. Hullo! who's this?'

This was Maria, feigning exhaustion, and noisily treading water at the boat's side.

'What, poor old Maria? Wanted to send her ashore, did he? Heartless ruffian!'

Thus was Maria installed on board the *Eileen Oge*, and the element of fatality had already begun to work.

There was just enough wind to take us out of Clountiss harbour, and with the last of the outrunning tide we crept away to the west. The party on board consisted of our host's sister, Miss Cecilia Shute, Miss Sally Knox, and ourselves; we sat about in conventional attitudes in deck chairs and on adamantine deck bosses, and I talked to Miss Shute with feverish brilliancy, and wished the patience-cards were not in the cabin; I knew the supreme importance of keeping one's mind occupied, but I dared not face the cabin. There was a long, almost imperceptible swell, with little queer seabirds that I have never seen before—and trust I never shall again—dotted about on its glassy slopes. The coast-line looked low, and grey and dull, as, I think, coast-lines always do when viewed from the deep. The breeze that Bernard had promised us we should find outside was barely enough to keep us moving. The burning sun of four o'clock focused its heat on the deck; Bernard stood up among us, engaged in what he was pleased to call 'handling the stick,' and beamed almost as offensively as the sun.

'Oh, we're slipping along,' he said, his odiously healthy face glowing like copper against the blazing blue sky. 'You're going a great deal faster than you think, and the men say we'll pick up a breeze once we're round the Mizen.'

I made no reply; I was not feeling ill, merely thoroughly disinclined for conversation. Miss Sally smiled wanly, and closing her eyes, laid her head on Philippa's knee. Instructed by a dread freemasonry, I knew that for her the moment had come when she could no longer bear to see the rail rise slowly above the horizon, and with an equal rhythmic slowness sink below it. Maria moved restlessly to and fro, panting and yawning, and occasionally rearing herself on her hind legs against the side, and staring forth with wild eyes at the headachy sliding of the swell. Perhaps she was meditating suicide; if so I sympathized with her, and since she was obviously going to be sick I trusted that she would bring off the suicide with as little delay as possible. Philippa and Miss Shute sat in unaffected serenity in deck chairs, and stitched at white things—tea cloths for the *Eileen Oge*, I believe, things in themselves a mockery—and talked untiringly, with that singular indifference to their marine surroundings that I have often observed in ladies who are not sea-sick. It always stirs me afresh to wonder why they have not remained ashore; nevertheless, I prefer their tranquil and total lack of interest in seafaring matters to the blatant Vikingism of the average male who is similarly placed.

Somehow, I know not how, we crawled onwards, and by about five o'clock we had rounded the Mizen, a gaunt spike of a headland that starts up like a boar's tusk above the ragged lip of the Irish coast, and the *Eileen Oge* was beginning to swing and wallop in the long sluggish rollers that the American liners know and despise. I was very far from despising them. Down in the west, resting on the sea's rim, a purple bank of clouds lay awaiting the descent of the sun, as seductively and as malevolently as a damp bed at a hotel awaits a traveller.

The end, so far as I was concerned, came at tea-time. The meal had been prepared in the saloon, and thither it became incumbent on me to accompany my hostess and my wife. Miss Sally, long past speech, opened, at the suggestion of tea, one eye, and disclosed a look of horror. As I tottered down the companion I respected her good sense. The *Eileen Oge* had been built early in the sixties, and head-room was not her strong point; neither, apparently, was ventilation. I began by dashing my forehead against the frame of the cabin door, and then, shattered morally and physically, entered into the atmosphere of the pit. After which things, and the sight of a plate of rich cake, I retired in good order to my cabin, and began upon the Yanatas.

I pass over some painful intermediate details and resume at the moment when Bernard Shute woke me from a drugged slumber to announce that dinner was over.

'It's been raining pretty hard,' he said, swaying easily with the swing of the yacht; 'but we've got a clinking breeze, and we ought to make Lurriga Harbour to-night. There's good anchorage there, the men say. They're rather a lot of swabs, but they know this coast, and I don't. I took 'em over with the ship all standing.

'Where are we now?' I asked, something heartened by the blessed word 'anchorage.'

'You're running up Sheepskin Bay—it's a thundering big bay; Lurriga's up at the far end of it, and the night's as black as the inside of a cow. Dig out and get something to eat, and come on deck——What! no dinner?'—I had spoken morosely,

with closed eyes—'Oh, rot! you're on an even keel now. I
promised Mrs. Yeates I'd make you dig out. You're as bad
as a soldier officer that we were ferrying to Malta one time in
the old *Tamar*. He got one leg out of his berth when we were
going down the Channel, and he was too sick to pull it in again
till we got to Gib!'

I compromised on a drink and some biscuits. The ship was
certainly steadier, and I felt sufficiently restored to climb weakly
on deck. It was by this time past ten o'clock, and heavy clouds
blotted out the last of the afterglow, and smothered the stars
at their birth. A wet warm wind was lashing the *Eileen Oge*
up a wide estuary; the waves were hunting her, hissing under her
stern, racing up to her, crested with the white glow of phosphorus, as she fled before them. I dimly discerned in the
greyness the more solid greyness of the shore. The mainsail
loomed out into the darkness, nearly at right angles to the
yacht, with the boom creaking as the following wind gave us
an additional shove. I know nothing of yacht sailing, but I
can appreciate the grand fact that in running before a wind the
boom is removed from its usual sphere of devastation.

I sat down beside a bundle of rugs that I had discovered to
be my wife, and thought of my whitewashed office at Shreelane and its bare but stationary floor, with a yearning that was
little short of passion. Miss Sally had long since succumbed;
Miss Shute was tired, and had turned in soon after dinner.

'I suppose she's overdone by the delirious gaiety of the
afternoon,' said I acridly, in reply to this information.

Philippa cautiously poked her head from the rugs, like a
tortoise from under its shell, to see that Bernard, who was
standing near the steersman, was out of hearing.

'In all your life, Sinclair,' she said impressively, 'you never
knew such a time as Cecilia and I have had down there! We've
had to wash *everything* in the cabins, and remake the beds, and
hurl the sheets away—they were covered with black finger-
marks—and while we were doing that, in came the creature
that calls himself the steward, to ask if he might get something
of his that he had left in Miss Shute's "birthplace"! and he
rooted out from under Cecilia's mattress a pair of socks and
half a loaf of bread!'

'Consolation to Miss Shute to know her berth has been well
aired,' I said, with the nearest approach to enjoyment I had

known since I came on board; 'and has Sally made any equally
interesting discoveries?'

'She said she didn't care what her bed was like; she just
dropped into it. I must say I am sorry for her,' went on
Philippa; 'she hated coming. Her mother made her accept.'

'I wonder if Lady Knox will make her accept *him*!' I said.
'How often has Sally refused him, does any one know?'

'Oh, about once a week,' replied Philippa; 'just the way I
kept on refusing you, you know!'

Something cold and wet was thrust into my hand, and the
aroma of damp dog arose upon the night air; Maria had issued
from some lair at the sound of our voices, and was now, with
palsied tremblings, slowly trying to drag herself on to my lap.

'Poor thing, she's been so dreadfully ill,' said Philippa.
'Don't send her away, Sinclair. Mr. Shute found her lying on
his berth not able to move; didn't you, Mr. Shute?'

'She found out that she was able to move,' said Bernard,
who had crossed to our side of the deck; 'it was somehow borne
in upon her when I got at her with a boot-tree. I wouldn't
advise you to keep her in your lap, Yeates. She stole half a
ham after dinner, and she might take a notion to make the only
reparation in her power.'

I stood up and stretched myself stiffly. The wind was
freshening, and though the growing smoothness of the water
told that we were making shelter of some kind, for all that I
could see of land we might as well have been in mid-ocean.
The heaving lift of the deck under my feet, and the lurching
swing when a stronger gust filled the ghostly sails, were more
disquieting to me in suggestion than in reality, and, to my surprise, I found something almost enjoyable in rushing through
darkness at the pace at which we were going.

'We're a small bit short of the mouth of Lurriga Harbour yet,
sir,' said the man who was steering, in reply to a question from
Bernard. 'I can see the shore well enough; sure I know every
yard of wather in the bay——'

As he spoke he sat down abruptly and violently; so did
Bernard, so did I. The bundle that contained Philippa col-
lapsed upon Maria.

'Main sheet!' bellowed Bernard, on his feet in an instant, as
the boom swung in and out again with a terrific jerk. 'We're
ashore!'

In response to this order three men in succession fell over me
while I was still struggling on the deck, and something that
was either Philippa's elbow, or the acutest angle of Maria's
skull, hit me in the face. As I found my feet the cabin skylight was suddenly illuminated by a wavering glare. I got
across the slanting deck somehow, through the confusion of
shouting men and the flapping thunder of the sails, and saw
through the skylight a gush of flame rising from a pool of fire
around an overturned lamp on the swing-table. I avalanched
down the companion and was squandered like an avalanche on
the floor at the foot of it. Even as I fell, McCarthy the steward
dragged the strip of carpet from the cabin floor and threw it
on the blaze; I found myself, in some unexplained way, snatching a railway rug from Miss Shute and applying it to the same
purpose, and in half a dozen seconds we had smothered the
flame and were left in total darkness. The most striking
feature of the situation was the immovability of the yacht.

'Great Ned!' said McCarthy, invoking I know not what
heathen deity, 'is it on the bottom of the say we are? Well,
whether or no, thank God we have the fire quinched!'

We were not, so far, at the bottom of the sea, but during the
next few minutes the chances seemed in favour of our getting
there. The yacht had run her bows upon a sunken ridge of rock,
and after a period of feminine indecision as to whether she were
going to slide off again, or roll over into deep water, she elected
to stay where she was, and the gig was lowered with all speed,
in order to tow her off before the tide left her.

My recollection of this interval is but hazy, but I can certify
that in ten minutes I had swept together an assortment of
necessaries and knotted them into my counterpane, had broken
the string of my eye-glass, and lost my silver match-box; had
found Philippa's curling-tongs and put them in my pocket;
had carted all the luggage on deck; had then applied myself to
the manly duty of reassuring the ladies, and had found Miss
Shute merely bored, Philippa enthusiastically anxious to be
allowed to help to pull the gig, and Miss Sally radiantly restored
to health and spirits by the cessation of movement and the
probability of an early escape from the yacht.

The rain had, with its usual opportuneness, begun again;
we stood in it under umbrellas, and watched the gig jumping on
its tow-rope like a dog on a string, as its crew plied the labouring

oar in futile endeavour to move the *Eileen Oge.* We had run on the rock at half-tide, and the increasing slant of the deck as the tide fell brought home to us the pleasing probability that at low water—viz, about 2 a.m.—we should roll off the rock and go to the bottom. Had Bernard Shute wished to show himself in the most advantageous light to Miss Sally he could scarcely have bettered the situation. I looked on in helpless respect while he whom I had known as the scourge of the hunting field, the terror of the shooting party, rose to the top of a difficult position and kept there, and my respect was, if possible, increased by the presence of mind with which he availed himself of all critical moments to place a protecting arm round Miss Knox.

By about 1 a.m. the two gaffs with which Bernard had contrived to shore up the slowly heeling yacht began to show signs of yielding, and, in approved shipwreck fashion, we took to the boats, the yacht's crew in the gig remaining in attendance on what seemed likely to be the last moments of the *Eileen Oge,* while we, in the dinghy, sought for the harbour. Owing to the tilt of the yacht's deck, and the roughness of the broken water round her, getting into the boat was no mean feat of gymnastics. Miss Sally did it like a bird, alighting in the inevitable arms of Bernard; Miss Shute followed very badly, but, by innate force of character, successfully; Philippa, who was enjoying every moment of her shipwreck, came last, launching herself into the dinghy with my silver shoe-horn clutched in one hand, and in the other the tea-basket. I heard the hollow clank of its tin cups as she sprang, and appreciated the heroism with which Bernard received one of its corners in his waist. How or when Maria left the yacht I know not, but when I applied myself to the bow oar I led off with three crabs, owing to the devotion with which she thrust her head into my lap.

I am no judge of these matters, but in my opinion we ought to have been swamped several times during that row. There was nothing but the phosphorus of breaking waves to tell us where the rocks were, and nothing to show where the harbour was except a solitary light, a masthead light, as we supposed. The skipper had assured us that we could not go wrong if we kept 'a westerly course with a little northing in it'; but it seemed simpler to steer for the light, and we did so. The dinghy climbed along over the waves with an agility that was safer than it felt; the rain fell without haste and without rest, the oars were as inflexible as crowbars, and somewhat resembled them in shape and weight; nevertheless, it was Elysium when compared with the afternoon leisure of the deck of the *Eileen Oge*.

At last we came, unexplainably, into smooth water, and it was at about this time that we were first aware that the darkness was less dense than it had been, and that the rain had ceased. By imperceptible degrees a greyness touched the back of the waves, more a dreariness than a dawn, but more welcome than thousands of gold and silver. I looked over my shoulder and discerned vague bulky things ahead; as I did so, my oar was suddenly wrapped in seaweed. We crept on; Maria stood up with her paws on the gunwale, and whined in high agitation. The dark objects ahead resolved themselves into rocks, and without more ado Maria pitched herself into the water. In half a minute we heard her shaking herself on shore. We slid on; the water swelled under the dinghy, and lifted her keel on to grating gravel.

'We couldn't have done it better if we'd been the Hydrographer Royal,' said Bernard, wading knee-deep in a light wash of foam, with the painter in his hand; 'but all the same, that masthead light is someone's bedroom candle!'

We landed, hauled up the boat, and then feebly sat down on our belongings to review the situation, and Maria came and shook herself over each of us in turn. We had run into a little cove, guided by the philanthropic beam of a candle in the upper window of a house about a hundred yards away. The candle still burned on, and the anaemic daylight exhibited to us our surroundings, and we debated as to whether we could at 2.45 a.m. present ourselves as objects of compassion to the owner of the candle. I need hardly say that it was the ladies who decided on making the attempt, having, like most of their sex, a courage incomparably superior to ours in such matters; Bernard and I had not a grain of genuine compunction in our souls, but we failed in nerve.

We trailed up from the cove, laden with emigrants' bundles, stumbling on wet rocks in the half-light, and succeeded in making our way to the house.

It was a small two-storeyed building, of that hideous breed of architecture usually dedicated to the rectories of the Irish Church; we felt that there was something friendly in the presence of a pair of carpet slippers in the porch, but there was a hint of exclusiveness in the fact that there was no knocker and that the bell was broken. The light still burned in the upper window, and with a faltering hand I flung gravel at the glass. This summons was appallingly responded to by a shriek; there was a flutter of white at the panes, and the candle was extinguished.

'Come away!' exclaimed Miss Shute, 'it's a lunatic asylum!'

We stood our ground, however, and presently heard a footstep within, a blind was poked aside in another window, and we were inspected by an unseen inmate; then someone came downstairs, and the hall door was opened by a small man with a bald head and a long sandy beard. He was attired in a brief dressing-gown, and on his shoulder sat, like an angry ghost, a large white cockatoo. Its crest was up on end, its beak was a good two inches long and curved like a Malay kris; its claws gripped the little man's shoulder. Maria uttered in the background a low and thunderous growl.

'Don't take any notice of the bird, please,' said the little man nervously, seeing our united gaze fixed upon this apparition; 'he's extremely fierce if annoyed.'

The majority of our party here melted away to either side of the hall door, and I was left to do the explaining. The tale of our misfortunes had its due effect, and we were ushered into a small drawing-room, our host holding open the door for us, like a nightmare footman with bare shins, a gnome-like bald head, and an unclean spirit swaying on his shoulder. He opened the shutters, and we sat decorously round the room, as at an afternoon party, while the situation was further expounded on both sides. Our entertainer, indeed, favoured us with the leading items of his family history, amongst them the facts that he was a Dr. Fahy from Cork, who had taken somebody's rectory for the summer, and had been prevailed on by some of his patients to permit them to join him as paying guests.

'I said it was a lunatic asylum,' murmured Miss Shute to me.

'In point of fact,' went on our host, 'there isn't an empty room in the house, which is why I can only offer your party the use of this room and the kitchen fire, which I make a point of keeping burning all night.'

He leaned back complacently in his chair, and crossed his legs; then, obviously remembering his costume, sat bolt upright again. We owed the guiding beams of the candle to the owner of the cockatoo, an old Mrs. Buck, who was, we gathered, the most paying of all the patients, and also obviously, the one most feared and cherished by Dr. Fahy. 'She has a candle burning all night for the bird, and her door open to let him walk about the house when he likes,' said Dr. Fahy; 'indeed, I may say her passion for him amounts to dementia. He's very fond of me, and Mrs. Fahy's always telling me I should be thankful, as whatever he did we'd be bound to put up with it!'

Dr. Fahy had evidently a turn for conversation that was unaffected by circumstance; the first beams of the early sun were lighting up the rep chair covers before the door closed upon his brown dressing-gown, and upon the stately white back of the coackatoo, and the demoniac possession of laughter that had wrought in us during the interview burst forth unchecked. It was most painful and exhausting, as much laughter always is; but by far the most serious part of it was that Miss Sally, who was sitting in the window, somehow drove her elbow through a pane of glass, and Bernard, in pulling down the blind to conceal the damage, tore it off the roller.

There followed on this catastrophe a period during which reason tottered and Maria barked furiously. Philippa was the first to pull herself together, and to suggest an adjournment to the kitchen fire that, in honour of the paying guests, was never quenched, and, respecting the repose of the household, we proceeded thither with a stealth that convinced Maria we were engaged in a rat hunt. The boots of paying guests littered the floor, the debris of their last repast covered the table; a cat in some unseen fastness crooned a war song to Maria, who feigned unconsciousness and fell to scientific research in the scullery.

We roasted our boots at the range, and Bernard, with all a sailor's gift for exploration and theft, prowled in noisome purlieus and emerged with a jug of milk and a lump of salt butter. No one who has not been a burglar can at all realize what it was to roam through Dr. Fahy's basement storey, with the rookery of paying guests asleep above, and to feel that, so far, we had repaid his confidence by breaking a pane of glass and a blind, and putting the scullery tap out of order. I have always maintained that there was something wrong with it before I touched it, but the fact remains that when I had filled

Philippa's kettle, no human power could prevail upon it to stop flowing. For all I know to the contrary it is running still.

It was in the course of our furtive return to the drawing-room that we were again confronted by Mrs. Buck's cockatoo. It was standing in malign meditation on the stairs, and on seeing us it rose, without a word of warning, upon the wing, and with a long screech flung itself at Miss Sally's golden-red head, which a ray of sunlight had chanced to illumine. There was a moment of stampede, as the selected victim, pursued by the cockatoo, fled into the drawing-room; two chairs were upset (one, I think, broken), Miss Sally enveloped herself in a window curtain, Philippa and Miss Shute effaced themselves beneath a table; the cockatoo, foiled of its prey, skimmed, still screeching, round the ceiling. It was Bernard who, with a well-directed sofa-cushion, drove the enemy from the room. There was only a chink of the door open, but the cockatoo turned on his side as he flew, and swung through it like a woodcock.

We slammed the door behind him, and at the same instant there came a thumping on the floor overhead, muffled, yet peremptory.

'That's Mrs. Buck!' said Miss Shute, crawling from under the table; 'the room over this is the one that had the candle in it.'

We sat for a time in awful stillness, but nothing further happened, save a distant shriek overhead, that told the cockatoo had sought and found sanctuary in his owner's room. We had tea *sotto voce*, and then, one by one, despite the amazing discomfort of the drawing-room chairs, we dozed off to sleep.

It was at about five o'clock that I woke with a stiff neck and an uneasy remembrance that I had last seen Maria in the kitchen. The others, looking, each of them, about twenty years older than their age, slept in various attitudes of exhaustion. Bernard opened his eyes as I stole forth to look for Maria, but none of the ladies awoke. I went down the evil-smelling passage that led to the kitchen stairs, and, there on a mat, regarding me with intelligent affection, was Maria; but what—oh, what was the white thing that lay between her forepaws?

The situation was too serious to be coped with alone. I fled noiselessly back to the drawing-room and put my head in; Bernard's eyes—blessed be the light sleep of sailors!—opened again, and there was that in mine that summoned him forth. (Blessed also be the light step of sailors!)

We took the corpse from Maria, withholding perforce the language and the slaughtering that our hearts ached to bestow. For a minute or two our eyes communed.

'I 'll get the kitchen shovel,' breathed Bernard, 'you open the hall door!'

A moment later we passed like spirits into the open air, and on into a little garden at the end of the house. Maria followed us, licking her lips. There were beds of nasturtiums, and of purple stocks, and of marigolds. We chose a bed of stocks, a plump bed, that looked like easy digging. The windows were all tightly shut and shuttered, and I took the cockatoo from under my coat and hid it, temporarily, behind a box border. Bernard had brought a shovel and a coal scoop. We dug like badgers. At eighteen inches we got down into shale and stones, and the coal scoop struck work.

'Never mind,' said Bernard; 'we 'll plant the stocks on top of him.' It was a lovely morning, with a new-born blue sky and a light northerly breeze. As we returned to the house, we looked across the wavelets of the little cove and saw, above the rocky point round which we had groped last night, a tri-angular white patch moving slowly along.

'The tide 's lifted her!' said Bernard, standing stock-still. He looked at Mrs. Buck's window and at me. 'Yeates!' he whispered, 'let 's quit!'

It was now barely six o'clock, and not a soul was stirring. We woke the ladies and convinced them of the high importance of catching the tide. Bernard left a note on the hall table for Dr. Fahy, a beautiful note of leave-taking and gratitude, and apology for the broken window (for which he begged to enclose half a crown). No allusion was made to the other casualties. As we neared the strand he found an occasion to say to me:

'I put in a postscript that I thought it best to mention that I had seen the cockatoo in the garden, and hoped it would get back all right. That 's quite true, you know! But look here, whatever you do, you must keep it all dark from the ladies——'

At this juncture Maria overtook us with the cockatoo in her mouth.

XI

OCCASIONAL LICENCES

'It's out of the question,' I said, looking forbiddingly at Mrs. Moloney through the spokes of the bicycle that I was pumping up outside the grocer's in Skebawn.

'Well, indeed, Major Yeates,' said Mrs. Moloney, advancing excitedly, and placing on the nickel plating a hand that I had good and recent cause to know was warm, 'sure I know well that if th' angel Gabriel came down from heaven looking for a licence for the races, your honour wouldn't give it to him without a charackther, but as for Michael! Sure, the world knows what Michael is!'

I had been waiting for Philippa for already nearly half an hour, and my temper was not at its best.

'Character or no character, Mrs. Moloney,' said I with asperity, 'the magistrates have settled to give no occasional licences, and if Michael were as sober as——'

'Is it sober! God help us!' exclaimed Mrs. Moloney with an upward rolling of her eye to the Recording Angel; 'I'll tell your honour the truth. I'm his wife, now, fifteen years, and I never seen the sign of dhrink on Michael only once, and that was when he went out o' good nature helping Timsy Ryan to whitewash his house, and Timsy and himself had a couple o' pots o' porther, and look, he was as little used to it that his head got light, and he walked away out to dhrive in the cows and it no more than eleven o'clock in the day! And the cows, the craytures, as much surprised, goin' hither and over the four corners of the road from him! Faith, ye'd have to laugh. "Michael," says I to him, "ye're dhrunk!" "I am," says he, and the tears rained from his eyes. I turned the cows from him. "Go home," I says, "and lie down on Willy Tom's bed——"'

At this affecting point my wife came out of the grocer's with a large parcel to be strapped to my handle-bar, and the history of Mr. Moloney's solitary lapse from sobriety got no further than Willy Tom's bed.

'You see,' I said to Philippa, as we bicycled quietly home through the hot June afternoon, 'we've settled we'll give no

licences for the sports. Why even young Sheehy, who owns
three pubs in Skebawn, came to me and said he hoped the
magistrates would be firm about it, as these one-day licences
were quite unnecessary, and only led to drunkenness and fighting, and every man on the Bench has joined in promising not to
grant any.'

'How nice, dear!' said Philippa absently. 'Do you know
Mrs. McDonnell can only let me have three dozen cups and
saucers; I wonder if that will be enough?'

'Do you mean to say you expect three dozen people?' said I.

'Oh, it's always well to be prepared,' replied my wife
evasively.

During the next few days I realized the true inwardness of
what it was to be prepared for an entertainment of this kind.
Games were not at a high level in my district. Football, of a
wild guerrilla species, was waged intermittently, blended in some
inextricable way with Home Rule and a brass band, and on
Sundays gatherings of young men rolled a heavy round stone
along the roads, a rudimentary form of sport, whose fascination
lay primarily in the fact that it was illegal, and, in lesser degree,
in betting on the length of each roll. I had had a period of
enthusiasm, during which I thought I was going to be the
apostle of cricket in the neighbourhood, but my mission
dwindled to single wicket with Peter Cadogan, who was indul-
gent but bored, and I swiped the ball through the dining-room
window, and someone took one of the stumps to poke the laundry
fire. Once a year, however, on that festival of the Roman
Catholic Church which is familiarly known as 'Pether and
Paul's day,' the district was wont to make a spasmodic effort at
athletic sports, which were duly patronized by the gentry and
promoted by the publicans, and this year the honour of a
steward's green rosette was conferred upon me. Philippa's
genius for hospitality here saw its chance, and broke forth into
unbridled tea-party in connection with the sports, even involving me in the hire of a tent, the conveyance of chairs and
tables, and other large operations.

It chanced that Flurry Knox had on this occasion lent the
fields for the sports, with the proviso that horse-races and a
tug-of-war were to be added to the usual programme; Flurry's
participation in events of this kind seldom failed to be of an
inflaming character. As he and I planted larch spars for the

high jump, and stuck furze-bushes into hurdles (locally known
as 'hurrls'), and skirmished hourly with people who wanted to
sell drink on the course, I thought that my next summer leave
would singularly coincide with the festival consecrated to St.
Peter and St. Paul. We made a grand stand of quite four feet
high, out of old fish-boxes, which smelt worse and worse as
the day wore on, but was, none the less, as sought after by those
for whom it was not intended, as is the royal enclosure at Ascot;
we broke gaps in all the fences to allow carriages on to the ground,
we armed a gang of the worst blackguards in Skebawn with
cart-whips, to keep the course, and felt that organization could
go no further.

The momentous day of Pether and Paul opened badly, with
heavy clouds and every indication of rain, but after a few
thunder showers things brightened, and it seemed within the
bounds of possibility that the weather might hold up. When
I got down to the course on the day of the sports the first thing
I saw was a tent of that peculiar filthy grey that usually en-
shrines the sale of porter, with an array of barrels in a crate
beside it; I bore down upon it in all the indignant majesty of
the law, and in so doing came upon Flurry Knox, who was
engaged in flogging boys off the grand stand.

'Sheehy's gone one better than you!' he said, without taking
any trouble to conceal the fact that he was amused.

'Sheehy!' I said; 'why, Sheehy was the man who went to
every magistrate in the country to ask them to refuse a licence
for the sports.'

'Yes, he took some trouble to prevent any one else having a
look in,' replied Flurry; 'he asked every magistrate but one,
and that was the one that gave him the licence.'

'You don't mean to say that it was you?' I demanded in
high wrath and suspicion, remembering that Sheehy bred
horses, and that my friend Mr. Knox was a person of infinite
resource in the matter of a deal.

'Well, well,' said Flurry, rearranging a disordered fish-box,
'and me that's a churchwarden, and sprained my ankle a
month ago with running downstairs at my grandmother's to
be in time for prayers! Where's the use of a good character
in this country?'

'Not much when you keep it eating its head off for want of
exercise,' I retorted; 'but if it wasn't you, who was it?'

'Do you remember old Moriarty out at Castle Ire?'

I remembered him extremely well as one of those representatives of the people with whom a paternal Government had leavened the effete ranks of the Irish magistracy.

'Well,' resumed Flurry, 'that licence was as good as a five-pound note in his pocket.'

I permitted myself a comment on Mr. Moriarty suitable to the occasion.

'Oh, that's nothing,' said Flurry easily; 'he told me one day when he was half screwed that his Commission of the Peace, was worth a hundred and fifty a year to him in turkeys and whisky, and he was telling the truth for once.'

At this point Flurry's eye wandered, and following its direction I saw Lady Knox's smart 'bus cleaving its way through the throngs of country people, lurching over the ups and downs of the field like a ship in a sea. I was too blind to make out the component parts of the white froth that crowned it on top, and seethed forth from it when it had taken up a position near the tent in which Philippa was even now propping the legs of the tea-table, but from the fact that Flurry addressed himself to the door, I argued that Miss Sally had gone inside.

Lady Knox's manner had something more than its usual bleakness. She had brought, as she promised, a large contingent, but from the way that the strangers within her gates melted impalpably and left me to deal with her single-handed, I drew the further deduction that all was not well.

'Did you ever in your life see such a gang of women as I have brought with me?' she began with her wonted directness, as I piloted her to the grand stand, and placed her on the stoutest looking of the fish-boxes. 'I have no patience with men who yacht! Bernard Shute has gone off to the Clyde, and I had counted on his being a man at my dance next week. I suppose you'll tell me you're going away too.'

I assured Lady Knox that I would be a man to the best of my ability.

'This is the last dance I shall give,' went on her ladyship, unappeased; 'the men in this country consist of children and cads.'

I admitted that we were but a poor lot, 'but,' I said, 'Miss Sally told me——'

'Sally's a fool!' said Lady Knox, with a falcon eye at her

daughter, who happened to be talking to her distant kinsman, Mr. Flurry of that ilk.

The races had by this time begun with a competition known as the 'Hop, Step, and Lep'; this, judging by the yells, was a highly interesting display, but as it was conducted between two impervious rows of onlookers, the aristocracy on the fish-boxes saw nothing save the occasional purple face of a competitor, starting into view above the wall of backs like a jack-in-the-box. For me, however, the odorous sanctuary of the fish-boxes was not to be. I left it guarded by Slipper with a cart-whip of flail-like dimensions, as disreputable an object as could be seen out of low comedy, with someone's old white cords on his bandy legs, butcher boots three sizes too big for him, and a black eye. The small boys fled before him; in the glory of his office he would have flailed his own mother off the fish-boxes had occasion served.

I had an afternoon of decidedly mixed enjoyment. My stewardship blossomed forth like Aaron's rod, and added to itself the duties of starter, handicapper, general referee, and chucker-out, besides which I from time to time strove with emissaries who came from Philippa with messages about water and kettles. Flurry and I had to deal single-handed with the foot-races (our brothers in office being otherwise engaged at Mr. Sheehy's), a task of many difficulties, chiefest being that the spectators all swept forward at the word 'Go!' and ran the race with the competitors, yelling curses, blessings, and advice upon them, taking short cuts over anything and everybody, and mingling inextricably with the finish. By fervent applications of the whips, the course was to some extent purged for the quarter-mile, and it would, I believe, have been a triumph of handicapping had not an unforeseen disaster overtaken the favourite—old Mrs. Knox's bath-chair boy. Whether as was alleged, his braces had or had not been tampered with by a rival was a matter that the referee had subsequently to deal with in the thick of a free fight; but the painful fact remained that in the course of the first lap what were described as 'his galluses' abruptly severed their connection with the garments for whose safety they were responsible, and the favourite was obliged to seek seclusion in the crowd.

The tug-of-war followed close on this *contretemps*, and had the excellent effect of drawing away, like a blister, the inflammation set up by the grievances of the bath-chair boy. I cannot at this moment remember of how many men each team consisted; my sole aim was to keep the numbers even, and to baffle the volunteers who, in an ecstasy of sympathy, attached themselves to the tail of the rope at moments when their champions weakened. . The rival forces dug their heels in and tugged, in an uproar that drew forth the innermost line of customers from Mr. Sheehy's porter tent, and even attracted 'the quality' from the haven of the fish-boxes, Slipper, in the capacity of Squire of Dames, pioneering Lady Knox through the crowd with the cart-whip, and with language whose nature was providentially veiled, for the most part, by the din. The tug-of-war continued unabated. One team was getting the worst of it, but hung doggedly on, sinking lower and lower till they gradually sat down; nothing short of the trump of judgment could have conveyed to them that they were breaking rules, and both teams settled down by slow degrees on to their sides, with the rope under them, and their heels still planted in the ground, bringing about complete deadlock. I do not know the record duration for a tug-of-war, but I can certify that the Cullinagh and Knockranny teams lay on the ground at full tension for half an hour, like men in apoplectic fits, each man with his respective adherents howling over him, blessing him, and adjuring him to continue.

With my own nauseated eyes I saw a bearded countryman, obviously one of Mr. Sheehy's best customers, fling himself on his knees beside one of the combatants, and kiss his crimson and streaming face in a rapture of encouragement. As he shoved unsteadily past me on his return journey to Mr. Sheehy's, I heard him informing a friend that 'he cried a handful over Danny Mulloy, when he seen the poor brave boy so shtubborn, and, indeed, he couldn't say why he cried.'

'For good nature ye'd cry,' suggested the friend.

'Well, just that, I suppose,' returned Danny Mulloy's admirer resignedly; 'indeed, if it was only two cocks ye seen fightin' on the road, yer heart'd take part with one o' them!'

I had begun to realize that I might as well abandon the tug-of-war and occupy myself elsewhere, when my wife's much harassed messenger brought me the portentous tidings that Mrs. Yeates wanted me at the tent at once. When I arrived I found the tent literally bulging with Philippa's guests; Lady Knox, seated on a hamper, was taking off her gloves, and loudly announcing her desire for tea, and Philippa, with a flushed face and a crooked hat, breathed into my ear the awful news that both the cream and the milk had been forgotten.

'But Flurry Knox says he can get me some,' she went on; 'he's gone to send people to milk a cow that lives near here. Go out and see if he's coming.'

I went out and found, in the first instance, Mrs. Cadogan, who greeted me with the prayer that the divil might roast Julia McCarthy, that legged it away to the races like a wild goose, and left the cream afther her on the servants' hall table. 'Sure, Misther Flurry's gone looking for a cow, and what cow would there be in a backwards place like this? And look at me shtriving to keep the kettle simpering on the fire, and not as much coals undher it as 'd redden a pipe!'

'Where's Mr. Knox?' I asked.

'Himself and Slipper's galloping the counthry like the deer. I believe it's to the house above they went, sir.'

I followed up a rocky hill to the house above, and there found Flurry and Slipper engaged in the patriarchal task of driving two brace of coupled and spancelled goats into a shed.

'It's the best we can do,' said Flurry briefly; 'there isn't a cow to be found, and the people are all down at the sports. Be d——d to you, Slipper, don't let them go from you!' as the goats charged and doubled like football players.

'But goats' milk!' I said, paralysed by horrible memories of what tea used to taste like at Gib.

'They'll never know it!' said Flurry, cornering a venerable nanny; 'here, hold this divil, and hold her tight!'

I have no time to dwell upon the pastoral scene that followed. Suffice it to say, that at the end of ten minutes of scorching profanity from Slipper, and incessant warfare with the goats, the latter had reluctantly yielded two small jugfuls, and the dairymaids had exhibited a nerve and skill in their trade that won my lasting respect.

'I knew I could trust *you*, Mr. Knox!' said Philippa, with shining eyes, as we presented her with the two foaming beakers. I suppose a man is never a hero to his wife, but if she could have realized the bruises on my legs, I think she would have reserved a blessing for me also.

What was thought of the goats' milk I gathered symptomatically from a certain fixity of expression that accompanied the first sip of the tea, and from observing that comparatively few ventured on second cups. I also noted that after a brief conversation with Flurry, Miss Sally poured hers secretly on to the grass. Lady Knox had throughout the day preserved an aspect so threatening that no change was perceptible in her demeanour. In the throng of hungry guests I did not for some time notice that Mr. Knox had withdrawn until something in Miss Sally's eye summoned me to her, and she told me she had a message from him for me.

'Couldn't we come outside?' she said.

Outside the tent, within less than six yards of her mother, Miss Sally confided to me a scheme that made my hair stand on end. Summarized, it amounted to this: That, first, she was in the primary stage of a deal with Sheehy for a four-year-old chestnut colt, for which Sheehy was asking double its value on the assumption that it had no rival in the country; that, secondly, they had just heard it was going to run in the first race; and thirdly, and lastly, that as there was no other horse available, Flurry was going to take old Sultan out of the 'bus and ride him in the race; and that Mrs. Yeates had promised to keep mamma safe in the tent, while the race was going on, and 'you know, Major Yeates, it would be delightful to beat Sheehy after his getting the better of you all about the licence!'

With this base appeal to my professional feelings, Miss Knox paused, and looked at me insinuatingly. Her eyes were greeny-grey, and very beguiling.

'Come on,' she said; 'they want you to start them!'

Pursued by visions of the just wrath of Lady Knox, I weakly followed Miss Sally to the farther end of the second field, from which point the race was to start. The course was not a serious one: two or three natural banks, a stone wall, and a couple of 'hurrls.' There were but four riders, including Flurry, who was seated composedly on Sultan, smoking a cigarette and talking confidentially to Slipper. Sultan, although something stricken in years and touched in the wind, was a brown horse who in his day had been a hunter of no mean repute; even now he occasionally carried Lady Knox in a sedate and gentlemanly manner, but it struck me that it was trying him rather high to take him from the pole of the 'bus after twelve miles on a hilly road, and hustle him over a country against a four-year-old. My acutest anxiety, however, was to start the race as quickly as possible, and to get back to the tent in time to establish an alibi; therefore I repressed my private sentiments, and, tying my handkerchief to a stick, determined that no time should be fashionably frittered away in false starts.

They got away somehow; I believe Sheehy's colt was facing the wrong way at the moment when I dropped the flag, but a friend turned him with a stick, and, with a cordial and timely whack, speeded him on his way on sufficiently level terms, and then somehow, instead of returning to the tent, I found myself with Miss Sally on the top of a tall narrow bank, in a precarious line of spectators, with whom we toppled and swayed, and, in moments of acuter emotion, held on to each other in unaffected comradeship.

Flurry started well, and from our commanding position we could see him methodically riding at the first fence at a smart hunting canter, closely attended by James Canty's brother on a young black mare, and by an unknown youth on a big white horse. The hope of Sheehy's stable, a leggy chestnut, ridden by a cadet of the house of Sheehy, went away from the friend's stick like a rocket, and had already refused his first bank twice before old Sultan decorously changed feet on it and dropped down into the next field with tranquil precision. The white horse scrambled over it on his stomach, but landed safely, despite the fact that his rider clasped him round the neck during the process; the black mare and the chestnut shouldered one another over at the hole the white horse had left, and the whole party went away in a bunch and jumped the ensuing hurdle without disaster. Flurry continued to ride at the same steady hunting pace, accompanied respectfully by the white horse and by Jerry Canty on the black mare. Sheehy's colt had clearly the legs of the party, and did some showy galloping between the jumps, but as he refused to face the banks without a lead, the end of the first round found the field still a social party personally conducted by Mr. Knox.

'That's a dam nice horse,' said one of my hangers-on, looking approvingly at Sultan as he passed us at the beginning of the second round, making a good deal of noise but apparently going at his ease; 'you might depind your life on him, and he have the crabbedest jock in the globe of Ireland on him this minute.'

'Canty's mare's very sour,' said another; 'look at her now, baulking the bank! she's as cross as a bag of weasels.'

'Begob, I wouldn't say but she's a little sign lame,' resumed the first; 'she was going light on one leg on the road a while ago.'

'I tell you what it is,' said Miss Sally, very seriously, in my ear, 'that chestnut of Sheehy's is settling down. I'm afraid he'll gallop away from Sultan at the finish, and the wall won't stop him. Flurry can't get another inch out of Sultan. He's riding him well,' she ended in a critical voice, which yet was not quite like her own. Perhaps I should not have noticed it but for the fact that the hand that held my arm was trembling. As for me, I thought of Lady Knox, and trembled too.

There now remained but one bank, the trampled remnant of the furze hurdle, and the stone wall. The pace was beginning to improve, and the other horses drew away from Sultan; they charged the bank at full gallop, the black mare and the chestnut flying it perilously, with a windmill flourish of legs and arms from their riders, the white horse racing up to it with a gallantry that deserted him at the critical moment, with the result that his rider turned a somersault over his head and landed, amidst the roars of the onlookers, sitting on the fence facing his horse's nose. With creditable presence of mind he remained on the bank, towed the horse over, scrambled on to his back again and started afresh. Sultan, thirty yards to the bad, pounded doggedly on, and Flurry's cane and heels remained idle; the old horse, obviously blown, slowed cautiously coming in at the jump. Sally's grip tightened on my arm, and the crowd yelled as Sultan, answering to a hint from the spurs and a touch at his mouth, heaved himself on to the bank. Nothing but sheer riding on Flurry's part got him safe off it, and saved him from the consequences of a bad peck on landing; none the less, he pulled himself together and went away down the hill for the stone wall as stoutly as ever. The high road skirted the last two fields, and there was a gate in the roadside fence beside the place where the stone wall met it at right angles. I had noticed this gate, because during the first round Slipper had been sitting on it, demonstrating with his usual fervour. Sheehy's colt was leading, with his nose in the air, his rider's hands going like a circular saw, and his temper, as a bystander remarked, 'up on end'; the black mare, half mad from spurring, was going hard at his heels, completely out of hand; the white horse was steering steadily for the wrong side of the flag, and Flurry, by dint of cutting corners and of saving every yard of ground, was close enough to keep his antagonists' heads over their shoulders, while their right arms rose and fell in unceasing flagellation.

'There 'll be a smash when they come to the wall! If one falls they 'll all go!' panted Sally. 'Oh!—— Now, Flurry! Flurry!——'

What had happened was that the chestnut colt had suddenly perceived that the gate at right angles to the wall was standing wide open, and, swinging away from the jump, he had bolted headlong out on to the road, and along it at top speed for his home. After him fled Canty's black mare, and with her, carried away by the spirit of stampede, went the white horse.

Flurry stood up in his stirrups and gave a view-holloa as he cantered down to the wall. Sultan came at it with the send of the hill behind him, and jumped it with a skill that intensified, if that were possible, the volume of laughter and yells around us. By the time the black mare and the white horse had returned and ignominiously bundled over the wall to finish as best they might, Flurry was leading Sultan towards us.

'That blackguard, Slipper!' he said, grinning; 'every one 'll say I told him to open the gate! But look here, I 'm afraid we 're in for trouble. Sultan 's given himself a bad overreach; you could never drive him home to-night. And I 've just seen Norris lying blind drunk under a wall!'

Now Norris was Lady Knox's coachman. We stood aghast at this 'horror on horror's head'; the blood trickled down Sultan's heel, and the lather lay in flecks on his dripping, heaving sides, in irrefutable witness to the iniquity of Lady Knox's only daughter. Then Flurry said:

'Thank the Lord, here 's the rain!'

At the moment I admit that I failed to see any cause for gratitude in this occurrence, but later on I appreciated Flurry's grasp of circumstances.

That appreciation was, I think, at its highest development about half an hour afterwards, when I, an unwilling conspirator (a part with which my acquaintance with Mr. Knox had rendered me but too familiar), unfurled Mrs. Cadogan's umbrella over Lady Knox's head, and hurried her through the rain from the tent to the bus, keeping it and my own person well between her and the horses. I got her in, with the rest of the bedraggled and exhausted party, and slammed the door.

'Remember, Major Yeates,' she said through the window, 'you are the *only* person here in whom I have any confidence. I don't wish *any* one else to touch the reins!' this with a glance towards Flurry, who was standing near.

'I'm afraid I'm only a moderate whip,' I said.

'My dear man,' replied Lady Knox testily, 'those horses could drive themselves!'

I slunk round to the front of the bus. Two horses, carefully rugged, were in it, with the inevitable Slipper at their heads.

'Slipper's going with you,' whispered Flurry, stepping up to me; 'she won't have me at any price. He'll throw the rugs over them when you get to the house, and if you hold the umbrella well over her she'll never see. I'll manage to get Sultan over somehow, when Norris is sober. That will be all right.'

I climbed to the box without answering, my soul being bitter within me, as is the soul of a man who has been persuaded by womankind against his judgment.

'Never again!' I said to myself, picking up the reins; 'let her marry him or Bernard Shute, or both of them if she likes, but I won't be roped into this kind of business again!'

Slipper drew the rugs from the horses, revealing on the near side Lady Knox's majestic carriage horse, and on the off, a thickset brown mare of about fifteen hands.

'What brute is this?' said I to Slipper, as he swarmed up beside me.

'I don't rightly know where Misther Flurry got her,' said Slipper, with one of his hiccoughing crows of laughter; 'give her the whip, major, and'—here he broke into song:

'Howld to the shteel,
Honamaundhiaoul; she'll run off like an eel!'

'If you don't shut your mouth,' said I, with pent-up ferocity, 'I'll chuck you off the 'bus.'

Slipper was but slightly drunk, and, taking this delicate rebuke in good part, he relapsed into silence.

Wherever the brown mare came from, I can certify that it was not out of double harness. Though humble and anxious to oblige, she pulled away from the pole as if it were red hot, and at critical moments had a tendency to sit down. However, we squeezed without misadventure among the donkey carts and between the groups of people, and bumped at length in safety out on to the high road.

Here I thought it no harm to take Slipper's advice, and I applied the whip to the brown mare, who seemed inclined to turn round. She immediately fell into an uncertain canter that no effort of mine could frustrate; I could only hope that Miss Sally would foster conversation inside the 'bus and create a distraction; but judging from my last view of the party, and of Lady Knox in particular, I thought she was not likely to be successful. Fortunately the rain was heavy and thick, and a rising west wind gave every promise of its continuance. I had little doubt but that I should catch cold, but I took it to my bosom with gratitude as I reflected how it was drumming on the roof of the 'bus and blurring the windows.

We had reached the foot of a hill, about a quarter of a mile from the race-course; the Castle Knox horse addressed himself to it with dignified determination, but the mare showed a sudden and alarming tendency to jib.

'Belt her, major!' vociferated Slipper, as she hung back from the pole chain, with the collar half-way up her ewe neck, 'and give it to the horse, too! He'll dhrag her!'

I was in the act of 'belting,' when a squealing whinny struck upon my ear, accompanied by a light pattering gallop on the road behind us; there was an answering roar from the brown mare, a roar, as I realized with a sudden drop of the heart, of outraged maternal feeling, and in another instant a pale-yellow foal sprinted up beside us, with shrill whickerings of joy. Had there at this moment been a bog-hole handy, I should have turned the 'bus into it without hesitation; as there was no accommodation of the kind, I laid the whip severely into everything I could reach, including the foal. The result was that we topped the hill at a gallop, three abreast, like a Russian troika; it was like my usual luck that at this identical moment we should meet the police patrol, who saluted respectfully.

'That the divil may blisther Michael Moloney!' ejaculated Slipper, holding on to the rail; 'didn't I give him the foaleen and a halther on him to keep him! I'll howld you a pint 'twas the wife let him go, for she being vexed about the licence! Sure that one's a March foal, an' he'd run from here to Cork!'

There was no sign from my inside passengers, and I held on at a round pace, the mother and child galloping absurdly, the carriage horse pulling hard, but behaving like a gentleman. I wildly revolved plans of how I would make Slipper turn the foal in at the first gate we came to, of what I should say to Lady Knox supposing the worst happened and the foal accompanied us to her hall door, and of how I would have Flurry's blood at the earliest possible opportunity, and here the fateful sound of galloping behind us was again heard.

'It's impossible!' I said to myself; 'she can't have twins!'

The galloping came nearer, and Slipper looked back.

'Murdher alive!' he said in a stage whisper; 'Tom Sheehy's afther us on the butcher's pony!'

'What's that to me?' I said, dragging my team aside to let him pass; 'I suppose he's drunk, like every one else!'

Then the voice of Tom Sheehy made itself heard.

'Shtop! Shtop thief!' he was bawling; 'give up my mare! How will I get me porther home!'

That was the closest shave I have ever had, and nothing could have saved the position but the torrential nature of the rain and the fact that Lady Knox had on a new bonnet. I explained to her at the door of the bus that Sheehy was drunk (which was the one unassailable feature of the case), and had come after his foal, which, with the fatuity of its kind, had escaped from a field and followed us. I did not mention to Lady Knox that when Mr. Sheehy retreated, apologetically, dragging the foal after him in a halter belonging to one of her own carriage horses, he had a sovereign of mine in his pocket, and during the narration I avoided Miss Sally's eye as carefully as she avoided mine.

The only comments on the day's events that are worthy of record were that Philippa said to me that she had not been able to understand what the curious taste in the tea had been till Sally told her it was turf-smoke, and that Mrs. Cadogan said to Philippa that night that 'the Major was that dhrinched that if he had a shirt between his skin and himself he could have wrung it,' and that Lady Knox said to a mutual friend that though Major Yeates had been extremely kind and obliging he was an uncommonly bad whip.

XII

'OH LOVE! OH FIRE!'

It was on one of the hottest days of a hot August that I walked over to Tory Lodge to inform Mr. Flurry Knox, M.F.H., that the limits of human endurance had been reached, and that either Venus and her family, or I and mine, must quit Shreelane. In a moment of impulse I had accepted her and her numerous progeny as guests in my stable-yard, since when Mrs. Cadogan had given warning once or twice a week, and Maria, lawful autocrat of the ashpit, had had—I quote the kitchenmaid—'tin battles for every male she 'd ate.'

The walk over the hills was not of a nature to lower the temperature, moral or otherwise. The grassy path was as slippery as glass, the rocks radiated heat, the bracken radiated horse-flies. There was no need to nurse my wrath to keep it warm.

I found Flurry seated in the kennel-yard in a long and un-clean white linen coat, engaged in clipping hieroglyphics on the ears of a young outgoing draft, an occupation in itself un-favourable to argument. The young draft had already mono-polized all possible forms of remonstrance, from snarling in the obscurity behind the meal sack in the boiler-house, to hysterical yelling as they were dragged forth by the tail; but through these alarms and excursions I denounced Venus and all her works, from slaughtered Wyandottes to broken dishes. Even as I did so I was conscious of something chastened in Mr. Knox's demeanour, some touch of remoteness and melancholy with which I was quite unfamiliar; my indictment weakened and my grievances became trivial when laid before this grave and almost religiously gentle young man.

'I 'm sorry you and Mrs. Yeates should be vexed by her. Send her back when you like. I 'll keep her. Maybe it 'll not be for so long after all.'

When pressed to expound this dark saying Flurry smiled wanly and snipped a second line in the hair of the puppy that was pinned between his legs. I was almost relieved when a hard try to bite on the part of the puppy imparted to Flurry's language a transient warmth; but the reaction was only temporary.

'It 'd be as good for me to make a present of this lot to old
Welby as to take the price he 's offering me,' he went on, as he
got up and took off his highly-scented kennel-coat, 'but I
couldn't be bothered fighting him. Come on in and have
something. I drink tea myself at this hour.'

If he had said toast and water it would have seemed no more
than was suitable to such a frame of mind. As I followed him
to the house I thought that when the day came that Flurry
Knox could not be bothered with fighting old Welby things
were becoming serious, but I kept this opinion to myself and
merely offered an admiring comment on the roses that were
blooming on the front of the house.

'I put up every stick of that trellis myself with my own hands,'
said Flurry, still gloomily; 'the roses were trailing all over the place
for the want of it. Would you like to have a look at the garden
while they're getting tea? I settled it up a bit since you saw it last.'

I acceded to this almost alarmingly ladylike suggestion,
marvelling greatly.

Flurry certainly was a changed man, and his garden was a
changed garden. It was a very old garden, with unexpected
arbours madly overgrown with flowering climbers, and a flight
of grey steps leading to a terrace, where a moss-grown sundial
and ancient herbaceous plants strove with nettles and briars;
but I chiefly remembered it as a place where washing was wont
to hang on black-currant bushes, and the kennel terrier matured
his bones and hunted chickens. There was now rabbit wire on
the gate, the walks were cleaned, the beds weeded. There was
even a bed of mignonette, a row of sweet pea, and a blazing
party of sunflowers, and Michael, once second in command in
many a filibustering expedition, was now on his knees, ingloriously tying carnations to little pieces of cane.

We walked up the steps to the terrace. Down below us the
rich and southern blue of the sea filled the gaps between scattered
fir-trees; the hillside above was purple with heather; a bay mare
and her foal were moving lazily through the bracken, with the
sun glistening on it and them. I looked back at the house,
nestling in the hollow of the hill, I smelled the smell of the
mignonette in the air, I regarded Michael's labouring back
among the carnations, and without any connection of ideas I
seemed to see Miss Sally Knox, with her golden-red hair and
slight figure, standing on the terrace beside her kinsman.

'Michael! Do ye know where 's Misther Flurry?' squalled a voice from the garden gate, the untrammelled voice of the female domestic at large among her fellows. 'The tay 's wet, and there 's a man over with a message from Aussolas. He was tellin' me the owld hairo beyant is givin' out invitations——'

A stricken silence fell, induced, no doubt, by hasty danger signals from Michael.

'Who 's "the old hero beyant?"' I asked, as we turned toward the house.

'My grandmother,' said Flurry, permitting himself a smile that had about as much sociability in it as skim milk; 'she 's giving a tenants' dance at Aussolas. She gave one about five years ago, and I declare you might as well get the influenza into the country, or a mission at the chapel. There won't be a servant in the place will be able to answer their name for a week after it, what with toothache and headache, and blathering in the kitchen!'

We had tea in the drawing-room, a solemnity which I could not but be aware was due to the presence of a new carpet, a new wall-paper, and a new piano. Flurry made no comment on these things, but something told me that I was expected to do so, and I did.

'I'd sell you the lot to-morrow for half what I gave for them,' said my host, eyeing them with morose respect as he poured out his third cup of tea.

I have all my life been handicapped by not having the courage of my curiosity. Those who have the nerve to ask direct questions on matters that do not concern them seldom fail to extract direct answers, but in my lack of this enviable gift I went home in the dark as to what had befallen my landlord, and fully aware of how my wife would despise me for my shortcomings. Philippa always says that she never asks questions, but she seems none the less to get a lot of answers.

On my own avenue I met Miss Sally Knox riding away from the house on her white cob; she had found no one at home, and she would not turn back with me, but she did not seem to be in any hurry to ride away. I told her that I had just been over to see her relative, Mr. Knox, who had informed me that he meant to give up the hounds, a fact in which she seemed only conventionally interested. She looked pale, and her eyelids were slightly pink; I checked myself on the verge of asking her if

she had hay fever, and inquired instead if she had heard of
the tenants' dance at Aussolas. She did not answer at first,
but rubbed her cane up and down the cob's clipped tooth-brush
of a mane. Then she said:

'Major Yeates—look here—there's a most awful row at
home!'

I expressed incoherent regret, and wished to my heart that
Philippa had been there to cope with the situation.

'It began when mamma found out about Flurry's racing
Sultan, and then came our dance——'.

Miss Sally stopped; I nodded, remembering certain episodes
of Lady Knox's dance.

'And—mamma says—she says——'

I waited respectfully to hear what mamma had said; the cob
fidgeted under the attentions of the horseflies, and nearly trod
on my toe.

'Well, the end of it is,' she said with a gulp, 'she said such
things to Flurry that he can't come near the house again, and
I'm to go over to England to Aunt Dora, next week. Will you
tell Philippa I came to say good-bye to her? I don't think I
can get over here again.'

Miss Sally was a sufficiently old friend of mine for me to take
her hand and press it in a fatherly manner, but for the life of
me I could not think of anything to say, unless I expressed my
sympathy with her mother's point of view about detrimentals,
which was obviously not the thing to do.

Philippa accorded to my news the rare tribute of speechless
attention, and then was despicable enough to say that she had
foreseen the whole affair from the beginning.

'From the day that she refused him in the ice-house, I suppose,' said I sarcastically.

'That *was* the beginning,' replied Philippa.

'Well,' I went on judicially, 'whenever it began, it was high
time for it to end. She can do a good deal better than Flurry.'

Philippa became rather red in the face.

'I call that a thoroughly commonplace thing to say,' she said.
'I dare say he has not many ideas beyond horses, but no more
has she, and he really does come and borrow books from
me——'

'*Whitaker's Almanack*,' I murmured.

'Well, I don't care, I like him very much, and I know what

you're going to say, and you're wrong, and I'll tell you why——'

Here Mrs. Cadogan came into the room, her cap at rather more than its usual warlike angle over her scarlet forehead, and in her hand a kitchen plate, on which a note was ceremoniously laid forth.

'But this is for you, Mrs. Cadogan,' said Philippa, as she looked at it.

'Ma'am,' returned Mrs. Cadogan with immense dignity, 'I have no learning, and from what the young man's afther telling me that brought it from Aussolas, I'd sooner yerself read it for me than thim gerrls.'

My wife opened the envelope, and drew forth a gilt-edged sheet of pink paper.

'Miss Margaret Nolan presents her compliments to Mrs. Cadogan,' she read, 'and I have the pleasure of telling you that the servants of Aussolas is inviting you and Mr. Peter Cadogan, Miss Mulrooney, and Miss Gallagher'—Philippa's voice quavered perilously—'to a dance on next Wednesday. Dancing to begin at seven o'clock, and to go on till five.—Yours affectionately, MAGGIE NOLAN.'

'How affectionate she is!' snorted Mrs. Cadogan; 'them's Dublin manners, I dare say!'

'P.S.,' continued Philippa; 'steward, Mr. Denis O'Loughlin; stewardess, Mrs. Mahony.'

'Thoughtful provision,' I remarked; 'I suppose Mrs. Mahony's duties will begin after supper.'

'Well, Mrs. Cadogan,' said Philippa, quelling me with a glance, 'I suppose you'd all like to go?'

'As for dancin',' said Mrs. Cadogan, with her eyes fixed on a level with the curtain-pole, 'I thank God I'm a widow, and the only dancin' I'll do is to dance to my grave.'

'Well, perhaps Julia, and Annie, and Peter——' suggested Philippa, considerably overawed.

'I'm not one of them that holds with loud mockery and harangues,' continued Mrs. Cadogan, 'but if I had any wish for dhrawing down talk I could tell you, ma'am, that the like o' them has their share of dances without going to Aussolas! Wasn't it only last Sunday week I wint follyin' the turkey that's layin' out in the plantation, and the whole o' thim hysted their sails and back with them to their lovers at the gate-house, and the kitchenmaid having a Jew-harp to be playing for them!'

'That was very wrong,' said the truckling Philippa. 'I hope you spoke to the kitchenmaid about it.'

'Is it spake to thim?' rejoined Mrs. Cadogan. 'No, but what I done was to dhrag the kitchenmaid round the passages by the hair o' the head!'

'Well, after that, I think you might let her go to Aussolas,' said I venturously.

The end of it was that every one in and about the house went to Aussolas on the following Wednesday, including Mrs. Cadogan. Philippa had gone over to stay at the Shutes', ostensibly to arrange about a jumble sale, the real object being (as a matter of history) to inspect the Scotch young lady before whom Bernard Shute had dumped his affections in his customary manner. Being alone, with every prospect of a bad dinner, I accepted with gratitude an invitation to dine and sleep at Aussolas and see the dance; it is only on very special occasions that I have the heart to remind Philippa that she had neither part nor lot in what occurred—it is too serious a matter for trivial gloryings.

Mrs. Knox had asked me to dine at six o'clock, which meant that I arrived, in blazing sunlight and evening clothes, punctually at that hour, and that at seven o'clock I was still sitting in the library, reading heavily-bound classics, while my hostess held loud conversations down staircases with Denis O'Loughlin, the red-bearded Robinson Crusoe who combined in himself the offices of coachman, butler, and, to the best of my belief, valet to the lady of the house. The door opened at last, and Denis, looking as furtive as his prototype after he had sighted the footprint, put in his head and beckoned to me.

'The misthress says will ye go to dinner without her,' he said very confidentially; 'sure she's greatly vexed ye should be waitin' on her. 'Twas the kitchen chimney cot fire, and faith she's afther giving Biddy Mahony the sack, on the head of it! Though, indeed, 'tis little we'd regard a chimney on fire here any other day.'

Mrs. Knox's woolly dog was the sole occupant of the dining-room when I entered it; he was sitting on his mistress's chair, with all the air of outrage peculiar to a small and self-important dog when routine has been interfered with. It was difficult to discover what had caused the delay, the meal, not excepting the soup, being a cold collation; it was heavily flavoured with soot, and was hurled on to the table by Crusoe in spasmodic bursts, contemporaraneous, no doubt, with Biddy Mahony's fits of hysterics in the kitchen. Its most memorable feature was a noble lake trout, which appeared in two jagged pieces, a matter lightly alluded to by Denis as the result of 'a little argument' between himself and Biddy as to the dish on which it was to be served. Further conversation elicited the interesting fact that the combatants had pulled the trout in two before the matter was settled. A brief glance at my attendant's hands decided me to let the woolly dog justify his existence by consuming my portion for me, when Crusoe left the room.

Old Mrs. Knox remained invisible till the end of dinner, when she appeared in the purple velvet bonnet that she was reputed to have worn since the famine, and a dun-coloured woollen shawl fastened by a splendid diamond brooch, that flashed rainbow fire against the last shafts of sunset. There was a fire in the old lady's eye, too, the light that I had sometimes seen in Flurry's in moments of crisis.

'I have no apologies to offer that are worth hearing,' she said, 'but I have come to drink a glass of port wine with you, if you will so far honour me, and then we must go out and see the ball. My grandson is late, as usual.'

She crumbled a biscuit with a brown and preoccupied hand; her claw-like fingers carried a crowded sparkle of diamonds upwards as she raised her glass to her lips.

The twilight was falling when we left the room and made our way downstairs. I followed the little figure in the purple bonnet through dark regions of passages and doorways, where strange lumber lay about; there was a rusty suit of armour, an upturned punt, mouldering pictures, and finally, by a door that opened into the yard, a lady's bicycle, white with the dust of travel. I supposed this latter to have been imported from Dublin by the fashionable Miss Maggie Nolan, but on the other hand, it was well within the bounds of possibility that it belonged to old Mrs. Knox. The coach-house at Aussolas was on a par with the rest of the establishment, being vast, dilapidated, and of unknown age. Its three double doors were wide open, and the guests overflowed through them into the cobble-stoned yard; above their heads the tin reflectors of paraffin lamps glared at us from among the Christmas decorations of holly and ivy that festooned the walls. The voices of a fiddle and a concertina, combined, were uttering a polka with shrill and hideous fluency, to which the scraping and stamping of hob-nailed boots made a ponderous bass accompaniment.

Mrs. Knox's donkey-chair had been placed in a commanding position at the top of the room, and she made her way slowly to it, shaking hands with all varieties of tenants and saying right things without showing any symptom of that flustered boredom that I have myself exhibited when I went round the men's messes on Christmas Day. She took her seat in the donkey-chair, with the white dog in her lap, and looked with her hawk's eyes round the array of faces that hemmed in the space where the dancers were solemnly bobbing and hopping.

'Will you tell me who that tomfool is, Denis?' she said, pointing to a young lady in a ball dress who was circling in conscious magnificence and somewhat painful incongruity in the arms of Mr. Peter Cadogan.

'That's the lady's-maid from Castle Knox, yer honour, ma'am,' replied Denis, with something remarkably like a wink at Mrs. Knox.

'When did the Castle Knox servants come?' asked the old lady, very sharply.

'The same time yer honour left the table, and—— Pillilew! What's this?'

There was a clatter of galloping hoofs in the courtyard, as of a troop of cavalry; and out of the heart of it Flurry's voice shouting to Denis to drive out the colts and shut the gates before they had the people killed. I noticed that the colour had risen to Mrs. Knox's face, and I put it down to anxiety about her young horses. I may admit that when I heard Flurry's voice, and saw him collaring his grandmother's guests and pushing them out of the way as he came into the coach-house, I rather feared that he was in the condition so often defined to me at Petty Sessions as 'not dhrunk, but having dhrink taken.' His face was white, his eyes glittered, there was a general air of exaltation about him that suggested the solace of the pangs of love according to the most ancient convention.

'Hullo!' he said, swaggering up to the orchestra, 'what's this humbugging thing they're playing? A polka, is it? Drop that, John Casey, and play a jig.'

John Casey ceased abjectly.

'What'll I play, Masther Flurry?'

'What the devil do I care? Here, Yeates, put a name on it! You 're a sort of musicianer-yourself!'

I know the names of three or four Irish jigs; but on this occasion my memory clung exclusively to one, I suppose because it was the one I felt to be peculiarly inappropriate.

'Oh, well, *Haste to the Wedding*,' I said, looking away.

Flurry gave a shout of laughter.

'That 's it!' he exclaimed. 'Play it up, John! Give us *Haste to the Wedding*. That 's Major Yeates's fancy!'

Decidedly Flurry was drunk.

'What 's wrong with you all that you aren't dancing?' he continued, striding up the middle of the room. 'Maybe you don't know how. Here, I 'll soon get one that 'll show you!'

He advanced upon his grandmother, snatched her out of the donkey-chair, and, amid roars of applause, led her out, while the fiddle squealed its way through the inimitable twists of the tune, and the concertina surged and panted after it. Whatever Mrs. Knox may have thought of her grandson's behaviour, she was evidently going to make the best of it. She took her station opposite to him, in the purple bonnet, the dun-coloured shawl, and the diamonds, she picked up her skirt at each side, affording a view of narrow feet in elastic-sided cloth boots, and for three repeats of the tune she stood up to her grandson, and footed it on the coach-house floor. What the cloth boots did I could not exactly follow; they were, as well as I could see, extremely scientific, while there was hardly so much as a nod from the plumes of the bonnet. Flurry was also scientific, but his dancing did not alter my opinion that he was drunk; in fact, I thought he was making rather an exhibition of himself. They say that that jig was twenty-pounds in Mrs. Knox's pocket at the next rent day; but though this statement is open to doubt, I believe that if she and Flurry had taken the hat round there and then she would have got in the best part of her arrears.

After this the company settled down to business. The dances lasted a sweltering half-hour, old women and young dancing with equal and tireless zest. At the end of each the gentlemen abandoned their partners without ceremony or comment, and went out to smoke, while the ladies retired to the laundry, where families of teapots stewed on the long bars of the fire, and Mrs. Mahony cut up mighty 'barm-bracks,' and the tea-drinking was illimitable.

At ten o'clock Mrs. Knox withdrew from the revel; she said that she was tired, but I have seldom seen any one look more wide awake. I thought that I might unobtrusively follow her example, but I was intercepted by Flurry.

'Yeates,' he said seriously, 'I 'll take it as a kindness if you 'll see this thing out with me. We must keep them pretty sober, and get them out of this by daylight. I—I have to get home early.'

I at once took back my opinion that Flurry was drunk; I almost wished he had been, as I could then have deserted him without a pang. As it was, I addressed myself heavily to the night's enjoyment. Wan with heat, but conscientiously cheerful, I danced with Miss Maggie Nolan, with the Castle Knox lady's-maid, with my own kitchenmaid, who fell into wild giggles of terror whenever I spoke to her, with Mrs. Cadogan, who had apparently postponed the interesting feat of dancing to her grave, and did what she could to dance me into mine. I am bound to admit that though an ex-soldier and a major, and therefore equipped with a ready-made character for gallantry, Mrs. Cadogan was the only one of my partners with whom I conversed with any comfort.

At intervals I smoked cigarettes in the yard, seated on the old mounting-block by the gate, and overheard much conversation about the price of pigs in Skebawn; at intervals I plunged again into the coach-house, and led forth a perspiring wallflower into the scrimmage of a polka, or shuffled meaninglessly opposite to her in the long double line of dancers who were engaged with serious faces in executing a jig or a reel, I neither knew nor cared which. Flurry remained as undefeated as ever; I could only suppose it was his method of showing that his broken heart had mended. •

'It 's time to be, making the punch, Masther Flurry,' said Denis, as the harness-room clock struck twelve; 'sure the night 's warm, and the men 's all gaping for it, the craytures!'

'What 'll we make it in?' said Flurry, as we followed him into the laundry.

'The boiler, to be sure,' said Crusoe, taking up a stone of sugar, and preparing to shoot it into the laundry copper.

'Stop, you fool, it 's full of cockroaches!' shouted Flurry, amid sympathetic squalls from the throng of countrywomen. 'Go get a bath!'

'Sure yerself knows there's but one bath in it,' retorted Denis, 'and that's within in the Major's room. Faith, the tinker got his own share yesterday with the same bath, shtriving to quinch the holes, and they as thick in it as the stars in the sky, and 'tis weeping still, afther all he done!'

'Well, then, here goes for the cockroaches!' said Flurry. 'What doesn't sicken will fatten! Give me the kettle, and come on, you Kitty Collins, and be skimming them off!'

There were no complaints of the punch when the brew was completed, and the dance thundered on with a heavier stamping and a louder hilarity than before. The night wore on; I squeezed through the unyielding pack of frieze coats and shawls in the doorway, and with feet that momently swelled in my pumps I limped over the cobble-stones to smoke my eighth cigarette on the mounting-block. It was a dark, hot night. The old castle loomed above me in piled-up roofs and gables, and high up in it somewhere a window sent a shaft of light into the sleeping leaves of a walnut-tree that overhung the gateway. At the bars of the gate two young horses peered in at the medley of noise and people; away in an outhouse a cock crew hoarsely. The gaiety in the coach-house increased momently, till, amid shrieks and bursts of laughter, Miss Maggie Nolan fled coquettishly from it with a long yell, like a train coming out of a tunnel, pursued by the fascinating Peter Cadogan brandishing a twig of mountain ash, in imitation of mistletoe. The young horses stampeded in horror, and immediately a voice proceeded from the lighted window above, Mrs. Knox's voice, demanding what the noise was, and announcing that if she heard any more of it she would have the place cleared.

An awful silence fell, to which the young horses' fleeing hoofs lent the final touch of consternation. Then I heard the irrepressible Maggie Nolan say: 'Oh God! Merry-come-sad!' which I take to be a reflection on the mutability of all earthly happiness.

Mrs. Knox remained for a moment at the window, and it struck me as remarkable that at 2.30 a.m. she should still have on her bonnet. I thought I heard her speak to someone in the room, and there followed a laugh, a laugh that was not a servant's, and was puzzlingly familiar. I gave it up, and presently dropped into a cheerless doze.

With the dawn there came a period when even Flurry showed

signs of failing. He came and sat down beside me with a yawn; it struck me that there was more impatience and nervousness than fatigue in the yawn.

'I think I 'll turn them all out of this after the next dance is over,' he said; 'I 've a lot to do, and I can't stay here.'

I grunted in drowsy approval. It must have been a few minutes later that I felt Flurry grip my shoulder.

'Yeates!' he said, 'look up at the roof. Do you see anything up there by the kitchen chimney?'

He was pointing at a heavy stack of chimneys in a tower that stood up against the grey and pink of the morning sky. At the angle where one of them joined the roof smoke was oozing busily out, and, as I stared, a little wisp of flame stole through.

The next thing that I distinctly remember is being in the van of a rush through the kitchen passages, every one shouting 'Water! Water!' and not knowing where to find it, then up several flights of the narrowest and darkest stairs it has ever been my fate to ascend, with a bucket of water that I snatched from a woman, spilling as I ran. At the top of the stairs came a ladder leading to a trap-door, and up in the dark loft above was the roar and the wavering glare of flames.

'My God! That's sthrong fire!' shouted Denis, tumbling down the ladder with a brace of empty buckets; 'we 'll never save it! The lake won't quinch it!'

The flames were squirting out through the bricks of the chimney, through the timbers, through the slates; it was barely possible to get through the trap-door, and the booming and crackling strengthened every instant.

'A chain to the lake!' gasped Flurry, coughing in the stifling heat as he slashed the water at the blazing rafters; 'the well 's no good! Go on, Yeates!'

The organizing of a double chain out of the mob that thronged and shouted and jammed in the passages and yard was no mean feat of generalship; but it got done somehow. Mrs. Cadogan and Biddy Mahony rose magnificently to the occasion, cursing, thumping, shoving; and stable buckets, coal buckets, milk pails, and kettles were unearthed and sent swinging down the grass slope to the lake that lay in glittering unconcern in the morning sunshine. Men, women, and children worked in a way that only Irish people can work on an emergency. All their cleverness, all their good-heartedness, and all their love of a ruction came to the front; the screaming and the exhortations were incessant, but so were also the buckets that flew from hand to hand up to the loft. I hardly know how long we were at it, but there came a time when I looked up from the yard and saw that the billows of reddened smoke from the top of the tower were dying down, and I bethought me of old Mrs. Knox.

I found her at the door of her room, engaged in tying up a bundle of old clothes in a sheet; she looked as white as a corpse, but she was not in any way quelled by the situation.

'I'd be obliged to you all the same, Major Yeates, to throw this over the balusters,' she said, as I advanced with the news that the fire had been got under. ''Pon my honour, I don't know when I've been as vexed as I've been this night, what with one thing and another! 'Tis a monstrous thing to use a guest as we've used you, but what could we do? I threw all the silver out of the dining-room window myself, and the poor peahen that had her nest there was hurt by an entrée dish, and half her eggs were——'

There was a curious sound not unlike a titter in Mrs. Knox's room.

"However, we can't make omelettes without breaking eggs—as they say—' she went on rather hurriedly; 'I declare I don't know what I'm saying! My old head is confused——'

Here Mrs. Knox went abruptly into her room and shut the door. Obviously there was nothing further to do for my hostess, and I fought my way up the dripping back-staircase to the loft. The flames had ceased, the supply of buckets had been stopped, and Flurry, standing on a ponderous cross-beam, was poking his head and shoulders out into the sunlight through the hole that had been burned in the roof. Denis and others were pouring water over charred beams, the atmosphere was still stifling, everything was black, everything dripped with inky water. Flurry descended from his beam and stretched himself, looking like a drowned chimney-sweep.

'We've made a night of it, Yeates, haven't we?' he said, 'but we've bested it anyhow. We were done for only for you!' There was more emotion about him than the occasion seemed to warrant, and his eyes had a Christy Minstrel brightness, not wholly to be attributed to the dirt of his face. 'What's the time?—I must get home.'

The time, incredible as it seemed, was half-past six. I could almost have sworn that Flurry changed colour when I said so. 'I must be off,' he said; 'I had no idea it was so late.' 'Why, what's the hurry?' I asked. He stared at me, laughed foolishly, and fell to giving directions to Denis. Five minutes afterwards he drove out of the yard and away at a canter down the long stretch of avenue that skirted the lake, with a troop of young horses flying on either hand. He whirled his whip round his head and shouted at them, and was lost to sight in a clump of trees. It is a vision of him that remains with me, and it always carries with it the bitter smell of wet charred wood.

Reaction had begun to set in among the volunteers. The chain took to sitting in the kitchen, cups of tea began mysteriously to circulate, and personal narratives of the fire were already foreshadowing the amazing legends that have since gathered round the night's adventure. I left to Denis the task of clearing the house, and went up to change my wet clothes, with a feeling that I had not been to bed for a year. The ghost of a waiter who had drowned himself in a bog-hole would have presented a cheerier aspect than I, as I surveyed myself in the prehistoric mirror in my room, with the sunshine falling on my unshorn face and begrimed shirt-front.

I made my toilet at considerable length, and, it being now nearly eight o'clock, went downstairs to look for something to eat. I had left the house humming with people; I found it silent as Pompeii. The sheeted bundles containing Mrs. Knox's wardrobe were lying about the hall; a couple of ancestors who in the first alarm had been dragged from the walls were leaning drunkenly against the bundles; last night's dessert was still on the dining-room table. I went out on to the hall-door steps, and saw the entrée dishes in a glittering heap in a nasturtium bed, and realized that there was no breakfast for me this side of lunch at Shreelane.

There was a sound of wheels on the avenue, and a brougham came into view, driving fast up the long open stretch by the lake. It was the Castle Knox brougham, driven by Norris, whom I had seen last drunk at the athletic sports, and as it drew up at the door I saw Lady Knox inside. 'It's all right, the fire's out,' I said, advancing genially and full of reassurance.

'What fire?' said Lady Knox, regarding me with an iron countenance.

I explained.

'Well, as the house isn't burned down,' said Lady Knox, cutting short my details, 'perhaps you would kindly find out if I could see Mrs. Knox.'

Lady Knox's face was many shades redder than usual. I began to understand that something awful had happened, or would happen, and I wished myself safe at Shreelane, with the bedclothes over my head.

'If 'tis for the misthress you 're looking, me lady,' said Denis's voice behind me, in tones of the utmost respect, 'she went out to the kitchen garden a while ago to get a blasht o' the fresh air afther the night. Maybe your ladyship would sit inside in the library till I call her?'

Lady Knox eyed Crusoe suspiciously.

'Thank you, I 'll fetch her myself,' she said.

'Oh, sure, that 's too throuble——' began Denis.

'Stay where you are!' said Lady Knox, in a voice like the slam of a door.

'Bedad, I 'm best plased she went,' whispered Denis, as Lady Knox set forth alone down the shrubbery walk.

'But *is* Mrs. Knox in the garden?' said I.

'The Lord preserve your innocence, sir!' replied Denis, with seeming irrelevance.

At this moment I became aware of the incredible fact that Sally Knox was silently descending the stairs; she stopped short as she got into the hall, and looked almost wildly at me and Denis. Was I looking at her wraith? There was again a sound of wheels on the gravel; she went to the hall door, outside which was now drawn up Mrs. Knox's donkey-carriage, as well as Lady Knox's brougham, and, as if overcome by this imposing spectacle, she turned back and put her hands over her face.

'She 's gone round to the garden, asthore,' said Denis in a hoarse whisper; 'go in the donkey-carriage. 'Twill be all right!' He seized her by the arm, pushed her down the steps and into the little carriage, pulled up the hood over her to its furthest stretch, snatched the whip out of the hand of the broadly-grinning Norris, and with terrific objurgations lashed the donkey into a gallop. The donkey-boy grasped the position, whatever it might be; he took up the running on the other side, and the donkey-carriage swung away down the avenue, with all its incongruous air of hooded and rowdy invalidism.

I have never disguised the fact that I am a coward, and therefore when, at this dynamitical moment, I caught a glimpse of Lady Knox's hat over a laurustinus, as she returned at high speed from the garden, I slunk into the house and faded away round the dining-room door.

'This minute I seen the misthress going down through the plantation beyond,' said the voice of Crusoe outside the window, 'and I 'm afther sending Johnny Regan to her with the little carriage, not to put any more delay on yer ladyship. Sure you can see him making all the haste he can. Maybe you.'d sit inside in the library till she comes.'

Silence followed. I peered cautiously round the window curtain. Lady Knox was looking defiantly at the donkey-carriage as it reeled at top speed into the shades of the plantation, strenuously pursued by the woolly dog. Norris was regarding his horses' ears in expressionless respectability. Denis was picking up the entrée-dishes with decorous solicitude. Lady Knox turned and came into the house; she passed the dining-room door with an ominous step, and went on into the library.

It seemed to me that now or never was the moment to retire quietly to my room, put my things into my portmanteau, and——

Denis rushed into the room with the entrée-dishes piled up to his chin.

'She 's diddled!' he whispered, crashing them down on the table. He came at me with his hand out. 'Three cheers for Masther Flurry and Miss Sally,' he hissed, wringing my hand up and down, 'and 'twas yerself called for *Haste to the Weddin'* last night, long life to ye! The Lord save us! There 's the misthress going into the library!'

Through the half-open door I saw old Mrs. Knox approach the library from the staircase with a dignified slowness; she had on a wedding garment, a long white burnous, in which she might easily have been mistaken for a small, stout clergyman. She waved back Crusoe, the door closed upon her, and the battle of giants was entered upon. I sat down—it was all I was able for—and remained for a full minute in stupefied contemplation of the entrée-dishes.

Perhaps of all conclusions to a situation so portentous, that which occurred was the least possible. Twenty minutes after Mrs. Knox met her antagonist I was summoned from strapping my portmanteau to face the appalling duty of escorting the combatants, in Lady Knox's brougham, to the church outside the back gate, to which Miss Sally had preceded them in the donkey-carriage. I pulled myself together, went downstairs, and found that the millennium had suddenly set in. It had apparently dawned with the news that Aussolas and all things therein were bequeathed to Flurry by his grandmother, and had established itself finally upon the considerations that the marriage was past praying for, and that the diamonds were intended for Miss Sally.

We fetched the bride and bridegroom from the church; we fetched old Eustace Hamilton, who married them; we dug out the champagne from the cellar; we even found rice and threw it.

The hired cariage that had been ordered to take the run-aways across country to a distant station was driven by Slipper. He was shaved; he wore an old livery coat and a new pot hat; he was wondrous sober. On the following morning he was found asleep on a heap of stones ten miles away; somewhere in the neighbourhood one of the horses was grazing in a field with a certain amount of harness hanging about it. The carriage and the remaining horse were discovered in a roadside ditch, two miles farther on; one of the carriage doors had been torn off, and in the interior the hens of the vicinity were con-ducting an exhaustive search after the rice that lurked in the cushions.

FURTHER EXPERIENCES OF AN IRISH R.M.

I

THE PUG-NOSED FOX

5 Turkies and their Mother
5 Ducks and the Drake
5 Hins and the Cock
              CATHARINE O'DONOVAN, Skeagh.

A LEAF from a copy-book, with these words written on it, was placed in my hand as I was in the act of dragging on a new pair of gloves in the stable-yard. There was something rhythmic in the category, suggestive of burnt-offerings and incantations; some 'touch of pathos, pointing to tragedy; something, finally, that in the light of previous events recalled to me suddenly and unpleasantly my new-born position of deputy M.F.H.

Not, indeed, that I was in need at that moment of circumstances to remind me of it. A new hunting-cap, pressing implacably upon my forehead, an equally new red coat, heavy as a coat of mail, a glittering horn, red hot from the makers, and so far totally unresponsive to my apoplectic wooings; these things in themselves, without the addition of a poultry bill, were sufficient to bring home to me my amazing folly in having succumbed to the wiles of Mr. Florence McCarthy Knox, and accepted the charge of his hounds, during his absence with the Irish Yeomanry at the South African War.

I had yielded in a burst of patriotic emotion to the spirit of volunteering that was in the air. It would be, Flurry had assured me, a purely nominal position.

'They 'll only go out one day a week, and Jerome Hickey and Michael 'll do all the work. I do secretary for myself, but that 'll be no trouble to you. There 's nothing at all to do but to send out the cards of the meets. It 'll be a comfort to me to think you were running the show.'

I suggested other names that seemed to me infinitely more comfortable, but found them blocked by intricate and insuperable objections, and when I became aware that Mr. Knox had so engineered his case as to get my wife on his side it seemed simpler to give in.

A week afterwards I saw Flurry off at the station. His last words to me were:

'Well, good-bye, Major. Be fighting my grandmother for her subscription, and whatever you do, don't give more than half a crown for a donkey. There 's no meat on them.'

Upon this touching farewell the train steamed out, and left me standing, shelterless, a reluctant and incapable Master of Hounds.

Exhaustive as Flurry's instructions had been on the subject of the cuisine and other details of kennel management, he had not even hinted at the difficulties that are usually composed by means of a fowl fund. My first experience of these had taken place but a week ago, when from the breakfast-table I had perceived a donkey and cart rambling, unattended, in the shrubberies, among the young hydrangeas and azaleas. The owner, a most respectable-looking old man, explained that he had left it there because he was 'dilicate' to bring it up to the house, and added that he had come for compensation for 'a beautiful milking goat' that the hounds had eaten last March, 'and she having two kids that died afther her.'

I asked why he had not long since been to Mr. Knox about it, and was favoured with an interminable history of the claimant's ill-health during the summer, consequent on his fretting after the goat; of how he had been anointed four times, and of how the donkey was lame this long while where a branch bet her in the thigh one day she ran into the wood from the hounds. Fearing that the donkey was about to be included in the bill, I made haste to settle for the goat and her offspring, a matter of fifteen shillings.

Next day two women took up a position on the steps at luncheon time, a course which experience has taught me indicates affairs too exalted and too personal to be transmitted via the kitchen. They were, according to their own showing, ruined proprietors of poultry yards, in proof of which they pointed to a row of decapitated hens, laid forth on the grass like the bag at a fashionable shoot. I was irritably aware of their triumph in the trophy.

'Sure he didn't make off with anny of them only three, but

he snapped the head off all that was in it, and faith, if Masther Flurry was at home, he'd give us the blood of his arm before he'd see our little hins desthroyed on us this way.'

I gave them thirty-two and sixpence as an alternative compensation, not, I admit, without an uneasy sense of something unusual in Peter Cadogan's expression, as he assiduously raked the gravel hard by.

It was Michael Leary, Flurry's Michael, who placed the matter of a fowl fund upon a basis. Catharine O'Donovan and her list of casualties had been dismissed at a cost of ten shillings, a price so inadequate, and so cheerfully accepted, as to confirm my dawning suspicions.

'Is it what would they get from Mr. Flurry?' replied Michael when I put the matter to him; 'it isn't ten shillings, no, nor thirty-two shillings that they'd get from him, but a pelt of a curse after their heels! Why wouldn't they keep their hens inside the house with themselves at night, the same as anny one that'd have sense, and not to leave them out enticing the fox this way.'

Michael was in a bad temper, and so, for the matter of that, was I, quite irrespective of dealings in poultry. Our red coats, our horses, and the presence of the hounds, did not betoken the chase, they merely indicated that the Hunt was about to be photographed. The local photographer, backed by Mrs. Sinclair Yeates, had extorted from me the privilege of 'a sitting,' a figurative expression, involving a ride of five miles to a covert, selected by my wife as being typical of the country, accompanied by the fourteen and a half couple of half-bred harriers who figured in hound lists as 'Mr. Knox's Foxhounds.'

It was a blazing day in late August, following on forty-eight hours of blanketing sea fog; a day for flannels and a languid game of croquet. Lady Jane, the grey mare lent to me by Flurry, had been demoralized by her summer at grass, and was in that peculiarly loathsome frame of mind that is a blend of laziness and bumptiousness. If I left her to her own devices she drowsed, stumbling, through the dust; if I corrected her, she pranced and pulled, and kicked up behind like a donkey. My huntsman, Doctor Jerome Hickey, who was to have been in the forefront of the photograph, was twenty miles off in an open boat, on his way to an island at the far end of his dispensary district, with fifteen cases of measles ahead of him.

I envied him; measles or no, he had on a turned down collar. As a result of his absence I rode in solitary dignity at the head of the pack, or, so speak more correctly, I preceded Michael by some thirty yards of unoccupied road, while the pack, callous to flogging, and disdainful of my cajoleries, clave to the heels of Michael's horse.

In this order we arrived at the tryst, a heathery hillside, flanked by a dense and rambling wood. A seagull scream from the hillside announced the presence of my wife, and summoned me to join her and the photographer at the spot where they were encamped. I put the mare at a suitable place in the wall by the roadside. She refused it, which was no more than I had expected. I sampled my new spurs on her fat sides, with the result that she charged the wall, slantways, at the exact spot where Philippa had placed her bicycle against it, missed the bicycle by a hair's breadth, landed in the field with a thump, on all four feet, and ended with two most distressing bucks. It was a consolation to me, when I came in touch again with the saddle, to find that one of the new spurs had ploughed a long furrow in her shoulder.

The photographer was a young man from Belfast, a newcomer to the neighbourhood; Philippa is also a photographer, a fact that did not tend as much as might have been expected to the harmony of the occasion.

'Mrs. Yeates has selected this hillock,' said Mr. McOstrich in tones of acrid resignation, indicating as he spoke a sugarloaf-shaped knoll, thickly matted with furze and heather. 'She considers the background characteristic. My own suggestion would have been the grass field yonder.'

It is an ancient contention of my wife that I, in common with all other men, in any dispute between a female relative and a tradesman, side with the tradesman, partly from fear, partly from masculine clannishness, and most of all from a desire to stand well with the tradesman. Nothing but the remembrance of this preposterous reproach kept me from accepting Mr. McOstrich's point of view, and, while I hesitated, Michael was already taking up his position on the hillock, perhaps in obedience to some signal from Philippa, perhaps because he had realized the excellent concealment afforded by the deep heather to his horse's fetlocks, whose outline was of a somewhat gouty type. It was part of Flurry Knox's demoniac gift for horseflesh that he should be able to buy screws and make them serve his exacting purposes. Michael's horse, Moses, had, at a distance, the appearance of standing upon four champagne bottles, but he none the less did the work of two sound horses and did it well.

I goaded Lady Jane through the furze, and established myself beside Michael on the sugarloaf, the hounds disposed themselves in an interval of bracken below, and Mr. McOstrich directed his camera upon us from an opposite slope.

'Show your teeth, please,' said Mr. McOstrich to Michael. Michael, already simmering with indignation at the senseless frivolity of the proceedings, glowered at his knuckles, evidently suspicious of an ill-timed pleasantry.

'Do you hear, Whip?' repeated Mr. McOstrich, raising his bleak northern voice, 'show your teeth, please!'

'He only wants to focus us,' said I, foreseeing trouble, and hurriedly displaying my own new front row in a galvanic smile.

Michael murmured to Moses' withers something that sounded like a promise to hocus Mr. McOstrich when occasion should serve, and I reflected on the hardship of having to feel apologetic towards both Michael and the photographer.

Only those who have participated in 'Hunt Groups' can realize the combined tediousness and tension of the moments that followed. To keep thirty hounds headed for the camera, to ensure that your horse has not closed its eyes and hung its head in a doze of boredom, to preserve for yourself that alert and workmanlike aspect that becomes a sportsman, and then, when these things have been achieved and maintained for what feels like a month, to see the tripod move in spider strides to a fresh position and know that all has to be begun over again. After several of these tentative selections of a site, the moment came when Mr. McOstrich swung his black velvet pall in the air and buried his head under its portentous folds. The hounds, though uneasy, had hitherto been comparatively calm, but at this manifestation their nerve broke, and they unanimously charged the glaring monster in the black hood with loud and hysterical cries.

Had not Michael perceived their intention while there was time awful things might have happened. As it was, the leaders were flogged off with ignominy, and the ruffled artist returned from the rock to which he had fled. Michael and I arranged

ourselves afresh upon the hillock; I squared my shoulders, and
felt my wonted photographic expression of hang-dog desperation settle down upon me.

'The dogs are not in the picture, Whip!' said Mr. McOstrich
in the chill tone of outraged dignity.

I perceived that the hounds, much demoralized, had melted
away from the slope in front of us, and were huddling in a wisp
in the intervening hollow. Blandishments were of no avail;
they wagged and beamed apologetically, but remained in the
hollow. Michael, in whose sensitive bosom the term 'Whip'
evidently rankled, became scarlet in the face and avalanched
from the hill-top upon his flock with a fury that was instantly
recognized by them. They broke in panic, and the astute and
elderly Venus, followed by two of the young entry, bolted for
the road. They were there met by Mr. McOstrich's carman,
who most creditably headed the puppies with yells and his
driving-whip, but was outplayed by Venus, who, dodging like
a football professional, doubled under the car horse, and fled
irrevocably. Philippa, who had been flitting from rock to rock
with her kodak, and unnerving me with injunctions as to the
angle of my cap, here entered the lists with a packet of sandwiches, with which, in spite of the mustard, she restored a
certain confidence to the agitated pack, a proceeding observed
from afar with trembling indignation by Minx, her fox-terrier.
By reckless expenditure of sandwich the hounds were tempted
to their proper position below the horses, but, unfortunately,
with their sterns to the camera, and their eyes fastened on
Philippa.

'Retire, madam!' said Mr. McOstrich, very severely, '*I* will
attract the dogs!'

Thus rebuked, madam scrambled hastily over the crest of
the hillock and sank in unseemly laughter into the deep heather
behind it.

'Now, very quiet; please,' continued Mr. McOstrich, and
then unexpectedly uttered the words, 'Pop! Pop! Pop!' in a
high soprano.

Michael clapped his hand over his mouth, the superseded
siren in the heather behind me wallowed in fresh convulsions;
the hounds remained unattracted.

Then arose, almost at the same moment, a voice from the
wood behind us, the voice of yet a third siren, more potent than

that of either of her predecessors, the voice of Venus hunting a line. For the space of a breath the hounds hung on the eager hacking yelps, in the next breath they were gone.

Matters now began to move on a serious scale, and with a speed that could not have been foreseen. The wood was but fifty yards from our sugar-loaf. Before Michael had got out his horn, the hounds were over the wall, before the last stern had disappeared the leaders had broken into full cry.

'Please God it might be a rabbit!' exclaimed Michael, putting spurs to his horse and bucketing down through the furze towards the wood, with blasts of the horn that were fraught with indignation and rebuke.

An instant later, from my point of vantage on the sugar-loaf, I saw a big and very yellow fox cross an open space of heather high up on the hill above the covert. He passed and vanished; in half a dozen seconds Venus, plunging through the heather, came shrieking across the open space and also vanished. Another all too brief an interval, and the remainder of the pack had stormed through the wood and were away in the open after Venus, and Michael, who had pulled up short on the hither side of the covert wall, had started up the open hillside to catch them.

The characteristic background chosen by Philippa, however admirable in a photograph, afforded one of the most diabolic rides of my experience. Uphill, over courses of rock masked in furze bushes, round the head of a boggy lake, uphill again through deep and purple heather, over a horrid wall of long slabs half buried in it; past a ruined cabin, with thorn bushes crowding low over the only feasible place in the bank, and at last, the top of the hill, and Michael pulling up to take observations.

The best pack in the kingdom, schoolmastered by a regiment of whips, could not have precipitated themselves out of covert with more academic precision than had been shown by Flurry Knox's irregulars. They had already crossed the valley below us, and were running up a long hill as if under the conventional tablecloth; their cry, floating up to us, held all the immemorial romance of the chase.

Michael regarded me with a wild eye; he looked as hot as I felt, which was saying a good deal, and both horses were puffing.

'He's all the ways for Temple Braney!' he said. 'Sure I know him well—that's the pug-nosed fox that's in it these last three seasons, and it's what I wish——'

(I regret that I- cannot transcribe Michael's wish in its own terms, but I may baldly summarize it as a desire minutely and anatomically specified that the hounds were eating Mr. McOstrich.)

Here the spurs were once more applied to Moses's reeking sides, and we started again, battering down the twists of a rocky lane into the steaming, stuffy valley. I felt as guilty and as responsible for the whole affair as Michael intended that I should feel; I knew that he even laid to my charge the disastrous appearance of the pug-nosed Temple Braney fox. (Whether this remarkable feature was a freak of nature, or of Michael's lurid fancy, I have never been able to ascertain.)

The valley was boggy, as well as hot, and the deep and sinuous ditch that by courtesy was supposed to drain it was blind with rushes and tall fronds of *Osmunda regalis* fern. Where the landing was tolerable, the take-off was a swamp, where the take-off was sound the landing was feasible only for a frog: we lost five panting minutes, closely attended by horse-flies, before we somehow floundered across and began the ascent of the second hill. To face tall banks, uphill, is at no time agreeable, especially when they are enveloped in a jungle of briars, bracken, and waving grass, but a merciful dispensation of cow-gaps revealed itself; it was one of the few streaks of luck in a day not conspicuous for such.

At the top of the hill we took another pull. This afforded to us a fine view of the Atlantic, also of the surrounding country and all that was therein, with, however, the single unfortunate exception of the hounds. There was nothing to be heard save the summery rattle of a reaping-machine, the strong and steady rasp of a corncrake, and the growl of a big steamer from a band of fog that was advancing, ghostlike, along the blue floor of the sea. Two fields away a man in a straw hat was slowly combing down the flanks of a haycock with a wooden rake, while a black and white cur slept in the young after-grass beside him. We broke into their silvan tranquillity with a heated demand whether the hounds had passed that way. Shrill clamour from the dog was at first the only reply; its owner took off his hat, wiped his forehead with his sleeve, and stared at us.

'I 'm as deaf as a beetle this three weeks,' he said, continuing to look us up and down in a way that made me realize, if possible, more than before, the absurdity of looking like a Christmas card in the heat of a summer's day.

'Did ye see the HOUNDS?' shouted Michael, shoving the chestnut up beside him.

'It 's the neurology I got,' continued the haymaker, 'an' the pain does be whistlin' out through me ear till I could mostly run into the say from it.'

'It 's a pity ye wouldn't,' said Michael, whirling Moses round, 'an' stop in it! Whisht! Look over, sir! Look over!'

He pointed with his whip along the green slopes. I saw, about half a mile away, two boys standing on a fence, and beyond them some cattle galloping in a field: three or four miles farther on the woods of Temple Braney were a purple smear in the hazy heat of the landscape. My heart sank; it was obvious even to my limited capacities that the pug-nosed fox was making good his line with a straightness not to be expected from one of his personal peculiarity, and that the hounds were still running as hard as ever on a scent as steamingly hot as the weather. I wildly thought of removing my coat and leaving it in charge of the man with neuralgia, but was restrained by the reflection that he might look upon it as a gift, flung to him in a burst of compassion, a misunderstanding that, in view of his affliction, it would be impossible to rectify.

I picked up my lathered reins and followed Michael at a gloomy trot in the direction of the galloping cattle. After a few fields a road presented itself, and was eagerly accepted by the grey mare, on whom the unbridled gluttonies of a summer's grass were beginning to tell.

'She 's bet up, sir,' said Michael, dragging down a rickety gate with the handle of his whip. 'Folly on the road, there 's a near way to the wood from the cross.'

Moses here walked cautiously over the prostrate gate.

'I 'm afraid you 'll kill Moses,' said I, by no means pleased at the prospect of being separated from my Intelligence Department.

'Is it him?' replied Michael, scanning the country ahead of him with hawk eyes. 'Sure he 's as hardy as a throut!'

The last I saw of the trout was his bottle fetlocks disappearing nimbly in bracken as he dropped down the far side of a bank.

I 'follied on the road' for two stifling miles. The heavy air was pent between high hedges hung with wisps of hay from passing carts (hay-carrying in the south-west of Ireland conforms to the leisure of the farmer rather than to the accident of season); phalanxes of flies arose as if at the approach of royalty, and accompanied my progress at a hunting jog, which, as interpreted by Lady Jane, was an effective blend of a Turkish bath and a churn.

The 'near way' from the cross-roads opened seductively with a lane leading to a farmhouse, and presently degenerated into an unfenced but plausible cart track through the fields. Breaches had been made in the banks for its accommodation, and I advanced successfully towards the long woods of Temple Braney, endeavouring, less successfully, to repel the attentions of two young horses, who galloped, squealed, and bucked round me and Lady Jane with the imbecile pleasantry of their kind. The moment when I at length slammed in their faces the gate of the wood, was one of sorely needed solace.

Then came the sudden bath of coolness and shade, and the gradual realization that I did not in the least know what to do next. The air was full of the deeply preoccupied hum of insects, and the interminable monologue of a wood pigeon; I felt as if I ought to apologize for my intrusion. None the less I pursued a ride that crossed the wood, making persevering efforts to blow my horn, and producing nothing but gramophonic whispers, fragmentary groans, and a headache. I was near the farther side of the wood when I saw fresh hoof-tracks on a path that joined the ride; they preceded me to a singularly untempting bank, with a branch hanging over it and a potato-field beyond it. A clod had been newly kicked out of the top of it; I could not evade the conviction that Michael had gone that way. The grey mare knew it too, and bundled on to and over the bank with surprising celerity, and dropped skilfully just short of where the potato beds began. An old woman was digging at the other side of the field, and I steered for her, making a long tack down a deep furrow between the 'lazy-beds.'

'Did you see the hounds, ma'am?' I called out across the intervening jungle of potato stalks.

'Sir!'

She at all events was not deaf. I amended my inquiry.

'Did you see any dogs, or a man in a red coat?'

'Musha, bad cess to them, then I did!' bawled the old woman, 'look at the thrack o' their legs down thro' me little pratie garden! 'Twasn't but a whileen ago that they come leppin' out o' the wood to me, and didn't I think 'twas the Divil and all his young ones, an' I thrun meself down in the thrinch the way they wouldn't see me, the Lord save us!'

My heart warmed to her; I also would gladly have lain down among the unbrageous stalks of the potatoes, and concealed myself for ever from Michael and the hounds.

'What way did they go?' I asked, regretfully dismissing the vision, and feeling in my pocket for a shilling.

'They went wesht the road, your honour, an' they screeching always; they crossed out the field below over-right the white pony, and faith ye couldn't hardly see Michael Leary for the shweat! God help ye, asthore, yourself is getting hardship from them as well as another!'

The shilling here sank into her earthy palm, on which she prayed passionately that the saints might be surprised at my success. I felt that as far as I was concerned the surprise would be mutual; I had had nothing but misfortune since ten o'clock that morning, and there seemed no reason to believe that the tide had turned.

The pony proved to be a white mule, a spectral creature, standing in malign meditation trace-high in bracken; I proceeded in its direction at a trot, through clumps of bracken and coarse grass, and as I drew near it uttered a strangled and heartbroken cry of greeting. At the same moment Lady Jane fell headlong on to her nose and the point of her right shoulder. It is almost superfluous to observe that I did the same thing. As I rolled on my face in the bracken something like a snake uncoiled itself beneath me and became taut; I clutched at it, believing it to be the reins, and found I was being hung up, like clothes on a line, upon the mule's tethering rope. Lady Jane had got it well round her legs, and had already fallen twice in her efforts to get up, while the mule, round whose neck the tether rope had been knotted, was backing hard, like a dog trying to pull its head through its collar.

In sunstroke heat I got out my knife, and having cut the rope in two places, an operation accomplished in the depths of a swarm of flies and midges, I pulled the mare on to her legs.

She was lame on the off fore, and the rope had skinned her shins in several places; my own shoulder and arm were bruised, and I had broken a stirrup leather. Philippa and the photographer had certainly provided me with a day of varied entertainment, and I could not be sure that I had even yet drained the cup of pleasure to the dregs.

I led Lady Jane out into the road, and considered the position. We were about nine miles from home, and at least five from any place where I could hire a car. To walk, and lead the mare, was an alternative that, powerless as events had proved me to be in the hands of misfortune, I still refused to consider. It was then given me to remember old McRory.

My acquaintance with old McRory was of the slightest. He was, it was understood, a retired Dublin coal merchant, with an enormous family, and a reputation for great riches. He had, within the last year or so, taken the derelict house of Temple Braney, and having by strenuous efforts attained that dubious honour, the Commission of the Peace, it had happened to me to sit on the Bench with him on one or two occasions. Of his family I knew little, save that whenever I saw an unknown young man buying cigarettes at Mr. Dannaher's in Skebawn, I was informed that it was one of the young McRorys, a medical student, and 'a bit of a lad, but nothing at all to the next youngest.' The Misses McRory were only occasionally viewed, whirling in large companies on glittering bicycles, and the legend respectfully ran that they had forty blouses apiece. Perhaps the most definite information about them was supplied by our cook, Mrs. Cadogan, who assured Philippa that Wild Pigs in America wouldn't be treated worse than what Mrs. McRory treated her servants. All these things together made an unpromising aggregate, but the fact remained that Temple Braney House was within a quarter of a mile of me, and its charity my only hope.

The lodge gates of Temple Braney were wide open, so was the door of the lodge; the weedy drive was scored with fresh wheel tracks, as also, for the matter of that, was the grass on either side. I followed it for a short distance, in the roomy shade of splendid beech-trees, servants of the old régime, preserving their dignity through the vicissitudes of the new. Near the house was a second open gate, and on a species of arch over it I was amazingly greeted by the word 'Welcome' in white letters on a blazing strip of Turkey red. This was an attention that I had not anticipated; did it mean a school feast?

I made a cautious survey, but saw nobody, and nerved by the increasing lameness of Lady Jane, I went on to the house and rang the bell. There was no response; the hall door was wide open, and from an inner hall two lanky red setter puppies advanced with their tails between their legs, barking uncertainly, and acutely conscious of the fact that upon the collar of each was fastened a flaunting though much chewed bow of white satin ribbon. Full of foreboding I rang again. The bell tinkled vigorously in some fastness of the house, but nothing else happened. I decided to try the stable yard, and, attended by the decorated puppies, set forth to find it.

It was a large quadrangle, of which one side was formed by a wing of the house; had there been a few more panes of glass in the windows and slates in the roof it might have been imposing. A cavernous coach-house stood open, empty save for the wheel-less body of an outside car that was seated on the floor, with wings outspread like a hatching hen. Every stable door gaped wide. Odds and ends of harness lay about, but neither horse nor human being was visible. A turkey-cock, in transports of wrath, stormed to and fro in front of his household, and to some extent dispelled the sentiment of desertion and stampede that pervaded the place. I led the limping mare into a stable wherein were two loose boxes. A sickly smell greeted me, and I perceived that in one of the boxes was a long low cage, alive with the red-currant-jelly eyes and pink noses of a colony of ferrets, and in the other was a pile of empty wine boxes and several bicycles. Lady Jane snorted heavily, and I sought elsewhere for a refuge for her. I found it at length in a long stable with six empty stalls, and proceeded to tie her up in one of them.

It was while I was thus engaged that a strange succession of sounds began overhead, heavy, shapeless sounds in which were blended the suggestions of shove and thump. There was a brief interval of silence, during which Lady Jane and I listened with equal intentness; then followed a hoarse bellow, which resolved itself into the inquiry:

'Is there any one there?'

Here was the princess of the enchanted palace waking up with a vengeance. More and angrier bellows followed; I went

* G 978

stealthily out into the yard, and took stock of the windows above
the stable. One of them was open, and it was from it that the
voice issued, loudly demanding release. It roared a string of
Christian names, which I supposed to be those of the McRory
family, it used most unchristian language, and it finally settled
down into shouts for help, and asseverations that it was smothering. I admit that my first and almost overwhelming impulse
was to steal a bicycle and wing my way to my far-away and
peaceful home, leaving Michael, the hounds, and the smothering
gentleman to work out their own salvation. Unfortunately for
me, the voice of conscience prevailed. There was a ladder
near at hand leaning against the wall, and I put it to the window,
and went up it as fast as my top boots would allow me, with a
vision before me of old McRory in apoplexy as the probable
reward of my labours. I thrust my head in, blocking the light
in so doing; the shouting ceased abruptly, and after the glare
of sunshine outside I could at first see nothing. Then was
revealed to me a long and darksome room, once, probably, a
loft, filled with broken chairs and varieties of primeval lumber.
In the middle of the floor lay an immense feather bed, and my
bewildered eyes discovered, at one end of it, a crimson face,
the face, not of old McRory, but that of a young gentleman of
my acquaintance, one Mr. Tomsy Flood of Curranhilty. The
mysteries were deepening. I straddled the window-sash, and
arrived in the room with a three-cornered tear in the shoulder
of my coat, inflicted by a nail in the frame, and one spur draped
with ancestral cobweb.

'Take me out of this!' howled Mr. Flood hysterically, accepting my pantomime entrance without question. 'Can't you see
I'm smothering in this damned thing?'

Fluff hung from his black moustache and clung to his eyebrows, his hair was full of feathers; earthquake throes convulsed
the feather bed, and the fact was suddenly revealed to me that
Mr. Flood was not under it, as I had at first imagined, but in it,
stitched in, up to the chin. The weaned child, or any other
conventional innocent, could not have failed for an instant to
recognize the handiwork of practical humorists of a high order.
I asked no questions, but got out my knife once more, and
beginning with due precaution somewhere near Mr. Flood's
jugular vein, proceeded to slit open the end of the 'tick.' The
stitches were long and strong, and as each one yielded, the

feathers burst forth in stifling puffs, and Tomsy Flood's allusions to the young McRorys were mercifully merged in sputtering. I did not laugh, not at least till I found that I had to drag him out like a mummy, accompanied by half the contents of the bed, and perceived that he was in full evening clothes, and that he was incapable of helping himself because the legs of his trousers were sewn together and his coat sleeves sewn to his sides; even then, I only gave way in painful secrecy behind the mighty calves of his legs as I cut the stitches out. Tomsy Flood weighed about fifteen stone and was not in a mood to be trifled with, still less to see the humour of the position. The medical students had done their work with a surgical finish, and by the time that I had restored to Tomsy the use of his legs and arms, the feathers had permeated to every recess of my being, and I was sneezing as if I had hay fever.

Having at length, and with considerable difficulty, got Mr. Flood on to his legs, I ventured, with the tact demanded by the situation, a question as to whether he had been dining at Temple Braney.

'Dining?' queried Mr. Flood, with an obvious effort of memory. 'Yes, I was, to be sure! Amn't I staying in the house?' Then, with an equally obvious shock of recollection: 'Sure I 'm Best Man at the wedding to-day!'

The scattered elements of the situation began to fall symmetrically into line, from the open gates to the white bows on the puppies' collars. My chief concern, however, bearing in mind Tomsy Flood's recent potations and provocations, was to let him down as easily as possible, and, reserving my conclusions to myself, to escape, swiftly and silently, while yet there was time. There was always that stall full of bicycles; I could borrow clothes from Tomsy, and leave this accursed tomfoolery of hunting kit to be fetched with the mare, I could write a beautifully explanatory note when I got home——

'Hadn't you better get out of your evening things as quickly as you can?' I suggested.

Mr. Flood regarded me with heavy and bloodshot eyes of imperfect intelligence.

'Oh! I 've time enough. Ye wouldn't get a pick of breakfast here before ten o'clock in the day. Now that I come to look into you,' he continued, 'you 're as big a show as myself! Is it for the wedding that you have the red coat on you?'

I do not now remember with what lies I composed Tomsy Flood, but I got him out of the room at last by a door into a passage of seemingly interminable length; he took my arm, he treated me as his only friend, he expressed his full confidence that I would see fair play when he got a hold of Stanley McRory. He also gave it as his private opinion that his cousin, Harry Flood, was making a hare of himself marrying that impudent little Pinkie McRory, that was as vulgar as a bag of straddles, in spite of the money. Indeed, the whole family had too many airs about them for his fancy. 'They take the English *Times*, if you please, and they all dress for dinner—every night I tell ye! I call that rot, y' know!'

We were all this time traversing the house by labyrinthine passages, flights of stairs, and strange empty lobbies; we progressed conversationally and with maddening slowness, followed by a fleecy train of feathers that floated from us as we went. And all the time I was trying to remember how long it took to get married. In my own case it seemed as if I had been in the church for two hours at least.

A swing door suddenly admitted us to the hall, and Tomsy stood still to collect his faculties.

'My room's up there,' he began, pointing vaguely up the staircase.

At this identical moment there was a loud and composite crash from behind a closed door on our right, followed by minor crashes, and noises as of chairs falling about.

'That's the boys!' said Tomsy, a sudden spark kindling in his eye; 'they're breakfasting early, I suppose.'

He dropped my arm unexpectedly, and flung the door open with a yell.

The first object that met my eyes was the original sinner, Venus, mounted on a long and highly adorned luncheon table, crunching and gulping cold chicken as fast as she could get it down; on the floor half a dozen of her brethren tore at a round of beef amid the débris of crockery and glass that had been involved in its overthrow. A cataract of cream was pouring down the table-cloth, and making a lake on the carpet for the benefit of some others; and President, the patriarch of the pack, was apparently seated on the wedding-cake, while he demolished a cold salmon. I had left my whip in the stable, but even had this paralysing sight left me the force to use it, its services would

not have been needed. The leaders of the revel leaped from
the table, mowing down colonies of wine glasses in the act, and
fled through the open window, followed by the rest of the party,
with a precipitancy that showed their full consciousness of sin
—the last scramblers over the sill yelping in agonized foretaste
of the thong that they believed was overtaking them.

At such a moment of catastrophe the craving for human
sympathy is paramount.

I turned even to the fuddled and feathered Tomsy Flood
as to a man and a brother, and was confronted in the doorway
by the Bride and Bridegroom.

Behind them the hall was filling, with the swiftness of an evil
dream, with glowing faces and wedding bonnets; there was a
turmoil of wheels and hoofs at the door, and through it all, like
'horns of Elfland faintly blowing,' Michael's blasts of summons
to his pirates. Finally, the towering mauve bonnet and equally
towering wrath of Mrs. McRory, as she advanced upon me and
Tomsy Flood. I thought of the Wild Pigs in America, and
wished I were with them.

Lest I should find myself the object of a sympathy more
acute than I deserve, it may be well to transcribe portion of a
paragraph from the *Curranhilty Herald* of the following week:

'. . . After the ceremony a reception was held at Temple
Braney House, where a sumptuous collation had been provided
by the hospitable Mr. and Mrs. McRory. The health of the
Happy Pair having been drunk, that of the Bridesmaids was
proposed, and Mr. T. Flood, who had been prevented by a slight
indisposition from filling the office of Best Man, was happily
sufficiently recovered to return thanks for them in his usual
sprightly vein. Major Sinclair Yeates, R.M., M.F.H., who,
in honour of the festive occasion had donned sporting attire,
proposed the health of the Bride's Mother in felicitous
terms. . . .'

II

A ROYAL COMMAND

WHEN I heard that Bernard Shute, of Clountiss, Esquire, late Lieutenant R.N., was running an Agricultural Show, to be held in his own demesne, I did not for a moment credit him with either philanthropy or public spirit. I recognized in it merely another outbreak of his exasperating health and energy. He bombarded the country with circulars, calling upon farmers for exhibits, and upon all for subscriptions; he made raids into neighbouring districts on his motor car, turning vague promises into bullion, with a success in mendicancy fortunately given to few. It was in a thoroughly ungenerous spirit that I yielded up my guinea and promised to attend the Show in my thousands : peace at twenty-one shillings was comparatively cheap, and there was always a hope that it might end there.

The hope was fallacious : the show boomed; it blossomed into a Grand Stand, a Brass Band, an Afternoon Tea Tent; finally, fortune, as usual, played into Bernard's hands and sent a celebrity. There arrived in a neighbouring harbour a steam yacht, owned by one of Mr. Shute's dearest friends, one Captain Calthorpe, and having on board a coloured potentate, the Sultan of X——, who had come over from Cowes to see Ireland and the Dublin Horse Show. The dearest friend—who, as it happened, having been for three days swathed in a wet fog from the Atlantic, was becoming something pressed for entertainment for his charge—tumbled readily into Bernard's snare, and paragraphs appeared with all speed in the local papers proclaiming the intention of H.H. the Sultan of X—— to be present at the Clountiss Agricultural Show. Following up this *coup*, Bernard achieved for his function a fine, an even sumptuous day, and the weather and the Sultan between them filled the Grand Stand beyond the utmost hopes (and possibly the secret misgivings) of its constructors.

Having with difficulty found seats on the topmost corner for myself, my wife, and my two children, I had leisure to speculate upon its probable collapse. For half an hour, for an hour, for an hour and a half, we sat on its hot bare boards and surveyed the wide and empty oval of grass that formed the arena of the show. Five 'made-up' jumps of varying dimensions and two vagrant fox-terriers were its sole adornment. A dark rim of spectators encircled it, awaiting developments, i.e. the arrival of the Sultan, with tireless patience, and the egregious Slipper, attired in a gala costume of tall hat, frock coat, white breeches, and butcher boots, gleanings, no doubt, from bygone jumble sales, swaggered and rolled to and fro, selling catalogues and cards of the jumping. Away under the tall elms near the gate, amid the rival clamour of the cattle sheds and the poultry pens, was stationed the green and yellow band of the 'Sons of Liberty'; at intervals it broke into an excruciating shindy of brass instruments, through which the big drum drove a ferocious and unfaltering course. Above the heads of the people, at the far end of the arena, tossing heads and manes moving ceaselessly backwards and forwards told where the 'jumping horses' were waiting, eaten by flies, inconsolably agitated by the band, becoming momently more jaded and stale from the delay. I thanked Heaven that neither my wife nor Bernard Shute had succeeded in inducing me to snatch my string of two from the paddock in which they were passing the summer, to take part in this purgatorial procession.

The Grand Stand, a structure bare as a mountain top to the assaults of sun and wind, was canopied with parasols and prismatic with millinery. The farmers, from regions unknown to me, had abundantly risen to the occasion; so also had their wives and daughters; and fashionable ladies, with comfortable brogues and a vigorous taste in scent, closed us in on every side. Throughout that burning period of delay went the searching catechisms of my two sons (aged respectively four and seven) as to the complexion, disposition, and domestic arrangements of the Sultan. Philippa says that I ought to have known that they were thoroughly overstrung; possibly my descriptions of the weapons that he wore and the cannibal feasts that he attended were a trifle lurid, but it seemed simpler to let the fancy play on such details than to decide, for the benefit of an interested *entourage* of farmers' daughters, whether the Sultan's face was the colour of my boots or of their mother's, and whether he had a thousand or a million wives. The inquiry was interrupted by the quack of a motor horn at the entrance gate.

'Here he is!' breathed the Grand Stand as one man. There was a flocking of stewards towards the gate, and the Sons of

Liberty, full of anxiety to say the suitable thing, burst into the melancholy strains of *My Old Kentucky Home Far Away*. To this somewhat 'hearse - like air' the group of green-rosetted stewards advanced across the arena, escorting the yacht party, in whose midst moved a squat figure, clad in grey flannel, and surmounted by a massive and snowy turban. My elder son became very pale; the younger turned an ominous crimson, and the corners of his mouth went down, slowly, but, as I well knew, fatally. The inevitable bellow, that followed in the inevitable routine, had scarcely died away in the heart of Philippa's feather boa, when Mr. Shute's red face and monstrous presidential rosette presented themselves on the stairs at my elbow.

'Mrs. Yeates!' he began, in a gusty whisper, 'Cecilia implores you to come and fling yourself to the Lion! She says she simply can't and won't tackle him single-handed, and she trusts to you to see her through! He talks French all right, and I know your French is top-hole! Do come——'

Incredible as it may appear, my wife received this suggestion with a reluctance that was obviously but half-hearted. Such it is to have the Social Gift.

I presently found myself alone with my offspring, both in tears, and deaf to my assurances that neither the Sultan, nor his lion, would eat their mother. Consolation, however, came with the entry of the 'jumping horses' into the arena, which followed with all speed upon that of the Sultan. The first competitor bucketed up to the starting-point, and at the same moment the discovery was made that there was no water in the water-jump, a space of perhaps a foot in depth by some five feet wide. Nothing but a thin paste of mud remained, the water having disappeared, unnoticed, during the hot hours of the morning. Swift in expedient, the stewards supplied the difficulty with quicklime, which was scattered with a lavish hand in the fosse, and shone like snow through the barrier of furze bushes on the take-off side. If, as I suppose, the object was to delude the horses into the belief that it was a water-jump, it was a total failure; they immediately decided that it was a practical joke, dangerous, and in indifferent taste. If, on the other side, a variety entertainment for the public was aimed at, nothing could have been more successful. Every known class of refusal was successfully exhibited. One horse endeavoured to climb the rails into the Grand Stand; another, having stopped dead at the critical point, swung round, and returned in consternation to the starting-point, with his rider hanging like a locket round his neck. Another, dowered with a sense of humour unusual among horses, stepped delicately over the furze bushes, and, amidst rounds of applause, walked through the lime with a stoic calm. Yet another, a ponderous war-horse of seventeen hands, hung, trembling like an aspen, on the brink, till a sympathizer, possibly his owner, sprang irrepressibly from his seat on the stand, climbed through the rails, and attacked him from behind with a large umbrella. It was during this three-cornered conflict that the green-eyed filly forced herself into the front rank of events. A chorus of 'Hi! Hi! Hi!' fired at the rate of about fifty per second, volleyed in warning from the crowd round the starting-point, and a white-legged chestnut, with an unearthly white face and flying flounces of tawny mane and tail, came thundering down at the jump. Neither umbrella nor war-horse turned her by a hair's breadth from her course, still less did her rider, a lean and long-legged country boy, whose single object was to keep on her back. Picking up her white stockings, she took off six feet from the jump, and whizzed like a driven grouse past the combatants and over the furze bushes and the lime. Beneath her creamy forelock I caught a glimpse of her amazing blue-green eyes.

She skimmed the hurdle, she flourished over the wall, flinging high her white heels with a twist that showed more consideration for their safety than that of her rider. She ramped over the big double bank, while the roars of approval swelled with each achievement, and she ended a faultless round by bolting into the heart of the crowd, which fled hilariously, and as hilariously, hived in round her again.

From my exalted seat I could see the Sultan clapping his hands in sweet accord with Philippa. Somewhere near me a voice yelled:

'Cripes! She's a monkey! When she jumped the wall she went the height of a tree over it!'

To which another voice replied that 'It'd be a good bird that'd fly the height she wouldn't lep; and John Cullinane'd be apt to get first with her at the Skebawn Show.' I remembered casually that John Cullinane was a neighbour of mine.

'Well, I wouldn't fancy her at all,' said a female voice. 'I'd say she had a very maleecious glance.'

'Ah! ye wouldn't feel that when the winkers 'd be on her,' said the first speaker; 'she 'd make a fine sweeping mare under a side-car.'

Meantime, the war-horse, much embittered by the umbrella, floundered through the lime, and, continuing his course, threw down the hurdle, made a breach in the wall that would, as my neighbour put it, give three hours' work to seven idlers, and came to a sudden conclusion in front of the bank, while his rider slowly turned a somersault that, by some process of evolution, placed him sitting on the fence, facing the large and gloomy countenance of his horse.

It was after this performance that my wife looked round to see if her sons were enjoying themselves, and waved her handkerchief. The snowy turban of the Sultan moved round too, and beneath its voluminous folds the round black disks of a pair of field glasses were directed at us. The effect was instant. With a simultaneous shriek of terror, my children flung themselves upon me and buried their faces in my breast. I shall never forget it to the farmers' daughters that, in this black hour, their sympathy was prompt and practical.

'Oh! Fie, fie! Oh! the creatures! 'Twas the spy-glasses finished them altogether! Eat a sweetie now, lovey! that 's the grand man! Pappy 'll not let the dirty fella near ye!'

A piece of the brown sugar-stick, known as 'Peggy's leg,' accompanied these consolations, and a tearful composure was gradually restored; but 'Pappy' had arrived at the conclusion that he had had about as much as he could stand. In shameful publicity I clambered down the steep tiers of seats, with one child under my arm, the other adhering to my coat-tail. Philippa made agitated signals to me; I cut her dead, and went to ground in the tea tent.

A couple of days later my duty took me to the farthest end of my district—a matter that involved a night's absence from home. I left behind me an infant family restored to calm, and a thoroughly domesticated wife and mother, pledged to one o'clock dinner with the children and tea in the woods. I returned in time for luncheon next day, bicycling from the station, as was my wont. It was a hot day, and as I walked my bicycle up the slope of the avenue, the shade of the beech-trees was passing pleasant; the dogs galloped to meet me over the soft after-grass, and I thought about flannels and an idle afternoon.

In the hall I met Margaret, the parlourmaid, engaged, with the housemaid, in carrying the writing-table out of my smoking-room. They were talking loudly to each other, and I noticed that their eyes were very bright and their complexions considerably above par. I am a man of peace, but the veriest dove will protect its nest, and I demanded with some heat the cause of this outrage.

'The mistress told us to clear this room for the servant of the—the gentleman's that's coming to lunch to-morrow, sir,' replied Margaret with every appearance of offence.

She and Hannah staggered onwards with my table, and the contents of the drawers rolled and rattled.

'Put down that table,' I said firmly. 'Where is the mistress?'

'I believe she's dressing, sir,' replied Margaret; 'she only came home about an hour ago. She was out all night on the sea, I believe.'

Instant on the heels of these astonishing statements the swing door to the kitchen was flung open and Mrs. Cadogan's angry voice was projected through it.

'Hannah! go tell the mistress the butcher's below, and he says he never heard tell of the like, and would she lend him one o' the Major's spears? How would the likes o' him have a spear! Such goings on!'

'What the devil is all this about?' I said with an equal anger. 'No one is to touch my spears!'

'Thanks be to God, the Major's come home!' exclaimed the ruler of the kitchen, advancing weightily into the hall. 'There's no fear I'd put a hand on your spears, sir, nor the butcher neither, the poor, decent man! He says he's supplying the gentry for twenty-five years, and he was never asked to do the like of a nasty thing like that!'

'Like what!' I said, with growing wrath and bewilderment.

'It's what the mistress said,' rejoined Mrs. Cadogan, the flush of injury mounting to her cap-frill. 'That what-shall-I-call-him—that king, wouldn't ate mate without it'd be speared! And it's what I say,' she went on, perorating loudly and suddenly, 'what's good enough for Christians and gentry is good enough for an owld Blackamoor!'

It was now sufficiently obvious that Philippa had, with incredible perfidy, taken advantage of my absence to embroil herself in the entertainment of barbaric royalty. 'Tell the butcher to wait,' was all I could trust myself to say, as I started in search of my wife.

'Wait, Sinclair! I 'm coming down!' cried an urgent voice from the upper landing, and Philippa, attired in what I may perhaps describe as a tempestuous dressing-gown, came swiftly downstairs and swept me before her into the drawing-room.

'My dear,' she said breathlessly, 'let me break it to you as gently as possible. The Shutes called for me in the motor after you left yesterday, and we went on board Bernard's yacht and sailed round to tea with Captain Calthorpe and the Sultan. We were becalmed coming back, and we were out all night— we had nothing to eat but the men's food—not that I wanted anything!' She gave a nauseated shudder of reminiscence. 'There was an awful swell. It rained, too. Cecilia and I tried to sleep in the cabin with all our clothes on; I never spent a more horrible night. The yacht crawled in with the tide at about ten o'clock this morning, and I got back here half dead, and was just going up to bed when Captain Calthorpe arrived on a car and said that the Sultan wanted to lunch here to-morrow. He says we *must* have him—it 's a kind of royal command—in fact, I suppose you *ought* to wear your frock-coat!'

'I 'm dashed if I do!' I said, with decision.

'Well, be that as it may,' resumed Philippa, discreetly evading this point, 'that green-eyed thing that got the first prize for jumping is to be here to meet him. He wants to buy it for his State carriage. I did my best to get out of it, and I told Captain Calthorpe it would be impossible to manage about the food. I forgot to tell you,' faltered Philippa, with a wan giggle, 'that he said he must have speared mutton!'

'I call it an infernal liberty of Calthorpe's!' I said, with indignation fanned by the spectacle of Philippa's sleepless black-rimmed eyes and pallid face, 'dumping his confounded menagerie upon us in this way! And I may tell you that those spears of mine are poisoned!'

'Oh! don't be so horrid, Sinclair,' said Philippa, 'inventing difficulties like that!'

I arose the following morning with a heart of lead—of boiling lead—as I went down early to the smoking-room to look for cigarettes and found that they, in common with every other thing that I wanted, had been tidied into oblivion. From earliest dawn I had heard the thumping of feet, and the swish of petticoats, and the plying of brooms; but for me the first shot of the engagement was not fired till 8.30, when, as I was moodily stropping my razor, I was told that John Cullinane was below, and would be thankful to see me. As I shaved I could see John Cullinane standing about in front of the house, in his Sunday clothes, waiting for me; and I knew that he would so wait, patiently, inexorably, if I did not come down till noonday.

I interviewed him, unsympathetically, on the hall-door steps, and told him, firstly, that, as I knew nothing of his filly, I could not 'say a good word' to the Sultan for her; and, secondly, that I certainly would not mention to the Sultan that, in my opinion, she was a cheap mare at eighty pounds. John Cullinane then changed the conversation by remarking that he had brought over a small little donkey for a present for the young gentlemen; to which, with suitable politeness, I responded that my children already had a donkey, and that I could not think of depriving him of his, and the interview closed.

Breakfast was late, and for the most part uneatable, the excitement of the household having communicated itself to the kitchen range.

'If I was to put my head under it it wouldn't light for me!' Mrs. Cadogan said to Philippa.

As a matter of fact, judging by a glimpse vouchsafed to me of her face as I struggled forth from the cellar with a candle and the champagne, one might have expected it to cause a conflagration anywhere.

My smoking-room had been dedicated to the Sultan's personal attendant, a gentleman who could neither lunch with his master nor with my servants; I was therefore homeless, and crept, an outcast, to the drawing-room to try to read the newspaper undisturbed. Sounds from above told me that trouble was brewing in the nursery; I closed the door.

At about eleven-thirty an outside car drove up to the house, and I saw a personable stranger descend from it, with a black bag in his hand, a forerunner, no doubt, of the Sultan, come over to see that the preparations were *en règle*. I saw no reason for my intervention, and, with a passing hope that providence might deliver him over to Mrs. Cadogan, I returned to my paper. The door was flung open.

'Sinclair, dear,' said my wife, very apologetically, 'here is Mr. Werner, the piano-tuner, from Dublin. He says he can't come again—he thinks he can finish it by luncheon time. I quite forgot that he was coming——'

Mr. Werner's spectacled and supercilious face regarded me over her shoulder; he evidently had a low opinion of me, I do not know why. With one Cenci-like glance of reproach at Philippa I rose and left the room. As I put on my cap I heard the first fierce chords break forth, followed by the usual chromatic passages, fluent and searching, which merged in their turn into a concentrated attack upon a single note. I hurried from the house.

It was a perfect August morning; the dogs lay on the hot gravel and panted politely as I spoke to them, but did not move. Rejected by all I betook myself to a plantation near the front gate to see how the work of clearing a ride was progressing. The cross-cut saw and a bill-hook lay on the ground, but of workmen there was no sign. From the high road came the sound of wheels and of rapid trotting, also something that seemed like cheering.

'Good heavens!' I thought, my blood running cold, 'here they are!'

I broke through the tall bracken and the larches to an opening from which the high road was visible. My two workmen were lying on their stomachs across the coping of the demesne wall, and a line of countrymen, with their best clothes on and crape 'weepers' on their hats, sat on the opposite fence and applauded what was apparently a trotting match between a long-legged bay colt and John Cullinane's chestnut filly, owners up.

I joined the entertainment, my two men melting like snow from the top of the wall, and it was explained to me that there had been a funeral in the locality, and that these were a few of the neighbours that had been at it, and were now waiting to see the Black Gentleman. An outside car rested on its shafts by the side of the road, and a horse with harness on it browsed voraciously on the shrubs inside my gate. Far away down the road I saw the receding figures of my two children, going forth to the picnic that had been arranged to allay their panic and to remove them from the sphere of action. Any Irish person will readily believe that one of them was mounted on 'the small little donkey,' the bribe which I had that morning irrevocably repudiated. I knew that John Cullinane saw them too, but I was too broken to interfere; I turned my back and walked rapidly away.

The rhythmic rasp of the cross-cut told me that work at the clearing had been resumed; I said to myself vindictively that I would see that it continued, and returned to the ride. The bill-hook was doing nothing, and picking it up I fell to snicking and chopping, with soothing destructiveness, among the briars and ash-saplings. Notwithstanding heat and horseflies, the time passed not disagreeably, and I was, at all events, out of range of the piano. I had paused for the fifteenth time to wipe a heated brow, and extract a thorn from my finger, when the familiar voice of the Shutes' motor-horn roused me to the appalling fact that it was nearly luncheon time, and that I was far from fit to receive royalty. As I hurriedly emerged from the wood there was a sound of hard galloping, and I beheld the green-eyed filly flying riderless up the avenue. She crossed the croquet ground, thoroughly, from corner to corner, and disappeared into the shrubbery in the direction of the flower garden. I ran as I have seldom run, dimly aware of a pursuing party of mourners on the avenue behind me, and, as I ran, I cursed profusely the Sultan, Calthorpe, and chiefly Bernard Shute and all his works.

The chase lasted for twenty minutes, and was joined in by not less than five-and-thirty people. The creamy mane of the filly floated like a banner before us through the shrubberies, with the dogs in full cry behind her; through it all went the reiterations of the piano, the monotonous hammerings, the majestic chords, the pyrotechnic scales; they expressed as fully as he himself could have desired the complete indifference of the tuner. The filly was ubiquitous; at one moment she was in the flower garden, the next, a distant uproar among the poultry told that she had traversed the yard, whence she emerged, *ventre à terre*, delivered herself of three bucks at sight of her original enemy the motor, at the hall door, and was away again for the croquet ground. At every turn I encountered a fresh pursuer; it was Bernard Shute and the kitchenmaid who slammed the flower-garden gate in her face; it was Philippa, in her very best dress, abetted by John Cullinane, very dusty, and waving a crushed and weepered hat, who, with the best intentions, frustrated a brilliant enveloping movement directed by me; finally the cross-cut-saw men, the tuner's car-driver, and a selection from the funeral, came so near cornering her that she charged the sunk fence, floated across its gulf with offensive ease, and scurried away, with long and defiant squeals, to assault my horses at the farther end of the paddock.

When we, i.e. Philippa, Bernard, and I, pulled ourselves together on the top of the steps, it was two o'clock. By the special favour of Providence the Sultan was late, but the position was desperate. Philippa had trodden on the front of her dress and torn it, Bernard had greened the knees of his trousers; I do not know what I looked like, but when Cecilia Shute emerged, cool and spotless, from the hall, where she had judiciously remained during the proceedings, she uttered a faint shriek and covered her face with her hands.

'I know,' I said, with deadly calm, stuffing my tie inside my waistcoat, 'I can't help it——'

'Here they are!' said Bernard.

The sound of wheels was indeed in the avenue. We fled as one man into the back hall, and Philippa, stumbling over her torn flounce, fell on her knees at the feet of Mr. Werner, the tuner, who stood there, his task finished, awaiting with cold decorum the reward of his labours. The wheels stopped. What precisely happened during that crowded moment I cannot pretend to explain, but as we dragged my wife to her feet I found that she had knelt on my eyeglass, with the result that may be imagined.

All was now lost save honour. I turned at bay, and dimly saw, silhouetted in the open doorway, a short figure in a frock coat, with a species of black turban on its head. I advanced, bowed, and heroically began:

'Sire! J'ai l'honneur——'

'Yerrah my law! Major!' said the bewildered voice of Slipper. 'Don't be making game of me this way! Sure I have a tallagram for you.' He removed the turban, which I now perceived to be a brown tweed cap, swathed in a crape 'weeper,' and handed me the telegram. 'I got it from the boy that was after breaking his bike on the road, an' I coming from the funeral.'

The telegram was from Calthorpe, and said, with suitable regrets, that the Sultan had been summoned to London on instant and important business.

I read it to the back hall, in a voice broken by many emotions.

'I saw the gentleman you speak of waiting for the Dublin train at Sandy Bay Station this morning,' remarked the tuner, condescending for a moment to our level.

'Then why did you not tell us so?' demanded Philippa, with sudden indignation.

'I was not aware, madam, that it was of any importance,' replied Mr. Werner, returning to his normal altitude of perpetual frost.

Incredible as it may seem, it was apparent that Philippa was disappointed. As for me, my heart was like a singing bird.

III

POISSON D'AVRIL

THE atmosphere of the waiting-room set at naught at a single glance the theory that there can be no smoke without fire. The station-master, when remonstrated with, stated, as an incontrovertible fact, that any chimney in the world would smoke in a south-easterly wind, and further, said there wasn't a poker, and that if you poked the fire the grate would fall out. He was, however, sympathetic, and went on his knees before the smouldering mound of slack, endeavouring to charm it to a smile by subtle proddings with the handle of the ticket punch. Finally, he took me to his own kitchen fire and talked politics and salmon fishing, the former with judicious attention to my presumed point of view, and careful suppression of his own, the latter with no less tactful regard for my admission that for three days I had not caught a fish, while the steam rose from my wet boots, in witness of the ten miles of rain through which an outside car had carried me.

Before the train was signalled I realized for the hundredth time the magnificent superiority of the Irish mind to the trammels of officialdom, and the inveterate supremacy in Ireland of the personal element.

'You might get a foot-warmer at Carrig Junction,' said a species of lay porter in a knitted jersey, ramming my suit-case upside down under the seat. 'Sometimes they're in it, and more times they're not.'

The train dragged itself rheumatically from the station, and a cold spring rain—the time was the middle of a most inclement April—smote it in flank as it came into the open. I pulled up both windows and began to smoke; there is, at least, a semblance of warmth in a thoroughly vitiated atmosphere.

It is my wife's habit to assert that I do not read her letters, and being now on my way to join her and my family in Gloucestershire, it seemed a sound thing to study again her latest letter of instructions.

'I am starting to-day, as Alice wrote to say we must be there two days before the wedding, so as to have a rehearsal for the pages. Their dresses have come, and they look too delicious in them——'

(I here omit profuse particulars not pertinent to this tale)——

'It is sickening for you to have had such bad sport. If the worst comes to the worst couldn't you buy one?——'

I smote my hand upon my knee. I had forgotten the infernal salmon! What a score for Philippa! If these *contretemps* would only teach her that I was not to be relied upon, they would have their uses, but experience is wasted upon her; I have no objection to being called an idiot, but, that being so, I ought to be allowed the privileges and exemptions proper to idiots. Philippa, had no doubt, written to Alice Hervey, and assured her that Sinclair would be only too delighted to bring her a salmon, and Alice Hervey, who was rich enough to find much enjoyment in saving money, would reckon upon it, to its final fin in mayonnaise.

Plunged in morose meditations, I progressed through a country parcelled out by shaky and crooked walls into a patchwood of hazel scrub and rocky fields, veiled in rain. About every six miles there was a station, wet and windswept; at one the sole occurrence was the presentation of a newspaper to the guard by the station-master; at the next the guard read aloud some choice excerpts from the same to the porter. The Personal Element was potent on this branch of the Munster and Connaught Railway. Routine, abhorrent to all artistic minds, was sheathed in conversation; even the engine-driver, a functionary ordinarily as aloof as the Mikado, alleviated his enforced isolation by sociable shrieks to every level crossing, while the long row of public-houses that formed, as far as I could judge, the town of Carrig, received a special and, as it seemed, humorous salutation.

The time-table decreed that we were to spend ten minutes at Carrig Junction; it was fifteen before the crowd of market people on the platform had been assimilated; finally, the window of a neighbouring carriage was flung open, and a wrathful English voice asked how much longer the train was going to wait. The station-master, who was at the moment engrossed in conversation with the guard and a man who was carrying a long parcel wrapped in newspaper, looked round, and said gravely:

'Well now, that's a mystery!'

The man with the parcel turned away, and convulsively studied a poster. The guard put his hand over his mouth.

The voice, still more wrathfully, demanded the earliest hour at which its owner could get to Belfast.

'Ye'll be asking me next when I take me breakfast,' replied the station-master, without haste or palpable annoyance.

The window went up again with a bang, the man with the parcel dug the guard in the ribs with his elbow, and the parcel slipped from under his arm and fell on the platform.

'Oh my! oh my! Me fish!' exclaimed the man, solicitously picking up a remarkably good-looking salmon that had slipped from its wrapping of newspaper.

Inspiration came to me, and I, in my turn, opened my window and summoned the station-master.

Would his friend sell me the salmon? The station-master entered upon the mission with ardour, but without success.

No; the gentleman was only just after running down to the town for it in the delay, but why wouldn't I run down and get one for myself? There was half a dozen more of them below at Coffey's, selling cheap; there would be time enough, the mail wasn't signalled yet.

I jumped from the carriage and doubled out of the station at top speed, followed by an assurance from the guard that he would not forget me.

Congratulating myself on the ascendancy of the personal element, I sped through the soapy limestone mud towards the public-houses. En route I met a heated man carrying yet another salmon, who, without preamble, informed me that

there were three or four more good fish in it, and that he was
after running down from the train himself.

'Ye have whips o' time!' he called after me. 'It's the first
house that's not a public-house. Ye'll see boots in the
window—she'll give them for tenpence a pound if ye're stiff
with her!'

I ran past the public-houses.

'Tenpence a pound!' I exclaimed inwardly, 'at this time of
year! That's good enough.'

Here I perceived the house with boots in the window, and
dived into its dark doorway.

A cobbler was at work behind a low counter. He mumbled
something about herself, through lengths of waxed thread that
hung across his mouth, a fat woman appeared at an inner door,
and at that moment I heard, appallingly near, the whistle of
the incoming mail. The fat woman grasped the situation in an
instant, and with what appeared but one movement, snatched a
large fish from the floor of the room behind her and flung a
newspaper round it.

'Eight pound weight!' she said swiftly. 'Ten shillings!'

A convulsive effort of mental arithmetic assured me that this
was more than tenpence a pound, but it was not the moment for
stiffness. I shoved a half-sovereign into her fishy hand, clasped
my salmon in my arms, and ran.

Needless to say it was uphill, and at the steepest gradient
another whistle stabbed me like a spur; above the station roof
successive and advancing puffs of steam warned me that the
worst had probably happened, but still I ran. When I gained
the platform my train was already clear of it, but the personal
element held good. Every soul in the station, or so it seemed
to me, lifted up his voice and yelled. The station-master put
his fingers in his mouth and sent after the departing train an
unearthly whistle, with a high trajectory and a serrated edge.
It took effect; the train slackened, I plunged from the platform
and followed it up the rails, and every window in both trains
blossomed with the heads of deeply interested spectators. The
guard met me on the line, very apologetic and primed with an
explanation that the gentleman going for the boat train wouldn't
let him wait any longer, while from our rear came an exultant
cry from the station-master.

'Ye *told* him ye wouldn't forget him!'

'There's a few countrywomen in your carriage, sir,' said the guard, ignoring the taunt, as he shoved me and my salmon up the side of the train, 'but they'll be getting out in a couple of stations. There wasn't another seat in the train for them!'

My sensational return to my carriage was viewed with the utmost sympathy by no less than seven shawled and cloaked countrywomen. In order to make room for me one of them seated herself on the floor with her basket in her lap, another, on the seat opposite to me, squeezed herself under the central elbow flap that had been turned up to make room. The aromas of wet cloaks, turf smoke, and salt fish formed a potent blend. I was excessively hot, and the eyes of the seven women were fastened upon me with intense and unwearying interest.

'Move west a small piece, Mary Jack, if you please,' said a voluminous matron in the corner, 'I declare we're as throng as three in a bed this minute!'

'Why then, Julia Casey, there's little throubling yourself,' grumbled the woman under the flap. 'Look at the way meself is! I wonder is it to be putting humps on themselves the gentry has them things down on top o' them! I'd sooner be carrying a basket of turnips on me back than to be scrooged this way!'

The woman on the floor at my feet rolled up at me a glance of compassionate amusement at this rustic ignorance, and tactfully changed the conversation by supposing that it was at Coffey's I got the salmon.

I said it was.

There was a silence, during which it was obvious that one question burnt in every heart.

'I'll go bail she axed him tinpence!' said the woman under the flap, as one who touches the limits of absurdity.

'It's a beautiful fish!' I said defiantly. 'Eight pounds weight. I gave her ten shillings for it.'

What is described in newspapers as 'sensation in court' greeted this confession.

'Look!' said the woman under the flap, darting her head out of the hood of her cloak, like a tortoise, 'tis what it is, ye haven't as much roguery in your heart as 'd make ye a match for her!'

'Divil blow the ha'penny Eliza Coffey paid for that fish!'

burst out the fat woman in the corner. 'Thim lads o' her's had a creel full o' thim snatchéd this morning before it was making day!'

'How would the gentleman be a match for her!' shouted the woman on the floor through a long-drawn whistle that told of a coming station. 'Sure a Turk itself wouldn't be a match for her! That one has a tongue that 'd clip a hedge!'

At the station they clambered out laboriously, and with groaning. I handed down to them their monster baskets, laden, apparently, with ingots of lead; they told me in return that I was a fine *grauver* man, and it was a pity there weren't more like me; they wished, finally, that my journey might well thrive with me, and passed from my ken, bequeathing to me, after the agreeable manner of their kind, a certain comfortable mental sleekness that reason cannot immediately dispel. They also left me in possession of the fact that I was about to present the irreproachable Alice Hervey with a contraband salmon.

The afternoon passed cheerlessly into evening, and my journey did not conspicuously thrive with me. Somewhere in the dripping twilight I changed trains, and again later on, and at each change the salmon moulted some more of its damp raiment of newspaper, and I debated seriously the idea of interring it, regardless of consequences, in my portmanteau. A lamp was banged into the roof of my carriage, half an inch of orange flame, poised in a large glass globe, like a gold fish, and of about as much use as an illuminant. Here also was handed in the dinner basket that I had wired for, and its contents, arid though they were, enabled me to achieve at least some measure of mechanical distension, followed by a dreary lethargy that was not far from drowsiness.

At the next station we paused long; nothing whatever occurred, and the rain drummed patiently upon the roof. Two nuns and some schoolgirls were in the carriage next door, and their voices came plaintively and in snatches through the partition; after a long period of apparent collapse, during which I closed my eyes to evade the cold gaze of the salmon through the netting, a voice in the next carriage said resourcefully:

'Oh, girls, I 'll tell you what we 'll do! We 'll say the Rosary!'

'Oh, that will be lovely!' said another voice; 'well, who 'll give it out? Theresa Condon, you 'll give it out.'

Theresa Condon gave it out, in a not unmelodious monotone, interspersed with the responses, always in a lower cadence; the words were indistinguishable, but the rise and fall of the western voices was lulling as the hum of bees. I fell asleep.

I awoke in total darkness; the train was motionless, and complete and profound silence reigned. We were at a station, that much I discerned by the light of the dim lamp at the far end of a platform glistening with wet. I struck a match and ascertained that it was eleven o'clock, precisely the hour at which I was to board the mail train. I jumped out and ran down the platform; there was no one in the train; there was no one even on the engine, which was forlornly hissing to itself in the silence. There was not a human being anywhere. Every door was closed, and all was dark. The name-board of the station was faintly visible; with a lighted match I went along it letter by letter. It seemed as if the whole alphabet were in it, and by the time I had got to the end I had forgotten the beginning. One fact I had, however, mastered, that it was not the junction at which I was to catch the mail.

I was undoubtedly awake, but for a moment I was inclined to entertain the idea that there had been an accident, and that I had entered upon existence in another world. Once more I assailed the station house and the appurtenances thereof, the ticket office, the waiting-room, finally, and at some distance, the goods store, outside which the single lamp of the station commented feebly on the drizzle and the darkness. As I approached it a crack of light under the door became perceptible, and a voice was suddenly uplifted within.

'Your best now agin that! Throw down your jack!'

I opened the door with pardonable violence, and found the guard, the station-master, the driver, and the stoker, seated on barrels round a packing-case, on which they were playing a game of cards.

To have too egregiously the best of a situation is not, to a generous mind, a source of strength. In the perfection of their overthrow I permitted the driver and stoker to wither from their places, and to fade away into the outer darkness without any suitable send-off; with the guard and the station-master I dealt more faithfully, but the pleasure of throwing water on drowned rats is not a lasting one. I accepted the statements that they thought there wasn't a Christian in the train, that a few minutes here or there wouldn't signify, that they would have me at the junction in twenty minutes, and it was often the mail was late.

Fired by this hope I hurried back to my carriage, preceded at an emulous gallop by the officials. The guard thrust in with me the lantern from the card table, and fled to his van.

'Mind the Goods, Tim!' shouted the station-master, as he slammed my door, 'she might be coming any time now!'

The answer travelled magnificently back from the engine.

'Let her come! She'll meet her match!' A war-whoop upon the steam whistle fittingly closed the speech, and the train sprang into action.

We had about fifteen miles to go, and we banged and bucketed over it in what was, I should imagine, record time. The carriage felt as if it were galloping on four wooden legs, my teeth chattered in my head, and the salmon slowly churned its way forth from its newspaper, and moved along the netting with dreadful stealth.

All was of no avail.

'Well,' said the guard, as I stepped forth on to the deserted platform of Loughranny, 'that owld Limited Mail's th' unpunctualest thrain in Ireland! If you're a minute late she's gone from you, and maybe if you were early you might be half an hour waiting for her!'

On the whole the guard was a gentleman. He said he would show me the best hotel in the town, though he feared I would be hard set to get a bed anywhere because of the '*Feis*' (a Feis, I should explain, is a festival, devoted to competitions in Irish songs and dances). He shouldered my portmanteau, he even grappled successfully with the salmon, and, as we traversed the empty streets, he explained to me how easily I could catch the morning boat from Rosslare, and how it was, as a matter of fact, quite the act of providence that my original scheme had been frustrated.

All was dark at the uninviting portals of the hotel favoured by the guard. For a full five minutes we waited at them, ringing hard: I suggested that we should try elsewhere.

'He'll come,' said the guard, with the confidence of the Pied Piper of Hamelin, retaining an implacable thumb upon the button of the electric bell. 'He'll come. Sure it rings in his room!'

The victim came, half awake, half dressed, and with an inch of dripping candle in his fingers. There was not a bed there, he said, nor in the town neither.

I said I would sit in the dining-room till the time for the early train.

'Sure there's five beds in the dining-room,' replied the boots, 'and there's mostly two in every bed.'

His voice was firm, but there was a wavering look in his eye.

'What about the billiard-room, Mike?' said the guard, in wooing tones.

'Ah, God bless you! we have a mattress on the table this minute!' answered the boots, wearily, 'and the fellow that got the First Prize for Reels asleep on top of it!'

'Well, and can't ye put the palliasse on the floor under it, ye omadhawn?' said the guard, dumping my luggage and the salmon in the hall, 'sure there's no snugger place in the house! I must run away home now, before Herself thinks I'm dead altogether!'

His retreating footsteps went lightly away down the empty street.

'Annything don't throuble *him*!' said the boots bitterly.

As for me, nothing save the Personal Element stood between me and destitution.

It was in the dark of the early morning that I woke again to life and its troubles. A voice, dropping, as it were, over the edge of some smothering over-world, had awakened me. It was the voice of the First Prize for Reels, descending through a pocket of the billiard-table.

'I beg your pardon, sir, are ye going on the 5 to Cork?'

I grunted a negative.

'Well, if ye were, ye'd be late,' said the voice.

I received this useful information in indignant silence, and endeavoured to wrap myself again in the vanishing skirts of a dream.

'I'm going on the 6.30 meself,' proceeded the voice, 'and it's unknown to me how I'll put on me boots. Me feet is swelled the size o' three-pound loaves with the dint of the little dancing-shoes I had on me in the competition last night. Me feet's delicate that way, and I'm a great epicure about me boots.'

H 97⁸

I snored aggressively, but the dream was gone. So, for al practical purposes was the night.

The First Prize for Reels arose, presenting an astonishing spectacle of grass-green breeches, a white shirt, and pearl-grey stockings, and accomplished a toilet that consisted of removing these and putting on ordinary garments, completed by the apparently excruciating act of getting into his boots. At any other hour of the day I might have been sorry for him. He then removed himself and his belongings to the hall, and there entered upon a resounding conversation with the boots, while I crawled forth from my lair to renew the strife with circumstances and to endeavour to compose a telegram to Alice Hervey of explanation and apology that should cost less than seven and sixpence. There was also the salmon to be dealt with.

Here the boots intervened, opportunely, with a cup of tea, and the intelligence that he had already done up the salmon in straw bottle-covers and brown paper, and that I could travel Europe with it if I liked. He further informed me that he would run up to the station with the luggage now, and that maybe I wouldn't mind carrying the fish myself; it was on the table in the hall.

My train went at 6.15. The boots had secured for me one of many empty carriages, and lingered conversationally till the train started; he regretted politely my bad night at the hotel, and assured me that only for Jimmy Durkan having a little drink taken—Jimmy Durkan was the First Prize for Reels—he would have turned him off the billiard-table for my benefit. He finally confided to me that Mr. Durkan was engaged to his sister, and was a rising baker in the town of Limerick; 'indeed,' he said, 'any girl might be glad to get him. He dances like whalebone, and he makes grand bread!'

Here the train started.

It was late that night when, stiff, dirty, with tired eyes blinking in the dazzle of electric lights, I was conducted by the Herveys' beautiful footman into the Herveys' baronial hall, and was told by the Herveys' imperial butler that dinner was over, and the gentlemen had just gone into the drawing-room. I was in the act of hastily declining to join them there, when a voice cried:

'Here he is!'

And Philippa, rustling and radiant, came forth into the hall, followed in shimmers of satin, and flutterings of lace, by Alice Hervey, by the bride elect, and by the usual festive rout of exhilarated relatives, male and female, whose mission it is to keep things lively before a wedding.

'Is this a wedding present for me, Uncle Sinclair?' cried the bride elect, through a deluge of questions and commiserations, and snatched from under my arm the brown paper parcel that had remained there from force of direful habit.

'I advise you not to open it!' I exclaimed; 'it 's a salmon!'

The bride elect, with a shriek of disgust, and without an instant of hesitation, hurled it at her nearest neighbour, the head bridesmaid. The head bridesmaid, with an answering shriek, sprang to one side, and the parcel that I had cherished with a mother's care across two countries and a stormy Channel fell, with a crash, on the flagged floor.

Why did it crash?

'A salmon!' screamed Philippa, gazing at the parcel, round which a pool was already forming, 'why, that 's whisky! Can't you smell it?'

The footman here respectfully interposed, and kneeling down, cautiously extracted from folds of brown paper a straw bottle-cover full of broken glass and dripping with whisky.

'I 'm afraid the other things are rather spoiled, sir,' he said seriously, and drew forth, successively, a very large pair of high-low shoes, two long grey worsted stockings, and a pair of grass-green breeches.

They brought the house down, in a manner doubtless familiar to them when they shared the triumphs of Mr. Jimmy Durkan, but they left Alice Hervey distinctly cold.

'You know, darling,' she said to Philippa afterwards, 'I don't think it was very clever of dear Sinclair to take the wrong parcel. I *had* counted on that salmon.'

IV

'THE MAN THAT CAME TO BUY APPLES'

It had been freezing hard all the way home, and the Quaker
skated perilously once or twice on the northerly stretches. As
I passed the forge near my gate I issued an order for frost-
nails, and while I did so the stars were kindling like diamonds
over the black ridge of Shreelane Hill.

The overture to the Frost Symphony had begun, with its
usual beauties and difficulties, and its leading theme was given
forth in a missive from Flurry Knox, that awaited me on the
hall table. Flurry's handwriting was an unattractive blend of
the laundress's bill and the rambling zigzags of the temperature chart, but he exhibited no more of it than was strictly
necessary in getting to the point. Would I shoot at Aussolas
the following day? There were a lot of cock in, and he had
whipped up four guns in a hurry. There was a postscript,
'Bernard Shute is coming. Tell Mrs. Yeates he didn't kill
any one yet this season.'

Since his marriage Flurry had been promoted to the position
of agent to his grandmother, old Mrs. Knox of Aussolas, and
through the unfathomable mazes of their dealings and fights
with each other, the fact remained that he had secured to himself the Aussolas shooting at about half its market value. So
Mrs. Knox said. Her grandson, on the other hand, had often
informed me that the privilege 'had him beggared, what with
beaters and all sorts, and his grandmother's cattle turned into
the woods destroying all the covert—let alone her poaching.'
Into the differences of such skilled combatants the prudent
did not intrude themselves, but they accepted without loss of
time such invitations to shoot at Aussolas as came their way.
Notwithstanding the buccaneerings of Flurry's grandmother,
the woods of Aussolas, in decent weather, were usually good for
fifteen to twenty couple of cock.

I sent my acceptance before mentioning to Philippa that
Bernard Shute was to be of the party. It was impossible to
make Philippa understand that those who shot Bernard's
pheasants at Clountiss could hardly do less than retaliate when
occasion served. I had once, in a moment of regrettable

expansion, entertained my wife with an account of how an entire shooting party had successively cast themselves upon their faces, while the muzzle of Bernard's gun had followed, half-way round the compass, a rabbit that had broken back. No damage had ensued, not even to the rabbit, but I had supplied Philippa with a fact that was an unfortunate combination of a thorn in her pillow and a stone in her sling.

The frost held; it did more than hold, it gripped. As I drove to Aussolas the fields lay rigid in the constraining cold; the trees were as dead as the telegraph poles, and the whistle of the train came thin and ghostly across four miles of silent country. Everything was half alive, with the single exception of the pony, which, filled with the idiotic exaltation that frost imparts to its race, danced upon its frost-nails, shied with un-tiring inventiveness, and made three several and well-conceived attempts to bolt. Maria, with her nose upon my gaiter, shuddered uninterruptedly throughout the drive, partly be-cause of the pinching air, partly in honour of the sovereign presence of the gun-case.

Old Mrs. Knox was standing on the steps as I walked round to the hall door of Aussolas Castle. She held a silver bowl in her hand; on her head, presumably as a protection against the cold, was a table-napkin; round her feet a throng of hens and pigeons squabbled for the bits that she flung to them from the bowl, and a furtive and distrustful peacock darted a blue neck in among them from the outskirts.

'"Good-morrow, old Sir Thomas Erpingham,"' was Mrs. Knox's singular greeting; '"a good soft pillow for that good grey head were better than a churlish turf of France"!'

My friendship with Mrs. Knox was now of several years' standing, and I knew enough of her to gather that I stood rebuked for being late.

' 'Flurry arrived only half an hour ago! my first intimation of a shooting party,' she continued, in the dictatorial voice that was always a shock when taken in connection with her beggar-woman's costume; 'a nice time of day to begin to look for beaters! And the other feather-bed sportsmen haven't arrived yet. In old times they would have had ten couple by this time, and then Mr. Flurry complains of the shooting!'

She was here interrupted by the twitching of the table-napkin from her head by her body-woman, who had advanced upon her from the rear, with the reigning member of the dynasty of purple velvet bonnets in her hand. The bonnet was substituted for the table-napkin, much as a stage property is shoved on from the wings, and two bony hands, advancing from behind, tied the strings under Mrs. Knox's chin, while she uninterruptedly fed the hens, and denounced the effeteness of modern cock-shooters. The hands descended and fixed a large pin in the uppermost of her mistress's shawls.

'Mullins, have done!' exclaimed Mrs. Knox, suddenly tearing herself from her captor, 'you're an intolerable nuisance!'

'Oh, very well, ma'am, maybe you'd sooner go out with your head naked and soak the cold!' returned Mullins, retiring with the honours of war and the table-napkin.

'Mullins and I get on famously,' observed Mrs. Knox, crushing an empty egg-shell with her yellow diamonded fingers and returning it to its original donors; 'we're both mad, you know!'

Comment on this might have been difficult, but I was preserved from it by the approach across the frozen gravel of a short, red-bearded man, Mrs. Knox's gardener, wood-ranger, and ruling counsellor, John Kane. He held in his hands two large apples of arsenical hue, and, taking off his hat to me with much dignity, addressed himself to the lady of the house.

'He says he'd sooner walk barefoot to Cork than to give three and fippence for the likes of them!'

'I'm sure I've no objection if he does,' responded Mrs. Knox, turning the silver bowl upside down over the scrimmaging hens and pigeons; 'I dare say it would be no novelty to him.'

'And isn't that what I told him!' said John Kane, his voice at once ascending to the concert pitch of altercation. 'I said to him if the Lord Left'nant and the Pope was follying me around the yard of Aussolas offering three and a penny for them apples they'd not get them! Sure the nuns gave us that much for windfalls that was only fit to be making cherubs with!'

I might have been struck by the fitness, as well as the ingenuity, of this industry, but in some remote byway of my brain the remembrance woke of a 'black-currant cherub' prescribed by Mrs. Cadogan for sore throats, and divined by Philippa to be a syrup. I turned away and lit a cigarette in order to conceal my feelings from John Kane, round whose red beard the smoke of battle hung almost palpably.

'What's between you?' asked his mistress sharply.

'Three and a penny he's offering, ma'am!' declaimed her deputy, 'for sheep's noses that there isn't one in the country has but yourself! And not a brown farthing more would he give!—the consecrated blagyard!'

Anything less like a sheep's nose than Mrs. Knox's hooked beak, as she received this information, could hardly be imagined.

'You're half a fool, John Kane!' she snapped, 'and the other half's not sensible! Go back and tell him Major Yeates is here and wants to buy every apple I have!' She dealt me a wink that was the next thing to a dig in the ribs. As she spoke a cart drawn by a cheerful-looking grey pony, and conducted by a tall, thin man, came into view from the direction of the yard. It rattled emptily, and proclaimed, as was intended, the rupture of all business relations.

'See here, sir,' said John Kane to me in one hoarse breath, 'when he's over-right the door I'll ask him the three and fippence again, and when he refuses your honour will say we should split the difference——'

The cart advanced, it passed the hall door with a dignity but little impaired by the pony's apprehensive interest in the peacock, and the tall man took off his hat to Mrs. Knox with as gloomy a respect as if she had been a funeral.

John Kane permitted to the salutation the full time due to it, in the manner of one who counts a semibreve rest, while the cart moved implacably onwards. The exact, the psychic instant arrived.

'HONOMAUNDHIAOUL! SULLIVAN!' he shouted, with a full-blown burst of ferocity, hurtling down the steps in pursuit, 'will ye take them or lave them?'

To manifest, no doubt, her complete indifference to the issue, Mrs. Knox turned and went into the house, followed by the majority of the hens, and left me to await my cue. The play was played out with infinite credit to both artists, and at the full stretch of their lungs; at the preordained moment I intervened with the conventional impromptu, and suggested that the difference should be split. The curtain immediately fell, and somewhere in the deep of the hall a glimpse of the purple bonnet told me that Mrs. Knox was in the auditorium.

When I rejoined her I found Flurry with her, and something i the atmosphere told that here also was storm.

'Well, take them! Take them all!' Mrs. Knox was saying in high indignation. 'Take Mullins and the maids if you like! I dare say they might be more use than the men!'

'They 'll make more row, anyhow,' said Flurry sourly. 'I wonder is it them that put down all the rabbit traps I 'm after seeing in the coach-house this minute!'

'It may be *they*, but it certainly is not *them*,' retorted Mrs. Knox, hitting flagrantly below the belt; 'and if you want beaters found for you, you should give me more than five minutes' warning——' She turned with the last word, and moved towards the staircase.

'I beg your pardon, ma'am,' said John Kane, very respectfully, from the hall door, 'that Sullivan brought this down for your honour.'

He placed on the table a bottle imperfectly wrapped in newspaper.

'Tell Sullivan,' said Flurry, without an instant's hesitation, 'that he makes the worst potheen in the country, and I 'll prosecute him for bringing it here, unless he comes out to beat with the rest of you.'

Remembering my official position I discreetly examined the barrels of my gun.

'You 'll give him no such message!' screamed Mrs. Knox over the dark rail of the staircase. 'Let him take himself and his apples off out of this!' Then, in the same breath, and almost the same key, 'Major Yeates, which do you prefer, curry, or Irish stew?'

The *cuisine* at Aussolas was always fraught with dark possibilities, being alternately presided over by bibulous veterans from Dublin, or aboriginal kitchen-maids off the estate. Feeling as Fair Rosamond might have felt when proffered the dagger or the bowl, I selected curry.

'Then curry it shall be,' said Mrs. Knox, with a sudden and awful affability. In this gleam of stormy sunshine I thought it well to withdraw.

'Did you ever eat my grandmother's curry?' said Flurry to me, later, as we watched Bernard Shute trying to back his motor into the coach-house.

I said I thought not.

'Well, you 'd take a splint off a horse with it,' said Mrs. Knox's grandson.

The Aussolas woods were full of birds that day. Birds bursting out of holly bushes like corks out of soda-water bottles, skimming low under the branches of fir-trees, bolting across rides at a thousand miles an hour, swinging away through prohibitive tree-tops, but to me had befallen the inscrutable and invincible accident of being 'off my day,' and, by an equal unkindness, Fate had allotted to me the station next Flurry. Every kind of bird came my way except the easy ones, and, as a general thing, when I had done no more than add a little pace to their flight, they went down to Flurry, who never in my experience had been off his day, and they seldom went farther afield. The beaters, sportsmen every man of them, had a royal time. They flailed the bushes and whacked the tree trunks; the discordant chorus of 'Hi cock! Hi cock! Cock! Cock! Prrrr!' rioted through the peaceful woods, and every other minute a yell of 'Mark!' broke like a squib through the din. The clamour, the banging of the guns, and the expectancy kept the nerves tingling; the sky between the grey branches was as blue as Italy's; despite fingers as icy as the gun-barrels, despite the speechless reproach of Maria, slinking at my heels in unemployed dejection, I enjoyed every breath of the frosty day. After all, hit or miss, a good day with the cock comes very near a good day with the hounds, without taking into consideration the comfortable fact that in the former the risk is all on the side of the birds.

Little Bosanquet, the captain of coast-guards, on my left, was doing remarkably well, so apparently, was Murray, the D.I. of Police; how Bernard Shute was faring I knew not, but he was certainly burning a lot of powder. At the end of the third beat I found myself beside Murray. His face was redder than usual, even his freckles conveyed an impression of impartially sprinkled cayenne pepper.

'Did you see Shute just now?' he demanded in a ferocious whisper. 'A bird got up between us, and he blazed straight at me! Straight bang in my face, I tell you! Only that I was in a dead line with the bird he 'd have got me!'

'I suppose that was about the safest place,' I said. 'What did you do?'

'I simply told him that if ever he puts a grain into me I shall let him have it back, both barrels.'

'Every one says that to Bernard sooner or later,' said I, pacifically; 'he 'll settle down after lunch.'

'We'll all settle down into our graves,' grumbled Murray; 'that'll be the end of it.'

After this it was scarcely composing to a husband and father to find Mr. Shute occupying the position on my right hand as we embarked upon the last beat of the Middle Wood. He was still distinctly unsettled, and most distressingly on the alert. Nothing escaped his vigilance, the impossible wood pigeon, clattering out of the wrong side of a fir-tree, received its brace of cartridges as instantly as the palpable rabbit, fleeing down the ride before him, and with an equal immunity. Between my desire to keep the thickest tree trunks between me and him, and the companion desire that he should be thoroughly aware of my whereabouts, my shooting, during that beat, went still more to pieces; a puff of feathers, wandering softly down through the radiant air, was the sum total of my achievements.

The end of the beat brought us to the end of the wood, and out upon an open space of sedgy grass and bog that stretched away on the right to the shore of Aussolas Lake; opposite to us, a couple of hundred yards away, was another and smaller wood, clothing one side of a high promontory near the head of the lake. Flurry and I were first out of the covert.

'We'll have time to run through the Rhododendron Wood before lunch,' he said, looking at his watch, 'Here! John Kane!' He put two fingers in his mouth and projected a whistle that cleft my head like a scimetar.

John Kane emerged, nymph-like, from a laurel bush in our immediate vicinity.

'"Tis only lost time to be beating them rosydandhrums, Master Flurry,' he said volubly, 'there wasn't a bird in that bit o' wood this winter. Not a week passes but I'm in it, making up the bounds fence against the cattle, and I never seen a one!'

'You might be more apt to be looking out for a rabbit than a cock, John,' said Flurry expressionlessly, 'but isn't it down in the lower paddocks you have the cattle and the young horses this hard weather?'

'Oh it is, sir, it is, of course, but indeed it's hard for me to know where they are, with the misthress telling this one and that one to put them in their choice place. Sure she dhrives me to and fro in my mind till I do have a headache from her!'

A dull rumble came to us across the marsh, and, as if Mrs.

Knox had been summoned by her henchman's accusation,
there laboured into view on the road that skirted the marsh a
long and dilapidated equipage, silhouetted, with its solitary
occupant, against the dull shine of the frozen lake.

'Tally-ho! Here comes the curry for you, Major! You'll
have to eat it, I tell you!' He paused. 'I'm dashed if she
hasn't got Sullivan's pony! Well, she'd steal the horns off
a cow!'

It was indeed the grey pony that paced demurely in the
shafts of Mrs. Knox's phaeton, and at its head marched Sullivan; fragments of loud and apparently agreeable conversation
reached us, as the procession moved onwards to the usual
luncheon tryst at the head of the lake.

'Come now, John Kane,' said Flurry, eyeing the cortège,
'you're half your day sitting in front of the kitchen fire. How
many of my rabbits went into that curry?'

'Rabbits, Master Flurry?' echoed John Kane almost pity-
ingly, 'there's no call for them trash in Aussolas kitchen!
And if we wanted them itself, we'd not get them. I declare
to me conscience there's not a rabbit in Aussolas demesne this
minute, with the way your honour has them ferreted—let alone
the foxes!'

'I suppose it's scarcely worth your while to put the traps
down,' said Flurry benignly; 'that's why they were in the
coach-house this morning.'

There was an undissembled titter from a group of beaters
in the background; Flurry tucked his gun under his arm and
walked on.

'It'd be no more than a charity if ye'd eat the lunch now,
sir,' urged John Kane at his elbow, in fluent remonstrance,
'and leave Sullivan go home. Sure it'll be black night on him
before the misthress will be done with him. And as for that
wood, it's hardly we can go through it with the threes that's
down since the night of the Big Wind, and briars, and all sorts.
Sure the last time I was through it me pants was in shreds,
and I was that tired when I got home I couldn't stoop to pick
a herrin' off a tongs, and as for the floods and the holes in the
western end——' John Kane drew a full breath, and with a
trawling glance gathered Bernard and me into his audience.
'I declare to ye, gintlemen, me boots when I took them off was
more than boots! They resimbled the mouth of a hake!'

'Ah, shut your own mouth,' said Flurry.

The big rhododendron was one of the glories of Aussolas. Its original progenitor had been planted by Flurry's great-grandmother, and now, after a century of unchecked licence, it and its descendants ran riot among the pine stems on the hillside above the lake, and, in June, clothed a precipitous half acre with infinite varieties of pale mysterious mauve. The farm road by which Mrs. Knox had traversed the marsh here followed obediently the spurs of the wood and creeks of the shore, in their alternate give and take. From the exalted station that had been given me on the brow of the hill, I looked down on it between the trunks of the pine-trees, and saw, instead of mysterious mauve blossoms, the defiant purple of Mrs. Knox's bonnet, glowing, motionless, in a sheltered and sunny angle of the road just where it met the wood. She was drawn up in her phaeton with her back to a tumbledown erection of stones and branches, that was supposed to bar the way into the wood; beside her was the great flat boulder that had for generations been the table for shooting lunches. How, in any area of less than a quarter of a mile, Sullivan had contrived to turn the phaeton, was known only to himself, but he had accomplished it, and was now adding to the varied and unforeseen occupations of his day the task of unpacking the luncheon basket. As I waited for the whistle that was the signal for the beat to begin, I viewed the proceedings up to the point where Sullivan, now warming artistically to his work, crowned the arrangement with the bottle of potheen.

It was at that moment that I espied John Kane break from a rhododendron bush beside the phaeton, with a sack over his shoulder. This, as far as I could see through the branches, he placed upon Mrs. Knox's lap, the invaluable Sullivan hurrying to his aid. The next instant I saw Murray arrive and take up his allotted station upon the road; John Kane retired into the evergreen thicket as abruptly as he had emerged from it, Flurry's whistle sounded, and the yells of 'Hi cock' began again.

We moved forward very slowly, in order to keep station with Murray, who had to follow on the road the outer curve of the wood, while we struck straight across it. It was a wood of old and starveling trees, strangled by ivy, broken by combat with each other in the storms that rushed upon them up the lake; it was two years since I had last been through it, and I re-

membered well the jungle of ferns and the undergrowth of
briars that had shredded the pants of John Kane, and had held
in their thorny depths what Flurry had described as 'a dose of
cock.' To-day the wood seemed strangely bare, and remarkably out of keeping with John Kane's impassioned indictment;
the ferns, even the bracken, had almost disappeared, the briar
brakes were broken down, and laced with black paths, and in
the frozen paste of dead leaves and peat mould the hoof marks
of cattle and horses bore witness against them, like the thumb-
prints of a criminal. In the first ten minutes not a gun had been
let off; I anticipated pleasantly, if inadequately, the remarks
that Flurry would address to John Kane at the conclusion of
the beat. To foreshadow John Kane's reply to Flurry was a
matter less simple. Bernard Shute was again the next gun on
my left, and kept, as was his wont, something ahead of his due
place in the line; of this I did not complain, it made it all the
easier to keep my eye on him. The idle cartridges in his gun
were obviously intolerable to him; as he crossed a little glade
he discharged both barrels into the firmament, where far above,
in tense flight and steady as a constellation, moved a wedge of
wild geese. The wedge continued its course unshaken, but, as if
lifted by the bang, the first woodcock of the beat got up in front
of me, and swung away into the rhododendrons. 'Mark!' I
shouted, loosing an ineffectual cartridge after him. Mr. Shute
was equal to the occasion, and let fly his usual postman's knock
with both barrels. In instant response there arose from behind
the rhododendrons the bray of a donkey, fraught with outrage
and terror, followed by crashing of branches and the thunderous
galloping of many hoofs, and I had a glimpse of a flying party
of cattle and horses, bursting from the rhododendron bushes
and charging down a grassy slope in the direction of the road.
Every tail was in the air, the cattle bellowed, and the donkey,
heading the flight, did not cease to proclaim his injuries.

'How many of them have you hit?' I shouted.

'I believe I got 'em all, bar the cock!' returned Mr. Shute,
with ecstasy scarcely tempered by horror.

I hastened to the brow of the hill, and thence beheld Mrs.
Knox's livestock precipitate themselves on to the road, and turn
as one man in the direction of home. With a promptitude for
which I have never been given sufficient credit, I shoved my
gun into the branches of a tree and ran back through the wood

at my best pace. In that glimpse of the rout I had recognized the streaming chestnut mane and white legs of the venerable Trinket, the most indomitable old rogue that had ever reared up generations of foals in the way they should not go, and I knew by repute that once she was set going it would take more to stop her than the half-demolished barricade at the entrance to the wood.

As I ran I seemed to see Trinket and her disciples hurling themselves upon Mrs. Knox's phaeton and Sullivan's pony, with what results no man could tell. They had, however, first to circumnavigate the promontory; my chance was by crossing it at the neck to get to the phaeton before them. The going was bad, and the time was short; I went for all I was worth, and Maria, mystified, but burning with zeal, preceded me with kangaroo leaps and loud and hysterical barks. A mossy wall ringed the verge of the hill; I followed Maria over it, and the wall, or a good part of it, followed me down the hill. I plunged onward amid the coiling stems and branches of the big rhododendrons, an illuminative flash of the purple bonnet giving me my bearings. A sort of track revealed itself, doubling and dodging and dropping down rocky slides, as if in flight before me. It was near the foot of the hill that a dead branch extended a claw, and with human malignity plucked the eyeglass from my eye and snapped the cord: the eyeglass, entering into the spirit of the thing, aimed for the nearest stone and hit it. It is the commonest of disasters for the short-sighted, yet custom cannot stale it; I made the usual comment, with the usual fervour and futility, and continued to blunder forward in all the discomfort of half-sight. The trumpeting of the donkey heralded the oncoming of the stampede; I broke my way through the last of the rhododendrons and tumbled out on to the road twenty yards ahead of the phaeton.

Sullivan's pony was on its hind legs, and Sullivan was hanging on to its head. Mrs. Knox was sitting erect in the phaeton with the reins in her hand.

'Get out, ma'am! Get out!' Sullivan was howling, as I scrambled to my feet.

'Don't be a fool!' replied Mrs. Knox, without moving.

The stampede was by this time confronted by the barrier. There was not, however, a moment of hesitation; Trinket came rocketing out over it as if her years were four, instead of four-

and-twenty; she landed with her white nose nearly in the back seat of the phaeton, got past with a swerve and a slip up, and went away for her stable with her tail over her back, followed with staglike agility by her last foal, her last foal but one, and the donkey, with the young cattle hard on their flying heels. Bernard, it was very evident, had peppered them impartially all round. Sullivan's pony was alternately ramping heraldically, and wriggling like an eel in the clutches of Sullivan, and I found myself snatching blindly at whatever came to my hand of his headstall. What I caught was a mingled handful of forelock and browband; the pony twitched back his head with the cunning that is innate in ponies, and the headstall, which was a good two sizes too large, slid over its ears as though they had been buttered, and remained, bit and all, in my hand. There was a moment of struggle, in which Sullivan made a creditable effort to get the pony's head into chancery under his arm; foreseeing the issue, I made for the old lady, with the intention of dragging her from the carriage. She was at the side farthest from me, and I got one foot into the phaeton and grasped at her.

At that precise moment the pony broke away, with a jerk that pitched me on to my knees on the mat at her feet. Simultaneously I was aware of Sullivan, at the opposite side, catching Mrs. Knox to his bosom as the phaeton whirled past him, while I, as sole occupant, wallowed prone upon a heap of rugs. That ancient vehicle banged in and out of the ruts with an agility that ill befitted its years, while, with extreme caution, and the aid of the side rail, I gained the seat vacated by Mrs. Knox, and holding on there as best I could, was aware that I was being seriously run away with by the apple-man's pony, on whom my own disastrous hand had bestowed his freedom.

The flying gang in front, enlivened no doubt by the noise in their rear, maintained a stimulating lead. We were now clear of the wood, and the frozen ditches of the causeway awaited me on either side in steely parallel lines; out in the open the frost had turned the ruts to iron, and it was here that the phaeton, entering into the spirit of the thing, began to throw out ballast. The cushions of the front seat were the first to go, followed, with a bomb-like crash, by a stone hot-water jar, that had lurked in the deeps of the rugs. It was in negotiating a stiffish outcrop of rock in the track that the back seat broke loose and fell to earth with a hollow thump; with a corresponding thump I returned to my seat from a considerable altitude, and found that in the interval the cushion had removed itself from beneath me, and followed its fellows overboard. Near the end of the causeway we were, into Trinket's rearguard, one of whom, a bouncing young heifer, slammed a kick into the pony's ribs as he drew level with her, partly as a witticism, partly as a token of contempt. With that the end came. The pony wrenched to the left, the off front wheel jammed in a rut, came off, and the phaeton rose like a live thing beneath me and bucked me out on to the road.

A succession of crashes told that the pony was making short work of the dashboard; for my part I lay something stunned, and with a twisted ankle, on the crisp whitened grass of the causeway, and wondered dully why I was surrounded by dead rabbits.

By the time I had pulled myself together Sullivan's pony was continuing his career, accompanied by a fair proportion of the phaeton, and on the road lay an inexplicable sack, with a rabbit, like Benjamin's cup, in its mouth.

Not less inexplicable was the appearance of Minx, my wife's fox-terrier, whom I had last seen in an arm-chair by the drawing-room fire at Shreelane, and now, in the role of the faithful St. Bernard, was licking my face lavishly and disgustingly. Her attentions had the traditional reviving effect. I sat up and dashed her from me, and in so doing beheld my wife in the act of taking refuge in the frozen ditch, as the cavalcade swept past, the phaeton and pony bringing up the rear like artillery.

'What has happened? Are you hurt?' she panted, speeding to me.

'I am; very much hurt,' I said, with what was, I think, justifiable ill-temper, as I got gingerly on to my feet, almost annoyed to find that my leg was not broken.

'But, dearest Sinclair, *has* he shot you? I got so frightened about you that I bicycled over to—— Ugh! Good gracious!' —as she trod on and into a mound of rabbits—'what are you doing with all these horrible things?'

I looked back in the direction from which I had come, and saw Mrs. Knox advancing along the causeway arm-in-arm with the now inevitable Sullivan (who, it may not be out of place to remind the reader, had come to Aussolas early in the morning,

with the pure and single intention of buying apples). In Mrs.
Knox's disengaged arm was something that I discerned to be
the bottle of potheen, and I instantly resolved to minimize the
extent of my injuries. Flurry, and various items of the shooting
party, were converging upon us from the wood by as many and
various short cuts. 'I don't quite know what I am doing with
the rabbits,' I replied, 'but I rather think I 'm giving them
away.'

As I spoke something darted past Mrs. Knox, something
that looked like a bundle of rags in a cyclone, but was, as a
matter of fact, my faithful water-spaniel, Maria. She came
on in zigzag bounds, in short maniac rushes. Twice she flung
herself by the roadside and rolled, driving her snout into the
ground like the coulter of a plough. Her eyes were starting
from her head, her tail was tucked between her legs. She bit,
and tore frantically with her claws at the solid ice of a puddle.

'She 's mad! She 's gone mad!' exclaimed Philippa,
snatching up as a weapon something that looked like a frying-
pan, but was, I believe, the step of the phaeton.

Maria was by this time near enough for me to discern a
canary-coloured substance masking her muzzle.

'Yes, she 's quite mad,' I replied, possessed by a spirit of
divination. 'She 's been eating the rabbit curry.'

V

A CONSPIRACY OF SILENCE

It has not often been my lot to be associated with a being of
so profound and rooted a pessimism as Michael Leary, Huntsman and Kennelman to Mr. Flurry Knox's Foxhounds. His
attitude was that of the one and only righteous man in a perfidious and dissolute world. With, perhaps, the exception of
Flurry Knox, he believed in no one save himself. I was
thoroughly aware of my inadequacy as Deputy-Master, and
cherished only a hope that Michael might look upon me as a
kind of Parsifal, a fool perhaps, yet at least a 'blameless fool'; but
during my time of office there were many distressing moments
in which I was made to feel not only incapable, but culpable.

Michael was small, sandy, green-eyed, freckled, and, I believe, considerably junior to myself; he neither drank nor smoked, and he had a blistering tongue. I have never tried more sincerely to earn any one's good opinion.

It was a pleasant afternoon towards the middle of December, and I was paying my customary Sunday visit to the kennels to see the hounds fed. What Michael called 'the Throch' was nearly empty; the greedier of the hounds were flitting from place to place in the line, in the undying belief that others were better off than they. I was studying the row of particoloured backs, and trying for the fiftieth time to fit each with its name, when I was aware of a most respectable face, with grey whiskers, regarding me from between the bars of the kennel door.

With an effort not inferior to that with which I had just discriminated between Guardsman and General, I recognized my visitor as Mr. Jeremiah Flynn, a farmer, and a cattle dealer on a large scale, with whom I had occasionally done business in a humble way. He was a District Councillor, and a man of substance; he lived twenty miles away, at a place on the coast called Knockeenbwee, in a flat-faced, two-storeyed house of the usual type of hideousness. Once, when an unkind fate had sent me to that region, I had heard the incongruous tinkle of a piano proceeding from Mr. Flynn's mansion, as I drove past fighting an umbrella against the wet wind that swept in from the Atlantic.

'I beg your pardon, Major Yeates,' began Mr. Flynn, with an agreeable smile, which I saw in sections between the bars; 'I had a little business over this side of the country, and I took the liberty of taking a stroll around to the kennels to see the hounds.'

I made haste to extend the hospitality of the feeding-yard to my visitor, who accepted it with equal alacrity, and went on to remark that it was wonderful weather for the time of year. Having obeyed this primary instinct of mankind, Mr. Flynn embarked upon large yet able compliments on the appearance of the hounds. His manners were excellent; sufficiently robust to accord with his grey frieze coat and flat-topped felt hat, and with just the extra touch of deference that expressed his respect for my high qualities and position.

'Ye have them in great form, Michael,' he remarked, surveying the hounds' bloated sides with a knowledgable eye; 'and upon me word there's our own poor Playboy! and a fine dog he is too!'

'He is; and a fine dog to hunt rabbits!' said Michael, without a relaxation of his drab countenance.

'I dare say, Major, you didn't know that it was in my place that fellow was rared?' continued Mr. Flynn.

Owing to his providentially distinctive colouring of lemon and white, Playboy was one of the hounds about whose identity I was never in doubt. I was able to bestow a suitable glance upon him, and to recall the fact of his having come from a trencher-fed pack, of which Mr. Flynn was the ruling spirit, kept by the farmers in the wildernesses beyond and around Knockeenbwee.

'Ah, Mr. Knox was too smart for us over that hound!' pursued Mr. Flynn pleasantly; 'there was a small difference between himself and meself in a matter of a few heifers I was buying off him—a thrifle of fifteen shillings it was, I believe——'

'Five-and-thirty,' said Michael to the lash of his thong, in which he was making a knot.

'And I had to give him the pup before we could come to terms,' ended my visitor.

Whether at fifteen or thirty-five shillings Playboy had been a cheap hound. Brief, and chiefly ornamental, as my term of office had been, I had learnt to know his voice in covert, and had learned also to act upon it in moments of solitary and helpless ignorance as to what was happening. This, however, was not the moment to sing his praises; I preserved a careful silence.

'I rared himself and his sister,' said Mr. Flynn, patting Playboy heavily, 'but the sister died on me. I think 'twas from all she fretted after the brother when he went, and 'twas a pity. Those two had the old Irish breed in them; sure you'd know it by the colour, and there's no more of them now in the country only the mother, and she had a right to be shot this long time.'

'Come hounds,' said Michael, interrupting this rhapsody, 'open the door, Bat.'

The pack swept out of the feeding yard and were away on their wonted constitutional in half a minute.

'Grand training, grand training!' said Mr. Flynn admiringly, 'they're a credit to you, Major! It's impossible to have hounds anyway disciplined running wild through the country the way our little pack is. Indeed it came into my mind on the

way here to try could I coax you to come over and give us a
day's hunting. We 're destroyed with foxes. Such marauding
I never saw! As for turkeys and fowl, they 're tired of them,
and it 's my lambs they 'll be after next!'

The moment of large and general acquiescence in Mr. Flynn's
proposal narrowed itself by imperceptible degrees to the
moment, not properly realized till it arrived, the horrid moment
of getting up at a quarter to seven on a December morning, in
order to catch the early train for Knockeenbwee.

In the belief that I was acting in the interest of sport I had
announced at the last meet that there was to be a by-day at
Knockeenbwee. To say that the fact was received without
enthusiasm is to put it mildly. I was assured by one authority
that I should have to hunt the hounds from a steam launch;
another, more sympathetic, promised a drag, but tempered the
encouragement by saying that the walls there were all made of
slates, and that by the end of the run the skin would be hanging
off the horses' legs like the skins of bananas. Nothing short
of a heart-to-heart appeal to my Whip, Dr. Jerome Hickey,
induced him to promise his support. Michael, from first to
last, remained an impenetrable thunder-cloud. The die, however, was cast, and the hospitality of Mr. Flynn accepted.
The eve of the by-day arrived, and the Thunder-cloud and the
hounds were sent on by road to Knockeenbwee, accompanied
by my ancient ally Slipper, who led my mare, and rode Philippa's
pony, which had been commandeered for the occasion.

Next morning at 9.45 a.m. the train stopped by signal at the
flag station of Moyny, a cheerless strip of platform, from which
a dead straight road retreated to infinity across a bog. An outside car was being backed hard into the wall of the road by a
long, scared rag of a chestnut horse as Dr. Hickey and I emerged
from the station, and its driver was composing its anxieties as
to the nature of trains by beating it in the face with his
whip. This, we were informed, was Mr. Flynn's equipage,
and at a favourable moment in the conflict Dr. Hickey and I
mounted it.

'It 's seldom the thrain stands here,' said the driver apologetically, as we started at a strong canter, 'and this one 's very
frightful always.'

The bog ditches fleeted by at some twelve miles an hour;

they were the softest, blackest, and deepest that I have ever seen, and I thanked heaven that I was not in my red coat.

'I suppose you never met the Miss Flynns?' murmured Dr. Hickey to me across the well of the car.

I replied in the negative.

'Oh, they 're very grand,' went on my companion, with a wary eye on the humped back of the driver, 'I believe they never put their foot outside the door unless they 're going to Paris. Their father told me last week that lords in the streets of Cork were asking who they were.'

'I suppose that was on their way to Paris,' I suggested.

'It was not,' said the driver, with stunning unexpectedness, ''twas when they went up on th' excursion last month for to have their teeth pulled. G'wout o' that!' This to the horse, who had shied heavily at a goat.

Dr. Hickey and I sank into a stricken silence, five minutes of which, at the pace we were travelling, sufficed to bring us to a little plantation, shorn and bent by the Atlantic wind, low whitewashed walls, an economical sweep of gravel, and an entrance gate constructed to fit an outside car to an inch. From the moment that these came within the range of vision the driver beat the horse with the handle of his whip, a prelude, as we discovered, to the fact that a minor gate, obviously and invitingly leading to the yard, lolled open on one hinge at the outset of the plantation. There was a brief dissension, followed by a hand gallop to the more fitting entrance; that we should find it too fitting was a foregone conclusion, and Dr. Hickey whirled his legs on to the seat at the moment when impact between his side of the car and the gate post became inevitable. The bang that followed was a hearty one, and the driver transmitted it to me in great perfection with his elbow as he lurched on to me; there was a second and hollower bang as the well of the car, detached by the shock, dropped on the axle and turned over, flinging from it in its somersault a harlequinade assortment of herrings, loaves of bread, and a bandbox. It was, I think, a loaf of bread that hit the horse on the hocks, but under all the circumstances even a herring would have been ample excuse for the two sledge-hammer kicks which he instantly administered to the footboard. While the car still hung in the gateway a donkey, with a boy sitting on the far end of its back, was suddenly mingled with the episode. The boy was off the donkey's back and the driver was off mine at apparently one and the same moment, and the car was somehow backed off the pillar; as we scraped through the boy said something to the driver in a brogue that was a shade more sophisticated than the peasant tune. It seemed to me to convey the facts that Miss Lynie was waiting for her hat, and that Maggie Kane was dancing mad for the soft sugar. We proceeded to the house, leaving the ground strewn with what appeared to be the elemental stage of a picnic.

'I suppose you're getting him into form for the hunt, Eugene?' said Dr. Hickey, as the lathered and panting chestnut came to a stand some ten yards beyond the hall door.

'Well, indeed, we thought it no harm to loosen him under the car before Master Eddy went riding him,' replied Eugene, 'and begannies I'm not done with him yet! I have to be before the masther at the next thrain.'

He shed us and our belongings on the steps, and drove away at a gallop.

The meet had been arranged for half-past eleven. It was half-past ten when Dr. Hickey and I were incarcerated in a dungeon-cold drawing-room by a breathless being in tennis shoes, with her hair down her back, doubtless Maggie Kane, hot from the war-dance brought on by the lack of soft sugar. She told us in a gusty whisper that the masther would be in shortly, and the ladies was coming down, and left us to meditate upon our surroundings.

A cascade of white paper flowed glacially from the chimney to the fender; the gloom was Cimmerian, and unalterable, owing to the fact that the blind was broken; the cold of a never occupied room ate into our vitals. Footsteps pounded overhead and crept in the hall. The house was obviously full of people, but no one came near us. Had it not been for my companion's biographical comments on the photographs with which the room was decked, all of them, it appeared, suitors of the Misses Flynn, I think I should have walked back to the station. At eleven o'clock the hurrying feet overhead were stilled, there was a rustling in the hall as of a stage storm, and the daughters of the house made their entry, wonderfully attired in gowns suggestive of a theatre, or a tropical garden party, and in picture hats. As I viewed the miracles of hairdressing, black as the raven's wing, the necklaces, the bracelets, and the lavish top-dressing of powder, I wildly wondered if Dr. Hickey and I should not have been in evening clothes.

We fell to a laboured conversation, conducted upon the highest social plane. The young ladies rolled their black eyes under arched eyebrows, and in almost unimpeachable English accents supposed I found Ireland very dull. They asked me if I often went to the London opera. They declared that when at home music was their only resource, and made such pointed reference to their Italian duets that I found myself trembling on the verge of asking them to sing. Dr. Hickey, under whose wing I had proposed to shelter myself, remained sardonically aloof. A blessed diversion was created by the entrance, at racing speed, of Maggie Kane, bearing a trayful of burning sods of turf; the cascade was torn from the chimney, and the tray was emptied into the grate. Blinding smoke filled the room, and Maggie Kane murmured an imprecation upon 'jackdahs,' their nests, and all their works.

The moment seemed propitious for escape; I looked at my watch, and said that if they would kindly tell me the way to the yard I would go round and see about things.

The arched eyebrows went up a shade higher; the Misses Flynn said they feared they hardly knew the way to the stables.

Dr. Hickey rose. 'Indeed it isn't easy to find them,' he said, 'but I dare say the Major and myself will be able to make them out.'

When we got outside he looked down his long nose at me.

'Stables indeed!' he said, 'I hate that dirty little boasting!'

Mr. Flynn's yard certainly did not at the first glance betray the presence of stables. It consisted of an indeterminate assembly of huts, with a long corrugated iron shed standing gauntly in the midst; swamp of varying depths and shades occupied the intervals. From the shed proceeded the lamentable and indignant clamours of the hounds, against its door leaned Michael in his red coat, enacting, obviously, the role of a righteous man constrained to have his habitation in the tents of Kedar. A reverential knot of boys admired him from the wall of a neighbouring pigsty; countrymen of all ages, each armed with a stick and shadowed by a cur, more or less resembling a foxhound, stood about in patient groups; two or three dejected horses were nibbling, unattended, at a hayrick. Of our host there was no sign.

At the door of the largest hut Slipper was standing.

'Come in and see the mare, Major,' he called to me in his

bantam-cock voice as I approached. 'Last night when we got in she was clean dead altogether, but this morning when I was giving the feed to the pony she retched out her neck and met her teeth in me poll! Oh, she's in great heart now!'

In confirmation of this statement a shrewish squeal from Lady Jane proceeded from the interior.

'Sure I slep' in the straw last night with herself and the pony. She'd have him ate this morning only for me.'

The record of his devotion was here interrupted by a tremendous rattling in the farm lane; it heralded the entrance of Mr. Flynn on his outside car, drawn at full gallop by the young chestnut horse.

'Oh, look at me, Major, how late I am!' shouted Mr. Flynn jovially, as he scrambled off the car. 'I declare you could light a candle at me eye with the shame that's in it, as they say! I was back in Curranhilty last night buying stock, and this was the first train I could get. Well, well, the day's long and drink's plenty!'

He bundled into a darksome hole, and emerged with a pair of dirty spurs and a Malacca crop as heavy as a spade handle.

'Michael! Did they tell you we have a fox for you in the hill north?'

'I wasn't speaking to any of them,' replied Michael coldly.

'Well, your hounds will be speaking to him soon! Here, hurry boys, pull out the horses!'

His eye fell on the chestnut, upon whose reeking back Eugene was cramming a saddle, while the boy who had met us at the entrance gate was proffering to it a tin basin full of oats.

'What are you doing with the young horse?' he roared.

'I thought Master Eddy would ride him, sir,' replied Eugene.

'Well, he will not,' said Mr. Flynn, conclusively; 'the horse has enough work done, and let you walk him about easy till he's cool. You can folly the hunt then.'

Two more crestfallen countenances than those of the young gentlemen he addressed it has seldom been my lot to see. The saddle was slowly removed. Master Eddy, red up to the roots of his black hair, retired silently with his basin of oats into the stable behind Slipper. Even had I not seen his cuff go to his eyes I should have realized that life would probably never hold for him a bitterer moment.

The hounds were already surging out of the yard with a

following wave, composed of every living thing in sight. As I took Lady Jane from the hand of Slipper, Philippa's pony gave a snort. Some touch of Philippa's criminal weakness for boys assailed me.

'That boy can ride the pony if he likes,' I said to Slipper.

I followed the hounds and their cortège down a deep and filthy lane. Mr. Flynn was just in front of me, on a broad-beamed white horse, with string-halt; three or four of the trencher-fed aliens slunk at his heels, the mouth of a dingy horn protruded from his coat pocket. I trembled in spirit as I thought of Michael.

We were out at length into large and furzy spaces that slanted steeply to the cliffs; like smuts streaming out of a chimney the followers of the hunt belched from the lane and spread themselves over the pale-green slopes. From this point the proceedings became merged in total incoherence. Accompanied, as it seemed, by the whole population of the district, we moved *en masse* along the top of the cliffs, while hounds, curs, and boys strove and scrambled below us, over rocks and along ledges, which, one might have thought, would have tried the head of a seagull. Two successive bursts of yelling notified the capture and slaughter of two rabbits; in the first hour and a half I can recall no other achievement.

It was, however, evident that hunting, in its stricter sense, was looked on as a mere species of side-show by the great majority of the field; the cream of the entertainment was found in the negotiation of such jumps as fell to the lot of the riders. These were neither numerous nor formidable, but the storm of cheers that accompanied each performance would have dignified the win of a Grand National favourite.

To Master Eddy, on Philippa's pony, it was apparent that the birthday of his life had come. Attended by Slipper and a howling company of boon companions, he and the pony played a glorified game of pitch and toss, in which, as it seemed to me, heads never turned up. It certainly was an adverse circumstance that the pony's mane had, the day before, been hogged to the bone, so that at critical moments the rider slid, unchecked, from saddle to ears, but the boon companions, who themselves jumped like antelopes, stride for stride with the pony, replaced him unfailingly with timely snatches at whatever portion of his frame first offered itself.

Music, even, was not wanting to our progress. A lame fiddler, on a donkey, followed in our wake, filling Michael's cup of humiliation to the brim, by playing jigs during our frequent moments of inaction. The sun pushed its way out of the grey sky, the sea was grey, with a broad and flashing highway to the horizon, a frayed edge of foam tracked the broken coastline, seagulls screamed and swooped, and the grass on the cliff summits was wondrous green. Old Flynn, on his white horse, moving along the verge, and bleating shrilly upon his horn to the hounds below, became idyllic.

I believe that I ought to have been in a towering passion, and should have swept the hounds home in a flood of blasphemy; as a matter of fact I enjoyed myself. Even Dr. Hickey admitted that it was as pleasant a day for smoking cigarettes as he had ever been out.

It must have been nearly three o'clock when one of Mr. Flynn's hounds, a venerable lady of lemon-and-white complexion, poked her lean head through furze-bushes at the top of the cliff, and came up on to the level ground.

'That's old Terrible, Playboy's mother,' remarked Dr. Hickey, 'and a great stamp of an old hound too, but she can't run up now. Flynn tells me when she's beat out she'll sit down and yowl on the line, she's that fond of it.'

Meantime Terrible was becoming busier and looking younger every moment, as she zigzagged up and across the trampled field towards the hillside. Dr. Hickey paused in the lighting of what must have been his tenth cigarette.

'If we were in a Christian country,' he said, 'you'd say she had a line——'

Old Flynn came pounding up on his white horse, and rode slowly up the hill behind Terrible, who silently pursued her investigations. Fifty or sixty yards higher up, my eye lighted on something that might have been a rusty can, or a wisp of bracken, lying on the sunny side of a bank. As I looked, it moved, and slid away over the top of the bank. A yell, followed by a frenzied tootling on Mr. Flynn's ancient horn, told that he had seen it too, and, in a bedlam of shrieks, chaos was upon us. Through an inextricable huddle of foot-people the hounds came bursting up from the cliffs; fighting every foot of ground with the country boys, yelping with the contagion of excitement, they broke through, and went screaming up the hill to old

Terrible, who was announcing her find in deep and continuous notes.

How Lady Jane got over the first bank without trampling Slipper and two men underfoot is known only to herself; as I landed, Master Eddy and the pony banged heavily into me from the rear, the pony having once and for all resolved not to be sundered by more than a yard from his stable companion of the night before. I can safely say that I have never seen hounds run faster than did Mr. Knox's and the trencher-feds, in that brief scurry from the cliffs at Knockeenbwee. By the time we had crossed the second fence the foot-people were gone, like things in a dream. In front of me was Michael, and, in spite of Michael's spurs, in front of Michael was old Flynn, holding the advantage of his start with a most admirable jealousy. The white horse got over the ground in bucks like a rabbit, the string-halt lending an additional fire to his gait; on every bank his great white hind quarters stood up against the sky, like the gable end of a chapel. Had I had time to think of anything I should have repented acutely of having lent Master Eddy the pony, who was practically running away. Twice I replaced his rider in the saddle with one hand, as he landed off a fence under my stirrup. Master Eddy had lost his cap and whip, his hair was full of mud, pure ecstasy stretched his grin from ear to ear, and broke from him in giggles of delight.

Providentially, it was, as I have said, only a scurry. It seemed that we had run across the neck of a promontory, and in ten minutes we were at the cliffs again, the company reduced to old Flynn, his son, and the Hunt establishment. Below us Moyny Bay was spread forth, enclosing in its span a big green island; between us and the island was a good hundred yards of mud, plump-looking mud, with channels in it. Deep in this the hounds were wading; some of them were already ashore on the island, struggling over black rocks thatched with yellow sea-weed, their voices coming faintly back to us against the wind. The white horse's tail was working like a fan, and we were all, horses and men, blowing hard enough to turn a windmill.

'That's better fun than to be eating your dinner!' puffed Mr. Flynn, purple with pride and heat, as he lowered himself from the saddle. 'There isn't a hound in Ireland would take that stale line up from the cliff only old Terrible!'

'What will we do now, sir?' said Michael to me, presenting

the conundrum with colourless calm, and ignoring the coat-tail trailed for his benefit; 'we'll hardly get them out of that island to-night.'

'I suppose you know you're bare-footed, Major?' put in Hickey, my other Job's comforter, from behind. 'Your two fore-shoes are gone.'

A December day is not good for much after half-past three. For half an hour the horns of Michael and old Flynn blew their summons antiphonally into the immensities of sea and sky, and summoned only the sunset, and after it the twilight; the hounds remained unresponsive, invisible.

'There's rabbits enough in that island to keep ten packs of hounds busy for a month,' said Mr. Flynn; 'the last time I was there I thought 'twas the face of the field was running from me. And what was it after all but the rabbits!'

'*My* hounds wouldn't hunt rabbits if they were throwing after them,' said Michael ferociously.

'Oh, I suppose it's admiring the view they are!' riposted Mr. Flynn; 'I tell ye now, Major, there's a man on the strand below has a flat-bottomed boat, and here's Eugene just come up; I'll send him over with the horn as soon as there's water enough, and he'll flog them out of it.'

The tide crept slowly in over the mud, and a young moon was sending a slender streak of light along it through the dusk before Eugene had accomplished his mission.

The boat returned at last across the channel with a precarious cargo of three hounds, while the rest splashed and swam after her.

'I have them all, only one,' shouted Eugene as he jumped ashore, and came scrambling up the steep slants and shaly ledges of the cliff.

'I hope it isn't Terrible ye left after ye?' roared Mr. Flynn.

'Faith, I don't know which is it it is. I seen him down from me floating in the tide. It must be he was clifted. I think 'tis one of Major Yeates's. We have our own whatever.'

A cold feeling ran down my back. Michael and Hickey silently conned over the pack in the growing darkness, striking matches and shielding them in their hands as they told off one hound after another, hemmed in by an eager circle of country-men.

'It's Playboy's gone,' said Michael, with awful brevity. 'I suppose we may go home now, sir?'

'Ah! hold on, hold on,' put in Mr. Flynn, 'are ye sure now, Eugene, it wasn't a sheep ye saw? I wouldn't wish it for five pounds that the major lost a hound by us.'

'Did ye ever see a sheep with yalla spots on her?' retorted Eugene.

A shout of laughter instantly broke from the circle of sympathizers. I mounted Lady Jane in gloomy silence; there was nothing for it but to face the long homeward road, minus Flurry Knox's best hound, and with the knowledge that while I lived this day's work would not be forgotten to me by him, by Dr. Hickey, and by Michael.

It was Hickey who reminded me that I was also minus two fore-shoes, and that it was an eighteen-mile ride. On my responding irritably that I was aware of both facts, and would get the mare shod at the forge by the station, Mr. Flynn, whose voluble and unceasing condolences had not been the least of my crosses, informed me that the smith had gone away to his father-in-law's wake, and that there wasn't another forge between that and Skebawn.

The steps by which the final disposition of events was arrived at need not here be recounted. It need only be said that every star went out of its course to fight against me; even the special luminary that presided over the Curranhilty and Skebawn branch railway was hostile; I was told that the last train did not run except on Saturdays. Therefore it was that, in a blend of match-light and moonlight, a telegram was written to Philippa, and, at the hour at which Dr. Hickey, the hounds, and Michael were nearing their journey's end, I was seated at the Knockeenbwee dinner table, tired, thoroughly annoyed, devoured with sleep, and laboriously discoursing of London and Paris with the younger Miss Flynn.

A meal that had opened at six with strong tea, cold mutton, and bottled porter, was still, at eight o'clock, in slow but unceasing progress, suggesting successive inspirations on the part of the cook. At about seven we had had mutton chops and potatoes, and now, after an abysmal interval of conversation, we were faced by a roast goose and a rice pudding with currants in it. Through all these things had gone the heavy sounds and crashes that betokened the conversion of the drawing-room into a sleeping-place for me. There was, it appeared, no spare room in the house; I felt positively abject at the thought of the trouble I was inflicting. My soul abhorred the roast goose, and was yet conscious that the only possible acknowledgment of the hospitality that was showered upon me was to eat my way unflinchingly through all that was put upon my plate.

It must have been nine o'clock before we turned our backs upon the pleasures of the table, and settled down to hot whisky punch over a fierce turf fire. Then ensued upon my part one of the most prolonged death-grapples with sleep that it has been my lot to endure. The conversation of Mr. Flynn and his daughters passed into my brain like a narcotic; after circling heavily round various fashionable topics, it settled at length upon croquet, and it was about here that I began to slip from my moorings and drift softly towards unconsciousness. I pulled myself up on the delicious verge of a dream to agree with the statement that 'croquet was a fright! You 'd boil a leg of mutton while you 'd be waiting for your turn!'

Following on this came a period of oblivion, and then an agonized recovery. Where were we? Thank heaven, we were still at the croquet party, and Miss Lynie's narrative was continuing.

'That was the last place I saw Mary. Oh, she was mad! She was mad with me! "I was born a lady," says she, "and I 'll die a lady!" I never saw her after that day.'

Miss Lynie, with an elegantly curved little finger, finished her wine-glass of toddy and awaited my comment.

I was, for the instant, capable only of blinking like an owl, but was saved from disaster by Mr. Flynn.

'Indeed ye had no loss,' he remarked. 'She 's like a cow that gives a good pail o' milk and spoils all by putting her leg in it!'

I said, 'Quite so — exactly,' while the fire, old Flynn, and the picture of a Pope over the chimney-piece swam back into their places with a jerk.

The tale, or whatever it was, wound on. Nodding heavily, I heard how 'Mary,' at some period of her remarkable career, had been found 'bawling in the kitchen' because Miss Flynn had refused to kiss her on both cheeks when she was going to bed, and of how, on that repulse, Mary had said that Miss Flynn was 'squat.' I am thankful to say that I retained sufficient control of my faculties to laugh ironically.

I think the story must then have merged into a description

of some sort of entertainment, as I distinctly remember Miss Lynie saying that they 'played "Lodging-houses"—it was young Scully from Ennis made us do it—a very vulgar game *I* call it.'

'I don't like that pullin' an' draggin',' said Mr. Flynn.

I did not feel called upon to intrude my opinion upon the remarkable pastime in question, and the veils of sleep once more swathed me irresistibly in their folds. It seemed very long afterwards that the clang of a fire-iron pulled me up with what I fear must have been an audible snort. Old Flynn was standing up in front of the fire; he had obviously reached the climax of a narrative, he awaited my comment.

'That—that must have been very nice,' I said desperately.

'Nice!' echoed Mr. Flynn, and his astounded face shocked me into consciousness; 'sure she might have burned the house down!'

What the catastrophe may have been I shall never know, nor do I remember how I shuffled out of the difficulty; I only know that at this point I abandoned the unequal struggle, and asked if I might go to bed.

The obligations of a troublesome and self-inflicted guest seal my lips as to the expedients by which the drawing-room had been converted into a sleeping-place for me. But though gratitude may enforce silence, it could not enforce sleep. The paralysing drowsiness of the parlour deserted me at the hour of need. The noises in the kitchen ceased, old Flynn pounded up to bed, the voices of the young ladies overhead died away, and the house sank into stillness, but I grew more wakeful every moment. I heard the creeping and scurrying of rats in the walls, I counted every tick, and cursed every quarter told off by a pragmatical cuckoo clock in the hall. By the time it had struck twelve I was on the verge of attacking it with the poker.

I suppose I may have dozed a little, but I was certainly aware that a long track of time had elapsed since it had struck two, when a faint but regular creaking of the staircase impressed itself upon my ear. It was followed by a stealing foot in the hall; a hand felt over the door, and knocked very softly. I sat up in my diminutive stretcher-bed and asked who was there. The handle was turned, and a voice at the crack of the door said: 'It's me!'

Even in the two monosyllables I recognized the accents of the son of the house.

'I want to tell you something,' pursued the voice.

I instantly surmised all possibilities of disaster; Slipper drunk and overlaid by Lady Jane, Philippa's pony dead from over-exertion, or even a further instalment of the evening meal, only now arrived at completion.

'What's the matter? Is anything wrong?' I demanded, raising myself in the trough of the bed.

'There is not; but I want to speak to you.'

I had by this time found the matches, and my candle revealed Eddy Flynn, fully dressed save for his boots, standing in the doorway. He crept up to my bedside with elaborate stealth.

'Well, what is it?' I asked, attuning my voice to a conspirator's whisper.

'Playboy's above stairs!'

'Playboy!' I repeated incredulously, 'what do you mean?'

'Eugene cot him. He's above in Eugene's room now,' said the boy, his face becoming suddenly scarlet.

'Do you mean that he wasn't killed?' I demanded, instantly allocating in my own mind half a sovereign to Eugene.

'He wasn't in the island at all,' faltered Master Eddy; 'Eugene cot him below on the cliffs when the hounds went down in it at the first go off, and he hid him back in the house here.'

The allotment of the half-sovereign was abruptly cancelled. I swallowed my emotions with some difficulty.

'Well,' I said, after an awkward pause, 'I'm very much obliged to you for telling me. I'll see your father about it in the morning.'

Master Eddy did not accept this as a dismissal. He remained motionless, except for his eyes that sought refuge anywhere but on my face.

There was a silence for some moments; he was almost inaudible as he said:

'It would be better for ye to take him now, and to give him to Slipper. I'd be killed if they knew I let on he was here.' Then, as an afterthought, 'Eugene's gone to the wake.'

The inner aspect of the affair began to reveal itself, accompanied by a singularly unbecoming sidelight on old Flynn. I perceived also the useful part that had been played by Philippa's pony, but it did not alter the fact that Master Eddy was showing

his gratitude like a hero. The situation was, however, too
delicate to admit of comment.

'Very well,' I said, without any change of expression, 'will
you bring the dog down to me?'

'I tried to bring him down with me, but he wouldn't let me
put a hand on him.'

I hastily got into the few garments of which I had not divested
myself before getting into the misnamed stretcher-bed, aware
that the horrid task was before me of burglariously probing the
depths of Eugene's bedroom, and acutely uncertain as to Playboy's reception of me.

'There's a light above in the room,' said Master Eddy, with
a dubious glance at the candle in my hand.

I put it down, and followed him into the dark hall.

I have seldom done a more preposterous thing than creep
up old Flynn's stairs in the small hours of the morning, in
illicit search for my own property; but, given the dual determination to recover Playboy, and to shield my confederate, I
still fail to see that I could have acted otherwise.

We reached the first landing; it vibrated reassuringly with
the enormous snores of Mr. Flynn. Master Eddy's cold paw
closed on my hand, and led me to another and steeper flight of
stairs. At the top of these was a second landing, or rather
passage, at the end of which a crack of light showed under a
door. A dim skylight told that the roof was very near my head;
I extended a groping hand for the wall, and without any warning
found my fingers closing improbably, awfully, upon a warm
human face. I defy the most hardened conspirator to have
refrained from some expression of opinion.

'Good Lord!' I gasped, starting back, and knocking my head
hard against a rafter. 'What's that?'

'It's Maggie Kane, sir!' hissed a female voice. 'I'm after
bringing up a bone for the dog to quieten him!'

That Maggie Kane should also be in the plot was a compli-
cation beyond my stunned intelligence; I grasped only the
single fact that she was an ally, endued with supernatural and
sympathetic forethought. She placed in my hand a tepid and
bulky fragment, which, even in the dark, I recognized as the
mighty drumstick of last night's goose; at the same moment
Master Eddy opened the door, and revealed Playboy, tied to
the leg of a low wooden bedstead.

I 978

He was standing up, his eyes gleamed green as emeralds, he looked as big as a calf. He obviously regarded himself as the guardian of Eugene's bower, and I failed to see any recognition of me in his aspect; in point of fact he appeared to be on the verge of an outburst of suspicion that would waken the house once and for all. We held a council of war in whispers that perceptibly increased his distrust; I think it was Maggie Kane who suggested that Master Eddy should proffer him the bone while I unfastened the rope. The strategy succeeded, almost too well in fact. Following the alluring drumstick Playboy burst into the passage, towing me after him on the rope. Still preceded by the light-footed Master Eddy, he took me down the attic stairs at a speed which was the next thing to a headlong fall, while Maggie Kane held the candle at the top. As we stormed past old Flynn's door I was aware that the snoring had ceased, but 'the pace was too good to inquire.' We scrimmaged down the second flight into the darkness of the hall, fetching up somewhere near the clock, which, as if to give the alarm, uttered three loud and poignant cuckoos. I think Playboy must have sprung at it, in the belief that it was the voice of the drumstick; I only know that my arm was nearly wrenched from its socket, and that the clock fell with a crash from the table to the floor, where, by some malevolence of its machinery, it continued to cuckoo with jocund and implacable persistence. Something that was not Playboy bumped against me. The cuckoo's note became mysteriously muffled, and a door, revealing a fire-lit kitchen, was shoved open. We struggled through it, bound into a sheaf by Playboy's rope, and in our midst the cuckoo clock, stifled but indomitable, continued its protest from under Maggie Kane's shawl.

In the kitchen we drew breath for the first time, and Maggie Kane put the cuckoo clock into a flour bin; the house remained still as the grave. Master Eddy opened the back door; behind his head the Plough glittered wakefully in a clear and frosty sky. It was uncommonly cold.

Slipper had not gone to the wake, and was quite sober. I shall never forget it to him. I told him that Playboy had come back, and was to be taken home at once. He asked no inconvenient questions, but did not deny himself a most dissolute wink. We helped him to saddle the pony, while Playboy crunched his hard-earned drumstick in the straw. In less than ten minutes he rode quietly away in the starlight, with Playboy trotting at his stirrup, and Playboy's rope tied to his arm.

I did not meet Mr. Flynn at breakfast; he had started early for a distant fair. I have, however, met him frequently since then, and we are on the best of terms. We have not shirked allusions to the day's hunting at Knockeenbwee, but Playboy has not on these occasions been mentioned by either of us.

I understand that Slipper has put forth a version of the story, in which the whole matter is resolved into a trial of wits between himself and Eugene. With this I have not interfered.

VI

THE BOAT'S SHARE

I was sitting on the steps of Shreelane House, smoking a cigarette after breakfast. By the calendar the month was November, by the map it was the south-west of Ireland, but by every token that hot sun and soft breeze could offer it was the Riviera in April.

Maria, my wife's water-spaniel, elderly now, but unimpaired in figure, and in character merely fortified in guile by the castigations of seven winters, reclined on the warm limestone flags beside me. Minx, the nursery fox-terrier, sat, as was her practice, upon Maria's ribs, nodding in slumber. All was peace.

Peace, I say, but even as I expanded in it and the sunshine, there arose to me from the kitchen window in the area the voice of Mrs. Cadogan, uplifted in passionate questioning.

'Bridgie!' it wailed. 'Where's me beautiful head and me lovely feet?'

The answer to this amazing inquiry travelled shrilly from the region of the scullery.

'Bilin' in the pot, ma'am.'

I realized that it was merely soup in its elemental stage that was under discussion, but Peace spread her wings at the cry; it recalled the fact that Philippa was having a dinner party that same night. In a small establishment such as mine, a dinner party is an affair of many aspects, all of them serious. The aspect of the master of the house, however, is not serious, it is merely contemptible. Having got out the champagne, and reverentially decanted the port, there remains for him no further place in the proceedings, no moment in which his presence is desired. If, at such a time, I wished to have speech with my wife, she was not to be found; if I abandoned the search and stationed myself in the hall, she would pass me, on an average, twice in every three minutes, generally with flowers in her hands, always with an expression so rapt as to abash all questionings. I therefore sat upon the steps and read the paper, superfluous to all save the dogs, to whom I at least offered a harbourage in the general stress.

Suddenly, and without a word of warning, Minx and Maria were converted from a slumbrous mound into twin comets—comets that trailed a continuous shriek of rage as they flew down the avenue. The cause of the affront presently revealed itself, in the form of a tall woman, with a shawl over her head, and a basket on her arm. She advanced unfalteringly, Minx walking on her hind legs beside her, as if in a circus, attentively smelling the basket, while Maria bayed her at large in the background. She dropped me a curtsy fit for the Lord Lieutenant.

'Does your honour want any fish this morning?' Her rippling grey hair gleamed like silver in the sunlight, her face was straight-browed and pale, her grey eyes met mine with respectful self-possession. She might have been Deborah the prophetess, or the Mother of the Gracchi; as a matter of fact I recognized her as a certain Mrs. Honora Brickley, mother of my present kitchen-maid, a lady whom, not six months before, I had fined in a matter of trespass and assault.

'They're lovely fish altogether!' she pursued, 'they're leppin' fresh!'

Here was the chance to make myself useful. I called down the area and asked Mrs. Cadogan if she wanted fish. (It may or may not be necessary to mention that my cook's name is locally pronounced 'Caydogawn.')

'What fish is it, sir?' replied Mrs. Cadogan, presenting at the kitchen window a face like a harvest moon.

'' Tis pollock, ma'am!' shouted Mrs. Brickley from the foot of the steps.

'' Sha! thim's no good to us!' responded the harvest moon in bitter scorn. 'Thim's not company fish!'

I was here aware of the presence of my wife in the doorway, with a menu slate in one hand, and one of my best silk pocket handkerchiefs, that had obviously been used as a duster, in the other.

'Filleted with white sauce—' she murmured to herself, a world of thought in her blue eyes, 'or perhaps quenelles——'

Mrs. Brickley instantly extracted a long and shapely pollock from her basket, and, with eulogies of its beauty, of Philippa's beauty, and of her own magnanimity in proffering her wares to us instead of to a craving market in Skebawn, laid it on the steps.

At this point a series of yells from the nursery, of the usual blood-curdling description, lifted Philippa from the scene of action as a wind whirls a feather.

'Buy them!' came back to me from the stairs.

I kept to myself my long-formed opinion that eating pollock was like eating boiled cotton wool with pins in it, and the bargain proceeded. The affair was almost concluded, when Mrs. Brickley, in snatching a fish from the bottom of her basket to complete an irresistible half-dozen, let it slip from her fingers. It fell at my feet, revealing a mangled and gory patch on its side.

'Why, then, that's the best fish I have!' declared Mrs. Brickley in response to my protest. 'That's the very one her honour Mrs. Yeates would fancy! She'd always like to see the blood running fresh!'

This flight of sympathetic insight did not deter me from refusing the injured pollock, coupled with a regret that Mrs. Brickley's cat should have been interrupted in its meal.

Mrs. Brickley did not immediately reply. She peeped down the area, she glanced into the hall.

'Cat is it?' she said, sinking her voice to a mysterious whisper. 'Your honour knows well, God bless you, that it was no cat done that!'

Obedient to the wholly fallacious axiom that those who ask no questions will be told no lies, I remained silent.

'Only for the luck of God being on me they'd have left meself no betther than they left the fish!' continued Mrs. Brickley. 'Your honour didn't hear what work was in it on Hare Island Strand last night? Thim Keohanes had the wooden leg pulled from undher me husband with the len'th o' fightin'! Oh! Thim's outlawed altogether, and the faymales is as manly as the men! Sure the polis theirselves does be in dhread of thim women! The day-and-night-screeching porpoises!' '

Seven years of Resident Magistracy had bestowed upon me some superficial knowledge of whither all this tended. I rose from the steps, with the stereotyped statement that if there was to be a case in court I could not listen to it beforehand. I then closed the hall door, not, however, before Mrs. Brickley had assured me that I was the only gentleman, next to the Lord Almighty, in whom she had any confidence.

The next incident in the affair occurred at about a quarter to eight that evening. I was tying my tie when my wife's voice summoned me to her room in tones that presaged disaster. Philippa was standing erect, in a white and glittering garment. Her eyes shone, her cheeks glowed. It is not given to every one to look their best when they are angry, but it undoubtedly is becoming to Philippa.

'I ask you to look at my dress,' she said in a level voice.

'It looks very nice——' I said cautiously, knowing there was a trap somewhere. 'I know it, don't I?'

'Know it!' replied Philippa witheringly; 'did you know that it had only one sleeve?'

She extended her arms; from one depended vague and transparent films of whiteness, the other was bare to the shoulder. I rather preferred it of the two.

'Well, I can't say I did,' I said helplessly, 'is that a new fashion?'

There was a spectral knock at the door, and Hannah, the housemaid, slid into the room, purple of face, abject of mien.

'It's what they're afther tellin' me, ma'am,' she panted. ''Twas took to sthrain the soup!'

'They took my sleeve to strain the soup!' repeated Philippa, in a crystal clarity of wrath.

'She said she got it in the press in the passage, ma'am, and she thought you were afther throwin' it,' murmured Hannah, with a glance that implored my support.

'Who are you speaking of?' demanded Philippa, looking quite six feet high.

The situation, already sufficiently acute, was here intensified by the massive entry of Mrs. Cadogan, bearing in her hand a plate, on which was a mound of soaked brownish rag. She was blowing hard, the glare of the kitchen range at highest power lived in her face.

'There's your sleeve, ma'am!' she said, 'and if I could fall down dead this minute it'd be no more than a relief to me! And as for Bridgie Brickley!' continued Mrs. Cadogan, catching her wind with a gasp, 'I thravelled many genthry's kitchens, but thanks be to God, I never seen the like of her! Five weeks to-morrow she's in this house, and there isn't a day but I gave her a laceratin'! Sure the hair's droppin' out o' me head, and the skin rollin' off the soles o' me feet with the heart scald I get with her! The big, low, dirty buccaneer! And I declare to you, ma'am, and to the Major, that I have a pain switching out through me hips this minute that'd bring down a horse!'

'Oh God!' said Hannah, clapping her hand over her mouth.

My eye met Philippa's; some tremor of my inward agony declared itself, and found its fellow on her quivering lips. In the same instant, wheels rumbled in the avenue.

'Here are the Knoxes!' I exclaimed, escaping headlong from the room with my dignity as master of the house still intact.

Dinner, though somewhat delayed by these agitations, passed off reasonably well. Its occasion was the return from the South African war of my landlord and neighbour, Mr. Florence McCarthy Knox, M.F.H., J.P., who had been serving his country in the Yeomanry for the past twelve months. The soup gave no hint of its cannibalistic origin, and was of a transparency that did infinite credit to the services of Philippa's sleeve; the pollock, chastely robed in white sauce, held no suggestion of a stormy past, nor, it need scarcely be said, did they foreshadow their influence on my future. As they made their circuit of the table I aimed a communing glance at my wife, who, serene in pale pink and conversation with Mr. Knox, remained unresponsive.

How the volcano that I knew to be raging below in the kitchen could have brought forth anything more edible than molten paving stones I was at a loss to imagine. Had Mrs. Cadogan sent up Bridget Brickley's head as an *entremet* it would not, indeed, have surprised me. I could not know that as the gong sounded for dinner Miss Brickley had retired to her bed in strong hysterics, announcing that she was paralysed, while Mrs. Cadogan, rapt by passion to an ecstasy of achievement, coped single-handed with the emergency.

At breakfast time next morning Philippa and I were informed that the invalid had at an early hour removed herself and her wardrobe from the house, requisitioning for the purpose my donkey-cart and the attendance of my groom, Peter Cado-, gan; a proceeding on which the comments of Peter's aunt, Mrs. Cadogan, left nothing to be desired.

The affair on the strand at Hare Island ripened, with infinite complexity of summonses and cross-summonses, into an imposing Petty Sessions case. Two separate deputations presented themselves at Shreelane, equipped with black eyes and other conventional injuries, one of them armed with a creelful of live lobsters to underline the argument. To decline the bribe was of no avail: the deputation decanted them upon the floor of the hall and retired, and the lobsters spread themselves at large over the house, and to this hour remain the nightmare of the nursery.

The next Petty Sessions day was wet; the tall windows of the Court House were grey and streaming, and the reek of wet humanity ascended to the ceiling. As I took my seat on the bench I perceived with an inward groan that the services of the two most eloquent solicitors in Skebawn had been engaged. This meant that justice would not have run its course till heaven knew what dim hour of the afternoon, and that that course would be devious and difficult.

All the pews and galleries (any Irish court house might, with the addition of a harmonium, pass presentably as a dissenting chapel) were full, and a line of flat-capped policemen stood like churchwardens near the door. Under the galleries, behind what might have answered to choir stalls, the witnesses and their friends hid in darkness, which could, however, but partially conceal two resplendent young ladies, barmaids, who were to appear in a subsequent Sunday drinking case. I was a little late, and when I arrived Flurry Knox, supported by a couple of other magistrates, was in the chair, imperturbable of countenance as was his wont, his fair and delusive youthfulness of aspect unimpaired by his varied experiences during the war, his roving, subtle eye untamed by four years of matrimony.

A woman was being examined, a square and ugly countrywoman, with wispy fair hair, a slow, dignified manner, and a slight and impressive stammer. I recognized her as one of the bodyguard of the lobsters. Mr. Mooney, solicitor for the Brickleys, widely known and respected as 'Roaring Jack,' was in possession of that much-enduring organ, the ear of the Court.

'Now, Kate Keohane!' he thundered, 'tell me what time it was when all this was going on?'

'About duskish, sir. Con Brickley was slashing the f-fish at me mother the same time. He never said a word but to take the shtick and fire me dead with it on the sthrand. He gave me plenty of blood to dhrink too,' said the witness with acid decorum. She paused to permit this agreeable fact to sink in, and added: 'His wife wanted to f-fashten on me the same time, an' she havin' the steer of the boat to sthrike me.'

These were not precisely the facts that Mr. Murphy, as solicitor for the defence, wished to elicit.

'Would you kindly explain what you mean by the steer of the boat?' he demanded, sparring for wind in as intimidating a manner as possible. The witness stared at him.

'Sure 'tis the shtick, like, that they pulls here and there to go in their choice place.'

'We may presume that the lady is referring to the tiller,' said Mr. Mooney, with a facetious eye at the Bench. 'Maybe now, ma'am, you can explain to us what sort of a boat is she?'

'She's that owld that if it wasn't for the weeds that's holding her together she'd bursht up in the deep.'

'And who owns this valuable property?' pursued Mr. Mooney.

'She's between Con Brickley and me brother, an' the saine is between four, an' whatever crew does be in it should get their share, and the boat has a man's share.'

I made no attempt to comprehend this, relying with well-founded confidence on Flurry Knox's grasp of such enigmas.

'Was Con Brickley fishing the same day?'

'He was not, sir. He was at Lisheen Fair; for as clever as he is he couldn't kill two birds under one slat!'

Kate Keohane's voice moved unhurried from sentence to sentence, and her slow pale eyes turned for an instant to the lair of the witnesses under the galléry.

'And you're asking the Bench to believe that this decent man left his business in Lisheen in order to slash fish at your mother?' said Mr. Mooney truculently.

'B'lieve me, sorra much business he laves afther him wherever he'll go!' returned the witness, 'himself and his wife had business enough on the sthrand when the fish was dividing, and it's then themselves put every name on me.'

* I 97⁸

'Ah, what harm are names!' said Mr. Mooney, dallying elegantly with a massive watch-chain. 'Come now, ma'am! will you swear you got any ill-usage from Con Brickley or his wife?' He leaned over the front of his pew, and waited for the answer with his massive red head on one side.

'I was givin' blood like a c-cow that ye'd shtab with a knife!' said Kate Keohane, with unshaken dignity. 'If it was yourself that was in it ye'd feel the smart as well as me. My hand and word on it, ye would! The marks is on me head still, like the prints of dog-bites!'

She lifted a lock of hair from her forehead, and exhibited a sufficiently repellent injury. Flurry Knox leaned forward.

'Are you sure you haven't that since the time there was that business between yourself and the postmistress at Munig? I'm told you had the name of the office on your forehead where she struck you with the office stamp! Try now, sergeant, can you read Munig on her forehead?'

The Court, not excepting its line of Churchwardens, dissolved into laughter; Kate Keohane preserved an offended silence.

'I suppose you want us to believe,' resumed Mr. Mooney sarcastically, 'that a fine hearty woman like you wasn't defending yourself!' Then with a turkey-cock burst of fury: 'On your oath now! What did you strike Honora Brickley with? Answer me that now! What had you in your hand?'

'I had nothing only the little rod I had afther the ass,' answered Miss Keohane, with childlike candour. 'I done nothing to them; but as for Con Brickley he put his back to the cliff and he took the flannel wrop that he had on him, and he threwn it on the sthrand, and he said he should have Blood, Murdher, or F-Fish!'

She folded her shawl across her breast, a picture of virtue assailed, yet unassailable.

'You may go down now,' said 'Roaring Jack' rather hastily, 'I want to have a few words with your brother.'

Miss Keohane retired, without having moulted a feather of her dignity, and her brother Jer came heavily up the steps and on to the platform, his hot, wary blue eyes gathering in the Bench and the attorneys in one bold comprehensive glance. He was a tall, dark man of about five and forty, clean-shaved, save for two clerical inches of black whiskers, and in feature of the type of a London clergyman who would probably preach on Browning.

'Well, sir!' began Mr. Mooney stimulatingly, 'and are you the biggest blackguard from here to America?'

'I am not,' said Jer Keohane tranquilly.

'We had you here before us not so very long ago about kicking a goat, wasn't it? You got a little touch of a pound, I think?'

This delicate allusion to a fine that the Bench had thought fit to impose did not distress the witness.

'I did, sir.'

'And how's our friend the goat?' went on Mr. Mooney, with the furious facetiousness reserved for hustling tough witnesses.

'Well, I suppose she's something west of the Skelligs by now,' replied Jer Keohane with great composure.

An appreciative grin ran round the court. The fact that the goat had died of the kick and been 'given the cliff' being regarded as an excellent jest.

Mr. Mooney consulted his notes:

'Well, now, about this fight,' he said pleasantly, 'did you see your sister catch Mrs. Brickley and pull her hair down to the ground, and drag the shawl off of her?'

'Well,' said the witness airily, 'they had a little bit of a scratch on account o' the fish. Con Brickley had the shteer o' the boat in his hand and says he: "Is there any man here that'll take the shteer from me?" The man was dhrunk, of course,' added Jer charitably.

'Did you have any talk with his wife about the fish?'

'I couldn't tell the words that she said to me!' replied the witness, with a reverential glance at the Bench, 'and she over-right three crowds o' men that was on the sthrand.'

Mr. Mooney put his hands in his pockets and surveyed the witness.

'You're a very refined gentleman upon my word! Were you ever in England?'

'I was part of three years.'

'Oh, that accounts for it, I suppose!' said Mr. Mooney, accepting this lucid statement without a stagger, and passing lightly on. 'You're a widower, I understand, with no objection to consoling yourself?'

No answer.

'Now, sir! Can you deny that you made proposals of marriage to Con Brickley's daughter last Shraft?'

The plot thickened. Con Brickley's daughter was my late kitchen-maid.

Jer Keohane smiled tolerantly.

'Ah! That was a thing o' nothing!'

'Nothing!' said Mr. Mooney, with the roar of a tornado, 'do you call an impudent proposal of marriage to a respectable man's daughter nothing! That's English manners, I suppose!'

'I was goin' home one Sunday,' said Jer Keohane, conversationally to the Bench, 'and I met the gerr'l and her mother. I spoke to the gerr'l in a friendly way, and asked her why wasn't she gettin' marrid, and she commenced to peg stones at me and dhrew several blows of an umbrella on me. I had only three bottles o' porther taken. There now was the whole of it.'

Mrs. Brickley, from under the gallery, groaned heavily and ironically.

I found it difficult to connect these coquetries with my impressions of my late kitchenmaid, a furtive and tousled being, who, in conjunction with a pail and scrubbing brush, had been wont to melt round corners and into doorways at my approach.

'Are we trying a breach of promise case?' interpolated Flurry, 'if so, we ought to have the plaintiff in.'

'My purpose, sir,' said Mr. Mooney, in a manner discouraging to levity, 'is to show that my clients have received annoyance and contempt from this man and his sister such as no parents would submit to.'

A hand came forth from under the gallery and plucked at Mr. Mooney's coat. A red monkey face appeared out of the darkness, and there was a hoarse whisper whose purport I could not gather. Con Brickley, the defendant, was giving instructions to his lawyer.

It was perhaps as a result of these that Jer Keohane's evidence closed here. There was a brief interval, enlivened by coughs, grinding of heavy boots on the floor, and some mumbling and groaning under the gallery.

'There's great duck-shooting out on a lake on this island,' commented Flurry to me, in a whisper. 'My grand-uncle went there one time with an old duck-gun he had, that he fired with a fuse. He was three hours stalking the ducks before he got the gun laid. He lit the fuse then, and it set to work sputtering and hissing like a goods engine till there wasn't a duck within ten miles. The gun went off then.'

This useful side light on the matter in hand was interrupted by the cumbrous ascent of the one-legged Con Brickley to the witness table. He sat down heavily, with his slouch hat on his sound knee, and his wooden stump stuck out before him. His large monkey face was immovably serious; his eye was small, light grey, and very quick.

McCaffery, the opposition attorney, a thin, restless youth, with ears like the handles of an urn, took him in hand. To the pelting cross-examination that beset him Con Brickley replied with sombre deliberation, and with a manner of uninterested honesty, emphasizing what he said with slight, very effective gestures of his big, supple hands. His voice was deep and pleasant; it betrayed no hint of so trivial a thing as satisfaction when, in the teeth of Mr. McCaffery's leading questions, he established the fact that the 'little rod' with which Miss Kate Keohane had beaten his wife was the handle of a pitchfork.

'I was counting the fish the same time,' went on Con Brickley, in his rolling *basso profondissimo*, 'and she said: "Let the divil clear me out of the sthrand, for there's no one else will put me out!" says she.'

'It was then she got the blow, I suppose!' said McCaffery venomously; 'you had a stick yourself, I dare say?'

'Yes. I had a stick. I must have a stick'—deep and mellow pathos was hinted at in the voice—'I am sorry to say. What could I do to her? A man with a wooden leg on a sthrand could do nothing!'

Something like a laugh ran round the back of the court. Mr. McCaffery's ears turned scarlet and became quite decorative. On or off a strand Con Brickley was not a person to be scored off easily.

His clumsy yet impressive descent from the witness stand followed almost immediately, and was not the least telling feature of his evidence. Mr. Mooney surveyed his exit with the admiration of one artist for another, and rising, asked the Bench's permission to call Mrs. Brickley.

Mrs. Brickley, as she mounted to the platform, in the dark and nun-like severity of her long cloak, the stately blue cloth cloak that is the privilege of the Munster peasant woman, was an example of the rarely blended qualities of picturesqueness and respectability. As she took her seat in the chair, she flung the deep hood back on to her shoulders, and met the gaze of the court with her grey head erect; she was a witness to be proud of.

'Now, Mrs. Brickley,' said 'Roaring Jack' urbanely, 'will you describe this interview between your daughter and Keohane.'

'It was the last Sunday in Shrove, your Worship, Mr. Flurry Knox, and gentlemen,' began Mrs. Brickley nimbly, 'meself and me little gerr'l was comin' from mass, and Jer Keohane come up to us and got on in a most unmannerable way. He asked me daughter would she marry him. Me daughter told him she would not, quite friendly like. I'll tell ye no lie, gentlemen, she was teasing him with the umbrella the same time, an' he raised his shtick and dhrew a sthroke on her in the back, an' the little gerr'l took up a small pebble of a stone and fired it at him. She put the umbrella up to his mouth, but she called him no names. But as for him, the names he put on her was to call her "a nasty long slopeen of a proud thing, and a slopeen of a proud tinker."'

'Very loverlike expressions!' commented Mr. Mooney, doubtless stimulated by ladylike titters from the barmaids; 'and had this romantic gentleman made any previous proposals for your daughter?'

'Himself had two friends over from across the water one night to make the match, a Sathurday it was, and they should land the lee side o' the island, for the wind was a fright,' replied Mrs. Brickley, launching her tale with the power of easy narration that is bestowed with such amazing liberality on her class; 'the three o' them had dhrink taken, an' I went to shlap out the door agin them. Me husband said then we should let them in, if it was a Turk itself, with the rain that was in it. They were talking in it then till near the dawning, and in the latther end all that was between them was the boat's share.'

'What do you mean by "the boat's share"?' said I.

''Tis the same as a man's share, me worshipful gintleman,' returned Mrs. Brickley splendidly; 'it goes with the boat always, afther the crew and the saine has their share got.'

I possibly looked as enlightened as I felt by this exposition.

'You mean that Jer wouldn't have her unless he got the boat's share with her?' suggested Flurry.

'He said it over-right all that was in the house, and he reddening his pipe at the fire,' replied Mrs. Brickley, in full-sailed response to the helm. '"D'ye think," says I to him, "that me daughter would leave a lovely situation, with a kind and tendher masther, for a mean, hungry blagyard like yerself," says I, "that's livin' always in this backwards place!" says I.'

This touching expression of preference for myself, as opposed to Mr. Keohane, was received with expressionless respect. by the Court. Flurry, with an impassive countenance, kicked me heavily under cover of the desk. I said that we had better get on to the assault on the strand. Nothing could have been more to Mrs. Brickley's taste. We were minutely instructed as to how Katie Keohane drew the shawleen forward on Mrs. Brickley's head to stifle her; and how Norrie Keohane was fast in her hair. Of how Mrs. Brickley had then given a stroke upwards between herself and her face (whatever that might mean) and loosed Norrie from her hair. Of how she then sat down and commenced to cry from the use they had for her.

"'Twas all I done,' she concluded, looking like a sacred picture, 'I gave a sthroke of a pollock on them.' Then, an afterthought, 'An' if I did, 'twas myself was at the loss of the same pollock!'

I fixed my eyes immovably on my desk. I knew that the slightest symptom of intelligence on my part would instantly draw forth the episode of the fish-buying on the morning of the dinner party, with the rape of Philippa's sleeve, and the unjust aspersion on Miss Brickley following in due sequence, ending with the paralytic seizure and dignified departure of the latter to her parents' residence in Hare Island. The critical moment was averted by a question from Mr. Mooney.

'As for language,' replied Mrs. Brickley, with clear eyes a little uplifted in the direction of the ceiling, 'there was no name from heaven and hell but she had it on me, and wishin'. the divil might burn the two heels off me, and the like o' me wasn't in sivin parishes! And that was the clane part of the discoorse, yer Worships!'

Mrs. Brickley here drew her cloak more closely about her, as though to enshroud herself in her own refinement, and presented to the Bench a silence as elaborate as a drop scene. It implied, amongst other things, a generous confidence in the imaginative powers of her audience.

Whether or no this was misplaced, Mrs. Brickley was not invited further to enlighten the Court. After her departure the case droned on in inexhaustible rancour, and trackless complications as to the shares of the fish. Its ethics and its arithmetic would have defied the allied intellects of Solomon and Bishop Colenso. It was somewhere in that dead hour of the afternoon, when it is too late for lunch and too early for tea, that the Bench, wan with hunger, wound up the affair by impartially binding both parties in sheaves 'to the Peace.'

As a sub-issue I arranged with Mr. Knox to shoot duck on the one-legged man's land on Hare Island as soon as should be convenient, and lightly dismissed from my mind my dealings, official and otherwise, with the House of Brickley.

But even as there are people who never give away old clothes, so are there people, of whom is Flurry Knox, who never dismiss anything from their minds.

VII

THE LAST DAY OF SHRAFT

It was not many days after the Keohane and Brickley trial that my wife's elderly step-brother, Maxwell Bruce, wrote to us to say that he was engaged in a tour through the Irish-speaking counties, and would look us up on his way from Kerry. The letter began '*O Bean uasal,*' and broke into eruptions of Erse at various points, but the excerpts from Bradshaw were, fortunately, in the vernacular.

Philippa assured me she could read it all. During the previous winter she had had five lessons and a half in the Irish language from the National Schoolmaster, and believed herself to be one of the props of the Celtic movement. My own attitude with regard to the Celtic movement was sympathetic, but a brief inspection of the grammar convinced me that my sympathies would not survive the strain of triphthongs, eclipsed consonants, and synthetic verbs, and that I should do well to refrain from embittering my declining years by an impotent and humiliating pursuit of the most elusive of pronunciations. Philippa had attained to the height of being able to greet the schoolmaster in Irish, and, if the day happened to be fine, she was capable of stating the fact; other aspects of the weather, however remarkable, she epitomized in a brilliant smile, and the schoolmaster was generally considerate enough not to press the matter.

My step-brother-in-law neither hunted, shot, nor fished, yet as a guest he never gave me a moment's anxiety. He possessed the attribute, priceless in guests, a good portable hobby, involving no machinery, accessories, or paraphernalia of any kind. It did not even involve the personal attendance of his host. His mornings were spent in proffering Irish phrases to bewildered beggars at the hall door, or to the respectfully bored Peter Cadogan in the harness room. He held *conversaziones* in the servants' hall after dinner, while I slept balmily in front of the drawing-room fire. When not thus engaged he sat in his room making notes, and writing letters to the Archimandrites of his faith. Truly an ideal visitor, one to whom neglect was a kindness, and entertainments an abomination; certainly not a person to take to Hare Island to shoot ducks with Flurry Knox.

But it was otherwise ordained by Philippa. Hare Island was, she said, and the schoolmaster said, a place where the Irish language was still spoken with a purity worthy of the Isles of Aran. Its folk-lore was an unworked mine, and it was moreover the home of one Shemus Ruadth, a singer and poet (and, I may add, a smuggler of tobacco) of high local renown: Maxwell should on no account miss such a chance. I mentioned that Hare Island was at present going through the measles phase of its usual rotation of epidemics. My wife wavered, in a manner that showed me that I had been on the verge of a family picnic, and I said I had heard that there was whooping-cough there too. The children had had neither. The picnic expired without a sound, but my step-brother-in-law had made up his mind.

It was a grey and bitter February morning when Maxwell and I, accompanied by Peter Cadogan, stood waiting on the beach at Yokahn for Flurry to arrive. Maria, as was her wont, was nosing my gun as if she expected to see a woodcock fly out of it; that Minx was beside her was due to the peculiar inveteracy of Minx. How she had achieved it is of no consequence; the distressing fact remained that she was there, seated, shuddering, upon a space of wet stone no larger than a sixpence, and had to be accepted as one of the party. It struck me that Mr. Cadogan had rather overdressed the part of dog-boy and bag-bearer, being attired in a striped blue flannel suit that had once been mine, a gaudy new cap, and yellow boots. The social possibilities of Hare Island had faded from my mind; I merely experienced the usual humiliation of perceiving how discarded garments can, in a lower sphere, renew their youth and blossom as the rose. I was even formulating a system of putting my old clothes out at grass, as it were, with Peter Cadogan, when a messenger arrived with a note from Flurry Knox, in which he informed me, with many regrets, that he was kept at home on unexpected business, but he had arranged that we should find a boat ready to take us to the island, and Con Brickley would look after us when we got there. The boat was even now nearing the beach, rowed by two men, who, in beautiful accord with our 'binding to the Peace,' proved to be the Widower, Jer Keohane, and his late antagonist, the one-legged Con Brickley. In view of this millennial state of affairs it seemed alarmingly probable that the boat which had come for us was that on which, as on a pivot, the late battle had turned. A witness had said, on oath, that 'if it wasn't for the weeds that's holding her together she'd bursht up in the deep.' I inspected her narrowly, and was relieved to see that the weeds still held their ground.

A mile of slaty water tumbled between us and the island, and an undue proportion of it, highly flavoured by fish, flowed in uneasy tides in the bottom of the boat, with a final disposition towards the well-laden stern. There were no bottom boards, and, judging by the depth of the flood over the keel, her draught appeared to be equal to that of a racing yacht. We sat precariously upon strips of nine-inch plank, our feet propped against the tarred sides just out of the wash; the boat climbed and wallowed with a three-cornered roll, the dogs panted in mingled nausea and agitation, and the narrow blades of the oars dipped their frayed edges in the waves in short and untiring jerks.

My brother-in-law, with a countenance leaden magenta from cold, struggled with the whirling leaves of a phrase book. He was tall and thin, of the famished vegetarian type of looks, with unpractical, prominent eyes, and a complexion that on the hottest day in summer imparted a chill to the beholder; in this aw November wind it was a positive suffering even to think of his nose, and my eyes rested, in unconscious craving for warmth, upon the changeless, impartial red of Con Brickley's monkey face.

We landed with a rush on the steep shingle of a sheltered cove. The island boasted a pier, built with 'Relief' money, but it was two miles from the lake where I was to shoot, and this small triangle of beach, tucked away in a notch of the cliff, was within ten minutes' walk of it. At the innermost angle of the cove, where the notch ended in a tortuous fissure, there was a path that zigzagged to the top of the cliff, a remarkably excellent path, and a well-worn one, with steps here and there. I commented on it to Mr. Brickley.

'Why, thin, it was in this same place that I losht the owld leg, sir,' he replied in his sombre voice. 'I took a shlip on a dark night and me landlord was that much sorry for me that he made a good pat' in it.' He was pitching himself up the steps on his crutches as he spoke, an object of compassion of the most obvious and silencing sort. Why, then, should Peter Cadogan smile furtively at the Widower?

At the top of the fissure, where it melted into a hollow between low, grassy hills, stood the Brickleys' cottage, long, low, and whitewashed, deep in shelter, with big stones, hung in halters of hay-rope, lying on its thatch, to keep the roof on in the Atlantic gales. A thick fuchsia hedge surrounded it; from its open door proceeded sounds of furious altercation; apparently a man and woman hurling invective and personalities at each other in Irish, at the tops of their voices. Con Brickley sprang forward on his crutch, a girl at the door vanished into the house, and a sudden silence fell. With scarcely a perceptible interval, Mrs. Brickley appeared in the doorway, a red shawl tied over her rippling grey hair, her manner an inimitable blend of deference and hospitality.

'Your honour's welcome, Major Yeates,' she said with a curtsy. A door banged at the back of the cottage. 'That was a poor man from across the water that came apologizin' to me for dhrawin' me name down in a little disagreement that he had about a settin' o' goose eggs.'

I suppose that it was contrition that caused the apologist to stumble heavily as he came round the corner of the house, and departed at a tangent through an opening in the fuchsia hedge.

Feeling that comment on the incident was too delicate a matter
for my capacities, I introduced Maxwell and his aspirations to
the lady of the house.   Any qualms that I might have had as to
how to dispose of him while I was shooting were set at rest by
Mrs. Brickley's instant grasp of the situation.   I regret to say
that I can neither transcribe nor translate the rolling periods
in which my brother-in-law addressed himself to her.   I have
reason to believe that he apostrophized her as 'O worthy woman
of cows!' invoking upon her and her household a comprehensive
and classic blessing, dating from the time of Cuchulain.

Mrs. Brickley received it without a perceptible stagger, and
in the course of the next few minutes, Miss Bridget Brickley
(who, it may be remembered, had but recently renounced
the office of kitchen-maid in my house) emerged, beautifully
dressed, from the cottage, and was dispatched, at full speed,
to summon Shemus Ruadth, the poet, as well as one or two of
'the neighbours' reputed to speak Irish of the purest kind.   If
to make a guest feel himself to be the one person in the world
whose welfare is of any importance is the aim of hostesses, they
can study the art in its perfection under the smoky rafters of
Irish cabins.   If it is insincere, it is equally to be respected; it
is often amiable to be insincere.

My own share of the day's enjoyment opened plausibly
enough, though not, possibly, as cloudlessly as Maxwell's.
Attended by Maria, Peter Cadogan, and the Widower, and by a
smell of whisky that floated to me on the chill breeze when the
Widower was to windward, I set forth, having—as I fatuously
imagined—disposed of Minx and of her intention to join the
shooting-party, by tying a stout piece of cord to her collar,
and placing its other end in my brother-in-law's hand.   I had,
by Flurry's advice, postponed the shooting of the lake till the
last thing before leaving the island, and turning my back upon
it, I tramped inland along half-thawed marshes in search of
snipe, and crept behind walls after plover, whose elusive
whistling was always two fields ahead.   After an unfruitful
hour or so the entertainment began to drag, and another plan
of campaign seemed advisable: I made a *cache* of my retinue
behind a rock, one of the many rocks that stood like fossilized
mammoths upon the ragged hill slopes, and, with Maria at my
heels, accomplished a long and laborious detour.   At length,
through the crannies of a wall, I perceived just within shot a

stand of plover, hopping, gobbling, squealing, quite unaware of my proximity. I cautiously laid my gun on the top of the wall. As I cocked it, a white form appeared on a fence behind the birds, poised itself for an instant with elf-like ears spread wide, then, volleying barks, the intolerable Minx burst like a firework into the heart of the plover. In lightning response to her comrade's tally-ho Maria rocketed over the wall; the plover rose as one man, and, as I missed with both barrels, swirled out of range and sight. By way, I suppose, of rounding off the jest effectively, Maria rushed in scientific zigzags through the field, in search of the bird that she well knew I had not shot, deaf as the dead to words of command, while Minx, stark mad with excitement, circled and shrieked round Maria. To take off Maria's collar and thrash her heavily with the buckle end of it was futile, except as a personal gratification, but I did it. To thrash Minx was not only absurd but impossible; one might as well have tried to thrash a grasshopper.

I whistled for Peter and the Widower without avail, and finally, in just indignation, went back to look for them. They were gone. Not a soul was in sight. I concluded that they had gone on towards the lake, and having sacrificed a sandwich to the capture of Minx I coupled her to Maria by means of the cord that still trailed from her collar, and again set forth. The island was a large one, three or four miles long by nearly as many wide; I had opened my campaign along its western shores, where heather struggled with bog, and stones, big and little, bestrewed any patch sound enough to carry them. Here and there were places where turf had been cut for fuel, leaving a drop like a sunk fence with black water at its foot, a matter requiring a hearty jump on to what might or might not be sound landing. When two maniacs are unequally yoked together by their necks, heartiness and activity are of less importance than unanimity, and it was in unanimity that Maria and Minx chiefly failed. At such moments, profoundly as I detested Minx, my sympathies reluctantly were hers. Conscious, as are all little dogs, of her superior astuteness, she yet had to submit to Maria's choice of pace, to Maria's professional quarterings and questings of obviously barren tracts of bogland. In bursts of squealing fury she hung from Maria's ear, she tore mouthfuls of brown wool from her neck, she jibbed with all her claws stuck into the ground; none the less she was swept across the ditches, and lugged over the walls, in seeming oneness of purpose, in total and preposterous absurdity. At one juncture a snipe, who must, I think, have been deaf, remained long enough within their sphere of action for me to shoot him. The couple, unanimous for once, charged down upon the remains; the corpse was secured by Maria, but was torn piecemeal from her jaws by Minx. They then galloped emulously back to me for applause, still bitterly contesting every inch of the shipe, and, having grudgingly relinquished the fragments, waited wild-eyed and panting, with tongues hanging like aprons to their knees.

It was towards the close of the incident that I was aware of a sibilant whispering near me, and found that I was being observed from the rear with almost passionate interest, by two little girls and a pair of goats. I addressed the party with an inquiry as to whether they had seen Jer Keohane.

The biggest little girl said that she had not seen him, but, in a *non sequitur* full of intelligence, added that she had seen Peter Cadogan a while ago, sitting down under a wall, himself and Pidge.

'What's Pidge?' said I cautiously. 'Is it a dog?'

'Oh Christians!' said the smaller child, swiftly covering her mouth with her pinafore.

The elder, with an untrammelled grin, explained that 'Pidge' was the name by which my late kitchen-maid was known in the home circle.

I postponed comment till Peter should be delivered into my hand, then, rightly concluding that the tendance of Hare Island goats would ensure the qualities necessary for dealing with even Maria and Minx, I engaged the pair as dog-boys.

My progress from this point to the lake might have been taken from the Old Testament, or *The Swiss Family Robinson.* In front of me paced the goats, who had sociably declined to be left out of the expedition; behind me strove the dogs, with the wiry and scarlet fingers of their attendants knotted in Mrs. Brickley's invaluable piece of string. It proved to be a thoroughly successful working arrangement; I even shot a plover, which was retrieved *en masse* by all except the goats.

In complete amity we reached the lake, a reedy strip of water that twisted in and out between low hills, its indeterminate shores cloaked with reeds. It was now past three o'clock, and the cold grey afternoon was already heaping into the west the pile of dark clouds that was to be its equivalent for sunset. I crept warily forward round the flank of the nearest hill, leaving the dogs and their keepers in death grapple, and the goats snatching mouthfuls of grass beside them, in the petulant, fractious manner of goats, that so ill assorts with their Presbyterian grey beards.

The frost had been preceded by a flood, and the swamp bordering the lake was very bad going; the tussocks were rotten, the holes were delusively covered with lids of white ice, and to traverse these in the attitude of a man with acute lumbago was no light matter. But the ducks were there. I could hear them quacking and splashing beyond the screen of reeds, and, straightening my back for an observation, caught sight of four or five swimming in a line, well within range. There was not an instant to lose; balancing precariously on a tussock, I flung up my gun and fired. Terrific quacking followed, interspersed by distant and heart-rending yells from the dogs, but the inexplicable feature of the case was that the ducks did not rise from the water. Had I slain the whole crowd? There was a sound as if the marsh behind me was being slashed with a flail; a brown body whizzed past me, closely followed by a white one. 'From his mountain home King James had rushing come,' in other words, my retrievers had hurled themselves upon their prey.

Maria's performance was faultless; in half a minute she had laid a bird at my feet, a very large pale drake, quite unlike any wild drake that I had ever——

Out of the silence that followed came a thin, shrill voice from the hill:

'Thim's Mrs. Brickley's ducks!'

In horrid confirmation of this appalling statement I perceived the survivors already landing on the far side of the lake, and hurrying homeward up the hill with direful clamours, while a wedge-shaped ripple in the grey water with a white speck at its apex, told of Minx in an ecstasy of pursuit.

'Stop the dog!' I shouted to my maids of honour; 'run round and catch her!'

Maria here, in irrepressible appropriation of the mission, bolted between my legs, and sent me staggering backwards into a very considerable bog-hole.

I will not labour the details. After some flounderings I achieved safety and the awestricken comments of the maids of honour, as wet as I have ever been in my life, and about five times as cold. One of my young ladies captured Minx in the act of getting ashore; the other collected the slaughtered drake and shrouded him in her pinafore, with a grasp of the position that did credit to both heart and head, and they finally informed me that Mrs. Brickley's house was only a small pieceen away.

I had left Mrs. Brickley's house a well-equipped sportsman, creditably escorted by Peter Cadogan and the Widower. I returned to it a muddy and dripping outcast, attended by two little girls, two goats, and her own eight ducks, whom my hand had widowed. My sodden clothes clung clammily about me; the wind, as it pierced them, carried with it all the iciness of the bog-hole. I walked at top speed to get up some semblance of a circulation; I should have run were it not for the confusion that such a proceeding would have caused to my cortège. As it was, the ducks fled before me in waddling panic, with occasional help from their wings, and panting and pattering in the rear told that the maids of honour, the goats, and the dogs were maintaining with difficulty their due places in the procession. As I neared the cottage I saw a boy go quickly into it and shut the door; I passed into the yard within the fuchsia hedge and heard someone inside howling and droning a song in Irish, and as I knocked, with frozen knuckles, the house gave the indefinable feeling of being full of people. There was no response; I lifted the latch. The door opened into the frieze-covered backs of several men, and an evenly blended smell of whisky, turf smoke, and crowded humanity steamed forth.

The company made way for me, awkwardly; I noticed a tendency amongst them to hold on to each other, and there was a hilarious light in Mrs. Brickley's eye as she hustled forward to meet me. My brother-in-law was sitting at a table by the window writing in a note-book by the last light of the waning day; he gave me a glance laden with affairs to which I was superfluous. A red-eyed, red-headed man, evidently the singer, was standing in the middle of the room; it must have been in conformity with some irresistible law of nature that his hair stood out round his head in the orthodox poetic aureole.

In spite of the painful publicity of the moment there was but one course open to me. I tendered to my hostess the corpse

of the drake, with abject apologies and explanations. To say
that Mrs. Brickley accepted them favourably is quite inadequate. She heaped insults upon the drake, for his age, for his
ugliness, for his temerity in getting in my way; she, in fact,
accepted his slaughter in the light of a personal favour and an
excellent jest combined, and passed rapidly on to explain that
the company consisted of a few of the neighbours that was
gathered to talk to the gentleman, and to be singing 'them ewld
songs' for him; their number and their zeal being entirely due
to the deep personal regard entertained for me by Hare Island.
She further mentioned that it was Shrove Tuesday, and that
people should 'jolly themselves' before Lent. I was hurriedly
conveyed to what is known as 'back in the room,' a blend of
best parlour and bedroom, with an immense bed in the corner.
A fire was lighted, by the simple method of importing most of
the kitchen fire, bodily, in a bucket, and placing it on the hearth,
and I was conjured to 'sthrip' and to put on a new suit of clothes
belonging to my host while my own were being dried. He
himself valeted me, inaugurating the ceremony with a tumbler
of hot whisky and water. The suit of new clothes was of the
thickest blue cloth, stiff as boards, and they smelt horribly of
stale turf smoke. The discovery that the trousers consisted of
but a leg and a half was startling; I had forgotten this aspect of
the case, but now, in the proprietor's presence, it was impossible
to withdraw from the loan. I could, at all events, remain
perdu. Through all these preparations I was aware of highly
incensed and fruitless callings for 'Pidge'; of Peter Cadogan no tidings were forthcoming, and although a conventional sense of honour withheld me from disclosing the
information I might have given about the young lady, it
did not deter me from mentally preparing a warm reception
for her squire.

I sat by the fire in regal seclusion, with my clothes steaming
on a chair opposite to me, and the strong glow of the red turf
scorching the shin that was unprotected. Maria and Minx,
also steaming, sat in exquisite serenity in front of the blaze,
retiring every now and then to fling themselves, panting, on a
cold space of floor. The hot whisky and water sent its vulgar
and entirely acceptable consolations into the frozen recesses
of my being, a feeling of sociability stole upon me; I felt magnanimously pleased at the thought that Maxwell, at least, had

had a perfectly successful day; I glowed with gratitude towards Con Brickley and his wife.

Judged by the usual test of hostesses, that is to say, noise, the *conversazione* in Maxwell's honour was a high success. Gabble and hum, harangue and argument, and, through all, Maxwell's unemotional educated voice in discussion with the poet. Scraps of English here and there presently told me that the talk had centred itself upon the tragedy of the drake. I had the gratification of hearing Mrs. Brickley inform her friends that 'if that owld dhrake was shot, itself, he was in the want of it, and divil mend him, going parading there till he had the Major put asthray! Sure that's the gintleman that's like a child! and Pidge could tell ye the same.'

'Faith and thrue for ye,' said another apologist, also female, 'and ye wouldn't blame him if he didn't leave duck nor dhrake livin' afther him, with the annoyance he got from thim that should be tinding him, and he bloated with the walk and all!'

(I may, in my own interest, explain that this unattractive description merely implied that I was heated from excessive exercise.)

'And as for the same Pidge,' broke in Mrs. Brickley with sudden fire, 'when I ketch her it isn't to bate her I'll go, no! but to dhrag her by the hair o' the head round the kitchen.'

These agreeable anticipations were interrupted by other voices. Someone named Paddy was called upon to sing the song about Ned Flaherty's drake.

'Sing up, Paddy boy, for the gentleman! Arrah, what ails ye, Paddy! Don't be ashamed at all!'

''Tis a lovely song, your honour, sir!' (this to my brother-in-law).

'Is it an ancient song?' I heard Maxwell inquire with serious eagerness.

'It is, your honour; 'twas himself made it up lasht year, and he sings it beautiful! Oh! Paddy's a perfect modulator!'

With curiosity stimulated by this mysterious encomium I rose softly and half opened the door in order to obtain a view of the Modulator. A lamp with a glaring tin reflector was on the table beside Maxwell; it illumined Paddy, the Modulator, an incredibly freckled youth, standing in front of my brother-in-law, with eyes fixed on the ground and arms hanging limply at his sides, like a prisoner awaiting sentence. It illumined

also the artistic contempt on the elder Poet's countenance, and
further revealed to me the fact that from twenty-five to thirty
men and women were packed into the small kitchen.

The Modulator opened with a long-drawn and nasal cadenza,
suggestive of the droning preliminary canter of a bagpipe,
which merged into the statement that

> The poor little fella',
> His legs they were yella',
> His bosom was blue, he could swim like a hake;   •
> But some wicked savage,
> To grease his white cabbage,.
> Murdered Ned Flaherty's beautiful drake!

Riotous applause followed on this startlingly appropriate
requiem. Maxwell coldly laid down his stylograph with the
manner of a reporter during an unimportant speech; the poet
took a clay pipe out of his pocket and examined its contents
with an air of detachment; Paddy, with a countenance of un-
diminished gloom, prepared the way for the next verse with
some half-dozen jig-steps, ending with a sledge-hammer
stamp on the earthen floor. Fresh thunders of approval greeted
the effort. It seemed to me that Con Brickley's hospitality had
been a trifle excessive; I even meditated a hint to that effect,
but neither my host nor my hostess was visible. They were
apparently holding an overflow meeting in a room at the other
end of the house, and I noticed that although there was a steady
flow of passers in and out between it and the kitchen, the door
was carefully closed after each opening.

Suddenly the lamp on Maxwell's table flared up smokily as
the door of the house was burst open. The second verse of
the drake's elegy ceased at its first line. A woman whom I
recognized as Kate Keohane, sister of the Widower, drove her
way into the kitchen, sweeping back the people on either side
of her with her arms, as though she was swimming. Her face
was scarlet.

'Is Jer Keohane within here?' she shouted.

'He is not!' replied several voices.

Instantly the door of the inner room flew open, and like a
stag (or a tom-cat, either simile would serve), answering the
challenge of a rival, Mrs. Brickley came forth.

'Is it yer brother you 're wantin', ma'am?' she said with
lofty politeness. 'Ye can search out the house for him if ye

like. It's little he troubles my house or myself now, thanks be to God, and to the magistrates that took my part before all that was in the Coort House! Me that he had goin' in dhread o' me life, with him afther me always in me thrack like a lap-dog!'

'And who has him enticed now but your own daughther?' shrieked Miss Keohane with lightning rapidity. 'Isn't Ellen, the chapel-woman, afther tellin' me she seen herself and himself shneakin' down behindside the chapel, like they'd be goin' aisht to the far sthrand, and she dhressed out, and the coat she stole from Mrs. Yeates on her and a bundle in her hand! Sure doesn't the world know she has her passage paid to Ameriky this two months!'

'Ye lie!' panted Mrs. Brickley, catching her antagonist by the arm, not in attack, but in the awful truce of mutual panic.

Miss Keohane flung her off, only the better to gather force for the prolonged and direful howl of which she delivered herself.

'If she didn't come here with him it's to Ameriky she's taken him! Look in yer box an' ye'll see where she got the passage money! She has the boat's share taken from ye in spite of yer teeth!' Miss Keohane here dropped upon her knees. 'An' I pray,' she continued, lyrically, 'that the devil may melt her, the same as ye'd melt the froth off porther——'

Groans, hoots, and drunken laughter overwhelmed the close of this aspiration. Oblivious of my costume, I stepped forward, with the intention of attracting Maxwell's attention, and withdrawing him and myself as swiftly and unobtrusively as possible from a position that threatened to become too hot to hold us.

Even as I did so I saw in the dark blue space of the open door a face that was strangely familiar, a face at once civilized and martial, whose gaze was set incredulously upon me.

'Here's the Polis!' squeaked a little girl.

The Poet blew out the lamp. The house was in an instant full of the voiceless and strenuous shoving and trampling of people trying to escape. I heard the table go over with a crash, and could only suppose that Maxwell had gone with it, and Maria and Minx, convinced that a cat-hunt was at the root of the matter, barked deafeningly and unceasingly.

In a blinding flash of insight I realized that my brother-in-law and I had been taken red-handed in a 'shebeen,' that is to say, a house in which drink is illicitly sold without a licence.

The Police Sergeant was egregiously tactful. During the conversation that I held with him in the inner room he did not permit his eye to condescend lower than the top button of Mr. Brickley's coat, a consideration that but served to make me more conscious of the humiliating deficiency below, nor did it deviate towards the empty tumbler, with the incriminating spoon in it, that stood on the table.

He explained to me and to Maxwell, whose presence I felt to be my sole link with respectability, that the raid had been planned in consequence of information received after the trial.

'I was going to you, sir, to sign the warrant, but Mr. Knox and Dr. Hickey signed it for us. It was Mr. Knox advised us to come here to-day. We 've found three half-barrels of porter under the bed in the room over there, and about two gallons of potheen hid under fishing nets. I 'll have about thirty summonses out of it.'

The Sergeant's manner was distressingly apologetic. I said nothing, but my heart burned within me as I recognized the hand of Flurry Knox.

'In case you might be looking for your man Cadogan, sir,' went on the Sergeant, 'we seen him in a boat, with two other parties, a man and a woman, going to the mainland when we were coming over. The man that was pulling the other oar had the appearance of having drink taken.'

A second flash, less blinding than the first, but equally illuminative, revealed to me that the brown boots, the flannel suit, had been a wedding garment, the predetermined attire of the Best Man, and a third recalled the fact that Shrove Tuesday was the last day between this and Easter on which a marriage could take place.

Maxwell and I went back with the police, and Maxwell explained to me at some length the origin of the word shebeen. As I neared the mainland, which to-morrow would ring with Flurry's artistic version of the day's events, the future held but one bright spot, the thought of putting Peter Cadogan to fire and sword.

But even that was denied to me. It must have been at the identical moment that my cook, Mrs. Cadogan (aunt of the missing Peter), was placing her wedding ring in the Shrove Tuesday pancakes that evening, that my establishment was felled as one man by tidings that still remain pre-eminent among the sensations of Shreelane. They reached me, irrepressibly, with the coffee.

Hard on the heels of the flushed parlour-maid followed the flat and heavy tread of Mrs. Cadogan, who, like the avenging deities, was habitually shod with felt.

'And now, sir, what do ye say to Pether Cadogan?' she began, launching the enigma into space from the obscurity of the deep doorway. 'What do ye say to him now? The raving scamp!'

I replied that I had a great deal to say to him, and that if I might so far trespass on his leisure as to request his presence in the hall I would say it.

'Hall is it!' echoed Peter's aunt in bitter wrath. 'It's my heart's grief that he ever stood in Shreelane hall to dhraw disgrace on me and on yer honour! God forgive me, when I heard it I had to spit! Himself and Bridget Brickley got married in Skebawn this evenin', and the two o' them is gone to Ameriky on the thrain to-night, and it's all I'll say for her, whatever sort of a thrash she is, she's good enough for him!' There was a pause while one might pant twice.

'I'll tell ye no lie. If I had a gun in me hand, I'd shoot him like a bird! I'd down the brat!'

The avenging deity retired.

What part the Widower proposed to play in the day's proceedings will never be clearly known. He was picked up next day in Hare Island Sound, drifting seaward in the boat whose 'share' had formed the marriage portion of Mrs. Peter Cadogan. Both oars were gone; there remained to him an empty bottle of 'potheen,' and a bucket. He was rowing the boat with the bucket.

VIII

'A HORSE! A HORSE!'

'OLD Jimmy Porteous!' I ejaculated, while a glow of the ancient enthusiasm irradiated my bosom, 'Philippa, I say! Do you see this? Jimmy Porteous is to command this district!'

'No, darling, *not* with an 'egg!' replied Philippa, removing the honey spoon from the grasp of her youngest child, just too late to avert disaster; 'we *don't* eat honey with eggs.'

The heavy hand of experience has taught me that at moments such as these the only possible course is to lie to, head to wind, till the squall passes, and then begin from the beginning again. I readdressed myself to my newspaper, while the incident went, like a successful burlesque, with a roar, sustained from the foot of the stairs to the point when the nursery door slammed upon it.

Philippa resumed her seat at the breakfast table.

'Yes, dear, what were you saying?' she said, yielding me the laborious but vague attention that is the best any husband can expect from any wife on such occasions.

I repeated my statement, and was scandalized to find that Philippa had but the most shadowy remembrance of Jimmy Porteous, who, in the days when I first joined my regiment, had been its senior subaltern, and, for me and my fellows, one of the most revered of its law-givers. As a captain he left us, and proceeded to do something brilliant on somebody's staff, and, what time I got my company, had moved on in radiance into a lofty existence in the War Office and newspaper paragraphs.

I recalled these things to my wife, coupling them with the information that she would have to call on Lady Porteous, when the door opened, and the face of Flurry Knox, unshaven and blue, with the miserable mother-o'-pearl blueness of fair people in cold weather, appeared in the opening.

He had looked in, he said, on his way home from the fair, to try would we give him a cup of tea, and he went on to remark that the wind was cold enough to cut the horns off a cow.

I asked him if he had seen my beasts there, and if they had been sold.

'Oh, they were, they were,' he said tolerantly; 'it was a wonderful good fair. The dealers were buying all before them. There was a man said to me: "If you had a little dog there, and he to be a calf, you'd have sold him."'

It was one of Flurry Knox's ruling principles in life to disparage the livestock of his friends; it was always within the bounds of possibility that the moment might arrive when he would wish to buy them.

'I met a man from Sir Thomas Purcell's country yesterday,' said Flurry presently; 'he says there's been the father and mother of a row down there between old Sir Thomas and Hackett, that's the man has the harriers. Sir Thomas is wild because they say the soldiers are giving Hackett as good a subscription as himself, and he says Hackett has all the foxes killed.'

'But surely—harriers don't hunt foxes?' said Philippa ingenuously.

Flurry looked at her for a moment in silence. 'Is it Hackett's harriers!' he said compassionately, 'sure he flogs them off hares.'

'Talking of soldiers, they've just sent a man who used to be in my regiment to command this district,' I said, plucking my own topic from the tangle of inter-hunt squabbles; 'a great man to hounds he used to be, too.'

'Would he buy the Dodger?' asked Flurry swiftly. 'Would he give a price?'

'I dare say he would if he liked the horse. If I got a chance I might tell him,' I said, magnanimously.

'I tell you what, Major,' said Flurry, with an eye on his ally, Philippa, 'you and me and Mrs. Yeates will go up and have a day with Sir Thomas's hounds, and you'll say the word for me to the General!'

Looking back at it all now I recognize that here was the moment for firmness. I let the moment slip, and became immersed in tracking General Sir James Porteous, K.C.B., through the pages of an elderly army list. By the time I had located him in three separate columns I found that Philippa and Flurry had arranged unalterably the details of what my wife is pleased to call a ramp—i.e. an expedition that, as its name implies, suggests a raid made by tramps.

'—Why, my gracious! aren't they cousins of my own?

They'll be only delighted! Sure, Sally had measles there three
years ago, and 'twas as good as a play for them!—Put us up, is
it? Of course they will! The whole lot of us. D'ye think
Sally 'd stay at home?—No, you 'll not take your own horses
at all. Hire from Flavin; I 'll see he does you well.'

'And you know, Sinclair'—thus the other conspirator—'it
would be an excellent chance for you to meet your beloved
Jimmy Porteous!'

It was not Mr. Knox's habit to let the grass grow under his
feet. Before I had at all grasped the realities of the project
my wife heard from Mrs. Sally Knox to say that she had
arranged it all with the Butler-Knoxes, and that we were to
stay on for a second night in order to go to a dance at which
we should meett he General. At intervals during the following
week I said to Philippa that it was preposterous and monstrous
to dump ourselves upon the Butler-Knoxes, unknown people
whom we had but once met at a function at the Bishop's. My
remembrance of them, though something blurred by throngs
of the clergy and their wives, did not suggest the type of person
who might be expected to keep open house for stray fox-
hunters. I said all this to Philippa, who entirely agreed with
me, and continued her preparations, after the manner of
experienced wives.

It was raining hard one afternoon in the following week
when a four-wheeled inside car—an admirable vehicle, which
I wish in no way to disparage—disgorged its burden at the
door of Garden Mount House. One item of the burden was
experiencing a sensation only too familiar, such a sensation as
a respectable seaman might feel on being pressed into a crew of
buccaneers. The house loomed over us, large, square, and
serious, in the wet moonlight of the January evening; the husky,
over-fed bark of an elderly dog was incessant in the hall. If
by laying hold of the coat-tails of the leading pirate, as he got
out to ring the bell, I could then and there have brought the
expedition to a close, I would thankfully have done so.

The door was opened by a melancholy old gentleman with a
grey moustache and whiskers; he might have been Colonel
Newcome in his decadence, but from the fact that he wore an
evening coat and grey trousers, I gathered that he was the
butler, and for any one skilled in Irish households, he at
once placed the establishment—rich, godly, Low Church, and

K 978

consistently and contentedly dull. As we entered the hall there arose from some fastness in the house a shrill clamour that resolved itself into the first line of a hymn.

Flurry dug me in the ribs with his elbow. 'They 've found!' he whispered; 'you needn't look so frightened. It 's only Lucy and Louisa having the choir practice!'

To these strains Colonel Newcome ushered us into the drawing-room. There was no one in it. It was a large double drawing-room, and nothing but heavy maroon curtains now separated us from the choir practice. The hymn continued, a loud and long-drawn proclamation, and, pending its conclusion, my wife and Mrs. Flurry Knox swiftly and stealthily circumnavigated the room, and appraised all its contents, from a priceless Battersea basket filled with dusty bulbs, to a Chippendale card-table with a sewing machine clamped on to it, while Flurry, in a stage whisper, dilated to me upon the superfluous wealth that Providence had seen fit to waste upon the Butler-Knoxes. The household, as I had gradually learnt, consisted of an elderly bachelor, Mr. Lucius Butler-Knox (commonly known as 'Looshy'), his unmarried sister, Miss Louisa, his widowed sister, Mrs. Hodnett, and a corpulent, grey-muzzled black-and-tan terrier. Their occupations were gardening, and going to what they called 'the city,' i.e. the neighbouring county town, to attend charitable committee meetings; they kept a species of philanthropic registry office for servants; their foible was hospitality, disastrously coupled with the fact that they dined at half-past six. It was one of the mysteries of kinship that Flurry Knox and our host and hostess should possess a nearer relative in common than Adam. That he should have established their respectable home as his hostelry and house of call was one of the mysteries of Flurry Knox.

The hymn ceased, the raiders hastily formed into line, the maroon drapery parted, and the ladies of the house, flushed with song, and importing with them a potent sample of the atmosphere of the back drawing-room, were upon us, loud in hospitable apologies, instant in offers of tea; the situation opened and swallowed us up.

The half-past six o'clock dinner came all too swiftly. Glared upon by an unshaded lamp that sat like a ball of fire in the centre of the table, we laboured in the trough of a sea of the thickest

ox-tail soup; a large salmon followed; with the edge of dubious
appetite already turned, we saw the succeeding items of the
menu spread forth on the table like a dummy hand at bridge.
The boiled turkey, with its satellite ham, the roast saddle of
mutton, with its stable companion the stack of cutlets;
the succeeding course, where a team of four wild-duck
struggled for the lead with an open tart and a sago pudding.   Like Agag, we went delicately, and, like Agag, it
availed us nothing.

I watched my *vis-à-vis*, little Mrs. Flurry, furtively burying
a slab of turkey beneath mashed potatoes as neatly as a little
dog buries a bone; her green kitten's eyes met mine without a
change of expression, and turned to her glass, which Colonel
Newcome had filled with claret.   'The beaded bubbles, winking
at the brim,' had a greyish tinge.

'Cousin Lucius!' observed Mrs. Flurry, in a silence that
presently happened to fall, 'can you remember who painted
that picture of our great-grandfather—the one over the door
I mean?'

Mr. Butler-Knox, a small, grey-bearded, elderly gentleman,
wholly, up to the present, immersed in carving, removed the
steam of the ducks from his eye-glasses, and concentrated them
upon the picture.

'It's by Maclise, isn't it?' went on Sally, leaning forward
to get a nearer view.

In that moment, when all heads turned to the picture, I
plainly saw her draw the glass of claret to the verge of the table;
it disappeared beneath it and returned to its place empty.
Almost simultaneously, the black-and-tan terrier sprang from
a lair near my feet, and hurried from the room, shaking his ears
vigorously.   Mrs. Flurry's eyes wavered from the portrait to
mine, and her face became slowly and evenly pink, like an
afterglow.

It was but one of the many shameless acts of my party during
the age-long evening.   At ten o'clock we retired to rest, for
my own part, thoroughly overfed, not in the least sleepy, worn
with conversation, and oppressed by the consciousness of
flippant, even brutal, ingratitude.

The weather had cleared next morning to mild greyness, that
softened even the asperity of half-past eight breakfast.   I
lumbered stiffly downstairs in a pair of new butcher boots, and

found with thankfulness that our hosts, exhausted possibly by their efforts, had kept their rooms.

Marshalled in order upon the sideboard stood the remains of all the more enduring items of last night's dinner, cold indeed, but firm and undefeated; hot dishes of ancient silver roasted before the noble brass-mounted fireplace; there were vats of lethargic cream, a clutch of new-laid eggs, a heap of hot scones.

'It's easy seen it wasn't cracking blind nuts made Lucy Hodnett and Louisa the size they are!' remarked Flurry, as the party, feeling more piratical than ever, embarked upon this collation. 'Mrs. Yeates, do you think I am bound to dance with the pair of them to-night? *You* are, Major, anyway! But I might get off with Louisa.'

'Oh, Sinclair's card is full,' said my wife, who was engaged in trying to decipher the marks on the cream jug without upsetting the cream; 'he and the General are plighted to one another for the evening.'

'I wonder if the claret has stained the carpet!' said Mrs. Flurry, diving under the table. 'It has! How awful!' Mrs. Flurry's voice indicated the highest enjoyment. 'Never mind, they'll never see it! They're too fat to get under the table!'

'If they did, it'd be the first time old Looshy's claret ever put any one there!' said Flurry.

We have never known the precise moment in this speech at which 'Old Looshy's' butler entered the room; we only know that while Mrs. Flurry, much hampered by habit and boots, was in the act of struggling from beneath the table, he was there, melancholy and righteous, with a telegram on a salver.

It was from Flavin, the livery stableman, and its effect upon the spirits of the company was that of a puncture in a tyre.

'Regret horses not available am trying to procure others will send by next train if possible.'

We said that there was no answer, and we finished our breakfasts in a gravity scarcely lightened by Flurry's almost religious confidence in Flavin's infallibility, and in his power of making horses out of rushes, like the fairies, if need be.

I was, I may admit, from the first thoroughly pessimistic. I almost went up and got into ordinary clothes; I at least talked of doing so, as a means of preparing Philippa for the worst. I

said it was a mere waste of time to send the Butler-Knox coachman to the station, as had been arranged, and I did my best to
dissuade Flurry from his intention of riding to the meet by way
of the station to help in unboxing animals that could not possibly
be there.

In abysmal dejection my wife and I surveyed the departing
forms of Mr. and Mrs. Florence Knox; the former on the
Dodger, a leggy brown four-year-old, the planting of whom
upon General Porteous had been the germ of the expedition;
while Sally skipped and sidled upon a narrow, long-tailed
chestnut mare, an undefeated jumper, and up to about as much
weight as would go by parcel post for ninepence. There then
ensued a period of total desolation, in which we looked morosely
at old photograph books in the drawing-room, and faced the
prospect of a long day with the Butler-Knoxes, while heavy
footsteps overhead warned us that our entertainers were
astir, and that at any moment the day's conversation might
begin.

I was engaged, not, I fancy, for the first time, in telling
Philippa that I had always said that the entire expedition was a
mistake, when Colonel Newcome again entered the room.

'The master sent me to ask you, sir, if you'd like to have the
pony-phaeton to drive down to the station to meet the half-past
ten train. Flavin might be sending the horses on it, and it'd
save you time to meet them there.'

We closed with the offer; at its worst, the pony-carriage
could be smoked in, which the drawing-room could not; at its
best, it might save half an hour in getting to the meet. We
presently seated ourselves in it, low down behind an obese
piebald pony, with a pink nose, and a mane hogged to the
height of its ears. As I took up the whip it turned and regarded us with an unblinkered eye, pink-lidded and small
as a pig's.

'You should go through Fir Grove, sir,' said the boy who
had brought the equipage to the door, 'it's half a mile of a short
cut, and that's the way Tom will come with the horses. It's
the first gate-lodge you'll meet on the road.'

The mud was deep, and the piebald pony plodded through it
at a sullen jog. The air was mild and chilly, like an uninteresting woman; the foreknowledge of fiasco lay heavily upon
us; it hardly seemed worth while to beat the pony when he sank

into a walk; it was the most heart-broken forlorn hope that ever took the field.

The gate-lodge of Fir Grove fulfilled the assignation made for it by the stable boy, and met us on the road. The gates stood wide open, and the pony turned in as by an accustomed route, and crawled through them with that simulation of complete exhaustion that is the gift of lazy ponies. Loud narrative in a male voice proceeded form the dark interior of the lodge, and, as we passed, a woman's voice said, in horrified rejoinder:

'The Lord save us! She must be Antichrist!'

Here, apparently, the speaker became aware of our proximity, and an old woman looked forth. Her face was apprehensive.

'Did ye see the police, sir?' she asked.

We replied in the negative.

'Please God, she'll not come our way!' she said, and banged the door.

We moved on, heavily, in the deep gravel of the avenue.

'Isn't this rather awful? Shall we go on?' said Philippa.

I replied with truth that there was no room to turn. On either side of the narrow drive laurels and rhododendrons were crammed as thickly as they could be planted, their dark foliage met overhead; if the inexpressible 'she' referred to by the lodge-keeper did come our way, retreat would be out of the question. The tunnel ran uphill, and I drove the pony up it as one drives a hoop, by incessant beating; had I relaxed my efforts he would probably, like a hoop, have lain down. Presently, and still uphill, we turned a corner, the tunnel ceased, and we were face to face with a large pink house.

As we advanced, feeling to the full the degradation of making a short cut past a strange house, in tall hats and a grovelling pony-carriage, we beheld figures rushing past the windows of one of the rooms on the ground floor, as if in headlong flight. Was this the fulfilment of the dark sayings of the lodge-keeper, and was 'she' 'coming our way'? The bouncing strains of a measure, known, I believe, as *Whistling Rufus*, came forth to us hilariously as we drew nearer. The problem changed, but I am not sure that the horror did not deepen.

Divining the determination of the piebald pony to die, if necessary, rather than pass a hall door without stopping at it, yet debarred by the decencies from thrashing him past the long line of windows, I administered two or three rousing tugs to his wooden mouth. At the third tug the near rein broke. The pony stopped dead. Simultaneously the hall door was flung open, and a young and lovely being, tall, and beautifully dressed, fluttered out on to the steps and peered at us through long-handled eye-glasses.

'Oh! I thought you were the police!' exclaimed the being, with unaffected disappointment.

The position seemed, from all points, to demand an apology. I disengaged myself from the pony-carriage and proffered it; I also volunteered any help that a mere man, not a policeman, might be capable of rendering.

The young lady aimed her glasses at the piebald, motionless in malign stupor, and replied irrelevantly:

'Why! That's the Knoxes' pony!'

I made haste to explain our disaster and the position generally, winding up with a request for a piece of string.

'You're staying at the Butler-Knoxes'!' exclaimed the lady of the house. "How funny that is! Do you know you're coming to our dance to-night, to meet your old friend the General! I know all about it, you see!' She advanced with a beaming yet perturbed countenance upon Philippa. 'I'm so glad to meet you. Do come in! We've got an infuriated cook at bay in the kitchen, and things are rather disorganized, but I think we can rise to a bit of string! The pony's all right —he'll sleep there for months, he always does.'

We followed her into a hall choked with the exiled furniture of the drawing-room, and saw through an open door the whirling forms of two or three couples of young men and maidens.

'They're polishing the floor,' said our hostess, swiftly shutting the door; 'they make a hideous noise, but it keeps them quiet— if you know what I mean. It's most disastrous that my husband has gone out hunting,' she pursued; 'this odious cook only arrived two days ago, and——'

At this juncture a door at the end of the hall burst open, disclosing a long passage and a young and crimson housemaid.

'She's coming, my lady! She's coming! Mr. Ralph's sent me on to get the door open!' she panted.

At the same moment a loud and wrathful voice arose in the passage and a massive form, filling it from wall to wall, appeared;

the capitulating cook, moving down upon us with the leisurely and majestic truculence of a traction engine. As she came she chanted these words in measured cadence:

> 'Lady Flora,
> Gets her brother
> To do her dirty work.'

By the time this rune had been repeated three times she was in the hall, shepherded by a tall young man, obviously the brother referred to, and by the butler, the vista being filled in the rear by a wavering assortment of female domestics. As the cook tacked to weather a sofa, there was something about her that woke a vague and unpleasant chord of memory. Her ranging eye met mine, and the chord positively twanged as I recognized the formidable countenance of a female, technically known as a 'job-cook,' who for two cyclonic weeks had terrorized our household while Mrs. Cadogan was on leave. I backed convulsively into Lady Flora, in futile and belated attempt to take cover, but even as I did so the chanting ceased and I knew the worst had happened.

'Is that my darlin' Major Yeates?' shouted the cook, tacking again and bearing down on me full-sailed. 'Thanks be to God I have the gentleman that 'll see I get justice! And Mrs. Yeates, a noble lady, that 'd never set foot in my kitchen without she 'd ask my leave! Ah, ha! As Shakespeare says, I 'd know a rale lady as soon as I 'd put an eye on her, if she was boiling cabbage!'

She caught my reluctant hand and waved it up and down, and the muffled triumphings of *Whistling Rufus* in the drawing-room filled up the position.

Through them came a sound of wheels on the gravel, and through this again a strangled whisper from behind:

'Take her out to the steps; I hear the car with the police!'

Holding the fervid hand of the job-cook, I advanced with her through the furniture, skew-wise, as in the visiting figure of the Lancers; there was an undoubted effort on her part to keep time to the music, and she did not cease to inform the company that Major and Mrs. Yeates were the real old nobility, and that they would see she got her rights.

Followed closely by the shepherd and the butler we moved forth on to the steps. The police were not there. There was nothing there save a complicated pattern of arcs and angles on the gravel, as of a four-wheeled vehicle that has taken an uncommonly short turn. At the bend of the avenue the pony-carriage, our link with the world without, was disappearing from view, the piebald pony heading for home at a pig-like but determined gallop. The job-cook clasped her hands on my arm and announced to the landscape that she would live and die with the Major.

IX

'A HORSE! A HORSE!'

PART II

A QUARTER of an hour later Philippa and I stood in the high road, with the sense of deliverance throbbing in every grateful nerve, and viewed the car, with the job-cook and the policeman, swing heavily away towards the railway station.

Mine was the strategy that had brought about our escape, mine were the attractions that had lured the cook to mount the policeman's car with me, and still more inalienably mine was the searing moment when, still arm-in-arm with the cook, we drove away from the deeply appreciative party on the doorsteps. Philippa and a policeman were on the opposite side of the car; the second policeman, very considerately, walked.

We were close to the station, the cook had sung herself to sleep, and Philippa and I had relapsed into the depths of abysmal despondency, when our incredulous eyes beheld the Butler-Knoxes' coachman coming towards us at a trot, riding a bay horse, and leading a grey, on which was a side-saddle. Flavin, the horse dealer, had, after all, been as good as Flurry's word—the hirelings were here, and all was right with the world.

The car slackened to a walk, we slid from it silently, and it and its burden passed into that place of shadows to which all extraneous affairs of life betake themselves on a hunting morning, when the hour is come, and the horse.

Looshy's coachman delivered to me the bay horse, a large

* K 97⁸

and notable-looking animal, with a Roman nose adorned with a crooked blaze, a tranquil eye, and two white stockings. In his left hand he held a compact iron-grey mare, hogged and docked, who came up to the bank by the roadside, to be mounted, as neatly as a man-o'-war boat comes alongside. Hirelings of so superior a class it had never before been my privilege to meet, and I made up my mind that they were either incurably vicious or broken-winded.

'It's easy known that this mare's carried a lady before, sir,' said the coachman, a young man with a soul for higher things than driving the Butler-Knox covered car, 'and the big horse is the best I ever seen come out of Flavin's! He's in grand condition, he's as slick as a mouse! Only for Mr. Flurry being there we'd hardly have got them,' he continued, while he lengthened my stirrup-leathers; 'the chap Flavin sent with them had drink taken, and the porters had the box shunted and himself in it, stretched, and the bottle of whisky with him!'

Flavin's man and his bottle of whisky were now negligible incidents for me. Philippa was already under way, and the time was short. The bay horse, arching his neck and reaching pleasantly at his bit, went away at a rhythmic and easy trot, the grey flitted beside him with equal precision; it was, perhaps, rather fast for riding to a meet, but we were late, and were they not hirelings?

We followed our guides, the telegraph posts, for some four miles of level road; they dropped down a deepening valley to a grey and brimming river, and presently came slate roofs and whitewashed houses, staring at each other across an empty village street. We had arrived at Kilbarron, the scene of the meet, and the meet was not.

'They've gone on! they've gone on!' screamed an old woman from a doorway, 'away up over the hill!'

Evidently every other live thing had followed the hunt, and we did not spare Mr. Flavin's horses in doing the same. We reached the top of the long hill in a remarkably brief space of time, and, having done so, realized that we were not too late. A couple of fields away a row of figures, standing like palings along the top of a bank, with their backs to us, told that the hounds were still in view; even as we sighted them, the palings plunged *en masse* from their standpoint with that composite yell that in Ireland denotes the breaking (and frequently the

heading) of a fox, and vanished. Whatever was happening, it
was not coming our way. I turned my hireling at the bank by
the roadside, he came round with a responsive swing, and in two
large and orderly bounds he was over. Before I had time to
look round the grey mare, with the faintest hint of a buck,
galloped emulously past me.   ~

'Perfection!' panted Philippa, putting her hat straight. •

As we came up on to the next bank, recently vacated by its
human palisade, we found that fortune had smiled upon us.
Just below, on our right, was a long strip of gorse covert; three
big-fields beyond it, gliding from us like a flock of seagulls, were
the clamouring hounds, and in the space between us and them
bucketed the hunt, in the first fine frenzy of getting away.
Flavin's bay immediately caught hold, not implacably, but
with the firmness of superior knowledge; the grey mare, having
ascertained that Philippa was not going to interfere, thought
better of going on alone, and took the time from her stable
companion. The field was already sorting itself into the usual
divisions of the forward, the cunning, and the useless; our luck
stood to us; the forward division, carried away by the enthusiasm of a good start and a sympathetic fall of ground, succeeded in less than a quarter of a mile in hustling the hounds
over the line, and brought about a check. We joined the rearguard, and worked our way towards the front, unobtrusively,
because Sir Thomas Purcell's comments on the situation were
circling like a stock-whip among the guilty, and were not
sparing the innocent. At this moment we found Flurry Knox
beside us.

'Sir Thomas is giving the soldiers their tea in a mug!' he
said; 'and they were in the want of it! How are those horses
doing with you?' he went on, looking our steeds up and down.
'They look up to your weights, anyhow! I suppose you didn't
see your friend, the general? He was at the meet in a motor.'

'In a motor!' repeated Philippa. 'I thought he was such a
wonderful rider.'

'He knows how to get a motor along, anyhow,' replied Flurry,
his attentive eyes following the operations of the hounds;
'maybe he has the gout. You 'd say he had by the colour of
his face. Hullo! Boys! They 're away again! Come on,
Mrs. Yeates! Knock your two guineas' worth out of Flavin!'

Short as it was, the burst had been long enough to tranquillize my anxieties as to our hirelings' wind, and when we started again we found them almost excessively ready for the stone-faced bank that confronted us at the end of the field. Some twenty of us, including the chidden, but wholly unabashed soldiers, went at it in line, and, after the manner of stone-faced banks, it grew very tall as we approached it. Flavin's bay strode unfalteringly over it; it was as though he grasped it and flung it behind him. The grey mare, full of jealousy and vain-glory, had a hard try to fly the whole thing, but retained suffi-cient self-control to change feet at the last possible instant; with or without a scramble or a peck, we all arrived somehow in the next field, and saw, topping the succeeding fence, the bulky chestnut quarters of Sir Thomas Purcell's horse and the square scarlet back of Sir Thomas. Away to the left, on an assortment of astute crocks, three of the Misses Purcell followed the First Whip, at as considerable a distance from their parent as was consistent with a good place. Their voices came con-fusedly to us; apparently each was telling the others to get out of her way.

For a quarter of an hour the hounds ran hard over the clean pasture-land, whose curves rose before us and glided astern like the long rollers under an Atlantic liner. Innocent of rocks or pitfalls, unimpeachable as to surface, it was a page of fair print as compared with the black-letter manuscript to which the country of Mr. Flurry Knox's hounds might be likened. Never before have I crossed fences as sound, as seductive; it was like jumping large and well-upholstered Chesterfield sofas; Chester-fieldian also were the manners of Flavin's bay. I found myself in the magnificent position of giving a lead to Flurry and the Dodger, of giving several leads to the soldiery; once, when a wide and boggy stream occurred, the Misses Purcell and the crocks looked to me as their pioneer. The hustle and the hurry never relaxed; the hounds had fastened on the line and were running it as though it were a footpath; but for the check at the start, no fox could have held his lead for so long at such a pace, and whatever the pace, the tails of the horses of Sir Thomas and the First Whip never failed to disappear over the bank just ahead.

For me, in the unwonted glory of heading the desperadoes of the first flight, life and the future were contained in the question of how much longer I could count on my hireling. I was just able to spare a hasty thought or two to Philippa and the grey, and I remember that it was after a heavy drop into a road that I noticed, with the just and impotent wrath of a husband, that her hair was beginning to come down.

It was just then that I first saw the motor. The fox had run the road for some little distance; we clattered and splashed along it, until an intimidating roar from Sir Thomas and the sight of his right arm in the air, brought us, bumping and tugging, to a standstill. The hounds were for a moment at fault, swarming, with their heads down, over every inch of the road, and beyond them, about a hundred yards from us, was a resplendent scarlet motor, whose nearer approach was summarily interdicted by the First Whip. I am short-sighted, but I caught an impression of two elderly gentlemen, one of whom, wearing a white moustache and a tall hat, was responding warmly to the fulminations of Sir Thomas. If this were my ancient brother-in-arms, Jimmy Porteous, following hounds in a motor, times were indeed changed. I dismissed the possibility from my mind. Just then I caught sight of Flurry's face; it had in it the fearful joy of a schoolboy who has seen a squib put into the tail pocket of the schoolmaster, and awaits the result. Mrs. Flurry, in the heroic act of plucking a hairpin from her own unshaken golden-red plaits, and yielding it to Philippa, met his eye with a glance that was so expressionless as to amount to a danger signal.

At this moment the hounds jostled over the wall with a clatter of falling stones; they spread themselves in the field like the opening of a fan, they narrowed to the recovered line like the closing of one; Sir Thomas's chestnut hoisted himself and his fifteen-stone burden out of the road with the heave of an earthquake. The riders shoved after him, and we were swept again into the current of the hunt.

As we thundered away up the field threatening shouts from the checked motorists followed us; apparently, after the manner of their kind, they had not a moment to spare, and the delay had annoyed them. The next fence arrived, and they, and all else, were forgotten.

There was a wood ahead of us, cresting a long upland, and for it the hounds were making, at a pace that brutally ignored the rise of ground, and the fact that in these higher levels the fields were smaller, and the fences had to be faced up a hill that momently grew steeper.

'Hold on, Mrs. Yeates, till I take down that pole for you!' Flurry's voice followed us up the hill, and there was that in it that told he was making heavy weather of it. He was leading the dripping Dodger, and I have seldom seen a redder face than his as he laboured past Philippa and dragged away the shaft of a cart that barred a gap. 'Bad luck to this for a close country!' he puffed. 'You're not off one fence before you're on top of the next!' Flavin's horses were certainly lathering pretty freely, but were otherwise making no remark on the situation, and neither of them had so far made a mistake of any kind. I saw the First Whip regard the bay with obvious respect, and turn with a confidential comment to the nearest Miss Purcell. It hall-marked my achievements.

Philippa and I, were among the first into the wood; even Flurry had been left three fields behind, and the glory of our position radiated from us, as we stood at the end of the main ride, sublimely surveying the arrival of the rest of the streaming hunt. Sir Thomas and the hounds had dived out of sight into the recesses of the wood; a period of inaction ensued, and for a few balmy minutes peace with honour was ours.

Balmy, however, as were the minutes, there crept into them an anxiety as to what the hounds were doing. A great and complete silence had fallen as far as they and Sir Thomas were concerned, and Philippa and I, conscious of our high estate as leaders of the hunt, melted away from the crowd to investigate matters. We followed a path that took us across the wood, and the deeper we went the deeper was the silence, and the more acute became our fears that we had been left behind. Sir Thomas had an evil reputation for slipping his field and getting away alone.

'There's the horn!' cried Philippa. 'It's outside the wood! They *have* gone away. Hurry!'

We were squeezing along the farther edge of the covert, looking for a way out, and I, too, heard the note, faint, yet commanding. I hurried. That is to say, with my hat over my eyes, and my cheek laid against the bay's neck, I followed my wife up an alley that was barely wide enough for a woodcock.

On our left was an impassable hedge of small trees, crowning a heavy drop into the field outside the wood; our faces were rowelled by the branches of young spruce firs. It was all very well for Philippa, riding nearly two hands lower than I, to

twist her way in and out through them like a squirrel, but for
me, on a 16.2 horse, resolved on following his stable companion
through a keyhole if necessary, it was anything but well.   My
eyes were tightly shut, my arm was in front of them, and my
eye-glass was hanging down my back, when I felt the bay stop.

'Here's a way out,' said my wife's voice, apparently from
the middle of a fir-tree, 'there's a sort of a cattle-track here.'

There followed a scramble and a slide, then Philippa's voice
again, enjoining me to keep to the right.

She has since explained that she really meant the left, and
that, in any case, I might have known that she always said right
when she meant left; be that as it may, when the bay and I had
committed ourselves to the steep descent—half water-course,
half cattle-track—I was smitten in the face by a holly branch.
Before I had recovered from its impact, a stout beechen bough,
that it had masked, met me violently across the waistcoat and
held me in mid-air, as the gorilla is reputed to grasp and hold
the traveller, while my horse moved firmly downward from
beneath me.   After a moment of suspense, mental and physical,
I fell to earth, like the arrow in the song, I knew not where, and
tobogganed painfully down something steep and stony, with
briars in it.

As I rose to my feet the mellow note of the horn that had
beguiled us from the wood again sounded; nearer now, and
with a harsher cadence, and I perceived, at the farther end of
the field in which I had arrived, a bullock, with his head over a
gate, sending a long and lamentable bugle note to the companions
from whom he had been separated.   Simultaneously the hounds
opened far back in the wood behind me, and I knew that the
flood-tide of luck had turned against us.

Flavin's bay had not waited for me.   He was already well
away, going with head and tail high held, a gentleman at large,
seeking for entertainment at a lively and irresponsible trot.
Pursuing him, with more zeal than discretion, was Philippa
on the grey mare; he broke into a canter, and I had the pleasure
of seeing them both swing through a gateway and proceed at
a round gallop across the next field.   I followed them at the
best imitation of the same pace that my boots permitted, and
squelched through the mire of the gateway in time to see the
bay horse jump a tall bank, and drop with a clatter into a road.
At the same moment the drumming and hooting of a motor-car

broke upon my ear, and three heads, one of them wearing a tall hat, slid at high speed along the line of the fence. At sight of this apparition the bay horse gave a massive buck, and fled at full speed up a lane. To my surprise and gratification, the motor-car instantly stopped, and one of its occupants—the wearer of the tall hat—sprang out and gave chase to my horse.

My attention was here abruptly transferred to my wife, who, having followed the chase, whether by her own wish or that of the grey mare I have never been able to discover, was now combating the desire of the latter to jump the bank at the exact spot calculated to land them both in the lap of the motor-car. The dispute ended in a slanting and crab-like rush at a place twenty yards lower down, and it was then that the figure of our host, Mr. Lucius Butler-Knox, rose, amazingly, in the motor-car, making semaphore gestures of warning.

The mare jumped crookedly on to the bank, hung there for half a second, and launched herself into space, the launch being followed, appropriately, by a mighty splash. Neither she nor Philippa reappeared.

Throughout these events I had not ceased to run, and the next thing I can distinctly recall is scrambling, thoroughly blown, on to the fence, whence a moving scene presented itself to me. The grey mare and Philippa had, with singular ingenuity, selected between them the one place in the fence where disaster was inevitable; and I now beheld my wife prone in two feet of yellow water, the overflow of a flooded ditch that had turned a hollow by the roadside into a sufficiently imposing pond. Mr. Butler-Knox and the chauffeur were already rendering all the assistance possible, short of wetting their feet, and were hauling her ashore; while the grey mare, recumbent in deeper water, surveyed the operation with composure, and made no attempt to move. When I joined the party—a process involving a wide circuit of the flood — Philippa had sunk, dripping, upon a heap of stones by the roadside, in laughter as inexplicable as it was unsuitable. There was, at all events, no need to ask if she were hurt.

'The most appalling thing that you ever knew in your life has happened!' she wailed, and instantly fell again into unseemly convulsions.

Whatever the jest might be, it did not appeal to the chauffeur, who withdrew in silence to his motor, coldly wiping the vicarious

duckweed from his knees with a silk pocket-handkerchief.
Still less did it appeal to me. Any fair-minded person will
admit that I had cause to be excessively angry with Philippa.
That a grown woman, the mother of two children, should mistake the bellow of a bullock for the note of a horn was bad
enough; but that when, having caused a serious accident by
not knowing her right hand from her left, and having, by further
insanities, driven one valuable horse adrift into the country,
probably broken the back of another, laid the seeds of heart
disease in her husband from shock and over-exertion, and of
rheumatic fever in herself; when, I repeat, after all these out-
rages, she should sit in a soaking heap by the roadside, laughing
like a maniac, I feel that the sympathy of the public will not be
withheld from me.

The mystery of Mr. Butler-Knox's appearance in the motor-
car passed by me like a feather in a whirlwind; I strode without
a word into the yellow flood in which the mare was lying, and
got hold of her reins with the handle of my crop; I might as
well have tried to draw out Behemoth with a hook. Her hind
quarters were well fixed in the hidden ditch, she made not the
slightest effort to stir, and continued to recline, contentedly,
not to say defiantly.

'That's a great sign of fine weather,' said a voice behind me
in affable comment, 'when a horse will lie down in wather that
way.'

I turned upon my consoler, and saw a young countryman with
a fur-lined coat hanging upon his arm.

'I got this thrown in the *bohireen* above,' he said, 'the other
gentleman, that's follying the bay horse, stripped it off him,
and God knows it's itself that's weighty!'

'My dear Major!' began Looshy, addressing me agitatedly
from the bank, as a hen might address a refractory duckling,
'there has been a most unfortunate mistake.'

'There has! There has! It's all Flurry's fault!' gasped
Philippa, staggering towards me like a drunken woman.

'I fear the General is terribly annoyed,' continued Looshy,
wiping his grey beard and mopping his collar to remove the
muddy imprint of Philippa's arm; 'he rushed into Garden
Mount in search of his horses when he found they were not at
the meet nor at the station—he left Lady Porteous with my
sisters and took me to identify you; I mentioned your name, but

he did not seem to grasp it—indeed his language was—er—was such that I thought it unwise to press the point.'

I dropped the reins and began, slowly, to wade out of the pool.

'I understand he has but just paid three hundred pounds for these horses—it was an unpardonable mistake of Flurry's,' went on Looshy; 'he found the General's horses at the station and thought that they were Flavin's.'

'Dear Flurry!' sobbed Philippa, shamelessly, reeling against me and clutching my arm.

'Begor', he have the horse!' said the young countryman, looking up the hill.

A stout figure in a red coat and tall hat was approaching by way of the *bohireen,* followed by a man leading a limping horse.

'I think,' said Looshy nervously, 'that Mrs. Yeates had better have my seat in the motor-car and hurry home. I will walk—I should really prefer it. The General will be quite happy now that he has found his horses and his old friend.'

The chauffeur, plying a long-necked oil-can, smiled sardonically.

X

SHARPER THAN A FERRET'S TOOTH

'My dear Philippa,' said Miss Shute gloomily, 'I have about as much chance of spending next winter in Florence as I have of spending it in the moon. I despair of ever getting Bernard married. I look upon him as hopeless.'

'I don't agree with you at all,' replied Philippa; 'don't you remember how demented he was about Sally Knox? And when we all thought he was on the verge of suicide, we discovered that he was deep in a flirtation with that American girl. It seems to me he 's ready to be devoted to any one who takes him in hand. He has none of that deadly helpless fidelity about him.'

'I ought never to have allowed him to take up gardening,'

said Miss Shute, despondently pursuing her own line of thought; 'it only promotes intimacies with dowagers.'

'Yes, and it makes men elderly, and contented, and stay-at-home,' agreed Philippa; 'it's one of the worst signs! But I can easily make Sybil Hervey think she's a gardener. She's a thoroughly nice, coercible girl. Alice has always been so particular about her girls. Of course with their money they've been run after a good deal, but they're not in the least spoilt.'

'I don't think,' I murmured privately to Maria, who was trying to hypnotize me into letting her crawl on to the sofa beside me, 'that we'll borrow half a crown to get drunk with her.'

Maria wagged her tail in servile acquiescence.

'Nonsense!' said my wife largely.

A month from the date of this conversation, Sybil Hervey, my wife's pretty, young, and well-dowered niece, was staying beneath our roof. I had not changed my mind about the half-crown, though Maria, perfidious as ever, feigned for her the impassioned affection that had so often imposed upon the guileless guest within my gates.

'Why, this dog has taken the most extraordinary fancy to me!' Sybil Hervey (who was really a very amiable girl) would say, and Maria, with a furtive eye upon her owners, would softly draw the guest's third piece of cake into the brown velvet bag that she called her mouth.

This was all very well from Maria's point of view, but a friendship with Maria had not been the object of Miss Hervey's importation. I evade, by main strength, the quotation from Burns proper to this state of affairs, and proceed to say that the matrimonial scheme laid by my wife and Miss Shute was not prospering. Sybil Hervey, the coercible, the thoroughly nice, shied persistently at the instructive pages of Robinson's *English Flower Garden*, and stuck in her toes and refused point-blank to weed seedlings for her Aunt Philippa. Nor was a comprehensive garden party at Clountiss attended with any success; far otherwise. Miss Shute unfortunately thought it incumbent on her to trawl in deep waters, and to invite even the McRory family to her entertainment, with the result that her brother Bernard—I quote my wife verbatim—made a ridiculous spectacle of himself by walking about all the afternoon with a fluffy-haired, certainly rather pretty little abomination, a creature who was staying with the McRorys. Worse even than this, Sybil had disappointed, if not disgraced, her backers, by vanishing from the ken of un-gentle men with Mr. De Lacy McRory, known to his friends as 'Curly.'

I have before now dealt, superficially, and quite inadequately, with the McRorys. It may even be permitted to me to recall again the generic description of each young male McRory. 'A bit of a lad, but nothing at all to the next youngest.' Since that time the family had worn its way, unequally and in patches, into the tolerance of the neighbourhood. It was said, apologetically, that the daughters danced, and played tennis and golf as well, and the sons did the same and were such excellent shots, and that Mrs. McRory bought, uncomplainingly, all that was offered to her at bazaars, and could always be counted on for a whole row of seats at local concerts. As for old McRory, people said that he was certainly rather awful, but that he was better than his family in that he knew that he was awful, and kept out of the way. As a matter of history, there were not many functions where a McRory of some kind, in accordance with its special accomplishment, did not find, at all events, standing room; fewer still where they did not form a valued topic of conversation.

Curly McRory was, perhaps, the pioneer of his family in their advance to cross what has been usefully called 'the bounder-y line.' He played all games well, and he was indisputably good-looking, he knew how to be discreetly silent; he also, apparently, knew how to talk to Sybil what time her accredited chaperon, oblivious of her position, played two engrossing sets of tennis.

After this fiasco came a period of stagnation, during which Mr. De Lacy McRory honoured us with his first visit to Shree-lane, bicycling over to see me, on business connected with the golf club; in my regretted absence he asked for Mrs. Yeates, and stayed for tea. Following upon this Sybil took to saying: 'I will,' in what she believed to be a brogue, instead of 'yes,' and was detected in fruitless search for the McRorys of Temple Braney in the pages of Burke's *Irish Landed Gentry*.

It was at this unsatisfactory juncture that Mrs. Flurry Knox entered into the affair with an invitation to us to spend three days at Aussolas Castle, one of which was to be devoted to the destruction of a pack of grouse, fabled by John Kane, the keeper,

to frequent a mountain back of Aussolas: the Shutes were also
to be of the party. I seemed to detect in the arrangement a
hand more diplomatic than that of Providence, but I said
nothing.

The Flurry Knoxes were, for the moment, in residence at
Aussolas, while old Mrs. Knox made her annual pilgrimage to
Buxton. They were sent there to keep the servants from
fighting, and because John Kane had said that there was no
such enemies to pigs as servants on board wages. (A dark
saying, bearing indirectly on the plenishing of pig-buckets.)

Between servants and pigs, as indeed in most affairs of life,
little Mrs. Flurry held the scales of justice with a remarkably
steady hand, and under her régime one could at all events be
reasonably sure of having one's boots cleaned, and of getting
a hot bath in the morning. We went to Aussolas, and Flurry
and Bernard Shute and I put in a blazing September day on
the mountain, wading knee deep in matted heather and furze,
in pursuit of the mythical grouse, and brought home two hares
and a headache (the latter being my contribution to the bag).
The ladies met us with tea; Sybil, in Harris tweed and admirable
boots, looked, I must admit, uncommonly smart. Even Flurry
was impressed, and it was palpable to the most superficial
observer that Bernard was at length beginning, like a baby, to
'take notice.' After tea he and she moved away in sweet
accord to wash teacups in a bog-hole, from whence their prattle
came prosperously to the ears of the three diplomatists, seated,
like the witches in *Macbeth*, upon the heath, and, like them,
arranging futures for other people. Bearing in mind that one
of the witches had (in a previous incarnation as Miss Sally
Knox) held Bernard in her thrall, and still retained him in a
Platonic sphere of influence, any person of experience would
have said that the odds were greatly against Mr. Shute.

The hot bath that was the *fine fleur* of Mrs. Flurry's régime
at Aussolas failed conspicuously next morning. It was the
precursor of a general slump. When, at a liberal 9.30, I arrived
in the dining-room, of neither host, hostess, nor breakfast was
there any sign. The host, it appeared, had gone to a fair;
having waited for a hungry half-hour we were coming to the
conclusion that the hostess had gone with him, when the door
opened and Mrs. Flurry came swiftly into the room. Her face
was as a book, where men might read strange matters; it was

also of a hue that suggested the ardent climate of the kitchen;
in her hand she carried a toast-rack, and following hard on her
heels came three maids, also heavily flushed, bearing various
foods, and all, apparently, on the verge of tears. This cortège
having retired, Mrs. Flurry proceeded to explain. The butler,
Johnny, a dingy young man, once Mrs. Knox's bath-chair
attendant, had departed at 8 a.m., accompanied by Michael
the pantry boy, to dig a grave for a cousin. To those acquainted
with Aussolas-there was nothing remarkable in this, but Sybil
Hervey's china-blue eyes opened wide, and I heard her ask
Bernard in a low voice if he thought it was anything agrarian.
The annoyance of the cook at the defection of the butler and
pantry boy was so acute that she had retired to her room and
refused to send in breakfast.

'That was no more than I should have expected from the
servants here,' said Mrs. Flurry vindictively, 'but what was
just a little too much was finding the yard-boy cramming the
toast into the toast-rack with his fingers.'

At this my wife's niece uttered the loud yell which all young
women with any pretension to smartness have by them for use
on emergencies, and exclaimed:

'Oh, *don't!*'

'You needn't be frightened,' said Mrs. Flurry, giving Miss
Hervey the eighth part of a glance of her greeny-grey eyes; 'I
made this stuff myself, and you may all think yourselves lucky
to get anything,' she went on, 'as one of the herd of incapables
downstairs said, "to get as much milk as 'd do the tea itself,
that was the stratagem"!'

Hard on the heels of the quotation there came a rushing
sound in the hall without, a furious grappling with the door
handle, and the cook herself, or rather the Tragic Muse in
person, burst into the room. Her tawny hair hung loose about
her head; her yellow-brown eyes blazed in an ashen and extremely handsome face; she shook a pair of freckled fists at the
universe. I cannot pretend to do more than indicate the drift
of her denunciation. Brunhilde, ascending the funeral pyre,
with full orchestral accompaniment, could not more fully and
deafeningly have held her audience, and the theme might have
been taken out of the darkest corner of any of the Sagas.

The burying-ground of her clan was—so she had been informed by a swift runner—even now being broken into by the

butler and the pantry boy, and the graves of her ancestors were
being thrown open to the Four Winds of the World, to make
room for the Scuff of the Country (whatever that might mean).
Here followed the most capable and comprehensive cursings
of the butler and the pantry boy that it has ever been my lot to
admire, delivered at lightning speed, and with gestures worthy
of the highest traditions of classic drama, the whole ending
with the statement that she was on her way to the graveyard
now to drink their blood.

'I trust you will, Kate,' cordially responded Mrs. Flurry;
'don't wait a moment!'

The Tragic Muse, startled into an instant of silence, stared
wildly at Mrs. Flurry, seemed to scént afar off the possibility
that she was not being taken seriously, and whirled from the
room, a Vampire on the war-path.

'I meant every word I said to her!' said Sally, looking round
upon us defiantly, 'I was very near offering her your motor,
Mr. Shute! The sooner she kills Johnny and Michael the
better pleased I shall be! And I may tell you all,' she added,
'that we shall have no luncheon to-day, and most probably no
dinner!'

'Oh, that's all right!' said Philippa, seeing her chance, and
hammering in her wedge with all speed; 'now there's nothing
for it but sandwiches and a picnic!'

The lake at Aussolas was one of a winding chain of three,
connected by narrow channels cut through the bog for the
passage of boats that carried turf to the lakeside dwellers. The
end one of these, known as Braney's Lake, was a recognized
place for picnics; a ruined oratory on a wooded point supplying
the pretext, and a reliable spring well completing the equipment.
The weather was of the variety specially associated in my mind
with Philippa's picnics, brilliantly fine, with a falling glass, and
twelve o'clock saw us shoving out from the Aussolas turf quay,
through the reeds and the rocks.

We were a party of six in two boats; diplomacy, whose I
know not, had so disposed matters that Bernard Shute and
Sybil Hervey were dispatched together in a dapper punt, and I,
realizing to the full the insignificance of my position as a married
man, found myself tugging at a tough and ponderous oar, in a
species of barge, known to history as 'The-Yellow-Boat-that-
was-painted-black.' My wife and Mrs. Flurry took turns in

assisting my labours by paddling with a scull in the bow, while Miss Shute languidly pulled the wrong string at intervals, in the stern. Why, I grumbled contentiously, should, as it were, fish be made of Bernard and flesh be made of me (which was a highly figurative way of describing a performance that would take a stone off my weight ere all was done)? Why, I repeated, should not Bernard put his broad back into it in the heavy boat with me, and leave the punt for the ladies? My wife tore herself from *sotto voce* gabblings with Sally in the bow to tell me that I was thoroughly unsympathetic, what time she dealt me an unintentional but none the less disabling blow in the spine, in her effort to fall again into stroke. Mrs. Flurry, in order to take turns at the oar with Philippa, had seated herself on the luncheon basket in the bow, thereby sinking the old tub by the head, and, as we afterwards found, causing her to leak in the sun-dried upper seams. To us travelled the voice of Bernard, lightly propelling his skiff over the ruffled and sparkling blue water.

'He's telling her about all the alterations he's going to make at Clountiss!' hissed Sally down the back of Philippa's neck.

'Almost actionable!' responded my wife, and in her enthusiasm her oar again took me heavily between the shoulder blades.

We laboured out of the Aussolas lake, and poled down the narrow channel into the middle lake, where shallows, and a heavy summer's growth of reeds, did not facilitate our advance. The day began to cloud over; as we wobbled out of the second channel into Braney's Lake the sun went in, a sharp shower began to whip the water, and simultaneously Miss Shute announced that her feet were wet, and that she thought the boat must be leaking. I then perceived that the water was up to the bottom boards, and was coming in faster than I could have wished. A baler was required, and I proceeded with confidence to search for the rusty mustard tin, or cracked jam-crock, that fills that office. There was nothing to be found.

'There are plenty of cups in the luncheon basket,' said Sally, tranquilly; 'Flurry once had to bale this old boat out with one of his grandmother's galoshes.'

Philippa and I began to row with some vigour, while Sally wrestled with the fastening of the luncheon basket in the bow.

The lid opened with a jerk and a crack. There was one long and speechless moment, and then Sally said in a very gentle voice:

'They 've sent the washing basket, with all the clean clothes!'

Of the general bearings of this catastrophe there was no time to think; its most pressing feature was the fact that there were no cups with which to bale the boat. I looked over my shoulder and saw Bernard dragging the punt ashore under the ruined oratory, a quarter of a mile away; there was nothing for it but to turn and make for the shore on our right at the best pace attainable. Sally and Philippa double-banked the bow oar, and the old boat, leaking harder at each moment, wallowed on towards a landing stage that suddenly became visible amid the reeds—the bottom boards were by this time awash, and Miss Shute's complexion and that of her holland dress matched to a shade.

'Could you throw the washing overboard?' I suggested over my shoulder, labouring the while at my massy oar.

'My—new—night-gowns!' panted Mrs. Flurry; 'never!'

Just then big rocks began to show yellow in the depths, the next moment the boat scraped over one, and, almost immediately afterwards, settled down quietly and with dignity in some three feet of brown water and mud.

Only those who have tried to get out of a submerged boat can form any idea of what then befell. Our feet and legs turned to lead, the water to glue, all that was floatable in the boat rose to the surface, and lay about there impeding our every movement. We had foundered in sight of port and were not half a dozen yards from the landing stage, but to drag myself and three women, all up to our waists in water, and the ladies hopelessly handicapped by their petticoats, over the gunwale of a sunken boat, and to flounder ashore with them in mud, over unsteady rocks, and through the ever-hampering reeds, was infinitely more difficult and exhausting than it may seem.

Clasping a slimy post to my bosom with one arm, I was in the act of shoving Miss Shute up on to the landing stage, when I heard the unmistakable Dublin light tenor voice of a McRory hail me, announcing that he was coming to our rescue. More distant shouts, and the rapid creaking of hard-pulled oars told that Bernard and Sybil were also speeding to our aid. The three diplomats, dripping on the end of the pier, looked at each other bodefully, and Philippa murmured:

'The worst has happened!'

After that the worst continued to happen, and at a pace that overbore all resistance. Mr. De Lacy McRory, tall and beautiful, in lily-white flannels, took the lead into his own hands and played his game faultlessly. Philippa was the object of his chief solicitude, Sally and Miss Shute had their share of a manly tenderness that resolutely ignored the degrading absurdity of their appearance; his father's house, and all that was therein, was laid at our feet. Captive and helpless, we slopped and squelched beside him through the shrubberies of Temple Braney House, with the shower, now matured into a heavy downpour, completing our saturation, too spiritless to resent the heavy pleasantries of Bernard, the giggling condolences of Sybil.

We have never been able to decide at which moment the knife of humiliation cut deepest, whether it was when we stood and dripped on the steps, while Curly McRory summoned in trumpet tones his women-kind, or when, still dripping, we stood in the hall and were presented to Mrs. McRory and a troop of young men and maidens, vociferous in sympathy and hospitality; or when, having progressed like water carts through the house, we found ourselves installed, like the Plague of Frogs, in the bedchambers of the McRorys, face to face with the supreme embarrassment of either going to bed, or of arraying ourselves in the all too gorgeous garments that were flung before us with a generous *abandon* worthy of Sir Walter Raleigh.

I chose the latter course, and, in process of time, found myself immaculately clothed in what is, I believe, known to tailors as 'a Lounge Suit,' though not for untold gold would I have lounged, or by any carelessness endangered the perfection of the creases of its dark grey trousers.

The luncheon gong sounded, and, like the leading gentleman in any drawing-room drama, I put forth from my dressing-room, and at the head of the stairs met my wife and Miss Shute. They were, if possible, grander than I, and looked as if they were going to a wedding.

'We had the choice of about eighty silk blouses,' breathed Philippa, gathering up a long and silken train, 'Sally has to wear Madame's clothes, nothing else were short enough. We're in for it, you know,' she added, 'a luncheon is inevitable, and goodness knows when we can get away, especially if this rain lasts——' her voice broke hysterically; I turned and saw Mrs.

Flurry shuffling towards us in velvet slippers, holding up with both hands a flowing purple brocade skirt. I pointed repressively downwards, to where, in the window seat of the hall below, were visible the crispèd golden curls of Mr. De Lacy McRory, and the shining rolls and undulations of Miss Sybil Hervey's *chevelure*. Their heads were in close proximity, and their voices were low and confidential.

'This must be put a stop to!' said Philippa, rustling swiftly downstairs.

We all moved processionally in to lunch, arm in arm with the McRorys. To Philippa had fallen old McRory, who was the best of the party (in being so awful that he knew he was awful). He maintained an unbroken silence throughout the meal, but whistled jigs secretly through his teeth, a method of keeping up his courage of which I believe he was quite unconscious. Of the brilliance of the part that I played with Mrs. McRory it would ill become me to speak; what is more worthy of record is the rapid and Upas-like growth of intimacy between Curly McRory and my wife's niece. She had probably never before encountered a young man so anxious to be agreeable, so skilled in achieving that end. The fact that he was Irish accounted, no doubt, in her eyes, for all that was unusual in his voice and manners, and his long eyelashes did the rest. Sybil grew momently pinker and prettier as the long, extraordinary meal marched on.

Of its component parts I can only remember that there was a soup tureen full of custard, a mountainous dish of trifle, in whose veins ran honey, instead of jam, and to whose enlivenment a bottle at least of whisky had been dedicated; certainly, at one period, Philippa had on one side of her plate a cup of soup, and on the other a cup of tea. Cecilia Shute was perhaps the member of our party who took it all hardest. Pale and implacable, attired in a brilliant blue garment that was an outrage alike to her convictions and her complexion, she sat between two young McRorys, who understood no more of her language than she did of theirs, and was obliged to view, with the frigid tranquillity boasted of by Doctor Johnson, the spectacle of her brother devoting himself enthusiastically to that McRory cousin whom Philippa had described as a fluffy-haired abomination. Everything, in fact, was occurring that was least desired by the ladies of my party, with the single exception of my niece by marriage; and the glowing satisfaction of the McRory family was not hid from us, and did not ameliorate the position.

When luncheon was at length brought to a close, nothing could well have been blacker than the outlook. The rain, and the splendour of our borrowed plumes, put a return by boat out of the question. It was a good seven miles round by road, and the McRory family, fleet and tireless bicyclists, had but one horse, which was lame. A telegram to Aussolas had been dispatched an hour ago, but as Mrs. Flurry was gloomily certain that every servant there had gone to the funeral, the time of our release was unknown.

I do not now distinctly remember what occurred immediately after lunch, but I know there came a period when I found myself alone in the hall, turning over the pages of a dreary comic paper, uncertain what to do, but determined on one point, that neither principalities nor powers should force me into the drawing-room, where sat the three unhappy women of my party, being entertained within an inch of their lives by Mrs. McRory. Sybil and Bernard and their boon companions had betaken themselves to that distant and dilapidated wing of the house in which I had once unearthed Tomsy Flood, there to play squash racquets in one of the empty rooms. I was consequently enacting the part laid down for me by my lounge suit; I was lounging, as a gentleman should, without for an instant disturbing the creases of my trousers.

At times I was aware of the silent and respectful surveillance of Mr. McRory in the inner hall, but I thought it best for us both to feign unconsciousness of his presence. Through a swing door that, true to its definition, swung wheezily to the cabbage-laden draughts from the lower regions, I could hear the tide of battle rolling through the disused wing. The squash racquets seemed to be of a most pervading character; the thunder of rushing feet, blent with the long, progressive shriek of an express train, would at intervals approach almost to the swing door, but I remained unmolested. I had entered upon my second cigarette, and a period of comparative peace, when I heard a stealing foot, and found at my elbow a female McRory of about twelve as years go, but dowered with the accumulated experience of six elder sisters.

'Did Pinkie and Mr. Shute come in this way to hide?' she began, looking at me as if 'Pinkie,' whoever she might be, was in my pocket. 'We 're playing hide-'n-go-seek, and we can't find them.'

I said I knew nothing of them.

The McRory child looked at me with supernal intelligence from under the wing of dark hair that was tied over one ear.

'They 're not playing fair anyhow, and there 's Curly and Miss Hervey that wouldn't play at all!' She eyed me again. 'He took her out to show her the ferrets and they never came back. I was watching them; she said one of the ferrets bit her finger, and Curly kissed it!'

'I suppose you mean he kissed the ferret,' I said repressively, while I thought of Alice Hervey, mother of Sybil, and trembled.

'Ah, go on! what a fool you 're letting on to be!' replied the McRory child, with elegant sarcasm. She swung round on her heel and sped away again upon the trail, cannoning against old McRory in the back hall.

'I tell you, that 's the lady!' soliloquized old McRory, from the deep of the back hall. I gathered that he was referring to the social capacity of his youngest daughter and thought he was probably right.

It was at this moment that deliverance broke like a sunburst upon us; I saw through the windows of the hall a dogcart and an outside car whirl past the door and onwards to the yard. The former was driven by Flurry Knox, the car by Michael the Aussolas pantry boy, apparently none the worse for his en-counter with the vampire cook. I snatched an umbrella, and, regardless of the lounge suit, followed with all speed the golden path of the sunburst.

Flurry, clad in glistening yellow oilskins, met me in the yard, wearing an expression of ill-concealed exultation worthy of Job's comforters at their brightest.

'D' ye know who opened your wire?' he began, regarding me with an all-observant eye from under his sou'wester, while the raindrops ran down his nose. 'I can tell you there 's the Old Gentleman to pay at Aussolas — or the old lady, and that 's worse! That 's a nice suit—you ought to buy that from Curly.'

'Who opened my telegram?' I said. I was not at all amused.

'"When she got there, the cupboard was bare,"' returned Flurry. '"Not a servant in the house, not a bit in the larder! If it wasn't that by the mercy of Providence I found the picnic

basket that you bright boys had left after you, she 'd have torn
the house down!'

'I suppose you mean that your grandmother has come back,'
I said stonily.

'She fought with her unfortunate devil of a doctor at Buxton,'
said Flurry, permitting himself a grin of remembrance; 'he
told her she was too old to eat late dinner, and she told him she
wasn't going to be a slave to her stomach or to him either, and
she 'd eat her dinner when she pleased, and she landed in at
Aussolas by the midday train without a word.'

'What did she say when she opened my telegram?' I faltered.

'She said, "Thank God I 'm not a fool!"' replied her grandson.

The proposition was unanswerable, and I took it, so to speak,
lying down.

'Here!' said Flurry, summoning the pantry boy. 'These
horses must go in out of the rain. I 'll look over there for some
place I can put them.'

'I see Michael got back from the funeral,' I said, following
Flurry across the wide and wet expanse of the yard. 'I suppose
the cook killed Johnny?'

'Ah, not at all,' said Flurry; 'anyway, my grandmother had
the two of them up unpacking her trunks when I left. Here,
this place looks like a stable——'

He opened a door, in front of which a cascade from a broken
water-shoot was splashing noisily. The potent smell of ferrets
greeted us.

Seated on the ferrets' box were Mr. De Lacy McRory and
Sybil, daughter of Alice Hervey. Apparently she had again
been bitten by the ferret, but this time the bite was not on her
finger.

XI

OWENEEN THE SPRAT

I WAS labouring in the slough of Christmas letters and bills, when my wife came in and asked me if I would take her to the Workhouse.

'My dear,' I replied, ponderously, but, I think, excusably, 'you have, as usual, anticipated my intention, but I think we can hold out until after Christmas.'

Philippa declined to pay the jest the respect to which its age entitled it, and replied inconsequently that I knew perfectly well that she could not drive the outside car with the children and the Christmas tree. I assented that they would make an awkward team, and offered, as a substitute for my services, those of Denis, the stopgap.

Those who live in Ireland best know the staying powers of stopgaps. Denis, uncle of Michael Leary the Whip, had been imported into the kennels during my ministry, to bridge a hiatus in the long dynasty of the kennel-boys, and had remained for eighteen months, a notable instance of the survival of what might primarily have been considered the unfittest. That Denis should so long have endured his nephew's rule was due not so much to the tie of blood, as to the privileged irresponsibility of a stopgap. Nothing was expected of him, and he pursued an unmolested course, until the return of Flurry Knox from South Africa changed the general conditions. He then remained submerged until he drifted into the gap formed in my own establishment by Mr. Peter Cadogan's elopement.

Philippa's Workhouse Tea took place on Christmas Eve. We were still hurrying through an early luncheon when the nodding crest of the Christmas tree passed the dining-room windows. My youngest son immediately upset his pudding into his lap; and Philippa hustled forth to put on her hat, an operation which, like the making of an omelette, can apparently only be successfully performed at the last moment. With feelings of mingled apprehension and relief I saw the party drive from the door, the Christmas tree seated on one side of the car, Philippa on the other, clutching her offspring, Denis on the box, embosomed, like a wood-pigeon, in the boughs of the spruce fir. I congratulated myself that the Quaker, now white with the snows of many winters, was in the shafts. Had I not been too deeply engaged in so arranging the rug that it should not trail in the mud all the way to Skebawn, I might have noticed that the lamps had been forgotten.

It was, as I have said, Christmas Eve, and as the afternoon wore on I began to reflect upon what the road from Skebawn would be in another hour, full of drunken people, and, what was worse, of carts steered by drunken people. I had assured Philippa (with what I believe she describes as masculine *esprit de corps*) of Denis's adequacy as a driver, but that did not alter the fact that in the last rays of the setting sun I got out my bicycle and set forth for the Workhouse. When I reached the town it was dark, but the Christmas shoppers showed no tendency to curtail their operations on that account, and the streets were filled with an intricate and variously moving tide of people and carts. The paraffin lamps in the shops did their best, behind bunches of holly, oranges, and monstrous Christmas candles, and partially illumined the press of dark-cloaked women and more or less drunken men, who swayed and shoved and held vast conversations on the narrow pavements. The red glare of the chemist's globe transformed the leading female beggar of the town into a being from the Brocken; her usual Christmas family, contributed for the festival by the neighbours, as to a Christmas number, were grouped in fortunate ghastliness in the green light. She extracted from me her recognized tribute, and pursued by her assurance that she would forgive me now till Easter (i.e. that further alms would not be exacted for at least a fortnight), I made my way onward into the outer darkness, beyond the uttermost link in the chain of public-houses.

The road that led to the Workhouse led also to the railway station; a quarter of a mile away the green light of a signal post stood high in the darkness, like an emerald. As I neared the Workhouse I recognized the deliberate footfall of the Quaker, and presently his long pale face entered the circle illuminated by my bicycle lamp. My family were not at all moved by my solicitude for their safety, but, being in want of an audience, were pleased to suggest that I should drive home with them. The road was disgustingly muddy; I tied my bicycle to the back of the car with the rope that is found in wells of all outside cars. It was not till I had put out the bicycle lamp that I noticed that the car lamps had been forgotten, but Denis, true to the convention of his tribe, asseverated that he could see better without lights. I took the place vacated by the Christmas tree, the Quaker pounded on at his usual stone-breaking trot, and my offspring, in strenuous and entangled duet, declaimed to me the events of the afternoon.

It was without voice or warning that a row of men was materialized out of the darkness, under the Quaker's nose; they fell away to right and left, but one, as if stupefied, held on his way in the middle of the road. It is not easy to divert the Quaker from his course; we swung to the right, but the wing of the car, on my side, struck the man full in the chest. He fell as instantly and solidly as if he were a stone pillar, and, like a stone, he lay in the mud. Loud and inebriate howls rose from the others, and, as if in answer, came a long and distant shriek from an incoming train. Upon this, without bestowing an instant's further heed to their fallen comrade, the party took to their heels and ran to the station. It was all done in a dozen seconds; by the time the Quaker was pulled up we were alone with our victim, and Denis was hoarsely suggesting to me that it would be better to drive away at once. I have often since then regretted that I did not take his advice.

The victim was a very small man; Denis and I dragged him to the side of the road, and propped him up against the wall. He was of an alarming limpness, but there was a something reassuring in the reek of whisky that arose as I leaned over him, trying to diagnose his injuries by the aid of a succession of lighted matches. His head lay crookedly on his chest; he breathed heavily, but peacefully, and his limbs seemed uninjured. Denis, at my elbow, did not cease to assure me, tremulously, that there was nothing ailed the man, that he was a stranger, and that it would be as good for us to go home. Philippa, on the car, strove as best she might with the unappeasable curiosity of her sons and with the pig-headed anxiety of the Quaker to get home to his dinner. At this juncture a voice, fifty yards away in the darkness, uplifted itself in song:

> 'Heaven's refle-hex! Killa-ar-ney!'

it bawled hideously.

It fell as balm upon my ear, in its assurance of the proximity of Slipper.

'Sure I know the man well,' he said, shielding the flame of a match in his hand with practised skill. 'Wake up, me *bouchaleen*!' He shook him unmercifully. 'Open your eyes, darlin'!'

The invalid here showed signs of animation by uttering an incoherent but, as it seemed, a threatening roar. It lifted Denis as a feather is lifted by a wind, and wafted him to the Quaker's head, where he remained in strict attention to his duties. It also lifted Philippa.

'Is he very bad, do you think?' she murmured at my elbow. 'Shall I drive for the doctor?'

'Arrah, what docthor?' said Slipper magnificently. 'Give me a half a crown, Major, and I'll get him what meddyceen will answer him as good as any docthor! Lave him to me!' He shook him again. 'I'll regulate him!'

The victim here sat up, and shouted something about going home. He was undoubtedly very drunk. It seemed to me that Slipper's ministrations would be more suitable to the situation than mine, certainly than Philippa's. I administered the solatium; then I placed Denis on the box of the car with the bicycle lamp in his hand, and drove my family home.

After church next day we met Flurry Knox. He approached us with the green glint in his eye that told that game was on foot, whatever that game might be.

'Who bailed you out, Mrs. Yeates?' he said solicitously. 'I heard you and the Major and Denis Leary were all in the lock-up for furious driving and killing a man! I'm told he was anointed last night.'

Philippa directed what she believed to be a searching glance at Flurry's face of friendly concern.

'I don't believe a word of it!' she said dauntlessly, while a very becoming warmth in her complexion betrayed an inward qualm. 'Who told you?'

'The servants heard it at first Mass this morning; and Slipper had me late for church telling me about it. The fellow says if he lives he's going to take an action against the Major.'

I listened with, I hope, outward serenity. In dealings with Flurry Knox the possibility that he might be speaking the truth could never safely be lost sight of. It was also well to remember that he generally knew what the truth was.

I said loftily that there had been nothing the matter with the man but Christmas Eve, and inquired if Flurry knew his name and address.

'Of course I do,' said Flurry, 'he's one of those mountainy men that live up in the hill behind Aussolas. Oweneen the Sprat is the name he goes by, and he's the crossest little thief in the Barony. Never mind, Mrs. Yeates, I'll see you get fair play in the dock!'

'How silly you are!' said Philippa; but I could see that she was shaken.

Whatever Flurry's servants may have heard at first mass, was apparently equalled, if not excelled, by what Denis heard at second. He asked me next morning, with a gallant attempt at indifference, if I had had any word of 'the man-een.'

' 'Twas what the people were saying on the roads last night that he could have the law of us, and there was more was saying that he'd never do a day's good. Sure they say the backbone is cracked where the wheel of the car went over him! But didn't yourself and the misthress swear black and blue that the wheel never went next or nigh him? And didn't Michael say that there wasn't a Christmas this ten years that that one hadn't a head on him the size of a bullawawn with the len'th o' dhrink?'

In spite of the contributory negligence that might be assumed in the case of any one with this singular infirmity, I was not without a secret uneasiness. Two days afterwards I received a letter, written on copybook paper in a clerkly hand. It had the Aussolas post-mark, in addition to the imprint of various thumbs, and set forth the injuries inflicted by me and my driver on Owen Twohig on Christmas Eve, and finally, it demanded a compensation of twenty pounds for the same. Failing this satisfaction the law was threatened, but a hope was finally expressed that the honourable gentleman would not see a poor man wronged; it was, in fact, the familiar mixture of bluff and whine, and, as I said to Philippa, the Man-een (under which title he had passed into the domestic vocabulary) had of course got hold of a letter-writer to do the trick for him.

In the next day or so I met Flurry twice, and found him so rationally interested, and even concerned, about fresh versions of the accident that had cropped up, that I was moved to tell him of the incident of the letter. He looked serious, and said he would go up himself to see what was wrong with Oweneen.

He advised me to keep out of it for the present, as they might open their mouths too big.

The moon was high as I returned from this interview; when I wheeled my bicycle into the yard I found that the coach-house in which I was wont to stable it was locked; so also was the harness-room. Attempting to enter the house by the kitchen door I found it also was locked; a gabble of conversation prevailed within, and with the mounting indignation of one who hears but cannot make himself heard, I banged ferociously on the door. Silence fell, and Mrs. Cadogan's voice implored Heaven's protection.

'Open the door!' I roared.

A windlike rush of petticoats followed, through which came sibilantly the words: 'Glory be to goodness! 'Tis the masther!'

The door opened, I found myself facing the entire strength of my establishment, including Denis, and augmented by Slipper.

'They told me you were asking afther me, Major,' began Slipper descending respectfully from the kitchen table, on which he had been seated.

I noticed that Mrs. Cadogan was ostentatiously holding her heart, and that Denis was shaking like the conventional aspen.

'What's all this about?' said I, looking round upon them. 'Why is the whole place locked up?'

'It was a little unaisy they were,' said Slipper, snatching the explanation from Mrs. Cadogan with the determination of the skilled leader of conversation; 'I was telling them I seen two men below in the plantation, like they'd be watching out for someone, and poor Mr. Leary here got a reeling in his head after I telling it——'

'Indeed the crayture was as white, now, as white as a masheroon!' broke in Mrs. Cadogan, 'and we dhrew him in here to the fire till your honour came home.'

'Nonsense!' I said angrily; 'a couple of boys poaching rabbits! Upon my word, Slipper, you have very little to do coming here and frightening people for nothing.'

'What did I say?' demanded Slipper, dramatically facing his audience; 'only that I seen two men in the plantation. How would I know what business they had in it?'

'Ye said ye heard them whishling to each other like curlews through the wood,' faltered Denis, 'and sure that's the whishle them Twohigs has always——'

'Maybe it's whistling to the girls they were!' suggested Slipper, with an unabashed eye at Hannah.

I told him to come up with me to my office, and stalked from the kitchen, full of the comfortless wrath that has failed to find a suitable victim.

The interview in the office did not last long, nor was it in any way reassuring. Slipper, with the manner of the confederate who had waded shoulder to shoulder with me through gore, could only tell me that though he believed that there was nothing ailed the Man-een, he wouldn't say but what he might be severely hurted. That I wasn't gone five minutes before near a score of the Twohigs come leathering down out of the town in two ass-butts (this term indicates donkey-carts of the usual dimensions), and when Oweneen felt them coming, he let the most unmarciful screech, upon which Slipper, in just fear of the Twohigs, got over the wall, and executed a strategic retreat upon the railway station, leaving the Twohigs to carry away their wounded to the mountains. That for himself he had been going in dread of them ever since, and for no one else in the wide world would he have put a hand to one of them.

I preserved an unshaken front towards Slipper, and I was subsequently sarcastic and epigrammatic to Philippa on the subject of the curlews who were rabbiting in the plantation, but something that I justified to myself as a fear of Philippa's insatiable conscientiousness made me resolve that I would, without delay, go 'back in the mountain,' and interview Oweneen the Sprat.

New Year's Day favoured my purpose, bringing with it clear frost and iron roads, a day when even the misanthropic soul of a bicycle awakens into sympathy and geniality. I started in the sunny vigour of the early afternoon, I sailed up the hills with the effortless speed of a seagull, I free-wheeled down them with the dive of a swallow, and, as it seemed to me, with a good deal of its grace. Had Oweneen the Sprat had the luck to have met me, when, at the seventh milestone from Shreelane, I realized that I had beaten my own best time by seven minutes, he could practically have made his own terms. At that point, however, I had to leave the high road, and the mountain lane that ensued restored to me the judicial frame of mind. In the first twenty yards my bicycle was transformed from a swallow to an opinionated and semi-paralysed wheelbarrow; struggling in a species of dry watercourse I shoved it up the steep gradients of a large and brown country of heather and bog, silent save for contending voices of the streams. A family of goats, regarding me from a rocky mound, was the first hint of civilization; a more reliable symptom presently advanced in the shape of a lean and hump-backed sow, who bestowed on me a side glance of tepid interest as she squeezed past.

The *bohireen* dropped, with a sudden twist to the right, and revealed a fold in the hillside, containing a half-dozen or so of little fields, crooked, and heavily walled, and nearly as many thatched cabins, flung about in the hollows as indiscriminately as the boulders upon the wastes outside. A group of children rose in front of me like a flight of starlings, and scudded with barefooted nimbleness to the shelter of the houses, in a pattering, fluttering stampede. I descended upon the nearest cabin of the colony. The door was shut; a heavy padlock linking two staples said Not at Home, and the nose of a dog showed in a hole above the sill, sniffing deeply and suspiciously. I remembered that the first of January was a holy-day, and that every man in the colony had doubtless betaken himself to the nearest village. The next cottage was some fifty yards away, and the faces of a couple of children peered at me round the corner of it. As I approached they vanished, but the door of the cabin was open, and blue turf smoke breathed placidly outwards from it. The merciful frost had glazed the inevitable dirty pool in front of the door, and had made practicable the path beside it; I propped my bicycle against a rock, and projected into the dark interior an inquiry as to whether there was any one in.

I had to repeat it twice before a small old woman with white hair and a lemon-coloured face appeared; I asked her if she could tell me where Owen Twohig lived.

'Your honour's welcome,' she replied, tying the strings of her cap under her chin with wiry fingers, and eyeing me with concentrated shrewdness. I repeated the question.

She responded by begging me to come in and rest myself, for this was a cross place and a backwards place, and I should be famished with the cold—'sure them little wheels dhraws the wind.'

I ignored this peculiarity of bicycles, and, not without exasperation, again asked for Owen Twohig.

'Are you Major Yeates, I beg your pardon?' I assented to what she knew as well as I did.

'Why then 'tis here he lives indeed, in this little house, and a poor place he have to live in. Sure he's my son, the crayture' —her voice at once ascended to the key of lamentation— 'faith, he didn't rise till to-day. Since Christmas Eve I didn't quinch light in the house with him stretched in the bed always, and not a bit passed his lips night or day, only one suppeen of whisky in its purity. Ye'd think the tongue would light out of his mouth with the heat, and ye'd see the blaze of darkness in his face! I hadn't as much life in me this morning as that I could wash my face!'

I replied that I wanted to speak to her son, and was in a hurry.

'He's not within, asthore, he's not within at all. He got the lend of a little donkey, and he went back the mountain to the bone-setter, to try could he straighten the leg with him.'

'Did Dr. Hickey see him?' I demanded.

'Sure a wise woman came in from Finnaun, a' Stephen's Day,' pursued Mrs. Twohig swiftly, 'and she bet three spits down on him, and she said it's what ailed him he had the Fallen Palate, with the dint o' the blow the car bet him in the poll, and that any one that have the Fallen Palate might be speechless for three months with it. She took three ribs of his hair then, and she was pulling them till she was in a passpiration, and in the latther end she pulled up the palate.' She paused and wiped her eyes with her apron. 'But the leg is what has him destroyed altogether; she told us we should keep sheep's butter rubbed to it in the place where the thrack o' the wheel is down in it.'

The blush of a frosty sunset was already in the sky, and the children who had fled before me had returned, reinforced by many others, to cluster in a whispering swarm round my bicycle, and to group themselves attentively in the rear of the conversation.

'Look here, Mrs. Twohig,' I said, not as yet angry, but in useful proximity to it, 'I've had a letter from your son, and he and his friends have been trying to frighten my man, Denis Leary; he can come down and see me if he has anything to say, but you can tell him from me that I'm not going to stand this sort of thing!'

If the Widow Twohig had been voluble before, this pronounce-ment had the effect of bringing her down in spate. She instantly and at the top of her voice called heaven to witness her inno-cence, and the innocence of her 'little boy'; still at full cry, she sketched her blameless career, and the unmerited suffering that had ever pursued her and hers; how, during the past thirty years, she had been drooping over her little orphans, and how Oweneen, that was the only one she had left to do a hand's turn for her, would be 'under clutches' the longest day that he'd live. It was at about this point that I gave her five shillings. It was a thoroughly illogical act, but at the moment it seemed inevitable, and Mrs. Twohig was good enough to accept it in the same spirit. I told her that I would send Dr. Hickey to see her son (which had, it struck me, a somewhat stemming effect upon her eloquence), and I withdrew, still in magisterial displeasure. I must have been half-way down the lane before it was revealed to me that a future on crutches was what Mrs. Twohig anticipated for her son.

By that night's post I wrote to Hickey, a strictly impartial letter, stating the position, and asking him to see Owen Twohig, and to let me have his professional opinion upon him. Philippa added a postscript, asking for a nerve tonic for the parlour-maid, a Dublin girl, who, since the affair of the curlews in the plantation, had lost all colour and appetite, and persisted in locking the hall door day and night, to the infinite annoyance of the dogs.

Next morning, while hurrying through an early breakfast, preparatory to starting for a distant Petty Sessions, I was told that Denis wished to speak to me at the hall door. This, as I before have had occasion to point out, boded affairs of the first importance. I proceeded to the hall door, and there found Denis, pale as the Lily Maid of Astolat, with three small fishes in his hand.

'There was one of thim before me in my bed lasht night!' he said in a hoarse and shaken whisper, 'and there was one in the windy in the harness-room, down on top o' me razor, and there was another nelt to the stable door with the nail of a horse's shoe.'

I made the natural suggestion that someone had done it for a joke.

'Thim's no joke, sir,' replied Denis, portentously, 'thim's Sprats!'

'Well, I'm quite aware of that,' I said, unmoved by what appeared to be the crushing significance of the statement.

'Oweneen the *Sprat !*' murmured Philippa, illuminatingly, emerging from the dining-room door with her cup of tea in her hand; 'it's Hannah, trying to frighten him!'

Hannah, the housemaid, was known to be the humorist of the household.

'He have a brother a smith, back in the mountain,' continued Denis, wrapping up the sprats and the nail in his handkerchief; ''twas for a token he put the nail in it. If he dhraws thim mountainy men down on me, I may as well go under the sod. It isn't yourself or the misthress they'll folly; it's meself'—he crept down the steps as deplorably as the Jackdaw of Rheims —'and it's what Michael's after telling me, they have it all through the country that I said you should throw Twohig in the ditch, and it was good enough for the likes of him, and I said to Michael 'twas a lie for them, and that we cared him as tender as if he was our mother itself, and we'd have given the night to him only for the misthress that was roaring on the car, and no blame to her; sure the world knows the mother o' children has no courage!'

This drastic generality was unfortunately lost to my wife, as she had retired to hold a court of inquiry in the kitchen.

The inquiry elicited nothing beyond the fact that since Christmas Day Denis was 'using no food,' and that the kitchen, so far from indulging in practical jokes at his expense, had been instant throughout in sympathy, and in cups of strong tea, administered for the fortification of the nerves. All were obviously deeply moved by the incident of the sprats, the parlour-maid, indeed, having already locked herself into the pantry, through the door of which, on Philippa's approach, she gave warning hysterically.

The matter remained unexplained, and was not altogether to my liking. As I drove down the avenue, and saw Denis carefully close the yard gates after me, I determined that I would give Murray, the District Inspector of Police, a brief sketch of the state of affairs. I did not meet Murray, but, as it happened, this made no difference. Things were already advancing smoothly and inexorably towards their preordained conclusion.

I have since heard that none of the servants went to bed that night. They, including Denis, sat in the kitchen, with locked doors, drinking tea and reciting religious exercises; Maria, as a further precaution, being chained to the leg of the table. Their fears were in no degree allayed by the fact that nothing whatever occurred, and the most immediate result of the vigil was that my bath next morning boiled as it stood in the can, and dimmed the room with clouds of steam — a circumstance sufficiently rare in itself, and absolutely without precedent on Sunday morning. The next feature of the case was a letter at breakfast time from a gentleman signing himself 'Jas. Fitzmaurice.' He said that Dr. Hickey having gone away for a fortnight's holiday, he (Fitzmaurice) was acting as his locum tenens. In that capacity he had opened my letter, and would go and see Twohig as soon as possible. He enclosed prescription for tonic as requested.

It was a threatening morning, and we did not go to church. I noticed that my wife's housekeeping *séance* was unusually prolonged, and even while I smoked and read the papers, I was travelling in my meditations to the point of determining that I would have a talk with the priest about all this infernal nonsense. When Philippa at length rejoined me, I found that she also had arrived at a conclusion, impelled thereto by the counsels of Mrs. Cadogan, abetted by her own conscience.

Its result was that immediately after lunch, long before the Sunday roast beef had been slept off, I found myself carting precarious parcels—a jug, a bottle, a pudding-dish—to the inside car, in which Philippa had already placed herself, with a pair of blankets and various articles culled from my wardrobe (including a pair of boots to which I was sincerely attached). Denis, pale yellow in complexion and shrouded in gloom, was on the box, the Quaker was in the shafts. There was no rain, but the clouds hung black and low.

It was an expedition of purest charity; so Philippa explained to me over again as we drove away. She said nothing of propitiation or diplomacy. For my part I said nothing at all, but I reflected on the peculiar gifts of the Dublin parlour-maid in valeting me, and decided that it might be better to allow Philippa to run the show on her own lines, while I maintained an attitude of large-minded disapproval.

The blankets took up as much room in the car as a man; I had to hold in my hand a jug of partly jellified beef-tea. A sourer Lady Bountiful never set forth upon an errand of mercy.

To complete establishment — in the words of the *Gazette* —
Maria and Minx, on the floor of the car, wrought and strove in
ceaseless and objectless agitation, an infliction due to the ferocity
of a female rival, who terrorized the high road within hail of my
gates. I thanked Heaven that I had at least been firm about not
taking the children; for the dogs, at all events, the moment of
summary ejectment would arrive sooner or later.

Seven miles in an inside car are seven miles indeed. The hills
that had run to meet my bicycle and glided away behind it now
sat in their places to be crawled up and lumbered down, at such
a pace as seemed good to the Quaker, whose appetite for the
expedition was, if possible, less than that of his driver. Appetite
was, indeed, the last thing suggested by the aspect of Denis.
His drooping shoulders and deplorable countenance proclaimed
apology and deprecation to the mountain-tops, and more
especially to the mountainy men. Looking back on it now, I
recognize the greatness of the tribute to my valour and omnipotence that he should have consented thus to drive us into
the heart of the enemy's country.

A steep slope, ending with a sharp turn through a cutting,
reminded me that we were near the mountain *bohireen* that was
our goal. I got out and walked up the hill, stiffly, because the
cramp of the covered car was in my legs. Stiff though I was,
I had outpaced the Quaker, and was near the top of the hill,
when something that was apparently a brown croquet-ball
rolled swiftly round the bend above me, charged into the rock
wall of the cutting with a clang, and came on down the hill with
a weight and venom unknown to croquet-balls. It sped past
me, missed the Quaker by an uncommonly near shave, and went
on its way, hotly pursued by the two dogs, who, in the next
twenty yards, discovered with horror that it was made of iron,
a fact of which I was already aware.

I have always been as lenient as the law, and other circumstances, would allow towards the illegal game of 'bowling.' It
consists in bowling an iron ball along a road, the object being
to cover the greatest possible distance in a given number of
bowls. It demands considerable strength and skill, and it is
played with a zest much enhanced by its illegality and by its
facilities as a medium for betting. The law forbids it, on
account of its danger to the unsuspecting wayfarer, in consideration of which a scout is usually posted ahead to signal the

approach of the police, and to give warning to passers-by. The mountainy men, trusting to their isolation, had neglected this precaution, with results that came near being serious to the Quaker, and filled with wrath, both personal and official, I took the hill at a vengeful run, so as to catch the bowler red-handed. At the turn in the cutting I met him face to face. As a matter of fact he nearly ran into my arms, and the yelp of agony with which he dodged my impending embrace is a lifelong possession. He was a very small man; he doubled like a rabbit, and bolted back towards a swarm of men who were following the fortunes of the game. He flitted over the wall by the roadside, and was away over the rocky hillside at a speed that even in my best days would have left me nowhere.

The swarm on the road melted; a good part of it was quietly absorbed by the lane up which I had dragged my bicycle two days before, the remainder, elaborately uninterested and respectable, in their dark blue Sunday clothes, strolled gravely in the opposite direction. A man on a bicycle met them, and dismounted to speak to the leaders. I wondered if he were a policeman in plain clothes on the prowl. He came on to meet me, leading his bicycle, and I perceived that a small black leather bag was strapped to the carrier. He was young, and apparently very hot.

'I beg your pardon,' he said in the accents of Dublin, 'I understand you 're Major Yeates. I 'm Dr. Hickey's "Locum," and I 've come out to see the man you wrote to me about. From what you said I thought it better to lose no time.'

I was rather out of breath, but I expressed my sense of indebtedness.

'I think there must be some mistake,' went on the 'Locum.' 'I 've just asked these men on the road where Owen Twohig lives, and one of them—the fellow they call Skipper, or some such name—said Owen Twohig was the little chap that 's just after sprinting up the mountain. He seemed to think it was a great joke. I suppose you 're sure Owen was the name?'

'Perfectly sure,' I said heavily.

The eyes of Dr. Fitzmaurice had travelled past me, and were regarding with professional alertness something farther down the road. I followed their direction, dreamily, because in spirit I was far away, tracking Flurry Knox through deep places.

On the hither side of the rock cutting the covered car had come to a standstill. The reins had fallen from Denis's hands; he was obviously having the 'wakeness' appropriate to the crisis. Philippa, on the step below him, was proffering to him the jug of beef-tea and the bottle of port. He accepted the latter.

'He knows what's what!' said the 'Locum.'

XII

THE WHITEBOYS

PART I

IT has been said by an excellent authority that children and dogs spoil conversation. I can confidently say that had Madame de Sévigné and Dr. Johnson joined me and my family on our wonted Sunday afternoon walk to the kennels, they would have known what it was to be ignored. This reflection bears but remotely on the matter in hand, but is, I think, worthy of record. I pass on to a certain still and steamy afternoon in late September, when my wife and I headed forth in the accustomed way, accompanied by, or (to be accurate), in pursuit of, my two sons, my two dogs, and a couple of hound puppies, to view that spectacle of not unmixed attractiveness, the feeding of the hounds.

Flurry Knox and Michael were superintending the operation when we arrived, coldly observing the gobbling line at the trough, like reporters at a public dinner. It was while the last horrid remnants of the repast were being wolfed that my wife hesitatingly addressed Mr. Knox's First Whip and Kennel Huntsman.

'Michael,' she said, lowering her voice, 'you know the children's old donkey that I spoke to you about last week—I'm afraid you *had* better——'

'Sure he's boiled, ma'am,' said Michael with swift and awful brevity; 'that's him in the throch now!'

Philippa hastily withdrew from the vicinity of the trough, murmuring something incoherent about cannibals or parricides,

I am not sure which, and her eldest son burst into tears that were only assuaged by the tactful intervention of the kennel boy with the jawbone of a horse, used for propping open the window of the boiler-house.

'Never mind, Mrs. Yeates,' said Flurry consolingly, 'the new hounds that I 'm getting won't be bothered with donkeys as long as there 's a sheep left in the country, if the half I hear of them is true!' He turned to me. 'Major, I didn't tell you I have three couple of O'Reilly's old Irish hounds bought. They 're the old white breed, y' know, and they say they 're terrors to hunt.'

'They 'd steal a thing out of your eye,' said Michael, evidently reverting to an interrupted discussion between himself and his master. 'There 's a woman of the O'Reillys married back in the country here, and she says they killed two cows last season.'

'If they kill any cows with me I 'll stop the price of them out of your wages, Michael, my lad!' said Flurry to his henchman's back. 'Look here, Major, come on with me to-morrow to bring them home!'

It was, I believe, no more than fifty miles across country to the mountain fastness of the O'Reillys, and a certain chord of romance thrilled at the thought of the old Irish breed of white hounds, with their truly national qualities of talent, rebelliousness, and love of sport. Playboy was one of the same race—Playboy, over whose recapture, it may be remembered, I had considerably distinguished myself during my term of office as M.F.H.

I went. At one o'clock next day two lines of rail had done their uttermost for us, and had ceded the task of conveying us to Fahoura to the inevitable outside car. And still there remained a long flank of mountain to be climbed; the good little slave in the shafts made no complaint, but save for the honour and glory of the thing we might as well have walked; certainly of the seven Irish miles of road, thrown over the pass like a strap over a trunk, our consciences compelled us to tramp at least three. A stream, tawny and translucent as audit ale, foamed and slid among its brown boulders beside us at the side of the road; as we crawled upwards the fields became smaller, and the lonely whitewashed cottages ceased. The heather came down to the wheel marks, and a pack of grouse suddenly whizzed across the road like a shot fired across our bows to warn us off.

At the top of the pass we stood, and looked out over half a county to the pale peaks of Killarney.

'There's Fahoura now, gentlemen,' said the carman, pointing downwards with his whip to a group of whitewashed farm buildings, that had gathered themselves incongruously about a square grey tower. 'I'm told old Mr. O'Reilly's sick this good while.'

'What ails him?' said Flurry.

'You wouldn't know,' said the carman; 'sure he's very old, and that 'fluenzy has the country destroyed; there's people dying now that never died before.'

'That's bad,' said Flurry sympathetically; 'I had a letter from him a week ago, and he only said he was parting the hounds because he couldn't run with them any more.'

'Ah, don't mind him!' said the carman, 'it's what it is he'd sooner sell them now, than to give the nephew the satisfaction of them, after himself 'd be dead.'

'Is that the chap that's been hunting them for him?' said Flurry, while I, for the hundredth time, longed for Flurry's incommunicable gift of being talked to.

'It is, sir; Lukey O'Reilly'— the carman gave a short laugh. 'That's the lad! They say he often thried to go to America, but he never got south of Mallow; he gets that drunk sayin' good-bye to his friends!'

'Maybe the old fellow will live a while yet, just to spite him,' suggested Flurry.

'Well, maybe he would, faith!' agreed the carman, 'didn't the docther say to meself that maybe it's walking the road I'd be, and I to fall down dead!' he continued complacently; 'but sure them docthors, when they wouldn't know what was in it, they should be saying something!'

We here turned into the lane that led to Mr. O'Reilly's house.

We pulled up at the gate of a wide farmyard, with outcrops of the brown mountain rock in it, and were assailed in the inevitable way by the inevitable mongrel collies. Blent with their vulgar abuse was the mellow baying of hounds, coming, seemingly, from the sky. The carman pointed to the tower which filled an angle of the yard, and I saw, about twenty feet from the ground, an arrow-slit, through which protruded white muzzles, uttering loud and tuneful threats.

'The kitchen door's the handiest way,' said Flurry, 'but I suppose for grandeur we'd better go to the front of the house.'

He opened a side gate, and I followed him through a wind-swept enclosure that by virtue of two ragged rose bushes, and a walk edged with white stones, probably took rank as a garden. At the front door we knocked; a long pause ensued, and finally bare feet thudded down a passage, a crack of the door was opened, and an eye glistened for a moment in the crack. It was slammed again, and after a further delay it was reopened, this time by a large elderly woman with crinkled black and grey hair and one long and commanding tooth in the front of her mouth.

'Why, then, I wasn't looking to see ye till to-morrow, Mr. Knox!' she began, beaming upon Flurry, 'but sure ye're welcome any day and all day, and the gentleman too!'

The gentleman was introduced, and felt himself being summed up in a single glance of Miss O'Reilly's nimble brown eyes. With many apologies, she asked us if we would come and see her brother in the kitchen, as he did not feel well enough to walk out to the parlour, and she couldn't keep him in the bed at all.

The kitchen differed more in size than in degree from that of the average cabin. There was the same hummocky earthen floor, the same sallow whitewashed walls, the same all-pervading turf smoke—the difference was in the master of the house. He was seated by the fire in an angular arm-chair, with an old horse-blanket over his knees, and a stick in his hand, and beside him lay an ancient white hound, who scarcely lifted her head at our entrance. The old man laboured to his feet, and, bent as he was, he towered over Flurry as he took his hand.

'Your father's son is welcome, Mr. Florence Knox, and your friend.' He was short of breath, and he lowered his great frame into his chair again. 'Sit down, gentlemen, sit down!' he commanded. 'Joanna! These gentlemen are after having a long drive——'

The clink of glasses told that the same fact had occurred to Miss O'Reilly, and a bottle of port, and another of what looked like water, but was in effect old potheen, were immediately upon the table.

'How well ye wouldn't put down a glass for me!' thundered old O'Reilly, 'I suppose it's saving it for my wake you are!'

'Or her own wedding, maybe!' said Flurry, shamelessly ogling Miss O'Reilly; 'we 'll see that before the wake, I 'm thinking!'

'Well, well, isn't he the dead spit of his father!' said Miss O'Reilly to the rafters.

'Here, woman, give me the kettle,' said her brother. 'I 'll drink my glass of punch with Mr. Florence Knox, the way I did with his father before him! The doctor says I might carry out six months, and I think myself I won't carry out the week, but what the divil do I care! I 'm going to give Mr. Knox his pick of my hounds this day, and that 's what no other man in Ireland would get, and be dam we 'll wet our bargain!'

'Well, well,' said Miss O'Reilly, remonstratingly, bringing the kettle, 'and you that was that weak last night that if you got Ireland's crown you couldn't lift the bedclothes off your arms!'

'Them hounds are in my family, seed and breed, this hundred years and more,' continued old O'Reilly, silencing his sister with one black glance from under his thick grey brows, 'and if I had e'er a one that was fit to come after me they 'd never leave it!' He took a gulp of the hot punch. 'Did ye ever hear of my brother Phil that was huntsman to the Charlevilles long ago, Mr. Knox? Your father knew him well. Many 's the good hunt they rode together. He wasn't up to forty years when he was killed, broke his neck jumping a hurl, and when they went to bury him it 's straight in over the churchyard wall they took him! They said he never was one to go round looking for a gate!'

'May the Lord have mercy on him!' murmured Miss O'Reilly in the background.

'Amen!' growled the old man, taking another pull at his steaming tumbler, as if he were drinking his brother's health. 'And look at me here,' he went on, reddening slowly through the white stubble on his cheeks, 'dying as soft as any owld cow in a bog-hole, and all they 'll be saying afther me is asking would they get their bellyful of whisky at my wake! I tell you this— and let you be listening to me, Joanna!—what hounds Mr. Knox doesn't take, I 'll not leave them afther me to be disgraced in the counthry, running rabbits on Sunday afternoons with them poaching blackguards up out of the town! No! But they 'll have a stone round their neck and to be thrown below in the lough!'

I thought of the nephew Luke, whose friends had so frequently failed to see him off, and I felt very sorry for old O'Reilly.

'They will, they will, to be sure!' said Miss O'Reilly soothingly, 'and look at you now, the way you are! Didn't I know well you had no call to be drinking punch, you that was coughing all night. On the face of God's earth, Mr. Knox, I never heard such a cough! 'Tis like a sheep's cough! I declare it's like the sound of the beating of the drum!'

'Well, Mr. O'Reilly,' said Flurry, ignoring these remarkable symptoms, but none the less playing to her lead, 'I suppose we might have a look at the hounds now.'

'Go, tell Tom to open the tower door,' said old O'Reilly to his sister, after a moment's silence. He handed her a key. 'And shut the gate, you.'

As soon as she had gone he got on to his feet. 'Mr. Knox, sir,' he said, 'might I put as much trouble on you as to move out this chair to the door? I'll sit there the way I can see them. Maybe the other gentleman would reach me down the horn that's up on the wall. He's near as tall as meself.'

Flurry did as he asked, and helped him across the room.

'Close out the half-door if you please, Mr. Knox, and give me the old rug that's there, my feet is destroyed with the rheumatics.'

He dropped groaningly into his chair, and I handed him the horn, an old brass one, bent and dinted.

Already the clamour of the hounds in the tower had broken out like bells in a steeple, as they heard the footsteps of their jailor on the stone steps of their prison.

Then Tom's voice, shouting at them in Irish to stand back, and then through the narrow door of the tower the hounds themselves, a striving torrent of white flecked with pale yellow, like one of their own mountain streams. There were about seven couples of them, and in a moment they overran the yard like spilt quicksilver.

'Look at them now, Mr. Knox!' said their owner; 'they'd take a line over the hob of hell this minute!'

Pending this feat they took a very good line into what was apparently the hen-house, judging by the hysterics that proceeded from within. Almost immediately one of them reappeared with an egg in his mouth. Old O'Reilly gave a laugh and an attempt at a holloa. 'Ah, ha! That's Whiteboy! The rogue!' he said, and putting the horn to his lips he blew a thin and broken note, that was cut short by a cough. Speechlessly he handed the horn to Flurry, but no further summons was needed; the hounds had heard him. They converged upon the doorway with a rush, and Flurry and I were put to it to keep them from jumping in over the half-door.

I had never seen hounds like them before. One or two were pure white, but most had some touch of faded yellow or pale grey about them; they were something smaller than the average foxhound, and were strongly built, and active as terriers. Their heads were broad, their ears unrounded, and their legs and feet were far from complying with the prescribed bedpost standard; but wherein, to the unprofessional eye, they chiefly differed from the established pattern, was in the human lawlessness of their expression. The old hound by the fire had struggled up at the note of the horn, and stood staring in perplexity at her master, and growling, with all the arrogance of the favourite, at her descendants, who yelped, and clawed, and strove, and thrust their muzzles over the half-door.

Flurry regarded them in silence.

'There's not a straight one among them,' he whispered in my ear through the din.

'There they are for you now, Mr. Knox,' said old O'Reilly, still panting after his fit of coughing. 'There isn't another man in Ireland would get them but yourself, and you've got them, as I might say, a present!'

Flurry and I went out into the yard, and the door was closed behind us.

The examination—I may say the cross-examination—of the hounds that followed, was conducted by Flurry and Michael to the accompaniment of a saga from Tom, setting forth their miraculous merits and achievements, to which, at suitable points, the carman shouted 'Selah,' or words to that effect, through the bars of the gate. At the end of half an hour Flurry had sorted out six of them; these were then coupled, and by dint of the exertions of all present, were bestowed in a cart with sides like a crate, in which pigs went to the fair.

We did not see our host again. His sister told us that he had gone to bed and wasn't fit to see any one, but he wished

Mr. Knox luck with his bargain, and he sent him this for a luck-penny. She handed Flurry the dinted horn.

'I'm thinking it's fretting after the hounds he is,' she said, turning her head away to hide the tears in her brown eyes. I have never until then known Flurry completely at a loss for an answer.

PART II

A fortnight afterwards—to be precise, it was the 10th of October—I saw the white hounds in the field. I had gone through the dreary routine of the cub-hunter. The alarm clock had shrilled its exulting and age-long summons in the pitchy dark. I had burnt my fingers with the spirit-lamp, and my mouth with hot cocoa; I had accomplished my bathless toilet, I had groped my way through the puddles in the stable yard, and got on to my horse by the light of a lantern, and at 5.30 a.m. I was over the worst, and had met Flurry and the hounds, with Michael and Dr. Jerome Hickey, at the appointed cross-roads. The meet was nine miles away, in a comparatively unknown land, to which Flurry had been summoned by tales of what appeared to be an absolute epidemic of foxes, accompanied by bills for poultry and threats of poison. It was still an hour before sunrise, but a pallor was in the sky, and the hounds, that had at first been like a gliding shoal of fish round the horses' feet, began to take on their own shapes and colours.

The white Irish hounds were the first to disclose themselves, each coupled up with a tried old stager. I had been away from home for the past ten days, and knew nothing of their conduct in their new quarters, and finding Flurry uncommunicative, I fell back presently to talk about them to Michael.

'Is it settling down they are?' said Michael derisively. 'That's the fine settling down! Roaring and screeching every minute since they came into the place! And as for fighting! They weren't in the kennel three days before they had Rampant ate, and nothing only his paws left before me in the morning! I didn't give one night in my bed since, with running down to them. The like o' them trash isn't fit for a gentleman's kennels. Them O'Reillys had them rared very pettish; it'd be as good for me to be trying to turn curlews as them!'

The indictment of 'The Whiteboys' (a title sarcastically

bestowed by Dr. Hickey), their sheep-killing, their dog-hunting, with the setting forth of Michael's trials, talents, and un-requited virtues, lasted, like an Arabian night's tale, till the rising of the sun, and also until our arrival at the place we were first to draw. This was a long and deep ravine, red with bracken, bushy with hazel and alders; a black stream raced downwards through it, spreading at the lower end into bog, green, undefined, entirely treacherous; a place that instantly assures the rider that if hounds get away on its farther side he will not be with them.

A couple of men were waiting for us at the lower end of the ravine.

'They 're in it surely!' they said, shoving down a stone gap for our benefit; 'there isn't a morning but we 'll see the owld fellow and his pups funning away for themselves down by the river. My little fellows, when they does be going to school in the morning, couldn't hardly pass his nest for the fume that 'd be from it.'

The first ten minutes proved that the foxes were certainly there, and during the following half hour pandemonium itself raged in the ravine. There were, I believe, a brace and a half of cubs on foot; they were to me invisible, but they were viewed about twice in every minute by Flurry and his subordinates, and continuously by a few early-rising countrymen, who had posted themselves along the edges of the ravine. The yells of the latter went up like steam whistles, and the hounds, among whom were five couple of newly entered puppies, were wilder than I had ever known them. They burst through the bracken and strove in the furze, in incessant full cry, and still the cubs doubled and dodged, and made detours round the valley, and Flurry and Michael roared themselves inside out, without producing the smallest effect upon anything save their own larynxes. No less than three times a fox was frantically halloaed away, and when, by incredible exertions on all our parts, the hounds, or a fair proportion of them, had been got together on to the line, a fresh outburst of yells announced that, having run a ring, he had returned to the covert.

Each of these excursions involved—

1. Scrambling at best speed down a rocky hillside.

2. Coercing a diffident horse across a noisy stream, masked by briars, out of bog, on to rock.

3. Reverse of the first proceedings.

4. Arrival, blown and heated, at the boggy end of the valley, to find the original conditions prevailing as before.

I should, perhaps, have already mentioned that I was riding a young horse, to whom I was showing hounds for the first time. My idea had been to permit him, strictly as an onlooker, to gather some idea of the rudiments of the game. He was a good young horse, with the large gravity of demeanour that is often the result of a domestic bringing up in the family of a small farmer; and when the moment came, and I was inexorably hustled into acting as Third Whip, he followed in the wake of Dr. Hickey with an anxious goodwill that made even his awkwardness attractive.

Throughout these excursions I noticed, as far as I was able to notice anything, the independent methods of the O'Reilly draft. They ignored the horn, eluded Michael, and laughed at Hickey and me; they hunted with bloodthirsty intentness and entirely after their own devices. Their first achievement was to run the earth-stopper's dog, and having killed him, to eat him. This horrid feat they accomplished, secure from interruption, in the briary depths of the ravine, and while the main body of the pack were industriously tow-rowing up and down the stream after their lawful fox, a couple of goats were only saved from the Whiteboys by miracles of agility and courage on the part of the countrymen. The best that could be said for them was that, 'linking one virtue to a thousand crimes,' whenever the hounds got fairly out of covert, the Whiteboys were together, and were in front.

It was about eight o'clock, and the fierce red and grey sunrise had been overridden by a regiment of stormy clouds, when one of the foxes met his fate, amid ear-piercing whoops, and ecstatic comments from the onlookers, who had descended from the hill-tops with the speed of ski-runners.

'Aha! that's the lad had many a fat duck under his rib!'

'He had, faith! I'll go bail 'twas him that picked me wife's fashionable cocks!'

'Well, I'm told that if ye'll see a fox taking a hen or a goose, and ye'll call to him in Irish, that he'll drop it,' remarked an older man to me, as we waited while Flurry and Hickey, in their capacity of butler and footman to the hounds' repast, snatched the few remaining morsels from the elder revellers and en-

deavoured to force them upon the deeply reluctant young
entry, who, having hunted with the innocent enthusiasm of
the *débutante*, thought as little of the ensuing meal as the
débutante thinks of supper at her first ball.

'I wonder why the deuce Michael can't get those Irish hounds,'
said Flurry, catching at the word and looking round. 'I only
have Lily here.'

(Lily, I should say, was the romantic name of one of the
Whiteboys.)

'I believe I seen a two-three of the white dogs running east
awhile ago,' said the elderly farmer, 'and they yowling!'

'They're likely killing a sheep now,' murmured Hickey
to me.

At the same moment I chanced to look up towards the western
end of the ravine, and saw what seemed to be five seagulls
gliding up a rift of grass that showed green between rocks and
heather.

'There are your white hounds, Flurry,' I called out, 'and
they're hunting.'

'Well, well,' said the farmer, 'they're afther wheeling round
the length of the valley in the minute! They're nearly able
to fly!'

A distant holloa from Michael, whose head alone was visible
above a forest of furze, rose like a rocket at the end of the
sentence, and every hound sprang to attention.

Once more we traversed the valley at full speed, and tackled
the ladder of mud that formed the cattle track up the ravine;
slough up to the horses' knees, furze bushes and briars meeting
over their heads and ours, hounds and country boys jostling
to get forward, with pistol shots behind from Hickey's thong,
and the insistent doubling of Flurry's horn in front. Up that
green rift I went on foot, and, as it were, hand in hand with
my admirable young horse. The rift, on closer acquaintance,
proved to be green with the deceitful verdure of swampy grass;
(in Ireland, it may be noted, water runs uphill, and the subtlest
bog-holes lie in wait for their prey on the mountain-tops). As
we ascended, the wind that had risen with the sun, fought us
every inch of the way, and by the time I had won to level
ground, I was speechless, and blowing like the bellows of a
forge. A country boy, whose grinning purple face remains a
fond and imperishable memory, caught me by the leg and

ramméd me into my saddle; just in front of me Flurry, also speechless, with his foot not as yet in his off stirrup, was getting up to his hounds. These were casting themselves uncertainly over a sedgy and heathery slope, on which, in this wind, the hottest scent would soon be chilled to its marrow. Of Michael and the Whiteboys nothing was to be seen.

At a little distance a young man was grasping by the ears and nose a donkey with a back-load of bracken, and a misplaced ardour for the chase.

'Did ye see the fox?' bellowed Flurry.

'I did! I did!'

'Which way did he go?'

'Yerrah! aren't yer dogs after ateing him below!' shouted the young man, waltzing strenuously with the donkey.

'Well, there's a pair of you!' replied Flurry, cracking his whip viciously at the donkey's tail, and thereby much stimulating the dance, 'and if I was given my choice of ye it's the ass I'd take! Here, come on out of this, Hickey!' He shoved ahead. 'Put those hounds on to me, can't you!'

During this interchange of amenities Lily had wandered aside, and now, far to the left of the rest of the pack, was thoughtfully nosing along through tufts of rushes; she worked her way down to a fence, and then, mute as a wraith, slid over it and slipped away across a grass field, still in jealous silence.

'Hark forrad to Lily, hounds!' roared Flurry, with electrical suddenness. 'Put them on to her, Jerome!'

'Well, those white hounds are the divil!' said Dr. Hickey, with a break of admiration in his voice, as the hounds, suddenly driving ahead, proclaimed to heaven that they had got the line. They were running up a fierce north-westerly wind, and their cry came brokenly back to us through it like the fragments of the chimes through the turmoil of Tschaikowsky's '1812' Overture. The young horse began to realize that there was something in it, and, with a monster and frog-like leap, flew over the ensuing heathery bank, landing, shatteringly, on all fours. We were travelling downhill, a fact that involved heavy drops, but involved also the privilege, rare for me, of seeing the hounds comfortably. Lily, leading the rest by half a field, was going great guns, so were Flurry and Hickey, so, I may say with all modesty, were the young horse and I. After an eventful and entirely satisfactory ten minutes of racing over the class of

country that has, on a low average, seventeen jumps to the
mile, we skated down a greasy path, and found ourselves in a
deep lane, with the hounds at fault, casting themselves eagerly
right and left. It was here that we came upon Michael, a
dolorous spectacle, leading his mare towards us. She was
dead lame.

'What happened her?' shouted Flurry through the rioting
wind.

'The foot's dropping off her, sir,' replied Michael, with his
usual optimism.

'Well, get away home with her as quick as you can,' interrupted Flurry, accepting the diagnosis with the usual discount
of 90 per cent. 'What way did those white hounds go?'

'The last I seen o' them they were heading west over the hill
beyond for Drummig. It might be he was making for an old
fort that's back in the land there behind Donovan's farm.
There was a fellow driving a bread van above in the road there
that told me if the hounds got inside in the fort we'd never see
them again. He said there were holes down in it that'd go
from here to the sea.'

'What the devil good were you that you didn't stop those
hounds?' said Flurry, cutting short this harangue with a
countenance as black as the weather. 'Here, come on!' he
called to Hickey and me, 'the road'll be the quickest for us.'

It was about a mile by the road to Donovan's farm, and as
Hickey and I pounded along in the rear of the disgusted hounds,
big pellets of rain were flung in our faces, and I began to realize,
not for the first time, that to turn up the collar of one's coat is
more of a protest than a protection.

The farmhouse of Donovan of Drummig was connected with
the high road by the usual narrow and stony lane; as we neared
the entrance of the lane we saw through the swirls of rain a
baker's van bumping down it. There were two men on the
van, and in the shafts was a raking young brown horse, who,
having espied the approach of the hounds, was honouring them
with what is politically known as a demonstration. One of the
men held up his hand, and called out a request to 'hold on
awhile till they were out on to the road.'

'Did you see any hounds?' shouted Flurry, holding back the
hounds, as the van bounded round the corner and into the main
road, with an activity rare in its species.

'We did, sir,' returned the men in chorus, clinging to the rail of their knife-board seat, like the crew of a racing yacht, 'they have him back in the fort above this minute! Ye can take your time, faith!'

The van horse reared and backed, and Flurry turned in his saddle to eye him as he ramped ahead in response to a slash from the driver; so did Dr. Hickey, and so also did Lily, who, with her white nose in the air, snuffed inquisitively in the wake of the departing van.

'You'd say she knew a good one when she saw him,' said Hickey as we turned the hounds into the lane.

'Or a good loaf of bread,' I suggested.

'It's little bread that lad carries!' answered Hickey, thonging the reluctant Lily on; 'I'll go bail, there's as much bottled porter as bread in that van! He supplies half the shebeens in the country.'

As we splashed into the farmyard a young man threw open a gate at its farther side, shouting to Flurry to hurry on. He waved us on across a wide field, towards a low hill or mound, red with wet withered bracken, and crested by a group of lean fir-trees, flinging their arms about in the wild gusts of wind and rain.

'The fox wasn't the length of himself in front of them!' shouted the young man, running beside us, 'and he as big as a donkey! The whole kit of them is inside in the fort together!'

Flurry turned his horse suddenly.

'Two and a half couple underground is enough for one while,' he said, riding back into the farmyard. 'Have you any place I could shove these hounds into?'

The door of a cow-house was open, and as if in anticipation of his wishes, the hounds jostled emulously into the darkness within. Again, guided by the young man, we faced the storm and rain. What Flurry's intentions were we neither knew nor dared to ask, and, as we followed him over the soaked fields, a back more expressive of profound and wrathful gloom it has never been my lot to contemplate.

The place in which the fox and the Irish hounds had entombed themselves, was one of the prehistoric earthen fortresses that abound in the south-west of Ireland. The fort at Drummig was like a giant flat-topped molehill; the spade work of a forgotten race had turned it into a place of defence, and, like

moles, they had burrowed into its depths. The tongue of the
young man who guided us did not weary in the recital of the
ways, and the passages, and the little rooms that was within in
it. He said that a calf belonging to himself was back in it for a
week, and she came out three times fatter than the day she went
in. He also, but with a certain diffidence, mentioned fairies.

Round and about this place of mystery went Flurry, blowing
long and dreary blasts at the mouths of its many holes, uttering
'Gone away' screeches, of a gaiety deplorably at variance with
his furious countenance. A more pessimistic priest never
trumpeted round the walls of a more impracticable Jericho.

Hickey led the dripping horses to and fro in the lee of the
fort, and I was deputed to listen at a rabbit hole from which the
calf was said to have emerged. After a period of time which I
was too much deadened by misery to compute, Flurry appeared,
and told me that he was going home. Judging from his appearance, he had himself been to ground; what he said about the
white hounds and the weather was very suitable, but would not
read as well as it sounded.

We returned to the farmyard with the wind and rain chivying
us from behind.

'I asked a man, one time,' said Dr. Hickey, as side by side,
and at a well-maintained distance, we followed our leader across
the field, 'why his father had committed suicide, and he said,
"Well, your honour, he was a little annoyed." I'm thinking,
Major, it'd be no harm for us to keep an eye on Flurry.'

I stooped my head to let the water flow out of the brim of
my hat.

'You needn't neglect me either,' I said.

While Hickey was getting the hounds out of the cow-house
my young horse shivered with cold, and gave an ominous cough.
I reflected upon the twelve long miles that lay between him
and home, and asked our saturated guide if I could get a warm
drink for him. There was no difficulty about that; to be sure
I could and welcome. I abandoned my comrades; regret, if it
were felt, was not expressed by Flurry. When the hounds had
paddled forth from the cow-house I put my horse into it, and
before they had accomplished half a mile of their direful progress, I was standing with my back to a glowing turf fire, with
my coat hanging on a chair, and a cup of scalding tea irradiating
the inmost recesses of my person.

My hostess, Mrs. Jeremiah Donovan, was a handsome young woman, tall, fair, and flushed, agonized with hospitality, shy to ferocity. The family dog was lifted from the hearth with a side kick worthy of an International football match; her offspring, clustered, staring, in the chimney-corner, were dispersed with a scorching whisper, of which the words, 'ye brazen tinkers,' gave some clue to its general trend. Having immured them in an inner room she withdrew, muttering something about another 'goleen o' turf,' and I was left alone with an excellent cake of soda-bread and two boiled eggs.

Presently a slight and mouse-like rattle made me aware that one of the offspring, aged about five, had escaped from captivity, and was secretly drawing my whip to him along the floor by the thong.

'What have ye the whip for?' said the offspring, undaunted by discovery.

'To bate the dogs with,' I replied, attuning my speech to his as best I could.

'Is it the big white dogs?' pursued the offspring.

I paused midway in a mouthful of soda-bread.

'Did you see the white dogs?' I asked very gently.

'God knows I did!' said the offspring, warming to his work, 'an' they snapped the bit o' bread out of Joola's hand within in the cow-house! And Joola said they were a fright!'

I sat still and waited while one might count five, fearful of scaring the bird that had perched so near me.

'Are the white dogs here now?' I ventured, wooingly.

'They are not.'

The crook of my crop was beginning to prove dangerously engrossing, and the time was short.

'Where did they go?' I persevered.

'Jimmy Mahony and me uncle Lukey took them away in the van,' said the offspring with clearness and simplicity, slashing with my whip at a member of the guild of Brazen Tinkers whom I assumed to be the already injured Julia.

.   .   .   .   .   .

As I bestowed at parting a benefaction upon Jeremiah Donovan, I said that I hoped he would let Mr. Knox know if any of the white hounds came out of the fort. He assured me that he would do so. He was, like his wife, a thoroughly good fellow, and he had wisped the young horse until one would have said he had never been out of the stable.

The storm had blown itself away, and the rain was nearly over. I rode home quietly, and in peace and goodwill towards all men; after all, there was no hurry. This was a thing that was going to last me for the rest of my life, and Flurry's.

I overtook Michael on the way home. Michael said that sure he knew all through it was a drag, and if Mr. Flurry had been said by him, he 'd have had neither cut, shuffle, nor deal with them O'Reillys. In the course of his life Michael had never been known to be in the wrong.

Dr. Hickey told me (but this was some time afterwards) that often he had to get out of his bed to laugh, when he thought of Flurry getting Jeremiah Donovan to screech in Irish down the holes in the fort, for fear old O'Reilly's hounds had no English. It is hardly necessary to say that Dr. Hickey also had been convinced by the way the hounds ran that it was a drag, but has omitted to mention the fact at the time.

Flurry was lost to home and country for three days. It was darkly said that he had gone to Fahoura to break every bone in young O'Reilly's body, and, incidentally, to bring back the white hounds. At the end of the three days he telegraphed for a man and a saddle to meet the afternoon train. There was nothing in the telegram about hounds. Next day I met him riding a young brown horse, with a wildish eye, and a nasty rub from a misfitting collar.

'I got him in a sort of a swap,' said Flurry tranquilly.

'I suppose he got that rub in the bread-van?' I remarked, drawing a bow at a venture.

'Well, that might be, too,' assented Flurry, regarding me with an eye that was like a stone wall with broken glass on the top.

Printed in July 2023
by Rotomail Italia S.p.A., Vignate (MI) - Italy